a gift to the Kennedy Library

from Anne T. Donaghy

May 2019

THE
VOICE
OF
AMERICA

Also by Mitchell Stephens

Beyond News: The Future of Journalism

Imagine There's No Heaven:
How Atheism Helped Create the Modern World

Journalism Unbound:
New Approaches to Writing and Reporting

the rise of the image the fall of the word

A History of News

Broadcast News

Writing and Reporting the News (with Gerald Lanson)

THE
VOICE
OF
AMERICA

Lowell Thomas
and the Invention of 20th-Century
Journalism

Mitchell Stephens

St. Martin's Press
New York

All photographs are credited to James A. Cannavino Library, Archives & Special Collections, Marist College, USA, unless otherwise noted.

www.stmartins.com

Design by Meryl Sussman Levavi

The Library of Congress Cataloging-in-Publication Data is available upon request.

ISBN 978-1-137-27982-8 (hardcover)
ISBN 978-1-4668-7940-9 (e-book)

Our books may be purchased in bulk for promotional, educational, or business use. Please contact your local bookseller or the Macmillan Corporate and Premium Sales Department at 1-800-221-7945, extension 5442, or by e-mail at MacmillanSpecialMarkets@macmillan.com.

First Edition: June 2017

10 9 8 7 6 5 4 3 2 1

For Esther Davidowitz

It is human to enjoy fame, especially when you have reason to suspect that you have earned it.

—LOWELL THOMAS[1]

Contents

The Messenger

Two very different men began to circle each other in Jerusalem in February 1918. One was attired in "full Sheikh's costume," as an acquaintance put it, including robe, *keffiyeh* and dagger. He walked the streets barefoot. The British had just "liberated," as it was then put, Jerusalem from the Ottoman Empire, and, despite the outfit, this man was a major in the British Army.

The other man, always well turned out, would have been wearing a "good pair," as he put it, of English field boots and crisp, military-like garb, although he was not enlisted in any of the armies then fighting the First World War. His name was Lowell Thomas, and, according to a journal Thomas was keeping at the time, he had first met Major T. E. Lawrence in the office of the military governor of Jerusalem. Thomas—often ready to improve a story—later maintained, however, that he had started tracking down this mysterious blue-eyed, beardless man in Arab dress after spotting him on the streets of Jerusalem.[1]

Lawrence, who had graduated Oxford with first-class honors in modern history, was leading, or helping lead, or tagging along on (his biographers have long tussled over which) the daring and successful Arab Revolt against the Ottoman Empire. Lawrence too was known to fiddle with a story. He was almost 30, although Thomas noted in his journal—and this was probably Lawrence's fib—that he was 28.

What Lowell Thomas was doing in the Middle East was not entirely clear. He was a 25-year-old American from a gold-rush town in the Rocky Mountains who had recently resigned from the faculty at Princeton University. Thomas had attended law school and worked on newspapers before that. More recently he had enjoyed some success presenting illustrated travelogues. If this seems today a rather varied résumé, rest assured it seemed that way then too. Based on this hodgepodge of experiences and a formidable persuasiveness, Thomas had raised money to pay for his loosely defined effort at journalism—or propaganda—in support of the American, and by extension the British, war effort. He had brought along a skilled still and film cameraman, this more than four years before *Nanook of the North*, the first commercially successful full-length film documentary, was released. But there is no evidence that Thomas, though he took a lot of notes and shot a lot of film, sold any journalism while in the Middle East.

Why Thomas would want to be in this part of the world at this moment is easier to divine: Thomas was not the sort to miss a good story or a good adventure, and the capture of Jerusalem offered both. He also was not the sort to let doubt about what he was doing interfere with getting something done.

Thomas was introduced to Lawrence. They talked and talked again, with Thomas taking notes. Lowell recognized that an Englishman in Arab robes *leading* (Thomas acknowledged no controversy here) a group of Arabs on camels in successful desert raids against one of Britain and America's enemies was news. With cameraman in tow, he arranged to follow Lawrence into the desert.

This would prove a life-changing encounter for both men. To what extent it was responsible for the celebrity that was about to afflict "Lawrence of Arabia" is also a matter of controversy. Some of Lawrence's biographers maintain that even without Thomas he would have been recognized as one of the heroes of a war that produced few heroes and would have achieved considerable renown. It offends those biographers to cede much credit to the messenger—this entrepreneurial, storytelling, uncredentialed American messenger. And Lawrence's exploits, even subtracting those in dispute, were indeed dramatic; he was a fascinating man.

But there can be no argument as to how Lawrence actually did first come to the attention of the world—including most of his compatriots. The vehicle was a show combining narration and music with slides and documentary film footage. The show was conceived, reported, written, narrated and produced by Lowell Thomas—more than a year after he met Lawrence. Thomas thought of it as "a wholly new and spectacular form of entertainment." The genre? Part travelogue, part theater, part newsreel, part proto-documentary. It was also, by some definitions, the first multimedia work of journalism. And the star of Thomas' production—seen in slides and film shot in Jerusalem, Arabia and, secretly, London—was "Lawrence, the Uncrowned King of Arabia."

About two million people around the world paid to watch and listen to Thomas' show. The audiences in London included the queen, the prime minister and, on more than one occasion, Lawrence himself—doing his best not to be recognized. In 1924 a book on the subject, *With Lawrence in Arabia*, appeared and became an international best seller. It was written by the only journalist (or propagandist) to have interviewed and traveled with Lawrence in the Middle East: Lowell Thomas.

Lawrence died in a motorcycle accident 17 years after first meeting Thomas in Jerusalem. After the war he had made one other major historical contribution: lobbying at postwar conferences for Arab independence and in the process helping draw, for better or worse, the modern-day borders of the Middle East.

The Lawrence story obviously gave a hefty boost to Thomas' career. The shows and then the book, his first, were at the time the biggest successes in this young man's already extraordinary life. They provided his own first taste of fame. But Thomas would have many more successes and experience much greater fame.

In the 63 years he lived after first meeting Lawrence, Lowell Thomas' contributions to twentieth-century American journalism—on radio, in newsreels, on television—would be as significant as anyone's. Much of the distance between a wild "Hey, sweetheart, get me rewrite" Chicago-style journalism and the sober, Olympian "And that's the way it is" journalism of Walter Cronkite was covered by Lowell Thomas. Thomas became one of the handful of individuals who might claim to have been the most creative and most successful American journalist of the twentieth century. For a decade or two of that century, he was the best-known American journalist—his voice as familiar as anyone's through his nightly radio newscast, his face, with its neatly trimmed mustache, easily recognizable as that of the on-screen host and narrator of the most popular twice-weekly newsreels.

And Thomas never stopped racing hither and yon: to Europe and the Middle East; to India, Afghanistan, New Guinea and, among countless other places, Tibet—then closed to outsiders—where he met with the young Dalai Lama right before the Communists marched in. The Explorers Club has named its building, its awards and one of its main dinners after Lowell Thomas.

His memoir sometimes reads like the *Perils of Pauline*: an airplane in which Thomas is riding makes a crash landing; a large, angry crowd is about to go after him and his fellow foreigners; bullets whiz by or penetrate his hat. Mention these incidents to those who knew him, and they smile. "He liked a good story," they'll say softly. But Thomas *was* in all those early, rickety airplanes—when air travel was still brand new—and he *did* visit an extraordinary number of out-of-the-way, even dangerous places. On the way back from Tibet, Thomas' pony threw him, and with his leg broken in eight places, Thomas had to be carried down from the Himalayas.

In the 1970s someone calculated that no human had flown more miles as a passenger in airplanes than Lowell Thomas. We describe some individuals as "well traveled"; with Thomas we might say "best traveled." And usually he brought his microphone, and often a camera, along.

Indeed, as much as anyone, Thomas helped acquaint Americans in the "American century" with the world in which they were coming to play such a large role. He functioned, often enough, as America's eyes and ears. And while he tended to be open, interested and empathetic, he was not at all embarrassed, as he saw and heard, to be equipped with a sturdy set of American principles and prejudices. Thomas lived long enough to see scholars become more alert to the importance of messengers and their biases. He wasn't the sort to reflect too much on that sort of issue, but he surely did illustrate it.

Although Thomas was slow to understand this, T. E. Lawrence was an unusually quirky, complex, troubled man, capable of flipping from hubris to self-doubt, even self-loathing. Burdened with a nineteenth-century sense of honor and a twenty-first-century sensibility, Lawrence was perpetually uncomfortable in his own time. Thomas, on the other hand, rarely succumbed to self-doubt. He was buoyant not troubled. He fit wonderfully with his time. But I would argue that Thomas was no less fascinating and probably more influential and important than Lawrence.

Three years after Thomas published his book, a parade of books on

Lawrence began, more than a hundred of them by now—retelling the story, challenging the story, trying to untangle the man behind it or using him to make some larger point about Britain or the Middle East. David Lean's 1962 film version of Lawrence's story won the Academy Award for best picture. In 2013 Lawrence's name appeared in the title of yet another bestseller in the United States.[2]

Only four books have been published about Lowell Thomas: a young-adult book about his many adventures, a collection of reminiscences by his colleagues and Thomas' own rather fanciful two-volume memoir. Most Americans under the age of 65 do not recognize his name.

((•))

That Lowell Thomas would be mostly forgotten a few decades after his death would have shocked most of his contemporaries. For he was the one who had introduced a large proportion of them to the world's deserts, mountains and trouble spots; its dictators, warriors and heroes.

Thomas may not have been the most penetrating of journalists. He worked fast and tended to farm out much of the writing and research to others—even in his many dozens of books. He fell victim, upon occasion, to some of the prejudices of his time. But he told, always, great stories. He expanded, often, horizons. And he changed journalism.

Indeed, Lowell Thomas deserves a significant part of the credit for the journalism that came into being in America in the twentieth century—a fact-filled, story-based, ostensibly nonpartisan journalism, which traveled widely, examined energetically, proclaimed authoritatively and was not much concerned with what it failed to notice or understand. Thomas did much to create, in other words, the journalism out of which twenty-first-century journalism was born and against which twenty-first-century journalism has been trying to establish itself.

Thomas' career also demonstrates that technology was remaking journalism, again and again, long before the Internet. For no other twentieth-century journalist managed to hitch his wagon to as many swift and strong new technologies: the typewriter, film, the automobile, the airplane, radio, newsreels, remote broadcasting, television, Cinerama. Thomas took a special delight in new ways of getting and presenting the news and was always among the first to experiment with them. Indeed, it is hard to think of any journalist in the twenty-first century who can match Thomas' knack for being on the side of the disruptive. He certainly achieved some success as an entrepreneur: the little radio and television company Thomas helped found with his business advisor, Capital Cities, was eventually sold to Disney for $19 billion.

Thomas is, in addition, as good a representative as anyone of the strengths and limitations of the bigger-newer-faster, can-do, put-things-right twentieth-century American. We can find in him the optimism, the curiosity, the desire to lend a hand or to send some troops of that American. But Thomas likewise exhibited some of the lack of subtlety, limited peripheral vision and willingness to disregard inconvenient facts that have and continue to undercut America's often well-intentioned efforts.

After his one grand adventure and triumph, followed by his political efforts and frustrations on behalf of the Arabs, T. E. Lawrence spent most of the rest of his years hiding from his fame. His life after Arabia was sparse, constricted and tragically short. For Thomas, on the other hand, the adventures never stopped coming, and for a number of decades, the triumphs grew larger and larger. His long life was overstuffed with journeys and people, with impact and significance. This storyteller's life, even minus a few perils, is consequently a storyteller's dream.

A couple of dozen authors, from Lowell Thomas himself to, most recently, Michael Korda, have undertaken full-scale biographies of T. E. Lawrence; one, by John E. Mack, won the Pulitzer Prize. You are reading the first biography of Lowell Thomas.

1.

A Portrait of the Journalist as a Young Cowboy

Victor, Colorado, the gold-rush town where Lowell Thomas was raised, was a rough-and-tumble place. It had its ambitions: Victor managed to build and sometimes fill an almost-grand, brick opera house, where a range of early twentieth-century acts, including even some operas, could be enjoyed. Nonetheless—together with its sister city, Cripple Creek—it had more saloons and gambling halls than stores. And while all those pugnacious miners made a lot of news, Victor harbored only one newspaper, the *Victor Record*. Since this was before the Internet, before television, before radio newscasts, even before newsmagazines, that meant this small city had but one regular news source besides local scuttlebutt.

The historian Doris Kearns Goodwin has spoken of a "golden age of journalism" in the first decades of the twentieth century.[1] She is impressed with the contingent of thoughtful correspondents who would discuss policy with Theodore Roosevelt before and during his presidency and who were disappointed that they did not have the opportunity to engage in such discussions with his successor, William Howard Taft. And Goodwin is rightly impressed, too, by the handful of progressive, "muckraking" magazines, led by *McClure's*, that helped inspire Roosevelt's reforms by exposing

the situation of the poor, corruption in government and the evils of pred-
atory business monopolies or "trusts."

But those mostly progressive correspondents who participated in Teddy
Roosevelt's informal seminars worked for the most part for East Coast
newspapers. Their writings were hard to find in Victor, Colorado. And those
progressive magazines were relatively rare sights in Victor or similar towns.
The exposé on municipal corruption that Lincoln Steffens—among the
greatest of the muckrakers—published in *McClure's* investigated no city
south of St. Louis or west of Minneapolis.

In 1911, when Thomas was 19 and just returned from a sprint through
a university, the *Victor Record* featured the occasional story about a development in Washington or overseas—undoubtedly from, but not credited to,
a wire service. However, the newspaper's pages were mostly occupied with
local stories—"SIDEWALKS MUST BE FIXED, Iron Doors Declared Menace
by Council"—and recountings of life's tragedies: "BRIDE TWO WEEKS,
ATTEMPTS SUICIDE" (her new husband had been arrested for embezzlement)
or "KNOCKED OUT BY PIECE OF STEEL" (a mine accident). The headline
"BAND TO GIVE EXCELLENT CONCERT" recurred every Friday. The stories
arrayed on the pages of the *Record*, the point is, were diverting, often even
useful, but facilitated no great debates on the economic system or on America's place in the world; they fail somehow to call to mind a "golden age" of
journalism.

This was the journalism with which young Lowell Thomas, and much
of the rest of America, had to make do. You'd find it in bigger cities than
Victor—Denver, San Francisco, Chicago. You'd find it often enough, if
truth be told, in many New York newspapers. It was a journalism that too
often was not only benighted and shrill—neither new embarrassments for
journalism—but parochial. That was a problem, since, thanks in part to
Theodore Roosevelt, political power was beginning to concentrate in
Washington; since, led in part by Theodore Roosevelt, America was beginning to shoulder burdens overseas. Indeed, this was the journalism Lowell
had begun *practicing*—because in 1911, at the age of 19, he was the editor
of the *Victor Record*.

((•))

Once he left Victor, Lowell Thomas would, as much as anyone, travel the
world. He would, as much as anyone, expand Americans' view of the world.

In other words, once he found himself as a journalist, Thomas played a major role—perhaps the major role—in creating a journalism more suited to America's growing international power and responsibilities. He was, in some sense, the Teddy Roosevelt of journalism. But Thomas continued to see the world through a powerful set of American values—values that he owed mostly to his parents and to Victor.

Lowell's ancestors on both sides were primarily Welsh, English or Dutch and had immigrated to America as far back as the seventeenth century. His paternal grandfather had fought in the Civil War. While Lowell's mother, the former Harriet Wagner, was properly loving, supportive and devoted to education, she could, when disappointed, be a bit of a nag. His father, Harry George Thomas, had a depressive side and did not display much business sense. Yet in his obsession with learning and self-improvement, he recalls one of the most-distinguished American types: the Ben Franklin–like omnivore and tinkerer.

Lowell Jackson Thomas, their first child, was born on April 6, 1892. Jackson was his paternal grandmother's maiden name, but there is no record of anyone in the family with the name Lowell. His parents were renting rooms in the spring of 1892 in a house in Woodington, Ohio, near where their families lived.

When their son was born, Harriet and Harry Thomas were both schoolteachers in the area. But Harry was ambitious, or perhaps it is more accurate to say that his wife—who seems the stronger figure—was ambitious for him. Harry's dream had been to become a mining engineer, working out West and outdoors. But he convinced himself that there wasn't much future for independent mining engineers. Harry's next thought was law. Harriet, however, had another thought: medicine. "She realized," Harry explains in a late-life attempt at a memoir, "that science suited me better." Besides, he adds, "being a country girl, she had a suspicion of the legal mind."[2] So Harry took some medical courses, until he ran out of money for tuition.

Then the family moved to Kirkman, Iowa, population 350—a town so desperate for a doctor that the absence of a medical degree, not legally required to practice medicine in Iowa at the time, could be overlooked. Many locals, as Lowell explains in his memoir, "paid their medical bills in produce."[3] That was less touching than it may sound when you were trying not just to feed but to support a family. Harry reports that he also found Kirkman's small-town small-mindedness unpleasant: "Its citizens seemed

committed to an all-out defense against progress, original ideas, and especially against anything remotely resembling behavior to which they
were not accustomed."

Lowell's early memories were of cornfields and the whistles of trains
heading elsewhere. His father finished medical school at the University of
Nebraska, mostly through correspondence courses, and then was in a hurry
to ride one of those trains out of Kirkman.

Harry writes that his "first stop was Chicago, where I went to attend
postgraduate courses . . . at the Rush Medical School and then at the North-
western Medical School." You could never have enough education, Dr. Harry
Thomas always believed. Then he boarded a train in Chicago heading
west—to check out a pair of gold-rush towns in Colorado, which Harry's
brother Carl had suggested were full of opportunity. Ever since Carl and
he had spent a summer in Leadville 11 years earlier, Harry had felt the call
of Colorado mining towns.[4]

Dr. Thomas, who was 30 years old, liked what he saw of Cripple Creek
and, in particular, of its sister city, which sat atop the bulk of the gold
mines, Victor, Colorado. Harry rented an office and an apartment in a
brick building there and sent for his wife and son. Lowell was eight.

Victor squats on the southwestern flank of Pike's Peak—in an uneven
bowl surrounded by a half-dozen hills that look gentle until you consider
that they begin, just below the tree line, at nearly 10,000 feet. When the
Thomas family arrived, almost all the trees that had once eked out an existence on those hills had been chopped down—first primarily for the convenience of cattle, then primarily, before railroads brought coal in, as fuel
for the prospectors. The town's center had been fortified by a clump of brick
buildings—one four stories tall and all of them brand-new when the Thomas
family arrived. They had been built in response to a fire a year earlier
that had burned down much of the town. A scattering of wooden houses
surrounded the brick. And some of Victor's streets were shaded by the
headframes of mines.

About 500 people had lived in Cripple Creek and Victor. Then someone had found traces of gold, then lots more gold—a couple of extraordinarily rich lodes. Cripple Creek and neighboring Victor, Lowell would write
in his never-understated memoir, were sitting "atop the greatest concentration of gold ever mined by man." Not quite, but there was a tremendous
amount of the magic metal—thanks to a buried and long-dormant volcano,
which had lifted this relatively heavy metal up to within mining distance

of the surface. The Thomases arrived in the first year of the new century, a year when $18 million worth of gold was extracted from the local mines. Victor dubbed itself the "city of gold mines." Its streets and houses were *undermined* by the *levels*—the horizontal *workings*—of a half-dozen mines.

Soon there were 55,000 people in the Cripple Creek–Victor area— some to dig for the gold, some, like Dr. Thomas, to supply services to those who did. The high terrain was quickly penetrated by three different rail-roads, and two new trolley lines helped people make their way from town to town. To keep them content the area boasted 150 saloons. Dr. and Mrs. Thomas, however, were both teetotalers.

Quite a few doctors joined the migration into Cripple Creek and Vic-tor. Most did well. Injuries and illnesses were always plentiful, and some patients were well-heeled: 30 local mine owners had become millionaires. But most of those doctors then left. Harry Thomas stayed.

In photographs Dr. Thomas appears stern, with a long, thick mustache. In reality Harry seems to have been a bit dreamy, and he does not appear to have been there primarily for the money. Even his son, who tends to speak worshipfully of his father, calls him "inept" at "the business side of his practice. . . . He seemed constitutionally incapable of pressing anyone for payment of a bill," Lowell recalls, "and had devised a calming strategy for dealing with delinquent accounts: he simply forgot about them."[5] Cer-tainly, Harry could not match his son's outsized drive and ambition.

However, Dr. Thomas was an unusually bright and studious man, with a yearning for all sorts of learning. His interests ranged "from music to mathematics," is how Lowell would put it. As Ben Franklin had been and Lowell Thomas would be, Dr. Thomas was a Freemason—a member of a secret society with a cerebral as well as charitable bent. And as Franklin established the Junto Club, for mutual improvement, in Philadelphia, Dr. Thomas established the Century Club, a literary group, in the Cripple Creek area. This variety of American—and Harry Thomas' son was also of the type—was always busy improving at one thing or another. It wasn't necessarily what you might have thought they ought to be getting better at—say, in Harry's case, running his medical practice—but it was noble.

Harry invested in a telescope, but otherwise spent, as the young Frank-lin had, just about all of his extra money on books. Their little house in Victor, Colorado, was eventually stuffed, Lowell reports, with 3,000 vol-umes. Lowell claims to have been reading by the age of three.

While his moral compass was strong, Dr. Thomas does not seem to have been formally religious; his son labels him an agnostic. His wife, Harriet, had no such doubts: she was a fundamentalist. Harriet found herself a seat on the sawdust floor of a tent whenever a big-time evangelist—Billy Sunday, Carry Nation—managed to make it all the way to Cripple Creek. And she was no less principled than her husband. Her letters to her son, along with pleas that he attend church, would contain injunctions against "a life of ease and luxury" and the pursuit of "money above everything else," and she would express in those letters the hope that he might help others to a "higher and richer life."

A gold-rush town seems an odd place for the respectable (back when that description carried great weight) Dr. and Mrs. Thomas. And it is difficult to imagine Harry, not to mention Harriet, patronizing the honky-tonks. But they carved out a comfortable place for themselves in the community. And what a study those get-rich-quick, here-today towns must have made for an inquisitive man like Harry! And what treasures the surrounding mountains held for someone fascinated with geology and biology!

Young Lowell tagged along on his father's weekend specimen-gathering expeditions. And sometimes Lowell stood alone at one of the spots in Victor from which the view to the southwest was clear and stared at the gray and white ribbon of the Sangre de Cristo mountain range about 60 miles distant.[6]

((•))

In the summer of 1901, the newly elected vice president of the United States boarded the Short Line railroad in Colorado Springs. The owners of the gold mines in Cripple Creek and Victor had built this line, officially known as the Colorado Springs and Cripple Creek District Railroad. Its purpose: to break the monopoly held by the company that owned the other two railroads that carried (along with passengers) supplies and machinery for the mines up and gold ore down. Those lines followed roundabout but relatively gentle paths up to those two mining towns. The new Short Line took a steeper, shorter route. It zigged and zagged around the southern slope of Pike's Peak—through dark tunnels, around red and gray rock formations that looked even more handsome as they rose above the tall green grasses. Some of the huge, rounded cliff formations were of national-park quality.

The white peaks of the Sangre de Cristo range flickered in and out of view as the steam train, carrying the new vice president, neared Victor.[7]

"This is the ride that bankrupts the English language," Theodore Roosevelt announced after he disembarked.

Teddy Roosevelt was one of those politicians who genuinely enjoyed the ritual that inevitably accompanied his appearance in an American city: He settled himself in the wood-paneled lobby of one of Victor's brick buildings—the Gold Coin Club, right across the street from the Gold Coin Mine. And a line formed to meet him—a long line; for this was TR. The new president, William McKinley, was not popular in Victor: he had talked during the campaign about fixing the price of gold; miners wanted it free to rise. But Teddy Roosevelt—war hero, horseman, nature lover, outdoorsman—may have been the most charismatic vice president the country had ever elected and the one best suited to win over Coloradans. The vice president shook hand after hand. He exchanged banter—an activity at which he excelled. He made sure he had a lump of sugar as a special treat for each of the children.

The tough but affable, outdoorsy, global-minded, forward-looking TR seemed perfectly suited, too, to inspire one of those on line that day in Victor. Although he was still young enough to qualify for a lump of sugar, Lowell Thomas reports that he had read Roosevelt's four-volume *The Winning of the West*—read it again and again. Nine-year-old Lowell waited on the long line, shook the vice president's hand, benefited from a bit of banter and received his treat. Then—Thomas would always try to increase his proximity to the accomplished—he went back to the end of the line, waited and shook Teddy Roosevelt's hand again.[8]

When old enough to vote, Thomas, with the rarest of exceptions, would cast his ballot for—and befriend—internationalist Republicans for the rest of his life.

$((\bullet))$

Lowell's mother gave birth to a girl—who soon died of pneumonia—then to another girl, his sister Pherbia, 12 years younger than Lowell. Her unusual name was borrowed from Lowell's paternal grandmother. Just about every day Harry read serious literature to both son and, when she grew older, daughter. And "Papa," as he was called in the house, was obsessed with another self-improvement strategy—one mostly forgotten today: mastering elocution. Lowell was constantly drilled on proper diction, enunciation ("Aspirate your h's!") and projection.

Elocution would serve him well. And Lowell combined it with a naturally deep, resonant, bold voice. His voice's strength he may have inherited from his mother, who, he later recalled, had perfect pitch, and "when she sang in the choir you could hear her above all others."[9]

In 1904, the year Lowell's sister was born, to the excitements of a mining town were added the horrors of a miners' strike, complete with beatings, shootings and a deadly bombing. This was part of an American and international conflict that would be fought again and again in the twentieth century: rapacious bosses versus militant workers, capitalism versus something more egalitarian and unproven, the status quo versus radical change, right versus left. The mines in Cripple Creek and Victor certainly were brutal and dangerous, the workers underpaid: most made three dollars a day. The union, the Western Federation of Miners, was led by Big Bill Haywood, who was something of a Marxist. (His ashes would one day be interred in the Kremlin Wall in Moscow.) Haywood demanded a lot for his members, pushed hard and made enemies beyond the mine owners.

One day, as Lowell tells the story, he and a cousin watched from a window in his father's office as an anti-union crowd confronted the strikers. A fiery orator riled them up. Punches were thrown. Then shots, many shots, were fired. The window rattled. The militia moved in. Two men lay on the ground dead. If Lowell's account in his much later memoir is to be believed, his father raced out to treat the wounded. Dr. Thomas found one bloody miner who had been shot in the stomach. Someone helped the doctor drag him by the armpits back to the office. After his father placed the man on the operating table, Lowell's job was to remove his gun. Then he turned toward the wall as his father began trying to extract the bullet.

The strike was broken. Harry Thomas had been sympathetic with the miners, but—although one of the 3,000 books Dr. Thomas owned was Karl Marx's Das Kapital[10]—he had no use for Haywood and the other union leaders. Lowell's own unwavering anti-communism may have gotten a start here. His United States was a global defender of capitalism.

Lowell's introduction to a couple of other American values did not come from his parents. Harry and Harriet had done what Americans often did: they had moved west. But this studious man and his deeply religious wife were not infused with much of the bet-your-bottom-dollar, stake-your-claim, always-ready-to-move-on American mentality that was so much on display in Cripple Creek and Victor. Their son, on the other hand, soaked up quite a bit of it as he wandered the honky-tonk streets and played the slot machines. For much of his life, Lowell would bet on long shots, on the new and unproven. His pleasures mostly involved risk—navigating rapids, scaling or skiing down mountains, going somewhere exotic or trying his hand at something unfamiliar. And he was never afraid of spending big—even if the money he was spending had been borrowed.

Unlike his father, but like many of the local prospectors, and in line with the world's image of Americans, Lowell Thomas had an outsized faith in himself. Life has a way of disabusing people—most prospectors, for example—of such a bullheaded self-confidence. Life never got around to doing that for Thomas. He always managed to repay (if only with the help of another loan) and to earn and spend more. He was not entirely lacking in insecurities and displayed a self-effacing sense of humor, but at heart Thomas was always brash.

When the doctor's son stopped growing, he was about five feet eight. His face was square, his nose and eyebrows a bit thick and his head a bit large for his shoulders. He was then, and remained for most of his life, comely, attractive without being excessively handsome. Heads inevitably turned, however, as soon as he unleashed that magnificent, resonant, dynamic, carefully controlled voice. Ben Hecht, the journalist and dramatist, described Thomas' voice as "juicy."[11] He may have picked the wrong liquid. The extensive audio archives reveal a voice that is rich and bracing, even a bit tart. Coffee seems the better simile. And his voice would prove—like Franklin Roosevelt's, like Frank Sinatra's—not only captivating for Americans but habit-forming.

Lowell does not seem to have been particularly aggressive romantically—no "threat to the local Lotharios," as he put it. Nonetheless, once he began noticing the girls around him, Lowell pined; he played "post office," a kissing game. He collected his share of invigorating, if often awkward, experiences in haylofts or, for a time, in the living room of a young lady named Gertrude Oliver. Lowell's stays in the latter setting often extended late into the evening—until her father, by Lowell's account, would lower an alarm clock over a second-floor railing. After some months of this, that father, in the traditional fashion, followed the young man home one evening and asked the traditional question: "My boy, do you think you can support my daughter?"[12] But this was a boy whose ambitions extended well beyond supporting a wife in Victor, Colorado. His amorous adventures continued, but his visits to Gertrude Oliver's living room ceased.

((•))

Victor, with its brick buildings, was more developed than most of the cowboy towns (or Hollywood sets) that later appeared in movies and on television. But the range was never more than a few blocks away. And the gambling halls were right in the center of things, as were the dance halls. The town had its red-light district—just a few blocks from where the upright doctor and his family lived. In sixth grade Lowell began waking up very early to deliver newspapers, so he could buy a burro to better explore the mountains and the range, and he found himself chatting with the friendly young women who, also for business reasons, had stayed up very late.

Unlike most of his friends, young Lowell didn't drink. His father, as Lowell tells the story, only had to get him out of jail once—after a well-aimed snowball collided with a local businessman. And only once did his father have to pull Lowell away from a loose woman—and undertake a lecture about venereal disease (an important component of Dr. Thomas' practice).

But still Lowell lived the life. Dressed in the requisite "boots, flannel shirt and broad-brimmed Stetson," he wandered the mountains and, with his buddies, explored caves and mines. One summer he found a job on a cattle ranch but ran off when he found himself "clearing a boulder-strewn field" rather than roping steers.

Other summers, he rotated through most of the jobs in the gold mines. Two of those summers he rode "assay." That was a good job: nine hours a day on horseback filling his saddlebags with ore samples from new strikes so their gold content could be evaluated. He sported that round, flat hat and wore denim bib-overalls, rolled up at the cuff. Sometimes Lowell would doze off in the saddle on the treeless slopes. Sometimes he'd head up to a lookout and gaze across the Rockies.[13]

Americans were beginning to romanticize the cowboy. Lowell had more or less become one. Wild Bill Hickok was two generations older than he; Annie Oakley one. But Hickok was raised in Illinois, Oakley in Ohio, right near where Lowell was born. Teddy Roosevelt, that cowboy president, had grown up in Manhattan. Lowell Thomas had an authentic free-range, wild-West childhood.

That childhood, combined with the adventurous spirit with which Lowell seems to have been born, conferred on him the impulse to conquer the world's deserts and jungles as well as its mountains—which he would do, often taking his audiences along on his journeys, often implying that a possibility-grabbing, resourceful, cowboy America might be able to do something to help out "over there."

(((•)))

When Lowell left Victor for college at Valparaiso University, in Northern Indiana, he made sure not to surrender his identity as a man from the West: he continued to wear his Stetson.

Lowell had not started out as an impressive student. His elementary school teachers scribbled remarks like "poor work," "conduct poor" or "average" next to his name. But he had begun to apply himself more at Victor High School. He had always been young for his class; still, although never a particularly gifted athlete, he played end and quarterback on the football team. And one of his teachers, Mabel Barbee Lee, writes that even as a sophomore Lowell stood out in the classroom by posing a "continuous challenge" to her "meager knowledge of modern history": "He was quiet mannered and fine-looking," she writes, "with dark wavy hair and serious eyes that seemed to see through my thin pretensions. Before long I was immersed in cramming my head with world history, fortifying myself against his unexpected questions."[14]

Lee is another unreliable memoirist, and hers is hardly an unbiased account: Lowell Thomas wrote the foreword to her memoir of living in Cripple Creek and Victor; her book is dedicated to him. But Lowell had begun to shine in class. And, of course, he had that great voice. There must not have been much doubt about who would deliver the commencement address when he graduated from Victor High School.

Valparaiso University was a no-frills institution—no intercollegiate sports teams, not even a gym. It kept its focus on learning and catered to older students and less well-off students. "The institution was organized," an advertisement for the university at the time explains, "with the idea of giving to every person, whether rich or poor, a chance to obtain a thorough, practical education at an expense within his reach." Tuition was $15 per quarter, room and board between $1.70 and $2.25 per week—less than a third of what an Ivy League college cost. The emphasis on studies—as well as the low fees—must have appealed to Dr. Thomas.

Lowell was 17 when he started college, hardly exceptionally young. But what happened when he registered for classes at Valparaiso University was indeed out of the ordinary. The young man looked over the schedule of freshman courses that first semester and decided they didn't look all that difficult. So Harry's son signed up for some sophomore courses as well.

He sat in these classes, behind wood and wrought-iron desks, with other young, or not so young, men and a scattering of women. The men wore dark suits and ties or bow ties and often had their hair parted in the middle. The women were in plain dresses, with their hair pulled back in buns. Outside the classroom some of the students—the men at least—looked jaunty. Inside, their faces, if the surviving photos are a reliable guide, were sober.

The fact that Lowell was sitting in an excessive number of these classes, including some for which he was not qualified, went unnoticed until half the semester had passed. Then the university's vice president called the young man in to put a stop to this foolishness. But when that administrator examined Lowell's grades, he realized that Lowell seemed to be having no difficulty handling the more advanced courses and the extra course load. Indeed, his grades at Valparaiso ranged from the low 80s to the high 90s, plus one rare 100, in a course called "Letter Writing."

The vice president was reduced to pointing out, in Thomas' recollection, that "at this rate you'll have your bachelor's degree in little more than a year." But Thomas' account of what happened next, in his memoir and elsewhere, seems wrong. Thomas reports having replied, "Then I'll stay two and take a master's." And he reports having fulfilled that boast.[15] But there is no evidence that Lowell Thomas ever obtained anything beyond a bachelor's degree at Valparaiso. He did, however, obtain that degree in much less than the usual time, graduating in two years.

In Valparaiso Lowell also demonstrated his knack for cozying up to celebrities. He had three advantages in this endeavor: First, of course, he was the opposite of shy. William Jennings Bryan had been the Democratic Party's presidential nominee in three of the last four elections and—of additional interest to this eloquent young student—was considered perhaps the best orator in the United States. When Bryan came to Valparaiso to deliver a speech, Lowell raced to the front of the room the moment that speech ended, and soon this small-boned college student was having a chat with that imposing, square-jawed, broad-chested man—among the best-known individuals in the nation.

Lowell was also exceedingly personable—well-mannered, good-humored, interested in others and always prepared to hold up his end of a conversation. Bryan, as Thomas tells the story, invited the young student to ride with him in the carriage to the railroad station.

The third secret of Lowell's success with celebrities was his skill at spotting and allying himself with other young people of talent. While at Valparaiso, Lowell befriended Eddie Rickenbacker, who later became America's most renowned World War I flying ace and a lifelong buddy of Thomas'. This ability to charm larval celebrities supported another of Lowell's proclivities: he was, throughout his life, an inveterate name-dropper.

Lowell met Rickenbacker, then one of the early race-car drivers, at a track near Valparaiso. Automobiles were a relatively new invention at the time. And Thomas, like a twenty-first-century venture capitalist, was unusually alert to what were not then called "new technologies"—particularly those that could take people places farther and faster than burros or horses: automobiles, airplanes, film, radio, television. These machines, which shaped the twentieth century, were not all invented in the United States, but they became, all of them, associated with the United States.

Most students then, as now, worked to help support themselves while going to college. Even as he was marching double-time through Valparaiso, Lowell Thomas held down a variety of jobs: While he boarded in Stiles Hall—an unremarkable brick dormitory with small, arched windows—he also served as one of the building's janitors. He was paid to milk someone's cow. He worked as a waiter and then as a short-order cook. In his memoir he doesn't report that he was suffering from overwork, but we have a letter from his mother making clear that this was indeed a problem.

None of those jobs led in the direction of any future he was contemplating. So after Lowell graduated and returned home to Victor, he did what he had done before he raced through his college education—he got a job in a gold mine, for three dollars a day.

Harry Thomas thought his son ought to consider a medical career. That plan, Lowell reports, was abandoned when father brought son into an operating room. He recalls "white shrouded figures," "a shaven and shining skull," something that "looked like a hacksaw," a "bloody mass of brain."

"And that's all I remember," Thomas explains, in what has the hallmarks of one of his too-good stories, "because at that point I interrupted the operation by keeling over."

But shortly after Lowell's return to Victor, he received a phone call that opened a new possibility: he was asked—out of the blue, he insists—to be a reporter on the *Victor Record*. Given the fact that the newspaper— circulation about 3,000—did not employ any other reporters or editors (a sister publication, the *Cripple Creek Times*, had its own small staff), that essentially meant that this 19-year-old would be putting out a daily newspaper himself, at a salary barely higher than he was earning in the mines. [16]

((•))

Lowell Thomas has credited to William Randolph Hearst the discovery of the audience-grabbing capabilities of newspaper stories reveling in crime or sex or, better, both—the sort of stories emphasized at the *Victor Record* and the *Cripple Creek Times*: ". . . BLOOD STAINED CLOTHES ARE FOUND . . . ," "MAN FALLS IN FIT ON STREET, WOMEN SCARED." Hearst actually had *rediscovered* this formula—first at the *San Francisco Examiner*, then at the *New York Journal*. Joseph Pulitzer, whom Hearst openly imitated, had rediscovered it some years earlier at the *St. Louis Post-Dispatch*, then at the *New York World*. This brand of sensationalism became known as *yellow journalism* in the late 1890s in New York—after Hearst and Pulitzer began one-upping each other in coverage of murders and incitements to war with Spain over Cuba (and after they began a tug-of-war over rights to a cartoon character known as the Yellow Kid). But it was not their invention.

To one English visitor to America in 1842, it seemed a very American invention. Charles Dickens was unsparing in his critique of many of the journalists he found on this side of the Atlantic. Among the deprecations he hurled at the American press: "foul," "licentious," "abject," "vicious," "a disgrace," a spreader of "moral poison," a "frightful engine" and a "monster of depravity."[17] In other words, there was little to which Hearst, Pulitzer or even their wildest imitators stooped to which some of their predecessors on American newspapers had not previously stooped.

Indeed, James Gordon Bennett Sr., probably the most creative nineteenth-century American journalist, had rediscovered the power of sex and crime in 1836, when his investigation of the ax murder of a well-known and attractive prostitute tripled the circulation of his *New York Herald*. And

Bennett, raised in Scotland, had learned some of these tricks from early nineteenth-century British newspapers, which could be pretty "foul" and "licentious" themselves. One hundred and five years before Bennett's investigation, Ben Franklin had also rediscovered this formula: his *Pennsylvania Gazette*, for example, indulged in the tale of a man who, having found his wife "napping" with a stonecutter, then attempted to decapitate said stonecutter.

This formula, the point is, is as old as news itself.[18] Nonetheless, it is true that with the success of Pulitzer and Hearst, this formula was being employed with renewed vigor in the United States in the early decades of the twentieth century. Cripple Creek and Victor, while somewhat removed from the wellsprings of journalistic innovation, were amply supplied with the raw materials for this brand of journalism. A single front page of the *Cripple Creek Times* during these months includes stories on three separate local mine accidents (two of them fatal), a murder trial in Denver and the sudden death of a young local man. And this does not appear to have been an unusually bloody day. "In any given ten-day period," Lowell recalls in his memoir, "you could count on a shooting spree in a gambling hall or one of the red-light districts, a holdup, a fire, a mine accident and an indignant reader proposing to horsewhip the editor"—this last, of course, not necessarily being fodder for Lowell's newspaper but a hazard of the career into which Lowell had dipped his toe.

Clearly he had a talent for it. Industry and curiosity helped. Courage helped. Brashness and salesmanship helped—although Lowell's weakness for hyperbole diminished somewhat the journalistic merit of his publication: a fire in three structures became, in type three inches high, "BLAZE SWEEPS LOCAL BUILDINGS." After about six months on the *Record*, Lowell was wooed away by the publisher of the *Victor Daily News*—a new newspaper, the town's second—for about twice what he had earned in the mines and with something vaguely resembling a staff. Here his most notable headline was "MAYOR'S NEPHEW SHOT IN LOVE NEST." The mayor, while he shared a name with that amorous shooting victim, turned out not to be related to him. As Thomas tells the story, he came after Lowell with a gun. In the journalism business as practiced in a gold-rush town in 1912, a talent for being able to talk yourself out of trouble also came in handy.

((•))

H. L. Mencken, 12 years Lowell's senior, had first stumbled into a position on a newspaper in Baltimore at the age of 18. He later rhapsodized about "the gaudy life that young newspaper reporters led in the major American cities at the turn of the century. . . . I was at large in a wicked seaport of a half a million people," Mencken recalled, "with a front seat at every public show, as free of the night as of the day, and getting earfuls and eyefuls of instruction in a hundred giddy arcana, none of them taught in schools." Mencken, eschewing his characteristic crustiness, concluded that it was "the maddest, gladdest, damndest existence ever enjoyed by mortal youth. . . . The days chased one another like kittens chasing their tails."[19]

Lowell, at about the same age, was "at large" in a smaller, landlocked but no less "wicked" town. He had similar fun.

The United States—born with the considerable assistance of a crusading, hotheaded press—had long been a newspaper country: in 1870, by one estimate, one-third of all the newspapers in the world were published here. And the number of newspapers in the United States peaked just about when Lowell was getting his introduction to journalism. If sheer numbers are the measure, then this may actually qualify as something of a "golden age" for newspapers. Each day more or less everyone who could read read one—or two or three. In 1910 the average home in New York State received more than three newspapers a day.[20]

After all, unless you had a ticket to the opera house or were drawn to the dance halls, there weren't many other public forms of entertainment. And when it came to satisfying the ingrained human thirst for news, there wasn't much competition. Busybodies certainly couldn't keep up with the early twentieth-century daily newspaper—fortified by webs of telegraph lines, by cables under all the oceans, by news-wholesaling wire services, by accelerating presses, by labor-saving linotype machines, by cheap newsprint and by tireless young Henry Menckens and Lowell Thomases.

The also ridiculously young Guglielmo Marconi had gotten radio working in Italy three years after Lowell was born. But in 1912 it was just morphing from "wireless telegraphy," which communicated only through dots and dashes, to "wireless telephony"—carrying music, carrying voices. Few if any at that time imagined that radio could become a wireless newsmonger.

So if you wanted to know what was going on, you paid a penny or two for a newspaper. And if you wanted to talk about what was going on, you talked about what was in that newspaper.

Nonetheless, receiving and providing "instruction in" those "hundred giddy arcana" was not the most reputable way to earn a living in the early twentieth century, especially since so many of those arcana—in accordance with the old formula—involved sex and crime. Mencken's father had insisted that he take over the family cigar factory. But his father died, and Mencken was left to newspapering. Journalism also does not seem to have met Lowell's father's standards. No evidence survives of ultimatums or even harsh words, but it is clear from letters on other topics that Dr. Thomas gave advice to his son freely and expressed concern to him frequently. And it is clear that Lowell was consistently respectful and well understood his father's value system. After a year of this mad, glad, damned existence, Harry Thomas' son went off to accumulate more degrees.

((•))

This time—the year was 1912—Lowell stayed closer to home: Denver University. And this time Lowell did have a specific career in mind: government service. But while his family was comfortable, all those unsent medical bills meant that there was no excess money for room and board. Lowell would still need to support himself. At night he worked as a clerk in a hotel—long a job favored by students because of the opportunity to study and sleep. And, having finally gained some experience at something besides horseback riding and mining, and never being one to sit on his hands, Lowell also found a job as a part-time reporter for both the *Denver Times* and the *Rocky Mountain News*.

Now he *was* reporting in a "major" American city. Now this ace acquaintance-maker was covering stories alongside other up-and-coming members of the journalistic fraternity—many of whom he would befriend and some of whom he would encounter again in Chicago or New York. Denver, unlike Victor, was an express stop on the journalistic circuit. Picking out the stories Lowell himself wrote is not possible. Bylines in these newspapers were rare. But it seems safe to assume that his appearances in these two Denver papers contributed substantially to Lowell's development as a journalist. Because, for the first time, this newspaperman—now all of 20—was working under editors.

One of the more helpful was William L. Chenery, then city editor of the *Rocky Mountain News* (later publisher of *Collier's* magazine), who was wont to dispense, city editor–like, advice such as: "The teller of the tale is not always the best judge of its interest or significance." Lowell still had plenty of mistakes to make, but he was learning. And with veteran journalists now examining his copy, fewer of those mistakes would now appear on the front page.

Nonetheless, this remained local-first journalism: Of the 23 stories that appeared on the front page of the September 24, 1912, edition of the *Denver Times*—about the time Lowell would have begun doing some reporting for the paper—all but one featured local, state or national news. The exception was a small piece mentioning the German kaiser—but only because he had honored a Denver banker. And the paper practiced a version of the if-it-bleeds-it-leads journalism Lowell was introduced to in Victor. The most prominent headline in the *Denver Times* that day was "LEAPS TO DEATH UNDER AN ENGINE." And the train engine in question, of course, had been "speeding into Denver."

The *Rocky Mountain News* was a somewhat more substantial paper. Two of the 12 stories on its front page that day, despite the lack of a Denver angle, mentioned Europe. But five of those stories mentioned crime, tragedy or sex. National and local politics were covered in these Denver newspapers, but there was little evidence in them either of the progressive muckraking or the thoughtful journalist-politician seminars on public policy that Doris Kearns Goodwin found in Washington and New York newspapers in these years.

Back at the university Lowell's course of study followed a familiar pattern. He was there for a master's degree, but after the university's chancellor suggested that he might want to supplement his rather hurried BA with some additional undergraduate courses, Lowell soon was working toward a second BA, as well as that master's.

Both degrees were achieved in a year—although, due to university regulations, Lowell did not formally receive the master's until June 1914. However, the takeaway from his year at Denver University that would have the greatest effect upon his life was the memory of a freshman there who had become his friend: Frances Ryan. Despite his rapidly growing number of degrees, Lowell was only a couple of years older than most freshmen himself. He and Frances Ryan had never actually dated. Yet, as he later tried to explain it, Miss Ryan seemed to have "a kind of heightened sensitivity to life's promises"—which, with a stronger adjective, could also have been a description of himself.

((•))

Lowell's first stop after Denver was the mountains—not around Victor, but farther west. His father—no businessman—had purchased a cattle ranch at 7,000 feet in the San Juan Mountains of Colorado. His father's younger brother Ira and his family, escapees from Chicago, were trying to make a go of that ranch. Lowell went out to help: "This meant I spent most of the summer in the saddle," he later recalls, "helping with brandings and round-ups, sleeping on my saddle blanket under the stars."[21]

By the time summer ended, Lowell's career aspirations had shifted once again, this time toward the law, which would require a fourth degree. So Lowell decided to move in the opposite direction of that uncle, to Chicago and law school. But the young man, as always, would need to support himself. Perhaps it was for this reason, or perhaps it was because he had never quite quelled a craving for "the gaudy life" of the journalist, but Lowell's first stop after arriving in Chicago was not a law school but a newspaper office—at a time when that city was experiencing some of the most exuberant journalism the country has seen.

2.

Two Scoops in Chicago

W hen your desk at the *Chicago Daily Journal* is next to that of Ben Hecht, who would co-author *The Front Page*, you know you are in for some hijinks and low adventures.

This was at a time when ethical standards in journalism were still in the process of solidifying. In 1912, almost a year before Lowell Thomas arrived in Chicago, a group of editors heard Casper S. Yost, editorial director of the *St. Louis Globe Democrat*, argue for "creation of an ethical organization of American newspaper editors." It finally happened—a decade later: Yost founded the American Society of Newspaper Editors, which approved a "Code of Ethics or Canons of Journalism."

The first canon declared that "a journalist who uses his power for any selfish or otherwise unworthy purpose is faithless to a high trust." The fourth canon proclaimed the importance for newspapers of "SINCERITY, TRUTHFULNESS, ACCURACY." The sixth insisted that "a newspaper should not invade private rights or feeling without sure warrant of public right as distinguished from public curiosity."[1]

Of course, there were reasons the need was felt to canonize these standards at this time. Hecht wrote *The Front Page* with Charles MacArthur, who had also prowled Chicago as a young man, and in its various theatrical and cinematic incarnations over the decades, their play delighted in a no-holds-barred Chicago journalism in which such standards were, at best, smirked at in the process of being ignored: the play's main character is occupied with concealing a convicted murderer to preserve his (or, in one film version, her) exclusive.

To understand the journalism in which Lowell Thomas was marinating in Chicago, it is worth examining some of Hecht's own escapades. Hecht had gotten his start in Chicago as a teenaged "picture chaser"— photographs then being a relatively new and highly valued addition to the entertainments newspapers were providing. And this fledgling journalist had chased notoriously hard, most notably while hustling to obtain a photo of a young woman who had died in a suicide pact with a married clergyman. When her grieving family wouldn't provide a photo, and after his competitors had left, Hecht, the story goes, climbed to the roof of the family's home and blocked the chimney. Smoke then caused the family to rush out, after which Hecht snuck in and made off with an acceptable photo. So much for not invading "private rights and feelings" for mere "public curiosity." This shockingly insensitive behavior led Walter Howey, the respected editor of a rival newspaper, to contact Hecht . . . to offer him a job.[2]

In a memoir Hecht also admits to having, in print, reported as true a raven-haired gold digger's fib that the jewelry a gentleman friend had given her had then been stolen from her—this in return for the invitation to crawl into her bed.[3] So much for "SINCERITY, TRUTHFULNESS, ACCURACY." And printing such a lie in return for sex would certainly seem to qualify as "selfish or otherwise unworthy."

Of course it was not just Hecht, who at least could write with as much energy, wit and style as anyone. Nor was it just Chicago. Nor was it just these years. But journalism in Chicago when Lowell Thomas arrived was particularly unrestrained—in part because it was intensely competitive.

Competition is one way to encourage some enterprising journalism. Walter Howey, the editor who had tried to hire Ben Hecht after Hecht had snatched that suicide's photo, once sent a healthy undercover reporter into doctors' offices with a bankbook in his back pocket. The point was to demonstrate how often that reporter was diagnosed with a nonexistent venereal disease that just happened to cost as much to treat as he had in his bank account.[4] That sort of journalism sold papers as well as exposed abuses.

But competition among newspapers in Chicago in the early twentieth century sometimes got ugly. Trucks distributing other newspapers were occasionally hijacked. Circulation men and newsboys trying to sell other newspapers were occasionally beaten, kidnapped or even shot.[5] But the competition mostly expressed itself not through violence but through coverage of violence. William Randolph Hearst, master of yellow journalism, had started a sensational and successful newspaper in Chicago at the turn of the century, the *American*. That seemed to open the floodgates on crime reporting in a city, truth be told, that produced more than its share of crimes.

Chicago, like any other city, has always been many things, but when Ben Hecht and Lowell Thomas were there, this city was very definitely one thing: wild. Crime statistics are notoriously unreliable, but there is evidence that the number of arrests for felonies jumped in Chicago in the years Thomas was in residence (1913 to 1915), as Chicago was becoming, by some measures, "the most violent major urban center in the nation." The fact that police officers were being encouraged to "shoot first" and "shoot to kill" contributed to the violence, as did the reluctance of local juries to find defendants in murder cases guilty if the fights had been "fair" or the killings seemed in some way "justified." Lowell, for instance, covered the story of an alderman shot by a young woman claiming to be his "neglected wife" and noted in a journal he had begun keeping that "public sentiment is with the woman."[6]

Most Chicago newspapers at the time did not evince excessive interest in public policy, political theories or foreign affairs. Hecht himself confesses to "a total unawareness of any political problems or ideologies that did not involve Chicago's thieving aldermen, mayor or other officials."[7] Freed of the distraction of such extraneous events and notions, Hecht and Thomas could examine each day the wildest occurrences this vigorous city had to offer.

The newspaper for which these two crown princes of journalism performed such examinations was the *Chicago Daily Journal*—one of the town's ten or so English-language dailies. (Chicago also was enlivened by a dozen foreign-language dailies.) The *Journal* was neither the best nor the most successful of the lot but was a contender on most local slayings, scandals, scams, suicides and baseball games. Its 16 or so pages were hawked on the streets for a penny. Lowell stumbled into the paper's newsroom right upon arriving in Chicago at the beginning of September 1913. Perhaps, he suggests, selecting this newspaper, rather than the others also headquartered on Market Street, because he liked the building's "broad stairs and massive double doors."[8] (That building is long gone, as is Market Street—now replaced by the western extension of Wacker Drive.)

The man who brought Lowell on board was Richard J. Finnegan, soon promoted to city editor of the *Journal*.[9] Finnegan apparently made his hire on first sight, maybe because fellows sporting Stetson hats, fresh from a summer on a ranch, were rather exotic back in the Midwest. Or maybe the paper was simply in need of another aggressive, very young man willing to work for peanuts and able both to stitch together a coherent account of a crime and stay reasonably sober. Above the water cooler in the *Journal*'s city room, reports Hecht, hung the following notification over the signature of the paper's publisher: "ANY REPORTER WHO IS WORTH MORE THAN $35 A WEEK DOES NOT BELONG IN MY NEWSPAPER."[10]

Lowell had just turned 21. Ben was two years younger, less educated but more familiar with the intricacies of big-city reporting, more prone to theorizing and more likely to wax poetic. Here, in one fine simile, is Hecht's cynical take on the journalism of his era (and many others): "Trying to determine what is going on in the world by reading the newspapers is like trying to tell the time by watching the second hand of a clock."[11]

Ben succeeded in placing a short story in the tiny Chicago literary magazine that first published James Joyce's *Ulysses*.[12] He aspired to *art*. While feasting on Chicago's smorgasbord of sensations by day, Ben was concocting sentences and ruminations by night that might elevate him into contention with the heavyweights. Lowell was becoming adept at picking up the scent of and sinking his teeth into news, and he could devise pleasing, often clever wordings of his own. But Lowell's aspirations, though mighty, were not literary or theoretical. He was never much given to undue polishing or excessive mulling over. That is why I am borrowing some aperçus from Hecht as I follow the trail of Thomas.

"We," Hecht writes, using a "we" easily broad enough to include Lowell, "interviewed thieves, swindlers, murderers, lunatics, fire bugs, bigamists, gangsters and innumerable sobbing ladies who had taken successful potshots at their married lovers."[13] (Actually Thomas, also not averse to leaning on Hecht, himself quotes this list in his memoir.) Lowell jotted down in his journal that he, for example, "handled actress suicide story involving charges against wealthy . . . clubman, threats of Mann Act prosecution and white slavery."

Given this pageant of colorful miscreants—of whom Chicago had an inexhaustible supply—it was hard, whatever one's ambitions, not to be enchanted by the swirl of the second hand. Hecht and Thomas would both retain a taste for larger-than-life characters—and each, in his way, eventually make considerable progress toward becoming one.

Hecht's halcyon days as a Chicago newspaper reporter—quite a few more years than Thomas managed—were not just exhilarating but formative. He would plunder them for characters, dialects and even plots as he took his poetic talent to movies, theater and novels. For Thomas, however, the *Chicago Daily Journal* was just another adventure in a life that would overflow with adventures.

The *Journal* was an afternoon paper, which meant the reporters who fed it worked more or less from six in the morning to three in the afternoon. This proved convenient for Hecht, whose evening routine not only included taking a whack at fiction but also, by his own account, entertaining a young prostitute he had installed in his apartment and was trying to reform. This early schedule proved convenient, too, for Thomas, who, after all, had come to Chicago with an additional purpose. Indeed, the prospect of having his evenings free may have been the real reason he walked into the *Journal* building. After all, another September would be arriving soon—and Dr. Thomas' son was hearing the call of another degree.

Reporters of the Chicago variety were "scorekeepers of the dead, injured and abused," to borrow another Hechtian formulation. Lawyers, like doctors, might have a bit more to offer such unfortunates. The lucky hall of learning was the Chicago-Kent School of Law, then on Michigan Avenue, a short walk from the *Journal* newsroom. Its students liked to refer to their school as "the largest night law school in the world."[14] Lowell was directed there by the *Journal*'s Dick Finnegan, who himself had squeezed a legal education into his evenings.

Lowell met with the appropriate academic officials and, being Lowell Thomas, was quickly accepted into Chicago-Kent. Then, a few days later, the consequences of what it meant to be Lowell Thomas—personable, poised, extraordinarily well spoken—became even clearer. The law school's dean, Edmund W. Burke, summoned him and announced that a vacancy had opened on the school's forensic oratory faculty.[15] Would the first-year student be interested in teaching a course on public speaking? Remaining undaunted was also a large part of what it meant, even at age 21, to be Lowell Thomas—so was answering "yes."

So first-year law student Lowell Jackson Thomas would lay claim to the title, which appeared now and again on his stationery or in local newspapers, "Professor of public speaking at the Kent School of Law" or, less grandly in school materials, "instructor of the public speaking class." This studying-plus-teaching load might just work for a person with a 6:00 a.m. to 3:00 p.m. reporting schedule—if that person was unnaturally energetic and heedless of sleep. "I've been busier than ever before in my life, and that is going some," Lowell writes to a friend from Denver University, Frances Ryan.[16]

Prodigious vitality was not uncommon in these young Chicago scribes: for a time, Ben Hecht claims, he secured, in an excess of ingenuity, that prostitute he was reforming a job as a reporter at the *Journal*; he also claims, equally dubiously, that he introduced her as a niece of Edith Wharton.[17] As Hecht tells it, that meant that, until she chose to revert to her old ways on a couch at the newspaper, his responsibilities each day included reporting her stories as well as his own.

The law-school course Lowell ran—in front of anywhere from 200 to 600 of his fellow students—went well. The course was built around a series of prominent guest speakers Lowell had persuaded to come by, including the man who was becoming the city's and probably the country's most revered defense attorney, Clarence Darrow. This eased somewhat the drain upon the instructor's vast but much-called-upon energies.

The courses Lowell took pleased him less, though he did well in them. "I couldn't get excited about torts and wills," he explains in his memoir. "But," he adds, "I guess my heart sang every morning when I reported to the city room."[18]

((•))

What made Lowell's heart sing was a city room devoted to informing the people of Chicago of such matters as—to confine myself to some of the headlines on the front page of the *Chicago Daily Journal* on July 6, 1914:

- HELEN MORTON HELD PRISONER IN HOME: HEIRESS, HELD INSANE, IS KEPT FROM FRIENDS
- SUSPECT ARRESTED AFTER FOUR ARE KILLED WITH AX: BABE AND KIN MURDERED AT BLUE ISLAND
- HOLD FIANCE OF DROWNED GIRL AS SLAYER
- PETRAS TAKES STAND IN TRIAL FOR HIS LIFE

This was, of course, a selection similar to that found in the *Victor Record* or the *Denver Times* when Lowell worked there, though, since the city was larger, the selection of crimes and tragedies was choicer. Foreign news was, as in those other papers, often absent from the *Journal*'s front page, even with Europe and eventually much of the world busy stumbling into war. That page that day did, however, include a reference to Sweden: a fellow from Chicago had just been named ambassador to that country.

News unconnected with Chicago, even news occurring outside of America, occasionally managed to command more attention. That world war often would. And Chicago produced its own incarnation of the dashing foreign correspondent, Floyd Gibbons, who traveled with the Mexican rebel leader Pancho Villa for four months in 1914, supplying the *Chicago Tribune* with intrepid and exclusive tales. Gibbons was widely praised for his boldness and fearlessness; Lowell would have noticed. But Gibbons, too, had started out covering the city's own juicy crimes and scandals. (Indeed, he was said to have been among the models for Hildy Johnson, the main character in *The Front Page*.[19]) And the goal in Chicago and elsewhere in American journalism at the time remained filling page one with as many such local sensations as events would allow.

Young Lowell found himself, in other words, engaged in a valued service: providing, as Hecht puts it, "our town . . . with its chief entertainment— newspaper headlines . . . the drama of facts in printer's ink." Movies and radio had not yet discovered that drama.

Since the competition among Chicago's plethora of dailies was intense, this required being quick. Getting a story before anyone else, getting an *exclusive*, meant your paper, plus the readers of your paper, could be the first to tell. And no one was going to do much business today hawking on the streets some bit of melodrama that the competition had hawked on the streets yesterday. Audiences and therefore publishers and therefore city editors and therefore reporters like Lowell Thomas wanted *scoops*.

Here's one journal entry from Lowell's days in Chicago:

> Interviewed "Dollie" Matters, 32-year-old wife of Fred Matters, age 70, who died suddenly Tuesday night leaving $150,000 estate to her. Posed as a police official in order to see her and talked to her as she lay sobbing in her bed, and scooped other afternoon papers.

Such misrepresentations, though they might be cause for dismissal today, were par for the course in Chicago journalism then. Lowell was not without qualms: "This reporter's life sure makes a sad bird of a fellow," he later admits in that journal. "You have to have a heart of stone; you have to lie like a trooper. . . ."[20] But he had gotten the interview, and it was an exclusive, albeit a minor one. In his two years in Chicago at the *Journal*, Lowell distinguished himself with two major exclusives. Only one of them was entirely made up.

Lowell's violation of the "SINCERITY, TRUTHFULNESS, ACCURACY" requirement that would soon be enshrined in the Canons of Journalism—his *fabrication*, as we would now label it—involved the largest of those headlines in the *Journal* on July 6, 1914: the one involving that allegedly "insane" heiress, Helen Morton, who was "HELD PRISONER IN HOME." Her father, the story explains, was "the millionaire salt magnate, Mark Morton." (You may recognize the last name from those dark-blue cylindrical packages still found in American pantries.) And the evidence that Helen was "suffering from mental derangement" included reports that she smoked, drank cocktails, had recently eloped over her father's vehement protests with a "Virginia gentleman," had chased her new husband, who by then seemed to have allied himself with her father, around with a knife and had threatened suicide.

That front-page story was probably written by Lowell Thomas, who had joined the scrum of reporters gathered in Wheaton, near the Morton family estates, to wait for tidbits on the travails of young Mrs. Bayly, Helen's new married name. The July 6 story was not an exclusive. And it was, within the epistemological limitations of such scandal mongering, true.

The *Journal*, like most early twentieth-century newspapers, made do without bylines, but Thomas has acknowledged his authorship of the report on the Morton scandal the paper published the next day. It appeared under the large front-page headline, "I WED FOR LOVE—HELEN MORTON." The subhead read, "'CRAZY? NOT I,' SAYS BRIDE OF ROGER BAYLY." Note the first person: Helen Morton—the hidden-away heiress—talking for herself! A scoop, indeed.

The story began: "Helen Morton Bayly was interviewed today by a *Journal* reporter for the first time since she was adjudged insane." Getting the thoughts of the "held prisoner" principal in one of the bigger scandals of the moment was a real coup for our youthful *Journal* reporter. And quotes from Mrs. Bayly were in good supply: She tells the reporter that if she is insane, "everybody in the world is also insane." She declares that her marriage to Roger Bayly was not unhappy. "It was a love match," she says.

The story explained that "to obtain the interview the *Journal* reporter outwitted the small army of burly guards" around the estate where Mrs. Bayly was being held. It explained that the reporter had approached the estate from the river behind it and then rowed down in an old dinghy, "climbed up the bank and stood before the house," where he came upon Mrs. Bayly. "My how you startled me," she was reported to have said before beginning to answer questions.

Such derring-do was hardly unknown in Chicago journalism. But the interview and the skullduggery behind it were entirely fictitious. Thomas had made the whole thing up. He had a partner in crime, Webb Miller of the *Chicago Evening American*, who ran his own apparently fictitious exclusive that day: a report on a party a reporter was said to have observed, which Helen Morton Bayly and Roger Bayly were said to have attended.[21]

Now, to be fair, fabrication was hardly the career-killer then that it is—or should be—in American journalism today. The notion that fiddling with the truth was a capital crime for journalists had yet to sink in. Indeed, there was a long history of clever and often even respected hoaxes, beginning with the *New York Sun*'s rather scholarly sounding account of the discovery of life on the moon in 1835.[22]

And Hecht, together with a photographer, Gene Cour, had turned hoaxes into something of an art form at the *Journal*: the goal more humor than deception. Perhaps their ultimate effort was the Great Chicago Earthquake, photographic evidence for which consisted of a trench in Lincoln Park the two men had dug, along with a shot of Hecht's landlady surrounded by some broken dishes. This elicited refutations but not much in the way of recriminations.[23] It added to the Hecht legend.

But Thomas wasn't bragging about having made up his interview with the heiress. He claims to have admitted his fabrication only to two chums at the paper: Dan C. Batchelor and Paul Crissey. The Morton family sued the *Journal* for libel, and indeed some potentially defamatory statements did appear in the story about this interview: allegations that one prominent member of her family had assaulted a photographer for the *Journal*, that Helen Morton had given her "affections" to others and that a family member had been Morton's "jailer," with what were mockingly referred to as "slaves" guarding her. The fact that the interview had never taken place might have created significant problems for the defense in that libel action.

Lowell was asked by the paper's managing editor, Martin J. Hutchens, if he had really interviewed Helen Morton. He said he had.[24]

(((•)))

After he arrived in Chicago, Lowell was allowed, for a small sum, to occupy a room in the home of the *Chicago Daily Journal*'s respected political editor, Joseph D. Salkeld. Also present were Salkeld's wife and their attractive and marriageable daughter, Elizabeth. She was 20.

With both characteristic cleverness and characteristic inaccuracy, Ben Hecht mentions engaging in a competition with Lowell for "the smiles" of one Betty Saltgelt, claiming to have "lost out to Lowell's superior diction." That would be Elizabeth *Salkeld*. Lowell called her Betty Jean or B.J. But Lowell denies in his memoir that Hecht was even pursuing "Miss Saltgelt." (He too gets her name wrong.[25]) In fact, after some months of dating, Lowell himself seemed mostly to be running from her too-ardent "smiles."

Being comely, confident and capable of commanding a room—in addition to possessing that remarkable "diction"—Lowell Thomas won the affections of a number of young women. But in romantic matters young Lowell, though normally so eager and accommodating, was not inclined to answer "yes." His relations with these young women often, consequently, followed this pattern: he'd flirt and engage enthusiastically in what he labels "some normal boy-girl fooling around," only to realize that the "girl" in question was taking it more seriously than the "boy." That is what transpired in the Salkeld home and on their evenings out and about in Chicago. It did not end well.

Betty began using the word "love." Her mother found some of the notes Lowell and her daughter exchanged and concluded—wrongly, Lowell insisted—that the "fooling around" had gone too far. "Mamma" demanded a marriage proposal and called Lowell (these wordings are from a later journal of his) a "trifler" and "a bum." Twenty-year-old Betty announced that "she felt so blue she wanted to jump in the lake."[26]

Lowell escaped from the Salkeld household to a cheap hotel room in the back of Michigan Avenue's Auditorium Building, which had its own drawback: continual opportunities to experience all the sights and sounds of one of the Loop's elevated train lines.[27] Letters from Betty, not one to take "no" for an answer, continued.

Lowell clearly had an eye for young women. He seemed particularly alert, by the evidence of one of his journals, to "pretty blondes." And he was aware of a category of woman he calls "sports"[28]—presumably meaning fun-loving if not loose. But we don't know whether Dr. and Mrs. Thomas' son managed or was disposed to go beyond mere "fooling around" or whether he ever paid for the privilege, as Hecht and a significant percentage of the journalists in Chicago apparently did. (Chicago engaged in these years in a war against "vice," with vice, perhaps, suffering some defeats. But a cease-fire was declared with the election of a new mayor in 1915.[29]) There is a hint in Thomas' memoir that he was prone to behaving with a prostitute as he would with "any other lady," which, while gentlemanly, presumably was not the point.[30]

Indeed, it is hard to read Lowell's sparse recollections on the subject without concluding that among his chief romantic goals up until that point was, as it had been with Betty Salkeld, avoiding entanglements. This remained, to be sure, a common concern at the time for eligible young men in the presence of marriageable ladies. Those ladies were expected to set the price for a consummated sexual relationship at a wedding—paid in advance. But there were other men who played the game differently— "triflers," Betty's mother appears to have called them; "lotharios" or "playboys" were Lowell's terms.

One such fellow—Paul Chamberlain, a roommate of Lowell's from Denver University—happened to pass through Chicago in March 1915. Chamberlain was something of a partyer and was confined, on that visit, to a wheelchair, having recently stumbled out of one such soiree directly into an elevator shaft, breaking both legs and both hips. Since he himself may have been somewhat freer in his relationships with women, Chamberlain may have found Lowell's fear of entanglements a bit excessive. Perhaps that explains why he posed what proved to be a portentous question: "Tommy"—long the name friends used for Thomas—"of all the girls we knew at DU which one did *you* like best?"

These are Lowell's italics and his recollection, more than 60 years later, of the question. We might wonder whether Chamberlain's query was really more along the lines of, "Tommy, was there anyone of all the girls we knew at DU whom you really *liked*?"

Whatever the emphasis and purport, Lowell seems to have surprised himself by answering without pause, "Fran Ryan." Frances Ryan, who was not blond and does not appear to have been a "sport," was the friend of a woman, Dorothy Allen, Lowell had dated. Fran, almost two years younger than he, had become his friend. Chamberlain suggested that Lowell might consider informing Miss Ryan of his feelings. In the letter he subsequently wrote to her, Lowell did not do that, but he did say he wanted to come to Denver for a "talk."[31]

((•))

Lowell Thomas' other big exclusive for the *Chicago Daily Journal*—five months after the Helen Morton "interview," five months before he set off for Denver and points beyond—was based on reporting he had actually done. The subject was Carleton Hudson, a Chicago financial advisor known for his support of the evangelical Moody Church. Hudson tended to offer his services to pious and wealthy widows.

Thomas' stories, like those of most great storytellers, improved in the telling. The reporting he did to expose Hudson in November and early December 1914 was quite enterprising, but by the time Thomas published the first volume of his memoir, in 1976, it sounded even more enterprising.

No, the *Journal's* city editor, Dick Finnegan, hadn't just handed Lowell a piece of paper with the name of an otherwise respectable man, Carleton Hudson, on it, and asked him to see what he could find. As the *Journal* reported in October 1914, Hudson was already being sued in Minneapolis by a widow for defrauding her of $120,000.[32] No, Lowell wasn't working on the story alone: other *Journal* reporters were helping get the goods on Hudson. And, no, Lowell hadn't just decided, because Hudson had an "Eastern" accent, to write "to every college president in New England" asking if they knew a Carleton Hudson. Hudson had told people he attended a small Vermont college, so Lowell had written the presidents of that much smaller group of possible alma maters and found someone who recalled a Carleton Hudson *Betts*, who had gone to New York.

Lowell took the train east and did do some energetic digging on his own in New York. He eventually discovered that Betts had jumped bail there 20 years earlier, after being accused of forging a check as part of a scheme to defraud another rich widow.[33] And Lowell did arrange to have

Hudson arrested in Chicago on the same day, December 3, 1914, that the article detailing his nefarious past in New York as Betts appeared on the front page of the *Journal*.[34]

Hudson lost the case in Minneapolis, but the charges against him in New York, where Clarence Darrow represented him, were eventually dismissed because no witnesses could be found for that two-decade-old case.[35] Nonetheless, Lowell Thomas, probably even better at self-promotion than he had proved at investigation, squeezed everything he could out of his exposé. A story detailing his scoop appeared not only in his hometown *Cripple Creek Times*, but—under the byline of his colleague and buddy, Paul Crissey—in *The Quill*, a respected national journalism publication: "It was the scoop of the year. . . . The story swept over the telegraph wires east, west, north and south."[36] This was a bit overstated, but Lowell had scored one large, honest triumph as a journalist in Chicago.

And he received one more reward for his efforts: a kind of IOU from one of the most powerful lawyers in Chicago, Silas Strawn, on behalf of some of the most powerful companies in Chicago, the meat packers. Hudson had been threatening to reveal illegal behavior he accused them of having committed if they didn't provide some money he insisted they owed him.[37] In helping expose Hudson, Lowell had, in other words, helped these companies escape a substantial blackmail threat. "If there is ever any way in which they can be helpful to you . . . ," Thomas quotes Strawn as telling him.[38]

((•))

Despite his lack of interest in the nuts and bolts of the law, Lowell had certainly made his mark at the Chicago-Kent School of Law. He was the first speaker at the banquet marking the end of the academic year there on May 1, 1915, the conclusion of his second year as a law student. Actually, he had organized the banquet himself, to much acclaim. Indeed, he had distinguished himself by inviting a Jewish judge to give a speech that night and a woman to deliver a toast.

In a new journal he began that day, Lowell noted two comments made about him right before he began to speak. The law school's dean, Edmund Burke, in introducing him, described Lowell as the "liveliest man he ever had connected with [at] Kent." And then Lowell overheard a blond woman sitting up front whisper, "Oh look, cutie's going to make a speech."[39]

However, as older men were wowed by his liveliness and young women succumbed to his diction or cuteness, a fair number of his contemporaries must have resented this golden boy, no matter how generous and self-mocking he tried to be. We know, thanks to an exchange of letters, of one of them: Lowell's erstwhile friend Dan C. Batchelor.

"My mission on earth is to help every other fellow as much as I possibly can," Lowell states in his letter, which came first. "If they make mistakes as I do, I intend to overlook them." This burst of self-praise is not without validity. Being nice *was* prominent among the missions Harriet and Harry's son had assigned himself. He did genuinely like people. He did tend to be obliging and forgiving. However, in this letter Lowell is quite critical of the behavior of Dan Batchelor, whom he accuses of a transgression he could not overlook: continually criticizing Lowell behind his back.

In his response Batchelor, in fact, agreed. "I wish to tell you that your letter has done me more good than anything that has happened to me since I arrived in Chicago," he declares, "in that it has shown me what an unspeakable cad I have been in my relations toward you." And Batchelor explains why he has behaved poorly: "I never before was jealous of anyone that I recall, but I confess that I have been jealous of you almost from your arrival in Chicago."

Lowell, of course, was nowhere near finished with inspiring jealousy. The motto on an earlier journal of his was "I WILL succeed."[40] Indeed, his travels back East in connection with the Hudson affair opened his eyes to worlds even larger than Chicago in which he might shine. They may have reminded him, in particular, that all degrees are not created equal. In March he had applied for a fellowship to the graduate program at Princeton University. A friend from Denver University, Harold M. Vinacke, had enrolled there and encouraged Lowell to join him. With the help of Vinacke and of Silas Strawn, he set about accumulating letters of reference.[41]

For now, however, with the academic year finishing up at law school, Lowell took a leave from the *Journal* and escaped Chicago, beginning what would become, after journalism, the most important activity in his life: travel.

3.

See America First

It was a rainy early-May night in Chicago in 1915, and Lowell Thomas was running late. He rarely missed engagements, but Lowell—gregarious and easily distracted—often almost missed them. He needed to make a train leaving from the Chicago and North Western Terminal at 10:45. Lowell grabbed a taxi, an indulgence for a young man taking a leave from an already low-paying job. But Lowell rarely skimped in pursuit of his goals, and he had big plans for the places this train and the ones that followed would take him. He was soon heading west.

Amongst the luggage Lowell had carried on board was one of the latest advances in human communication: a portable typewriter. Newspapermen had been early adopters of typewriters. Lowell would describe himself as "helpless" without one.[1] So before he set out on this journey, Lowell had managed to obtain a Corona 3. This "machine," as he often called it, had debuted in 1912 and had a carriage that folded down on top of its keyboard, enabling it to tuck inside a relatively trim case. The Corona was not quite, in today's terms, a *laptop*. Though Lowell sometimes balanced it there, effective operation required that it rest on something harder, flatter and higher than a pair of thighs. Nonetheless, this was the first decent typewriter someone—even someone perpetually running late—could comfortably lug around.

Shortly after he awoke the next morning somewhere in Iowa on the Chicago and North Western railway tracks, Lowell began "punching," as he put it, that Corona. He didn't stop typing until ten that evening. By then the tracks upon which he was riding were owned by the Union Pacific.

Lowell was also making use of somewhat older technologies on this train ride and as he continued on what became a two-and-a-half-month journey. He was writing with a pencil in a small, spiral notebook, keeping a journal he had begun after that law school banquet of a few days earlier. That pencil produced an almost always legible but sometimes irregular script—handwriting, unlike elocution, not being among his father's obsessions. And it was in this journal that Lowell recorded the initial versions of his tales, versions intended only for him. Or maybe not only for him. Perhaps some part of him imagined our eyes upon his scribblings, since Lowell had as much in front of him as he rode this train as he ever had, and he was sufficiently immodest to suspect that what he was about to experience might someday be of interest to others.

Lowell tells the journal that there was a "light rain" at eight the next morning as he "breezed into Denver," where, that evening, the event that would become the basis of one of his more significant stories unfolded.[2]

In his much later memoir, which seems to have been written without consulting this journal, Thomas offers three reasons why he headed west in May 1915: "I began to feel a certain restlessness, a sense of having been too long in the same place," he reports. "Throughout my life, it would catch up with me again and again, this urge to *do* something, to see some other part of the forest."[3] This explains a lot—much more than just Lowell's decision to leave Chicago that spring.

His second explanation is also revealing and also characteristic. Lowell had cooked up a scheme. He had gotten a few railroad publicists to fund a trip out West and back, in return for this young journalist's producing some pieces extolling the virtues of the places he would encounter along the way—thereby persuading others to ride the rails on similar journeys. Lowell would get to travel and write. The railroad companies, needful of passengers for their new lines in the still sparsely settled West, were open to this sort of deal.

Thomas' third explanation for his departure from Chicago that summer is love.

While passion routinely tossed about young men like Ben Hecht, romance had not previously been a schedule-altering force in Lowell's life. But, as Thomas tells us in that much later memoir, his conversation with Paul Chamberlain had him homing in on Frances Ryan in Denver. This was another advantage of that scheme—a train ticket west to Denver being, he reports, beyond his means. With free passage on these and other railroads, Lowell would be able to pay a call upon the newly acknowledged target of his affections and—being Lowell Thomas—also "see some other part of the forest," in this case, initially, the Pacific Coast.[4]

So he showed up in Frances Ryan's living room.

At least that's how Thomas ended up telling the story—another one that became more dramatic over the decades. In fact, Lowell was closer to Fran before Chamberlain's visit than he lets on. She had passed through Chicago with her mother during Lowell's first year there and paid him a visit. And some earlier chatty, clever, conspiratorial letters and one postcard from him to her survive. They are full of quips about the romantic struggles of their acquaintances.[5] In fact, their pre–May 1915 relationship has the appearance of a lively, almost intimate friendship. It is not entirely surprising that it became something more.

And that journal makes clear that Lowell's devotion to his family was at least as strong a motivation for his trip in the spring and early summer of 1915 as this torch he was, or decided he was, carrying for Frances Ryan. "Nothing like coming home to mother's cooking and mother's beds," he declares in the journal. He would have an opportunity to spend some time with his parents and sister in Victor after he left Denver. But beyond that, though he fails to mention this central aspect of his trip in his later recollections, Lowell was planning to take his mother, Harriet, and sister, Pherbia, along for most of the journey. His deal with the railroads presumably included passage for them. And the trip was to culminate in a visit to Lowell's uncle and his family in Portland, Oregon.

Nonetheless, Lowell clearly was exhilarated by the opportunity to reveal his heart to Fran in Denver at the beginning of this journey. He had left Chicago on May 3, 1915, and on May 5, after spending the afternoon "looking up" some other friends in Denver, Lowell showed up at Frances Ryan's house. His journal is our only contemporary source on how their conversation that evening went.

"I told Fran tonight," he writes. "My years of Chicago newspaper experience gave me the necessary nerve to say part of what I wanted. There is absolutely no doubt in my mind but [that] Fran is the one girl in all the world." Fran had certainly not been expecting whatever it was, exactly, that Lowell presented her with: a marriage proposal, or "part" of a marriage proposal, or, perhaps, a pledge of undying love.[6] "She was dumbfounded and greatly embarrassed," he admits. "She hadn't dreamed of what might happen."

Lowell, never one to leave future splendors unimagined, had clearly done plenty of dreaming. He acknowledged no doubts. "Every time I see her I fall further in love with her," he writes in that journal—although Lowell is supposed to have only recently realized that Fran was the girl for him. "It's not passion this time," he does concede, but adds, "I could write books about her . . . she is the type of girl I've always dreamed about." (Lowell's generally playful letters to friends are better at dodging sentimentality.)

Frances Ryan was solidly built with a round, warm face and a knowing look. The young woman with whom Lowell was suggesting he wanted to spend his life was not the most beautiful he had met, but she may have been the most self-possessed and the wisest. Her father was a railroad conductor; one of her two brothers would achieve success as a railroad executive. Fran's transcript at Denver University has the same mix of 90s and 80s as his, though she was following the more usual academic program: working on one degree at a time.

And her reserve and poise must have made Frances Ryan's heart, unlike those of the Betty Salkelds of the world, seem hard to win and therefore more worth winning. What probably also helped in this regard was Fran's lack of enthusiasm for the traditional romance game, in which the female contestant was supposed to be trying to secure the earliest possible marriage to the likeliest possible fellow.

How did Fran evaluate this suddenly amorous friend? There's no record of her initial impression of him. It would not have been surprising if she considered his bravado, although leavened by humor, a little excessive or his focus—given the hodgepodge of jobs, degrees and schemes—a little soft. But having been his friend, she couldn't have missed the prepossessing manner and personality, plus the alertness to opportunity. Lowell had no money and no clear career path, but this recent grad was reporting for a Chicago newspaper, teaching a law school course and getting free passage around the country. He made acquaintances and formed alliances with remarkable frequency and ease. In many ways it was hard to imagine a more likely prospect than the young fellow who had, if not proposed marriage, at least raised its possibility. He was probably figuratively, and certainly literally, going places. And Fran, too, had a yen for "the other part of the forest."

Still, she might very well have been wary of Lowell, who had in the end failed to reciprocate her friend Dorothy's feelings for him. And Fran had a right to be thrown by Lowell's metamorphosis from pal to suitor. "She says she doesn't know me well enough, and she's right," Lowell tells his journal. "She gave me no encouragement," he later explained. But Fran did not preclude further contact.

And Lowell, as always, proved undaunted. "I'm going to make doubly good in order to win her," he announces to himself, and then proclaims, "Two years from now I'm to marry Fran." He does add, "if she'll have me," but then pledges, "And believe me I'm going to fight hard to prove worthy of the grandest girl in the universe."

In his journal Lowell dubs his evening in Fran's living room "the greatest night of my life." But that was all the time they spent together. She turned down a last-minute invite to see a vaudeville show with him at the Orpheum Theater in Denver.[7] He sent letters and postcards from the road, which Fran, whatever her professed attitude toward him, began saving in a cedar chest.[8] Lowell even attempted a phone call. (He reached her mother.) But on a trip that lasted about two and a half months, Lowell ended up devoting only this one evening to visiting with the young woman with whom he proposed to spend the rest of his life.

((•))

What followed that intense encounter with Fran would be the initial travel adventure of Lowell Thomas' adult life.

Lowell had journeyed here or there for school or work or on a story. This time, though, the point was not to get somewhere but to experience the challenges and delights of travel itself—of unfamiliar places, people and experiences. Moreover, Lowell for once was heading west—the direction in which his family had set off a decade and a half earlier, the direction toward which the American adventure and the American destiny had always been oriented.

And the West was the great trump card the United States held in what the film historian Jennifer Lynn Peterson dubs a "contest with Europe that was being waged on the level of scenery." The slogan "See America First" was catching on, and high on the list of things to see were the spectacular mountains, canyons, geysers and glaciers of the American West—then beginning to be preserved in national parks. Peterson concludes that "a veritable Grand Tour of the American West was constructed." Lowell was early in taking and promoting it.[9]

As with all good adventures, his journey featured a considerable element of risk—not physical, in this case. Now that railroads had replaced stagecoaches and Native Americans had lost the battles for their lands, most of the danger had been subtracted from expeditions to the West. The risk Lowell undertook was entrepreneurial. "I'm making this trip on sheer bluff," he confided early on to his journal. The journey would not be possible—given his limited resources—without plenty of free meals, free lodging and free sightseeing to go along with the free travel. And such gifts would require convincing various businessmen and civic leaders that he would indeed come through with free publicity.

Lowell—unshy and preternaturally self-assured—always moved with extraordinary comfort and confidence among those older and more accomplished than he. The day after he began wooing the "grandest girl in the universe," Lowell paid a visit to the Denver Chamber of Commerce, during which he persuaded its officials to offer him a private tour around Denver. Then he traveled up to Victor, where his return would be celebrated not only by his family but by the *Cripple Creek Times*, which judged only a German U-boat's sinking of the *Lusitania* to be more newsworthy that day. "Mr. Thomas," the newspaper crowed, "will prepare a series of fifteen articles, four of which will deal with Colorado, which will be published in a number of the leading newspapers of the East." Four days later in the *Colorado Springs Gazette* it was "twenty-four articles on Colorado Springs, Denver and the various Pacific coast scenic places" for "a syndicate of eastern newspapers."

Local muckety-mucks provided this local boy who had apparently made good with a tour of a new mining drainage tunnel near Cripple Creek. "Greatest mining trip I ever made," he effuses in his journal. He was chauffeured around the tourist attractions near Colorado Springs in an automobile that impressed him by hitting a speed of "sixty miles per hour at times." "The greatest day's trip of my life," he gushes in that journal.

After he returned to Denver, representatives of a couple of newspapers—some of whom, to be sure, were old buddies of his—stopped by to pay their respects to what one local paper calls "one of the most prominent of the younger school of newspapermen."

Lowell admits to being taken aback by the attention: "This is a new stunt for me," he tells his journal, "to have big men salaaming to me and falling over themselves in an attempt to treat me good."[10] And he enjoyed it. Indeed, Lowell had found, in these initial days of his initial journey, the activity that most suited him: traveling with credentials, however inflated. His bluff seemed to be working.

There was, however, one problem: our "prominent" young journalist was still struggling to justify all the "salaaming," all the free trips, hotels and meals, by lining up newspapers for the "syndicate" that would print his articles—15 of them, or 24, or whatever number he wanted to pull out of the air. On that first train ride, from Chicago to Denver, what Lowell had been busy "punching" out on the Corona were letters asking newspapers if they might be interested in printing the travel pieces that this, in fact, mostly unknown 23-year-old sometime journalist had promised to publish.

Actually, there was also a second problem: Lowell was broke.

Along with free passage for himself and then his mother and sister, the young journalist had also been given $100 by one railroad and $125 by another to help fund his journey. Let the record show that accepting such "junkets" or "freebies," let alone actual cash, is now considered by many of the better news organizations to be unethical—because of an implied quid pro quo. But let the record also show that the meeting at which Casper S. Yost first presented a group of editors with his idea for the "creation of an ethical organization of American newspaper editors" was held at Glacier National Park—on a junket paid for by a railroad trying to encourage tourism there and enjoyed without embarrassment by those editors.

Lowell had also borrowed $200 from his father—always a soft touch, especially for his son or a brother.

His mother, Harriet, and sister, Pherbia, joined Lowell for the Colorado Springs and Denver tours. And the three then proceeded to Salt Lake City and Los Angeles. The assistant manager of their hotel in Salt Lake, also pleased at the prospect of mentions back East, announced that they could remain as his guests as long as they'd like. To which Lowell, who thought he might have to pay for their rooms, responds in his journal, "Yea!" He describes the hotel as the "finest I ever stopped at." A hotel in Long Beach, south of Los Angeles, offered a similar arrangement. The suite occupied there by the three Thomases looked out over the balmy Pacific—Lowell's first view of the reward won by generations of westbound travelers. "Finest suite I was ever in," he tells his journal.

Local tourist associations or business organizations generally covered the tours and tickets for Lowell and his mother and sister. Lowell, or some-times all three of them, received invitations to some lunches, dinners and banquets, including one at which the speakers included Charlie Chaplin, only three years older than Lowell and just establishing himself in Holly-wood. (Our "professor of public speaking" recorded this evaluation of Chaplin's oration in his journal: a "rotten speech.")

But sometimes as they traveled, mother, daughter and son had to house, feed or entertain themselves, or pay for the occasional taxi, with the son generally footing the bill. And a Corona portable would have cost, unless Lowell had a scheme going here too, $50. As was his pattern, he may also have used some of his new stake to pay off old debts. Anyway, the hundreds of dollars he had raised went fast. By May 20, a little more than two weeks after he set out from Chicago, Lowell discovered that his "pile" had "de-creased to fifty cents."[11]

This is a classic Lowell Thomas moment. Our "prominent . . . news-paperman," who had promised a series of articles for a "syndicate" of "leading" eastern newspapers, was struggling—since his name, in fact, was barely known in Chicago, let alone other eastern cities—to find news-papers interested in publishing what he wrote. This very young man was staying at classy hotels, eating at good restaurants and seeing the sights in style. He was being introduced as "a famous journalist." He was moving among the business, entertainment and journalism elite. He was present-ing his mother and sister with what might have qualified as the time of their lives, if those lives wouldn't continue to have Lowell Thomas in them. Yet he had nothing but small change in his pockets.

One might think this would be the moment to contemplate retreat or, at least, to cut losses. Lowell did not think that. Instead, he took being un-daunted to a new, almost confidence-man-like level. He enjoyed bluffing. Maybe that was because, even more than most confidence men, he sort of believed in the bluff, sort of fancied himself a prominent newspaperman. Or maybe he was comfortable with bluffing because, unlike most confidence men, he had the talent and devotion to make the bluff come true. Indeed, he would continue to pretend to have accomplished more, and to spend as if he had earned more, until he was so successful (which would happen quickly) or so rich (which would happen much more slowly) that he would no longer have to bluff. A maxim from our time seems to apply: "fake it 'til you make it."[12] However, in Los Angeles in late May 1915, Lowell—who definitely had not yet made it—was forced to scramble.

Right after taking a tour of Long Beach with the ex-mayor, Lowell had dinner, his journal reports, with Kimpton Ellis—a friend from Valparaiso, now a Los Angeles lawyer—and Lowell "tried to touch him for ten dollars." Ellis said he didn't have it. His dad back in Victor forwarded $25, an additional loan Lowell was quite pleased to receive. It wouldn't last long, however. He begins to record in his journal the price of meals—two dollars, "six bits"—and whether they were worth it. And then the problem of where to stay in San Diego arose.

San Diego would be an important stop on the trip because it was one of two West Coast cities hosting a world's fair at the time. The Panama-California Exposition would be a big tourist draw, and Lowell's sponsors would want him to contribute to making it bigger. But no one had come forward with any hotel rooms. The manager of the first hotel he telephoned, the Hotel Del Coronado, insisted that Lowell stop by if he wanted to talk about a deal. "To hell with him," Lowell mutters in his journal—a rare display of temper. The manager of the second hotel he called complained that he had already "made himself poor contributing to the fair." A third was only willing to cut the price of the rooms in half. Lowell decided he would make time to stop by the Del Coronado after all, and with the help of some fair officials, he scored "an elegant suite of four rooms" in this huge Victorian confection on the water, which would host former president Taft that summer. "Fifty dollars worth of accommodations free," Lowell exults in his journal.

As he was leaving San Diego, one of his sponsors handed Lowell $26 to cover any expenses he may have incurred. "I was down to my last four dollars," he notes in his journal, "with Portland, Oregon"—their destination—"nearly fifteen hundred miles away and with mother and sister to take care of. Some Relief."

San Francisco, their next stop, had its own, similarly named world's fair: the Panama-Pacific International Exposition. It not only honored, as did San Diego's version, the new canal, which promised to open the West to shipping from the East, but celebrated San Francisco's recovery from the great earthquake nine years earlier. Lowell was presented with the by-now expected collection of free tours and free passes to the fair. It is not clear from his journal whether he had to pay for his hotel, which may mean he did not.[13]

The next leg in their subsidized Pacific Coast travels was accomplished by ship, through the Golden Gate and up to Portland. Lowell's father's brother Carl now lived in Portland with his wife and two children. After a pleasant week with them in that city, Lowell set off on his own for Seattle. "Left mother and sister there last night," he writes on a postcard to Fran. "I never hated to leave anybody as bad in my life. We have had a high old time together." He would continue having "a high old time," but of a somewhat different variety.

The impresario for this part of Lowell's journey was George W. Hibbard, an executive with the Milwaukee and St. Paul Railroad, the northern route to the Pacific, which had rougher, less developed country to promote. Lowell's experiences accordingly got rougher: the Olympic Peninsula and, later, Mount Rainier National Park, where the clouds parted to reveal the monumentally out-of-scale mountain only for about ten minutes. And it rained. Water ran "in a torrent," he writes Fran, through his tent at night.[14]

The other destination to which Hibbard dispatched Lowell was even more remote and more exotic.

((•))

Lowell Thomas was demonstrating on this trip a number of the attributes that would rank him among the world's great travelers. Being one of the few passengers on that ship from San Francisco to Portland who did not get seasick was a good sign. His failure to complain when water rushed through his tent was a definite positive. So was his ability to carry on, mostly unfazed, with nothing but small change in his pockets. Perhaps most encouraging was the eagerness and composure with which he faced each new town, new hotel and new person, along with plenty of new challenges.

However, Lowell still had lots to learn. At one point in a letter to Fran he characterizes someone he calls a "Jap," with whom he was sharing a car ride outside San Diego, as displaying "that sickly oriental smile"—offensive even by the standards of an insensitive time. And when Lowell had crossed briefly into Mexico, he wasn't able to see beyond "dives and cutthroats."[15] A great traveler would need wider, more sensitive, more discerning eyes. But perhaps the best demonstration that Thomas the intrepid adventurer was not yet fully formed came in conversation with George Hibbard early in that visit to Seattle.

In his 1976 memoir, Thomas recalls their dialogue thusly: "When Mr. Hibbard asked if I was ready for more, I assured him that I was. 'Good,' he said crisply, 'because I've fixed it for you to go to Alaska.'" Thomas then writes, "Alaska! My heart sang at the very word." He describes himself as "aquiver with anticipation."

This is how we might have expected our great traveler to have responded. Thomas, however, is not remembering his reaction to Hibbard's proposal accurately. In his journal Lowell instead records this reply: "I said I was in a hurry and hadn't thought of it." Lowell Thomas, in other words, was suggesting that he was in too much of a hurry to make his first trip to Alaska! Fortunately, Hibbard "insisted," and Lowell soon enough came around and answered "yes."[16]

Four days later he was headed north. And if his heart had not initially sung, it must have soon enough.

Steamships provided the only easy access to Alaska in those days, before roads made some incursions or airplanes, still in their infancy, regularly undertook the hop. On May 18, 1915, in Seattle, Lowell boarded the *Alameda*—a long, coal-burning, steam-powered ship—and headed up the Inside Passage, weaving through the channels, which were mostly protected by islands from the North Pacific. When the fog and mist lifted, the journey was spectacular.

The voyage began among evergreen-covered islands large and small, supporting mountains that were small but sometimes decorated with snow. These were the western waters of the Canadian province of British Columbia.

Then the ship steamed into the territory of Alaska—purchased from Russia 48 years earlier, not to become a state for another 44 years. The ship docked in what were then fishing towns. Thomas lists them in his memoir: "Ketchikan, Petersburg, Wrangell, Sitka, the old Russian capital."[17] The coastline began to rise here and fracture into fjords. One rare flat stretch at the bottom of some massive peaks was occupied by Juneau, the American capital—a town battling for territory with some of the world's great glaciers.

As the *Alameda* steamed on, the mountains gained heft and snow. Seals likely floated by; porpoises rolled to the surface; humpbacked whales emitted their spouts and exhibited their tails. The snow in places crawled down to the shore. The scene here was spectacularly grand and mysterious even when water-soaked clouds, as was their wont, lolled about the channels and rolled around the cliffs.

Thomas explains in an autobiographical sketch that this was "the first rather distant part of the world that I headed for when I started my career (if you want to call it that) as a 'world traveler.'" Yet it was apparent on this first distant journey of that "career" that his main interest was not so much the faraway lands themselves but their occupants. Lowell Thomas admired the attractive and startling shapes into which the Earth's crust had been kneaded, but he was more fascinated by people—by "meeting new people constantly," as he would soon put it.[18] The humans on exhibit for the wide-ranging traveler included the inhabitants of exotic climes but also those curious and adventurous enough to visit them. One person in particular had caught his attention on this steamship navigating the Inside Passage to Alaska: a student on summer vacation from Vassar College, then an all-girls school.

Perhaps it is a mistake to expect too much of the male of the species, but this was a month and a half after Lowell declared Fran both "the grandest girl in the universe" and "the one girl in all the world." It came after some other flirtations—including one with a young woman, standing on the dock at Ketchikan, whom he describes in his journal as "an unusually stunning blonde." It came after he and his uncle's daughter Mae, with whom he spent a lot of time in Portland, "decided . . . that we were strong for each other in spite of our being first cousins."[19] But the young lady from Vassar on board the *Alameda*, Ruth Pennybacker, really seemed to get under Lowell's skin.

She was traveling with her mother and a friend from Vassar. And let's give them some credit: this was early in the history of nature-and-adventure travel. There were no souvenir shops and package tours on shore. Mrs. Pennybacker and her two young charges could afford to travel in style, but they definitely could have found more comforts, more services and more easily intelligible sights on the East Coast or in Europe. Not that their presence in these remote lands meant these three women were without airs. Lowell heard from someone who had been dining with them that they "had referred sneeringly to mixing with others on board."

"That doesn't make a hit with me," Lowell, affecting a bit of a sneer himself, explains in his journal. Whether he took their disdain as a personal affront or it simply roused his rather strong, Western egalitarian streak is not clear. But he certainly took it as a challenge. Lowell reports in that journal that he decided to walk up to Ruth Pennybacker, without introduction, and initiate a conversation. It didn't go well. "She . . . look[ed] questioningly out from under her blonde hair, with her pretty blue eyes, and answered, 'Ree-ay-lly' in a soft southern accent to everything I said," Lowell reports. "Then she disappeared on the excuse of looking for her mother."

Lowell considered this "a start." But toward what? His motivations here—as in other romantic, or apparently romantic, situations—are sometimes hard to divine. "Before this trip comes to an end I'm going to . . . ," he pledges in his journal. Yet Lowell does not complete this resolution the way many young men feeling slighted by an attractive young woman might—nowadays at least. Instead, he pledges to "have this bunch"—Ruth, her friend and her mom—"gathered around me as I read a few of Service's poems."

If you were going to read some poetry on a ship heading north through the Inside Passage, you couldn't do much better than Robert W. Service. Just eight years earlier Service had published in the Yukon the collection of poems, mostly about the Yukon, that had made him famous. And the desire to recite poetry to a group was perhaps appropriate for someone who would in 15 years be reciting the news to much of America. In a few days Lowell achieved his goal, as he usually did, splendidly. He entranced Ruth and the other two women with his rendition of some of Service's poems, including "The Cremation of Sam McGee"[20]:

> . . . . *The Northern Lights have seen queer sights,*
> *But the queerest they ever did see*
> *Was that night on the marge of Lake Lebarge*
> *I cremated Sam McGee.*

Lowell disembarked at Skagway. Ruth Pennybacker, her mother and friend would remain on the *Alameda* all the way to Valdez, where it reversed course. They suggested to Lowell that he board the ship again when it returned to Skagway and join them for the return trip to Seattle. He would—nine days later.

((•))

Skagway is a diminutive town surrounded by snowy mountains so tall and drifting clouds so low they are difficult to tell apart. This was a locale with a history designed to enchant Lowell. Together with its sister city, Dyea (pronounced DIE-ee), Skagway, in Alaska, was the jumping-off point for the trek, which began in 1897, to the Klondike gold fields in the Yukon, in Canada.

This became known as "the last great adventure." It was also among the more foolhardy adventures in human history. To get to the gold fields near Dawson from Skagway, the "Stampeders"—perhaps 100,000 humans behaving like a herd of hysterical horses—had to surmount the treacherous White Pass Trail, also known as "Dead Horse Trail" because of all the animals that gave out along the way. And they had to surmount it again and again in order to transport the year's worth of provisions initially required to convince the Canadian Mounties that they could survive when they arrived. And, yes, it got cold in Alaska, especially when crossing mountain passes.

Lowell Thomas was certainly not one to believe any great adventure could be the "last." But having been raised in Victor, Colorado, he knew something of the ability of the metal in question to mesmerize, and he was on his way to becoming a connoisseur of adventures. This one had the standard elements: it was mad, and it was dangerous. The Klondike gold rush was also unsurpassed in what, going back to Sisyphus, has been among the most poignant of human conditions: futility. Those among the gold-crazed Stampeders who actually made it to Dawson City, where the Klondike River met the Yukon River, found that claims had already been staked to just about all the promising territory.

Aspects of this story had already been well told by the novelist Jack London, who had made it to the Klondike via Dyea, as well as by Service, whose entry point had been Skagway. Lowell, also, was much taken by another author who had struggled to reach and then written about the far north, Rex Beach. Lowell took a lesson from their work: that adventurous travel could produce entertaining tales.

Indeed, somewhere between Seattle and Skagway he seems to have come up with the idea that he might have a career as a travel lecturer—a viable quasi-journalistic endeavor in the days before television and then the Internet regularly overloaded us with accounts and images of faraway places. And Alaska would be a reasonable, if not original, subject for these illustrated lectures. Lowell began taking photos.[21] (He doesn't explain where he got the camera.) On the *Alameda* he discussed his lecture idea with Clifford C. King, a salesman based in Portland, with whom, in the course of one six-hour conversation, Lowell became "close friends." King, who had worked for the government in Alaska, offered to give Lowell 208 slides he had taken of Alaska.

And Lowell began collecting not only information that would be of use in the newspaper travel articles he was trying to place but historical and economic data, plus the sort of tales—in good supply on the way to the Klondike—he might use to entertain an audience. Considerable space in his journal is devoted to the saga of one woodsman whose scalp was peeled back after he managed, if this story is to be credited, to extricate his head from a grizzly's jaws.[22]

Lowell arrived in Skagway more than a decade and a half after the Stampede had ended and Dyea and Skagway had begun losing their population. He arrived 14 years after the completion of the White Pass and Yukon Route railroad—a remarkable feat of engineering, ranking with the Short Line to Victor and Cripple Creek as a bankrupter of language. This railroad had taken all the danger (but none of the beauty) out of the journey over the mountains into Canada, though it was completed just after the Klondike strain of gold fever had broken. The White Pass and Yukon, which originated in Skagway, settled for good the competition with Dyea—some of whose last remaining buildings were dragged to Skagway.

Lowell, with his railroad sponsors, was there in part to publicize the White Pass and Yukon, which he boarded the same day he disembarked from the *Alameda*. The railroad, comfortable and filled with the effusion of cruise ships today, was less comfortable then. "If you can picture a combination of the roll of a river boat in a typhoon on the Yellow Sea, an auto going up Pike's Peak . . . and a train running on the ties instead of the rails you will get a faint idea of the movement of this car," Lowell would later inform Fran. The "wildlife" that snuck on the train was also bothersome: "This is the original home of the 'Elephantine-Mosquito' and several million of them, attracted by my youth and appetizing appearance, have just entered the car and are mobilizing for an attack." The railroad's tracks followed the green Skagway River, but the river ended up far below as they climbed up the mountains, across an extraordinarily high trestle and over—near what had become the Canadian border—the White Pass. Every few minutes brought another waterfall. One twisted, dived and shimmered for thousands of feet.

Lowell arrived in Whitehorse, a town that had grown where the Stampeders stopped before the next of their trials: rapids that, as they tried to ride the Yukon River north, reared so high, the story went, that they resembled white horses. Lowell's visit was recorded in the next edition of the Whitehorse *Weekly Star*, under the headline "Prominent Writer Here."[23] (He had "spent [the] day loafing around" with the paper's editor.)

After a night in a hotel—his first on land since he left Seattle—Lowell boarded the *Dawson*, a sternwheeler, which had to stop a couple of times a day for the wood needed to make the steam that turned its paddle wheel. The Yukon River, and therefore such steamships, passed through Lake Lebarge (now commonly spelled Laberge). Lowell noted its "marge" and recited Service's poem in his berth to an audience composed only of himself.

As the guest of various transportation companies, Lowell was ensconced in comfortable, even plush, quarters here as elsewhere on his journey. He was socializing with and benefiting from acquaintance with the most important folks on board—the general manager of a California business, a bishop, the wife of the manager of a gold-mining company. That caused this Colorado cowboy occasional twinges of embarrassment. "It's pretty soft to have influential friends," he admits in his journal. It "sort of goes against the grain." But this didn't stop Lowell from sleeping an extra night in his "soft" quarters on the *Dawson*—thereby saving himself the cost of a hotel room when they arrived in Dawson City, center of the Klondike gold rush.

This—the end of the line for the Stampeders—was another town built by gold. Lowell was fascinated by the place. Robert Service, after all, had been living and writing in a log cabin there just a few years earlier. Dawson had obvious similarities to Victor. And Lowell delighted in the irony that, as he puts it in his journal, "the Frozen North"—Dawson was near the Arctic Circle—could be "dusty" and "hot." It was now officially summer, and the sun was working around the clock. Lowell spent a very long and full day there: getting a tour of the gold dredges endeavoring to recover the last vestiges of gold from the Klondike River and watching a night baseball game in one of the only places one could then be played. But he didn't sleep in Dawson. Instead, that night Lowell caught another stern-wheeler back to Whitehorse, where he hopped on the next train back to Skagway.

After one night in a hotel there, Lowell again boarded the *Alameda* for the trip back to Seattle and a reunion with Ruth Pennybacker and her two companions. "I fear I am growing rather weary of this bunch," he writes in his journal. "They are too fussy, too particular and too different from most regular people to suit yours truly."[24] It didn't help that they could not disguise their annoyance that the "prominent," but hardly well-heeled, "writer" had been upgraded to the best stateroom on board—a room they coveted.

In some sense the upgrade to his stateroom was a sign of what these many weeks of navigating unfamiliar places, hobnobbing with accomplished people and impersonating a distinguished journalist had meant for Lowell. He had grown into the role he had been playing. He had upgraded himself. He would move through the world with even more sureness after his return from the West and Alaska.

Lowell Thomas' trip to "Alaska" had lasted 16 days. He had been in Canada, not Alaska, for half of those days. He had slept onshore only at the end of two of those days. Yet over the next year Lowell would establish a sideline giving lectures on Alaska. Clearly he was not done bluffing.

((•))

Lowell, his mother and sister having returned to Colorado, took a train from Seattle to Minneapolis. The *Minneapolis Tribune* was supposed to have been printing his travel pieces. Lowell explains that he "hunted through" the paper but "failed to find any of my articles."[25]

My researchers and I have had similar difficulties—including in Thomas' own paper, the *Chicago Daily Journal*. It is not possible to examine all the newspapers in America during this period. And, yes, there are some scattered articles that might have been his—on Mount Rainier, on Colorado Springs. But his byline does not appear on them, and there were others writing on the pleasures of America's increasingly accessible frontiers at the time.[26] Certainly, such travel pieces are conspicuous in their absence in the archives of a fellow who had already begun saving evidence of his accomplishments or forwarding such evidence to Fran, who saved it. Yet also conspicuously absent are complaints from the railroad companies who sponsored his trip about a failure to publish the promised articles.

By the middle of July Lowell was back in Chicago, where a letter was waiting from Princeton University: he had not received a fellowship but had been accepted into the graduate program to study history and politics. Princeton was not in the habit of accepting many graduate students from the Rocky Mountain states. Lowell would be one of only two there—the other being his old friend from Denver University, Harold Vinacke.

If his goal was impressing his education-obsessed father, it was hard to do better than a PhD program at Princeton.[27] However, this would mean that Lowell would be bidding adieu to the Chicago-Kent School of Law. Allowing a degree to go unfinished was frowned upon in the Thomas household. And Lowell still saw himself doing some sort of legal work— probably in Chicago. So he hatched a vague and ambitious plan to later finish his legal education at Harvard.

Lowell also had to resign from the *Chicago Daily Journal*. He surprised his editor, Dick Finnegan, with this news on August 17, 1915, and put in his last day at the paper—Thomas' last day working full-time for any newspaper—four days later. Lowell left Chicago on August 24. For once he was not running late. "I had more time on my hands tonight waiting for the train to leave than anytime since I came to Chicago . . . two years ago today lacking eight days," he writes in the new journal he had begun for his trip east.

Lowell also jotted down a career goal for which he must have received some encouragement: a position as a lawyer at the prestigious firm headed by Silas Strawn. They were—both being skilled at this sort of thing—staying in touch.

Lowell definitely had made a lot of influential friends in his almost two years in Chicago, Strawn prominent among them. Another mentor, N. H. Reed, was now an executive with Standard Oil. Reed gave Lowell some advice he probably did not need but certainly followed: focus on the "big things"; don't worry about "minor matters"; play only for big stakes. Another doyen of the business world—Nelson Lampart, a bank vice president— helped facilitate such plays by lending this currently unemployed graduate student $250, $150 of which Lowell used to pay off all but $25 of the money he still owed his father for his trip west.

"Chicago has been mighty kind to me," Lowell concludes in his journal, "and I look forward to returning in a year or two with great pleasure."[28] But plans change.

4.

Too Good to Be True

owell Thomas returned from his trip to the West Coast, Alaska and the Yukon with another new love besides Frances Ryan: gallivanting about. "I have the wanderlust in its worst form," he writes Fran. "And if my humble plans don't go awry, . . . I intend to visit every place on the map anyone else has seen and some that have never been explored."

His "humble plans"—for traveling and much else—were, in other words, anything but. The 23-year-old man who left Chicago in late August 1915 was looking for a larger map upon which to operate, larger stakes, larger challenges. This time the trains were taking him east. His ostensible destination, Princeton University, was very much devoted to educating the ruling class the country was still busy pretending not to have and to which Lowell had definitely not been born. Yet even Princeton would come to seem a little small.

Lowell had been assertive and assured even before he had accomplished much. Now, having hobnobbed and gotten around, he was ready to take that to new levels. He made sure his route took him through Washington, DC—to visit the city, of course, but also to introduce himself to it. His plan—as reported to Fran—was to meet with the secretary of the interior of the United States, Franklin K. Lane, and the president of the United

States, Woodrow Wilson. Upon arriving in town, Lowell walked over to the White House, where he failed to encounter the president but did attend a brief press briefing by Secretary of State Robert Lansing. That afternoon Lowell spent 40 minutes interviewing Secretary of the Interior Lane and discussing Alaska. They hit it off. Yes, it was a simpler time, when Washington operated on a more human scale . . . but still.

There was an incident in Washington—not involving any of the city's notables—that qualifies as one of the few mentioned in his letters or journals in which Lowell Thomas was daunted. It seems ridiculously minor. He did not see it that way. He had just ordered corned beef and cabbage, with graham bread, milk and cake at a Washington café and thought he might have underpaid by a dime. "I couldn't shake it off," Lowell explains in his journal. "The matter kept preying on my mind." In order to clear his conscience without having to sheepishly walk back in, Lowell hiked ten blocks back to the café, jotted down the address, hiked another 15 blocks to a post office, purchased five two-cent stamps and a three-cent stamped envelope and then mailed the stamps in the envelope to the café. It was worth it. "An enormous load had fallen from my shoulders," he notes in that journal.[1]

Wheedling himself into confabs with the country's leaders, on the other hand, did not weigh upon this young man at all. Nonetheless, despite its roster of star politicians, Washington was not the stage upon which Lowell was most interested in performing. The city that really drew him, as it had so many other young Americans with grand ambitions, was, of course, New York.

Lowell spent a few weeks there before setting himself up in Princeton. Accommodations were relatively cheap: he stayed across the East River in Brooklyn's Bedford YMCA for $3.50 a week. But he was also eating his meals out, and not all at corned-beef-and-cabbage prices. He contributed $2.50 for carfare to an unemployed journalist he met who claimed to have work as a copy editor in New Jersey but no way to get out there. He sought out interesting or influential people and occasionally sprang for dinner. About once a week he bought a theater ticket—not as expensive a proposition as it is today but still an expense. He was a regular at Carnegie Hall lectures. And once again Lowell got a shock when he examined his "pile." He had only one dollar left and still had not set foot in Princeton.

This necessitated pawning his Elgin watch, for which Lowell received four dollars. But the Lowell Thomas attitude toward financial matters was establishing itself by this point: he assumed he would get by and that, if he kept moving forward, everything would be okay. This was to some small extent a philosophical position, of a kind that fit with his mother's injunctions against the pursuit of "money above everything else" and was not uncommon in 23-year-olds: "The American ideal—worshipping at the shrine of Mammon and scrambling like wolves over a carcass for the mere coin of the realm," young Lowell proclaims to Fran, "seems like madness." Not that Lowell was prone to criticizing his country. And not that he was—as his mother was—particularly devoted to worship at other shrines.

"I'm not an atheist," he tells Fran and assumes she agrees. "I'm strong for churches and all institutions that do good. I like to go to church very much." Indeed, he particularly enjoyed evaluating sermons. "But," Lowell writes, "I'm not one of those who shouts 'amen' every time the honorable pastor pulls a little fireworks about the Ruler of the Universe." Lowell summed up his views on such theological matters to Fran thusly: "For more than four thousand years human beings have been trying to solve the problem of the unknown—usually by idle conjecture. I'd much rather spend my time with you and thinking about you Fran, and in helping solve the practical problems of the world."

So, no, Lowell's perpetual refusal to worry about "the coin of the realm" was not primarily philosophical, political or religious. It was mostly just his way, his disposition. He was too optimistic, too confident—in the way individuals with the gift of gab can get too confident—to fret much about what was, or was not, in his pocket at any given moment. The evening he pawned his watch, Lowell treated himself to a ticket to a big boxing match in Brighton Beach.

And he kept moving forward—meeting people, making connections and in general beginning the process of insinuating himself into New York life. Lowell called upon a couple of editors at the *New York Times*, hawking a profile he had written of the then well-known but aging Indiana poet James Whitcomb Riley, author of "Little Orphan Annie."[2] Lowell had visited Riley, of whose nostalgic and emotional poetry he was a fan, on his way east. Then one day he opened the *Times* to find a full page of its magazine section occupied by his story. "It naturally tickles me," he admits to his journal. The *Times* paid him $16.07.

After he importuned the dean and impressed a faculty member, Brooklyn College of Law agreed to allow him to offer two noncredit courses in public speaking for law students and lawyers there on Saturdays. The students would each pay Lowell ten dollars a semester. With 25 students in a class, that would be good money. He drew students, especially, to the afternoon session, but not that many. The money, consequently, was not that good. New York University's law school turned him down when he proposed a similar deal.[3]

((•))

On September 22, 1915, Lowell lugged his trunk, two suitcases, traveling bag, Corona typewriter and two cases filled with Alaska slides from Brooklyn to Princeton, New Jersey. What he came upon when he reached the university did not much resemble his alma maters, Valparaiso and Denver University. "I'm what Robert W. Service would call a 'misfit' in this dense atmosphere of deep learning," he murmurs to Fran, who was still completing her senior year at Denver University.

Princeton University fancied itself so dedicated to study, seriousness and tradition that it asked its young scholars to wear academic gowns to their meals. And those meals extended over multiple courses. Lowell also had taken a step up in social class. His "rooms," which he occupied by himself, included a bedroom plus a parlor with a bay window and fireplace. "It seems too good to be true," Lowell writes in his journal.

A selection of the sons of the ruling class lived down the hall or sat in his classes, among them, for example, Allen Dulles—grandson of one U.S. secretary of state and nephew of the then secretary of state, Robert Lansing. (Dulles himself would become the first civilian director of the Central Intelligence Agency, while his older brother, John Foster Dulles, another Princeton graduate, served as secretary of state.) The habits and entertainments of these American aristocrats were not Lowell's . . . yet. He did spend a little time out on the Princeton golf course, but only because he was looking for a secluded spot to recite "The Cremation of Sam McGee." Lowell—still partial to a Stetson and seeing himself as a regular guy from the West—flipped between being a little awed by his well-born fellow students and a little put off by them, until, thanks to his social skills and his enthusiasm for people of all sorts, his relations became entirely affable with them, Dulles included.

Still, his fellowship having been denied, and with recourse to just dribs and drabs of his father's meager savings, how could Lowell Thomas afford to sup and study with this crowd—among which were many young men who, as Lowell puts it in his journal, were "overburdened by their bank-rolls"? He appears to have paid his own non-university expenses through loans, a little assistance from his financially strapped father and what money he could earn—initially through tutoring and teaching, including a position at two Princeton dormitories instructing undergraduates in public speaking. And—in what may have been the key to the whole thing—Lowell's room, board and tuition at Princeton may have been paid by a benefactor: Silas Strawn. According to records at Strawn's law firm, Lowell was one of a number of promising young men whose education this prom-inent Chicago lawyer supported.

Lowell took courses in philosophy, history and the philosophy and his-tory of law. On the advice of one professor, he worked toward a thesis on freedom of the press—which would have been a fine idea, combining his two Chicago activities, if Lowell's interest in legal principles had run as deep as his interest in the stuff of journalism: people, places and stories.

He palled around with his friend from Denver, Harold Vinacke—"Nook" to his friends. This being a simpler time and he being Lowell Thomas, he dined with John G. Hibben, president of the university whose previous president, Woodrow Wilson, now sat in the White House. "I'm here to work, w-o-r-k, WORK," Lowell reminds himself in his journal early in his stay at Princeton.[4] And that he also did. Lowell reports needing less sleep than the other "fellows." Despite a burgeoning collection of jobs and schemes—which Lowell's father feared might cause him to slack off on his studies—Lowell did quite well in the graduate program.

Nonetheless, a significant percentage of the first semester Lowell ostensi-bly spent at Princeton—the weekends in particular—was really spent in New York.

On October 8, 1915, three months and four days after he returned from Alaska, Lowell gave his first lecture on Alaska—"Uncle Sam's Polar Paradise"—in the parlor of the YMCA in Brooklyn in which he had spent his first weeks in New York. He wasn't paid for it, and there were some prob-lems: his slides appeared too slowly, and he chided himself for being too "oratorical"—one of the cardinal errors a speaker could make, in Lowell's estimation, though less egregious than merely reading from a prepared text or going on too long. Still, this first talk went well enough to keep alive his dream of supporting himself through this line of work.

There were many competing dreams. Indeed, in letters to Fran and the privacy of his journal, while his personal aspiration remained the same—

"marry Fran"—his career aspirations morphed, multiplied and steadily expanded: write a textbook on public speaking, write a book on journalism and the law; "establish a 'New York School of Journalism,' and make myself its dean"; "get to where Elihu Root"—secretary of war and secretary of state under Theodore Roosevelt—"is in world affairs, and beyond"; and one more, "become . . . the greatest orator of my day."[5]

On November 27, 1915, this ambitious and fearless fellow who had spent eight days in Alaska, most of them on board a steamship, lectured again on "Uncle Sam's Polar Paradise"—this time for five dollars before a standing-room-only crowd of 400 people at New York's much larger West Side YMCA.[6]

((•))

Lowell may seem a young man ripe for a fall or at least a slip. And he was. The problem, however, was not the presumption involved in his lecturing on Alaska. As usual, Lowell backed up his bluff by applying himself, diligently. His capacity for hard "w-o-r-k," for preparation and study, got him through. He had spent dozens of hours in conversation with individuals who knew more than he about Alaska—including the secretary of interior—and put in many days in the New York Public Library researching the area. He snapped up any secondhand book on the subject he could find.[7] He invested time and money in perfecting his talk in consultation with another young expert on public speaking, Dale Carnagey, who, with his name recast as Carnegie, would write perhaps the first great self-help book: *How to Win Friends and Influence People.*

That second YMCA lecture went well. A good percentage of the audience stuck around to congratulate Lowell and ask questions. The YMCA asked him back. Lowell began lecturing on Alaska with increasing skill, regularity and, often, remuneration.

However, there were other issues in Lowell Thomas' life in the late fall and winter of 1915. The first had to do with his family. Less gold of high-enough concentration and easy-enough accessibility had been turning up under Victor, Colorado. Mines were still going, but as Lowell's father put it, "the prosperity was hardly general."[8] Victor and Cripple Creek, therefore, were doing what Skagway, Dyea and Dawson City had done: emptying out. By early 1916 Victor's respected, longtime doctor, in some desperation, hired a bill collector. Harry Thomas had also foolishly invested much

too much—"almost all the savings of twenty-five years," his wife moans—
in that cattle ranch in the San Juan Mountains, which was being run, di-
sastrously it appears, by Harry's younger brother Ira. Harriet Thomas was
not above harping upon her husband's financial failings in her frequent
letters to their son.[9]

The few letters Harry Thomas sent to Princeton are full of concern
about his son: "I fear, in fact am quite sure, you are overworking," he
writes—a regular theme. Dr. Thomas does remind Lowell, with more perti-
nence but no more effect, that "the absurd and impossible are not expected
of you."[10] In fact, at this time it was the son, much too early in life, who had
reason to be concerned about the father, who was no longer able to do what
was expected of him. Dr. Harry Thomas was no longer earning enough to
support his family.

Lowell's mother is surprisingly blunt in a letter to her son written from
Victor on October 24, 1915: "Business is almost entirely gone here for us,
Lowell." Two other doctors in town, she reports, had won the contracts
with the hospital and the mines, perhaps because Dr. Thomas had not
invested in an automobile or assistants. The title "City Physician" had been
crossed out by hand from the top of Dr. Thomas' stationery. "You cannot
imagine dear son how hard it is for your father to sit in the office day after
day without one thing to do," Harriet writes. "He says he is so tired of trying to practice medicine under difficulties that he feels like he never wants
to try again." His mother's portrait of his father then gets sadder still: "I
hate to tell you Lowell, but he cries so hard every day that he is never fit to
go on the street."

At about this time Lowell quips in a letter to Fran, "I haven't been able
to sleep the last few nights (or rather the last few years.) . . . I've always
heard that sleeplessness was the result of worry but Alienists"—early ap-
proximations of psychologists—"would have a hard time doping my case
out because I have never been known to worry." He reveals nothing of his
parents' difficulties to Fran, whom he is still energetically wooing. But if
Lowell were capable of worry, this would certainly seem to have been an
occasion for it. At the very least, a new responsibility had been added to
this 23-year-old's "absurd and impossible" list of ambitions: "I've got to get
busy and figure out some way of helping father out of his difficulties," Lowell tells himself in his journal. "I must do everything in my power for
mother, father and sister, and do it quick."[11]

Then, another topic—over which someone with the ability to worry might lose sleep—resurfaced. More than 16 months after Thomas had written up that interview with Helen Morton, the salt heiress, and three months after Lowell had left the *Chicago Daily Journal*, he received a letter from the paper's managing editor, Martin J. Hutchens.

"It is not pleasant for me to communicate the facts contained in this letter to you," Hutchens writes Lowell on November 24, 1915. "Lately I have been informed that the interview you reported to me as having been secured with Miss Helen Morton, and which is, in part, the basis of several libel suits against the *Journal*, was not a bona-fide interview, but a fake from start to finish." Perhaps because there were lawsuits involved, perhaps because he had been directly lied to, or perhaps because he had a precocious allegiance to truth, Hutchens did not think this had all been in good fun—just another example of wacky, anything-goes Chicago journalism. Here was one successful older man who was no longer impressed by Lowell Thomas.

There is no evidence that Lowell discussed this disturbing letter from Hutchens with Fran, Nook or anyone else. And his response to it, written on November 30, shows him at his worst. Indeed, it is an example of what has been called, based on a story told by Sigmund Freud, "kettle logic"— combining contradictory excuses. In the course of this three-page letter, Thomas argued:

- That he "had nothing to conceal" on the Helen Morton story, "except that" he "had been misled and had used poor judgment"; but also that when he had participated with three other reporters on another fake story, he had been told "that the office knew it was faked but merely laughed about it."
- That he had really interviewed a "good looking young woman" whom he thought was Helen Morton; but also that he had confessed to two friends at the *Journal* that his "story was a fake."
- That after a rewrite man had gotten through with his Helen Morton story, he had "hardly recognized it"; but also that he would have come clean and resigned from the paper if he had thought the libel case would ever go to trial.

Lowell added that he had been underpaid at the *Journal* but hadn't complained, that he was not "infallible" and that he had later tried to "make amends" to the *Journal* by "beating men from other papers merely by out-working them."[12]

The libel suits against the *Journal* would eventually disappear. And Lowell was still young enough to deserve some forbearance. Still, that letter qualifies as a tour de force of disingenuous self-justification.

It was also at this difficult time that Lowell's best buddy at Princeton and his companion on many New York excursions—the aforementioned Harold "Nook" Vinacke—was offered a job as a professor in China and decided to leave Princeton.

It is hard to read the inner life of someone whose main psychological trait seems to be moving forward so fast that he never has to be burdened with one. Still, we might wonder whether having been caught by Hutchens, on top of his family's problems and Nook's departure, left Lowell anxious, vulnerable, unable to sleep—even uncharacteristically insecure and lonely. We know he worried his mother by failing to send a letter home for a week.[13]

Then, on December 7, after all this bad news had arrived, Lowell wrote something in a letter to Frances Ryan that he probably should not have written—erring in the way he tended to err: by being too enthusiastic and therefore too pushy.

Lowell had regularly chided Fran for not writing enough. He had asked more than once whether he was writing too much. But in the seven months since he had surprised her by professing love and advancing plans—seven months in which they had not again seen each other—Lowell had been careful not to push Fran for the commitment she had staunchly refused to give in May. Now, perhaps under the influence of loneliness, he did.

He wrote Fran a long, mostly jaunty letter including news of Nook, who was scheduled to marry another friend of theirs in Denver before sailing for China. But after five pages the letter drops its jaunty tone. Lowell—"Tom" is how he signs his letters to Fran—begins relating his childhood fantasy of "someday meeting a princess." He attributes his drive for success to the "dream" of winning that "princess." Then he writes:

> I know as surely as I know I am here at Princeton that I have discovered who the wonderful princess is. Regarding every other girl I have known but you Fran, I always felt some mysterious force pulling me away and telling me "to wait a little longer." . . . But about two years ago it gradually dawned on me that you were the one. I've often been told I had a strange habit of changing my mind about girls, that I was inconsistent. And I was. But in the last two years there hasn't been a

moment when I doubted that I had found the wonderful girl of my boy-hood dreams.

"Tom" then offered Fran his fraternity pin—the acceptance of which would mean they were engaged. And he waited for her response, prefera-bly, he made clear, by telegram. No letter or telegram arrived.

Lowell followed up, on December 11, with a telegram of his own in which his enthusiasm became, as it occasionally would for the 99 percent of the world more tentative than he, overbearing. It read: "SILENCE FOR YES REMEMBER SILENCE IS GOLDEN."

Fran finally did respond—by mail. This letter is missing from the ar-chives. Perhaps a certain Princeton graduate student had crumpled it up and tossed it in the trash. But we know its purport from the letter Lowell wrote back on December 16.

He starts jauntily once again, with talk of Nook's departure. But the tone quickly changes. And we get another, much weightier example of that seldom-encountered phenomenon: Lowell Thomas daunted. "Thanks for being honest with me," he writes to Fran. "Now that I think it all over I see you didn't give me any reason for harboring the hopes I mentioned in my last letter. And I beg your pardon for being so presumptuous. . . . It was very nice of you to break the news so gently." Then Lowell, still maudlin, beats what may have been a strategic retreat: "If in declining my fraternity pin you had given me any idea that you thought more of me than any other fellow but thought we ought to wait a while, I wouldn't have been satisfied, but would have felt 'nearly' that. But . . . in your kind way you left no room for further remarks."

Lowell wrote Fran again the next night, too—in a rare introspective, even self-loathing, vein: "For years I've been merely trying to do things that would make people say nice things about me, so I could go off by myself and pat myself on the back." Then he adds, "By Jove it's appalling to look back and see what a poor dub you've been."

Fran's response to Lowell's responses to her response we do have, and it gives a sense of her dismay and also of her thinking:

My dear Tommy—I knew that letter would get me into trouble and all sorts of fiery words would come back at me—but that's what I get for not being able to tell people what I think—and always say[ing] what I don't mean. . . . Tommy I am not ready to be engaged or married. . . . You said you would be "nearly" satisfied if I told you something[,] and I can honestly say that I admire you more than any other person I know (and admiration is close kin to love). When I wish to pledge myself, it will be to you[,] but are you willing to wait until I get ready?

Clearly, there was reason even for a "poor dub" to find hope here.

More letters were exchanged. Nook, in Denver on the way to China, tried to help Fran and Lowell decipher each other's feelings. "I found, frankly, that Fran was a little sore about the suddenness and the rather peremptory tone of your letter, and of the telegram as well," he writes to Lowell. "She says she hardly knows you but is strong for you." But he adds, "I think she is rather afraid of the prospect of leaving her folks and all her friends far behind and going away to Chicago or New York. . . . As for you yourself, she said that she was a little afraid of you, that you seemed to be too good to be true; you had been so many places, and had seen so many things and accomplished so much." Nook's assessment offered additional reasons for hope: fears could be eased; time could be allowed to pass; Lowell and Fran might even try to see each other more clearly, if not more often.

Lowell decelerated and became a bit more serious in his letters to Fran. His feelings for her—which initially seemed somewhat random, particularly to her—congealed after this dash of rejection into something more profound, even more passionate. This was a love she could begin to trust. So Fran allowed herself to warm up and appreciate Lowell's dynamism and all that it offered. Lowell in the end did not have to be "willing to wait" for long. Less than a month after writing that she was "not ready," Fran gifted him with this line: "I have been dreaming wonderful dreams all my life; and suddenly you have made me see that they can all come true." To which Lowell retorted, his jauntiness restored, "I thought I had a copyright on the dream stunt." It wasn't a bad thing to have your dreams entwined with those of Lowell Thomas.

On January 18, 1916, Lowell informed his parents that there was an "understanding," as his mother put it, between him and a young woman in Denver, Frances Ryan.[14]

((•))

"I hope to never let a year go by without getting at least a flitting bird's-eye view of some far off corner of the Earth," Lowell wrote Fran at the end of

1915. Indeed, he had begun tossing around possible grand plans for the summer. But in the interim Lowell began undertaking excursions to places less "far off." Fran and his parents started receiving letters and postcards from Leesburg, Virginia; from Reading, Pennsylvania; from Baltimore, Maryland; from Freehold, New Jersey; from Poughkeepsie, New York—which just happened to be where Vassar College and the "fussy" Ruth Pennybacker could be found. Lowell had gotten himself some out-of-town lecturing gigs.

There was plenty of bluffing going on in publicizing these lectures. A promotional letter for his talk in Baltimore stated, "Lowell Jackson Thomas, author, journalist, geologist and lecturer . . . has made many expeditions through Alaska . . . having explored parts where no other white man has been." Even Lowell's mother dismissed this as a "whopper." The letter featured, as would most other advertisements for Thomas' lecture, a picture of him in a bulky, all-fur, hooded Eskimo outfit—which he had either obtained on the East Coast or cropped his face into. The whoppers were also picked up by the press. A review of his lecture in the *Reading News-Times* reported, "Mr. Thomas has spent many years traveling through the arctic and sub-arctic regions."

However, once again Lowell backed up his bluff. His lecture, which he continually refined, was well received. That review in the Reading news-paper called his talk "a delightful treat to all who heard it" and concluded that Thomas "showed that he is very familiar with the country on which he lectured." He was earning, by his own account, anywhere from 15 to zero dollars a night. But the opportunity "to see some other part of the forest" made it worthwhile. "I get more sport out of this roaming around than I could out of anything else that I know of," he explains to Fran.[15]

And then Lowell managed to schedule a handful of lectures that would take him—via Illinois and Iowa on the way out, and Kansas and Ohio on the way back—to Colorado. There were, of course, some people he wanted to see back in Colorado. He planned to meet Fran along the way in Hastings, Nebraska, where she was paying a visit, and accompany her back to Denver. Lowell, an increasingly unflappable traveler, was not at all calm about this rendezvous with Fran on April 21, 1916: he anxiously dashed off a last-minute telegram and formulated backup plans in case something went wrong. It would be the first time this newly engaged couple had seen each other since that one evening together almost a year earlier. Yet, in typical Lowell Thomas fashion, he had also stuffed other purposes into this trip: those lectures, a return to Chicago and an overdue reunion with his suffering family. Fran would accompany him to Victor to meet Dr. and Mrs. Thomas and Lowell's sister.

No journal from this period survives. And since Lowell and his betrothed were finally able to communicate tête-à-tête on those precious days, they wrote no letters that might tell us how the brief convergence of Tom and Fran went. Given the creeds and moralities hovering about these lovers, it seems unlikely that anything beyond "normal boy-girl fooling around" occurred. Still, judging from their tone after letter writing recommenced, neither party was disappointed.

We do have a letter to Lowell from his mother about the visit Lowell and Fran paid to the Thomas family in Victor. Harriet Thomas was quite disappointed.

Her husband may have been too depressed to share in the excitement, but Harriet and Pherbia had been thrilled about the long-awaited return of the much-missed son, who was perpetually oozing optimism and accumulating successes. Their home had not been witness to much of the above since they had seen Lowell last. And the appearance of his future wife would be a significant bonus. Lowell's focus, however, as is normal for those who are in love, was almost entirely on his beloved.

But these were not normal times in the Thomas household in Victor, Colorado, which was, after 16 years, about to be disassembled. Dr. Thomas had sold the shards of his practice to one of his competitors and was ready to leave for the East Coast, where he would attend a church conference and then try, with the considerable assistance of his dynamo of a son, to locate a future for himself—perhaps treating wounded soldiers in Europe. After Pherbia finished school, Harriet Thomas and her daughter would move to Ohio to stay with relatives, while waiting for whatever came next. Most of their belongings had to be sold, but they had wanted to keep the house in Victor together long enough to properly entertain their future daughter-in-law. And they badly needed a dose of their son's "spirit," as his mother put it.

Lowell Thomas had great love and respect for his parents. And he was, by all accounts, kind, eager to help and considerate. Yet on this visit, at this wrenching time for his dear mother, father and sister, he proved disturbingly inconsiderate. He and Fran stayed in Victor only a day and a half—making an excuse, which his mother saw through, in order to leave and spend more time together in Denver. "We had to each of us have a big cry," his mother states in her letter to him, "because you hurried away." And worse, while there Lowell, still straining to impress Fran, seemed to be going out of his way to distance himself from his woebegone, small-town family and what his mother called their "quaint old-fashioned ways and talk."

Harriet Thomas was almost always supportive of her son, but she was also forthright: "You criticize entirely too much," she concluded in her evaluation of the visit. "We certainly like your choice of a girl but hope when you come to see us again you can feel more at ease and be jolly and pleasant and stay longer."[16]

((•))

Before he had left for Colorado, Lowell had been informed by John Hibben, Princeton's president, that the faculty of the university no longer wanted him to continue as a PhD student. But this was good news, stunning in fact: Princeton's faculty had instead elected Lowell Thomas, who was just turning 24, a member of the university's faculty. Hibben's hope was, as Lowell puts it in a letter to Fran, that the new instructor "might build up a department of public speaking." Lowell said "yes," of course. But, he writes, "when the president called me in and asked me if I would be willing to settle down here and devote my life to work as a teacher and professor in Princeton, I told him frankly that I would NOT." For Lowell— still imagining larger stages—this was merely "a great stepping stone to something else."

For Dr. Harry Thomas, however, the fact that his son, because he was now on the faculty, would receive only a master's degree from Princeton was something of a disappointment. Thirty-five years later he was still talking about it. "I had hoped he would receive the doctor's degree," Lowell's father said.[17]

A medley of ambitions took turns as that "something else," but becoming a successful travel lecturer remained prominent among them. This particular profession offered, of course, plenty of opportunity for "roaming around"—getting the material and delivering the lectures. Lowell believed he could make good money at it. And he certainly enjoyed the performance aspects of it. Indeed, at a time when other forms of journalism were restricted to words printed on pages, the travel lecture offered an opportunity to make use of images and of the human voice—always a strong point of Lowell's.

Travel lectures had a long history in Europe, where, before the advent of photography, the images were provided by hand-painted slides, projected by what was then known as a "magic lantern." By the middle of the nineteenth century, photographic slides, of the sort Lowell had borrowed from Clifford C. King, began taking over. Often they were colored by hand. Although travel lectures enchanted with then-rare images of far-off places and exotic peoples (occasionally scantily clad), like school lectures and the most thoughtful journalism, they also presumed to instruct. They combined, in other words, entertainment with education in an age—and for Lowell a family—suspicious of mere entertainment.[18]

The top travel lecturers in the United States were Burton Holmes (for whom the term "travelogue" may have been coined), Dwight Elmendorf and E. M. Newman. On his visits to Carnegie Hall, in New York, Lowell attended and studied lectures by them all. He also went to the Waldorf Hotel to "have a look at the wares presented by" a direct competitor: Dr. Leonard S. Sugden, another Alaska lecturer.[19]

In May, after he returned from Colorado, Lowell passed what he— never one for understatement—described to Fran as "the most important test I have ever had." He lectured on Alaska before a particularly large crowd, with dozens standing in the aisles, at a particularly classy venue: the Brooklyn Academy of Music. This was under the auspices of the also-prestigious Brooklyn Institute of Arts and Sciences.

A typed script survives of a lecture, named "Alaska: Uncle Sam's Polar Paradise," that Lowell composed at about that time, seemingly for a Brooklyn audience. If it wasn't the exact talk he delivered that spring evening, it was a close cousin. The lecture includes a brief history of Alaska— actually of "white peoples" in Alaska. Lowell was not, alas, ahead of his time in sensitivity to indigenous peoples. And in these early twentieth-century travel lectures, a degree of chauvinism—*let me tell you about these odd heathens*—was pretty much de rigueur.[20]

Lowell's lecture, according to this script, also featured the story of the Klondike gold rush and used that as an excuse for him to recite all 15 stanzas of Robert Service's "The Cremation of Sam McGee." It introduced, with a photo, an odd, low-riding native boat called a "kiak." It included cues for about 60 additional images of Alaska on slides, most from Clifford King's collection, plus lots of maps.

The main point of Lowell's Alaska lecture was to extol the potential of the territory's fish, lumber, agricultural and mineral resources. (Oil and tourism were not yet deemed worthy of mention.) Lowell also failed to outperform his time in seeing the dangers for the environment in unbridled development of those resources. Indeed, his lecture—and this, too, was typical of the genre—not only was devoid of negativity, it set out to expunge it: "You have pictured it," Lowell writes of Alaska, "as a land where men starve, go snow-blind and freeze to death." But he was there to tell "you"—the second person was ubiquitous in this lecture—that there are flower gardens and girls picking pansies "way up north in the Arctic."[21] And he had a photo to prove it.[22]

Both Jack London and Robert Service found drama and poetry in the Yukon's habit of unleashing the mad, wild, feral side of men (or dogs). Lowell's focus, like that of the considerably less poetic or complex Rex Beach, remained instead on the entrepreneurial opportunities available to "big, strong, sane men with iron nerve who are willing to take chances."

Nonetheless, this lecture script exhibits notable writerly skills—a talent, in particular, for connecting with an audience. Yes, Lowell could tell stories. His lecture includes, with one embellishment, a long, dramatic version of the tale Lowell had recorded in his journal of that woodsman who was said to have extricated his head from a grizzly's jaws. The embellishment is that Lowell says he "used to know" that woodsman.[23]

And somewhere along the way from the *Victor Record* to the *Rocky Mountain News* to the *Chicago Daily Journal* to Princeton—perhaps under the tutelage of Dale Carnagey—Lowell Thomas had become unusually adept at using comparisons to the familiar to assist his audience in understanding the unfamiliar. His listeners, pondering an exotic northern land few had visited, were advised to "think of its being one fifth as large as the United States. And then think of it having a population about equal to that of Trenton, New Jersey, or Coney Island on a warm summer night." To help the audience make sense of the price the United States originally paid to purchase Alaska from Russia—$7,200,000—Lowell invoked New York's, and the world's, tallest building at the time: that's "about half what it cost to build the Woolworth building," he notes. And then he impressed that audience with this fact: "Since we bought Alaska it has netted the United States $525,000,000 or enough to build thirty-six Woolworth buildings."

Lowell explains to Fran that "if a man gets to lecturing for the Brooklyn Institute and makes good, he is assured of a fairly successful career in the lecture game." He made good. The Institute's director invited him back for five more presentations the next season and gave Lowell a little lecture

on why he should appear only at first-class venues and "quit lecturing before churches and YMCAs."[24]

((•))

Thomas' early career continued to be marked by uncanny temporal rever-
sals: he managed to accomplish what he claimed to have accomplished, but
only *after* having made the claim. His career as a lecturer on Alaska was
well under way when Lowell Thomas managed actually to spend considerable time there.

But before he made plans for another summer trip, there was one matter
to settle: his family. The now-adrift Harry Thomas found his way to Princeton in May 1916, right after his son's triumphant Brooklyn lecture. Lowell
had settled upon a plan for his father: "I intend," he announces to Fran,
"to talk him into leaving for Europe at an early date"—the number of people
in Europe in 1916 requiring a doctor's attention being, of course, horribly
high.

While waiting for the Europe scheme to come together, the son would
have the pleasure of showing his learning-obsessed father around. "Dad
thinks Princeton," Lowell informs Fran, "seems like . . . a part of paradise."
He also enjoyed showing the well-read doctor off: "In the evening I dolled
him up in a gown and put him beside the master of the house, Prof.
Butler."

And then Lowell asked for "letters" endorsing his father from his own
network of accomplished acquaintances—which, given his extraordinary
talent for "winning friends and influencing people," was already unusually
large and from which he was unusually comfortable asking for favors. Professor Butler was the first to agree, but Lowell set his sights higher. "I intend to jolly President Hibben [of Princeton] into writing a few letters of
introduction for him," he explains to Fran. Not everyone succumbed to
Lowell's persuasion, but some impressive letters were dutifully drafted.

Before Harry Thomas could sail for Europe, he would require a
passport—a trick to get during wartime, especially since the United States
was still actively trying to stay out of this bloody war. Lowell traveled to
Washington to help. "The letter I took down to Secretary [of State] Lansing
was the crowbar that did the deed," Lowell crows to Fran. Harry Thomas,
and his collection of letters of introduction, set sail for England on May 27,
1916.

Dr. Thomas was put in charge, Lowell reports, of an English army hospital in Sussex, and then he worked at one of London's war hospitals.[25]

His mother and sister still needed to be settled somewhere, and Lowell was clearly prepared to take on that responsibility as well. But at the end of May 1916, they were staying with relatives in Ohio, and Lowell was ready to set off for the second time to a "far off corner of the Earth." He might have joined his father for the summer in England, France or Germany, but the woman described in the salutation to one of his letters as "the Dearest SwEeTeSt, GRANDEST, and most W-O-N-D-E-R-F-U-L Girl in the world" still lived in Denver. So, since Denver was on the way, the lecturer said to have "made many expeditions through Alaska" decided to make his second journey there.

"I'm not the same fellow I was a year ago," he announces to Fran. This new fellow, in addition to having gotten her to accept his proposal, carried with him to Alaska, this time, real and substantial credentials: travel lecturer, member of the faculty at Princeton University. And he carried even larger ambitions: "I have a wonderful opportunity to become known as the greatest authority on Alaska," he insists in one letter to Fran, "and intend to play it to the limit."

Lowell left New York on June 3; he met his mother and sister in Chicago and then spent a few successful days with Fran in Denver before boarding a steamship in Seattle bound for Alaska on June 19, 1916.[26]

This would be a much more ambitious expedition. Lowell later reported having spent $1,798—much, most or all of this kicked in by railroad companies. Although he may not have published a lot of newspaper articles about his trip the previous year, Thomas had certainly demonstrated an ability to encourage Alaska travel through his lectures. And the fellow who undertook this second Yukon and Alaska trip knew what was needed to improve those lectures.

((•))

Since Lowell already was well supplied with anecdotes, facts and figures on Alaska and the Yukon, the main purpose of this trip in the summer of 1916 would be feeding two cameras—in particular a camera designed to record moving images on film. This was less than 21 years after the Lumière brothers helped invent commercial, nonfiction cinema with primitive, less-than-a-minute-long, home-video-like films such as *Feeding the*

Baby and *Workers Leaving the Lumière Factory.* This was just over a decade and a half after Burton Holmes first began integrating film into his "travelogues."[27] Moreover, this was just a couple of years after Robert Flaherty first set out with a Bell & Howell film camera to record Eskimo life, and it was six years before the film that resulted, *Nanook of the North*—celebrated as the first successful documentary film—was released.[28]

Thomas surely wasn't the first to document with film, but he was, as he usually would be, very early. And he was helping pave the way not only for future photo, film and video journalists but for the legions of Kodak-, 8mm-, camcorder- and smartphone-wielding tourists from America and elsewhere who would set off in the second half of that century and the next to photograph the world.

Filming on the road wasn't easy in those days. Lowell had purchased for $400 a German-made Ernemann moving-picture camera—essentially a rectangular wooden box with a lens in front, a strap on top and a crank handle on the side to move the film through it. Movie cameras and their accouterments—lights, tripods, multiple reels of film—were then extremely bulky. And Lowell had also taken along some sort of playback setup, which he ended up selling in Alaska. "The apparatus I have with me," he moans to Fran, ". . . weighs about 250 pounds, so you can figure what a classy job I have making a team of oxen and a freight truck out of myself while prowling through the land of the midnight sun."[29]

And, of course, the presumption that he might shoot this film himself was another bluff: Lowell had no training or experience in shooting film. After the fact, he admits to one of his sponsors that "all the expert moving-picture cameramen I talked to in New York, Chicago and Seattle before starting north prophesied failure for me owing to my being a neophyte."

Yet he shot some fine footage. Just before arriving in Juneau, for example, Lowell managed to observe, from the deck of the steamship, one of the world's more dramatic sights: the face of a calving glacier—and not just any glacier: Taku, among the thickest in the world outside the Arctic and Antarctica. "The light was perfect for taking pictures this morning . . . ," he notes. "I ground over a hundred feet of film."

Lowell's itinerary included a return to Skagway, Whitehorse and Dawson City, and since he was actually able to spend some time on land this time, Lowell's big adventure was enlivened by a lot of smaller adventures. With some new buddies, he climbed a mountain next to Skagway and gained a spectacular view of a glacier "shoving its nose out into the fiord."

In Whitehorse Lowell took a boat, with a reluctant local hotelier at the rudder, between the orange- and gray-basalt walls of narrow Miles Canyon and down the notorious Whitehorse rapids. These were the treacherous waters that had defeated so many of the Stampeders. "Spectators," Lowell recalls in a letter, "said all they could see were three white faces bobbing up occasionally and our hair, which they said was on end." Here we get one of the first instances of a behavior that would recur throughout Lowell's travels: courting danger. A local photographer, behind Lowell's camera, "ground the movie crank from the shore," so Lowell's lecture audiences would get to marvel and chuckle at his daring.

Perhaps Lowell was even beginning to learn something on this trip about the riches and strengths of cultures besides his own and people from races besides his own. It couldn't have hurt that he dined with the "next chief of the Chilkat Indians" and his wife—both of whom had attended Ivy League universities.

Most of the places Lowell visited—Seward, Fairbanks, Nome, Cordova—were new to him, which was catnip for him. "Seeing the streets lined with dog teams instead of Jitneys," he writes; ". . . riding on a narrow gauge railway through a flock of glaciers; battling against an army of mosquitoes that would make the German forces at Verdun run like a drove of rabbits; chased by a regiment of timber wolves; . . . and listening to the yarns pulled by Old Sourdoughs, any man ought to be re-invigorated and pul-motored back to life."

And the adventures did not stop after he returned to Seattle. Lowell and some of his acquaintances attempted to scale Mount Rainier but turned back only, he insists in a letter to Fran, because of "a big storm." Before he returned to Princeton—the start of classes there had been delayed by a polio outbreak—Lowell also managed to hike down and up the Grand Canyon.[30]

This was the journey that established the pattern for 60 years' worth of Lowell Thomas journeys, which meant that along with the physical exertions, flirtations with danger, exotic scenes and rarely seen sights it had to have one more element: larger-than-life characters. Among the individuals—Sourdoughs, real Alaska types—who played that role on this 1916 trip was Jack McCord, who had a hand in railroading, mining and cattle ranching and was said to have been a model for the hero of Lowell's favorite Rex Beach novel. The terms Thomas would later use to describe McCord would fit others of those to whom he attached himself over the

years: "seldom did anything the way most of us would do it . . . gifted raconteur. . . . the life of the party. . . . adventurer, entrepreneur."[31]

In his own effort to become such a character, Lowell had settled on a
new look for himself: just north of his upper lip he now displayed a thin,
neatly barbed line of hair. "Pherbie raised a great disturbance when she saw
my microscopic moustache and insists that I amputate it at once," he writes
Fran on the way back to Princeton. "It relieved her quite a bit to know that
you didn't like it either."[32] Pencil mustaches were not unknown in 1916.
George Beranger, for example, exhibited one in a film Lowell had seen,
Birth of a Nation. But Lowell grew his well before the dapper and dynamic
actors who would popularize this species of facial hair grew theirs: Clark
Gable, after all, was only 15 at the time, Errol Flynn seven and Douglas
Fairbanks Jr., six. Once again Lowell Thomas was early. And despite the
initial opposition of his fiancée and his sister, and with few interruptions,
Lowell sported a slender, well-trimmed mustache for the rest of his life.

((•))

Early in October 1916 Lowell settled his mother, sister and himself into an
apartment in Princeton. He had fixed it up but wasn't in it enough to suit
his mother—still forlorn due to the loss of her home, and both missing and
worrying about her husband. Lowell was teaching courses in public speaking and English at Princeton but spending much of his time in New York
getting film edited and colored, attending to the lecture business and flog-
ging other schemes. "Life for me seems to be one regular series of jumps
from Old Nassau to Father Knickerbocker's Isle," he informs Fran.

Having obtained her BA, Fran had taken a job as a grade school
teacher—"a school marm," is how she puts it—in Castle Rock, Colorado.
Her "jumps," accomplished by hitching a horse to a cart, were from the
farm where she was boarding to the "little red brick school." Each morning
upon arriving she brought water in from a well in the yard, lit the stove,
swept the floor and then taught 14 children "spread over nearly all eight
grades."

For Lowell, this period—from the end of his second Alaska trip through
the entrance of the United States into World War I, which altered many a
young man's plans—can roughly be divided in two: before and after
Lowell's lecture at Carnegie Hall.

During the 15 weeks that preceded that talk on January 13, 1917,

Lowell's lecture business was taking off. He worked his new film of Alaska into at least three different Alaska travelogues, which he presented for the Brooklyn Institute but also at other venues—YMCAs still among them— around the Northeast. Lowell hired a friend to handle his correspondence— hardly a standard move for a 24-year-old—and then replaced him with a young man who could perform these secretarial duties and work the projector during his lectures. Lowell persuaded Clifford King, the older businessman who had supplied his initial cache of Alaska slides, to leave the Northwest and come to New York as his manager, and he remained loyal to King, even after an established lecture agency offered to handle his bookings.

And then Lowell was invited to speak at a government conference on the National Parks in Washington. Other speakers included a senator, the secretary of the interior and Orville Wright, whose talk was entitled "Air Routes to the National Parks." Lowell's assigned topic, unfortunately, was not Alaska, which was just getting its first national park, but "Typical Development at Mount Rainier." Even he realized that was "funny": "having spent three days in Ranier [sic] I am not exactly what you would call an authority on the subject." He quips to Fran that before his talk he "had nine different brands of ague, nervous prostration and paralysis." But he pulled it off. "I think I did the best I ever did in my life. At any rate I got away without being . . . pelted with vegetables." Lowell's secret was turning the subject whenever possible to something upon which he now was an authority: Alaska.

The reviews of his Rainier talk—helpfully excerpted by Lowell from letters he received—were certainly positive: "An excellent address," concluded the naturalist and writer Enos Mills. Robert Sterling Yard, a magazine editor now working to promote the National Parks, wrote, "I was greatly pleased with it, and so was everybody who spoke to me about it— and many spoke." And, as always, success bred more schemes—perhaps including, in this case, renting Carnegie Hall.

Lowell had sent out "some sixty" Christmas packages to his nearest, dearest and best-connected. He had mailed Fran a diamond ring, to replace his fraternity pin. He was staying at hotels, not YMCAs. He spent and earned and spent sums that would have been unimaginable to him a year earlier. "Nothing suits me better than to pay bills like these," he explains to Fran, "and I hope they get bigger and bigger each year, but that my income will increase five times as fast."[33]

It was in that spirit that Clifford King and he financed the Carnegie Hall event together. It cost a thousand dollars to rent the place, plus lots more for ads in the newspapers:

ALASKA
WONDERFUL ILLUSTRATED LECTURE with
Remarkable Colored Motion Pictures by
LOWELL JACKSON THOMAS
THE EMINENT AUTHORITY ON ALASKA.
CARNEGIE HALL—TO-NIGHT
AT 8:30. Tickets 50c. to $1.50 at Box Office.[34]

Carnegie Hall was, as he reminds Fran, "the most important place of its kind in the country." It was also large. Thomas and King had about three thousand seats to fill, with a Burton Holmes travelogue in the same hall the next night as competition.

And while Lowell never quite admits it in his letters to Fran, it looks as if he and Mr. King, as Lowell calls him, took a bath. The hall must have been embarrassingly empty. They must have lost a lot of money. Four days later Lowell writes of "financial crises" and "deep gloom." And after Carnegie Hall, Thomas and Clifford King parted ways. Lowell had admitted to Fran before the Carnegie Hall debacle that "when it comes to making bonehead plays and bungling, I hold several championship belts." In imagining himself ready for Carnegie Hall, he—or King, or both of them—had bungled. Lowell had, as he was always capable of doing, overreached.

Lowell signed up with that lecture agency and ended up playing a lot more small East Coast cities and a lot more YMCAs. His repertoire now included, to shake out some more business, something on Mount Rainier and the Grand Canyon. There are no more mentions in his letters of that personal secretary. "This barnstorming lecture game is not all a path of roses, believe me," he complains to Fran.

And the teaching game, which he had stumbled into, failed to excite him. He voiced the academic's complaint: "I have a stack of exam papers three feet high with me to correct this afternoon." But he fails to voice the academic's enthusiasm for cerebration, reflection and the arcane. By early March he is writing Fran, "I've had about all the teaching I care for. It doesn't appeal to me at all and it isn't a good idea for a fellow to keep on

doing something he is not particularly interested in." Lowell had also begun to note the "paltry salaries" of "American college professors."

Business continued to interest him, as did politics, journalism and, of
course, travel. And the schemes kept flowing. He lists seven of them in a
letter to Fran written a month after his Carnegie Hall debacle. Lowell was
contemplating guiding a troop of Ivy League men—and Fran—on a grand
tour of Alaska. He was negotiating with two businessmen to form something christened "the Alaskan Development Company." He was taking
meetings on the possibility of taking charge of the speaking campaign in
support of John Purroy Mitchel, a young reformer, who was running for
reelection as New York's mayor. And Lowell was trying to convince either
the Interior Department, the U.S. Chamber of Commerce or Daniel Guggenheim, among the biggest of Alaska investors, to put him on salary as a
lecturer.

Lowell had a rare talent for coming up with ideas, but they were inevitably large ideas. "It's just as easy to shoot a bear as a rabbit," is how he
would later explain this. The grandiosity of so many of his plans, and their
number, made his success rate in actualizing them less impressive. None
of these schemes went anywhere.

But setbacks, even "financial crises," didn't deter him long. Lowell operated by the maxim that "everything has got to come out right." In his way
of looking at the world, something could be too *bad* to be true. The United
States declared war on Germany in April 1917. It would take Lowell a while
to figure out what doors this closed . . . and what doors it opened. But that
month he took one decisive step: he resigned from the faculty of Princeton
University.[35]

5.

===================

Something More Colossal
Than Anything of Its Kind Ever Tried

By the late spring of 1917, there was just one place to be for an American rapidly developing an adventure addiction: near "the Great War." Yes, it had actually been a horrid war—devoid of purpose, grindingly slow, "great" only in the number of countries involved and their casualties. But Lowell and many other American young men believed the entrance into that war of the reliably earnest and increasingly strong United States would somehow make it right. And war was offering its usual, though so often unfulfilled, promise of glory.

The obvious way for a young American man to get "over there" would have been by joining the military. Indeed, the government had instituted a draft designed to ensure men did just that. But Lowell did not join the military.

"I happened to be one of those unfortunates who was turned down by the army for some alleged physical reasons," he maintains in a letter to a dean at Princeton in 1919.[1] But that was not true. His draft registration form from June of 1917 clearly states that Lowell Jackson Thomas had decided to "claim exemption from [the] draft" because his mother was "solely dependent upon" him "for support."[2] It is hard to imagine Lowell—who dared rapids, precipices and wildernesses—wiggling out of the draft because of fear. And his mother and sister really did need his assistance. Still, it is not hard to imagine Lowell desiring to find a grander role for himself in the war than that of just another soldier.

That draft registration form does not list Lowell's "current trade, occupation or office" as anything connected with the university. Princeton was clearly behind him, though he was still prepared to invoke the connection when useful. Nor does that form describe him as a travel lecturer. That business had for the moment lost its attraction. "For the American people," Fran explains in her own journal, "were not in the mood to listen to talks on the quiet charms of nature when their minds were filled with war."[3] Instead on that form Lowell anointed himself a "war correspondent." He was after journalistic glory.

Reporting on wars was considered quite a dashing occupation in 1917. The first correspondents to achieve renown traipsing after soldiers—and this goes back to William Howard Russell of the *Times* of London in the middle of the nineteenth century—dressed like officers, like gentlemen. Russell was known for his well-polished high boots. The most renowned American war correspondent of Thomas' youth, the movie-star-handsome Richard Harding Davis, managed to be well turned out even as shots rang out around him: his standard outfit included a tie. Davis died of a heart attack in 1916, while still relatively young. Lowell read a book of his letters and listed Davis, along with Teddy Roosevelt, as a man he emulated.[4]

Floyd Gibbons of the *Chicago Tribune*—who had inhabited circles not far from Lowell's but whom Lowell later insisted he had never met—was another who covered wars with bravado and bravura, even before a wound from a German bullet in 1918 necessitated his wearing that swashbuckler's emblem: an eye patch. Gibbons' dispatches also appeared in the *New York Times*; Lowell must have read them.

Previous to assuming his duties as a mostly self-proclaimed war correspondent, Lowell bought himself a new suit and a pair of leather boots even higher than those filled by William Howard Russell.

((•))

Lowell would not be a typical war correspondent—assigned by one newspaper to cover one part of the war. He had in mind, as was his wont, something more ambitious—"something that is more colossal than anything of its kind ever tried," as he modestly put it to Fran. And, as had not been his wont, he began devoting all his energies to this one scheme. The plan was to report on how the world—some approximation of the whole world—was experiencing the First World War. This would be journalism: Lowell had lined up a magazine, *Leslie's Weekly*, and was lining up a bunch of news-papers to print his articles, which would later, he envisioned, be turned into a book. Lowell would also be traveling with film and still cameras, so this journalism could take a new form: he could apply the images-plus-voice techniques he had helped develop in his travel lectures to coverage of war.

And Lowell was not shy about proclaiming that his reporting also would provide publicity and encourage support for the war effort. It would function as what we would now call public relations, if not as what was then just beginning to be disparaged as propaganda. (Lowell still some-times dubbed himself a "propagandist.") Lowell's scheme was not, as many later would insist, initiated by the Wilson administration, which was undertaking—under the direction of a former journalist, George Creel—the first organized government publicity campaign for a war in American history. The idea was Lowell's. The plan was Lowell's. However, his trip did have the support of the Wilson administration. Creel and other top officials in Washington helped Thomas obtain passports and letters of introduction.

That his role as a publicist supporting the war might conflict with his obligations as a journalist reporting on the war does not appear to have concerned Thomas. It is not clear that such apparent conflicts of interest concerned many others at the time either. The "Canons of Journalism," which the American Society of Newspaper Editors would adopt in 1923, did decry "promotion of any private interest contrary to the general welfare." But it did not proscribe supporting a government initiative—a war.

Lowell envisioned his trip being funded by investors. The attraction for them—aside from the chance to share in any profits—would not be the op-portunity to support journalism but the chance to support the war. The funding he would require was significant: $40,000, which he soon boosted to $50,000—big money for those days, certainly big money for Thomas, who two years earlier had exulted when able to borrow $250. But Lowell had no interest in traveling cheap. And he was ready to travel far: beginning a circumnavigation of the globe with a steamship from the West Coast across the Pacific to Russia, which, Lowell noted with considerable excite-ment, "was on the verge of a second French Revolution."

Lowell would not be traveling alone. The key member of Lowell's team was an expert cameraman and whiz with the equipment, Harry A. Chase, who would relieve Lowell of responsibility for the care, feeding and operation of the still and movie cameras. Chase had played the same role for another of Lowell's competitors in the travelogue business, Frank R. Roberson, who had recently died. Lowell, in yet another bold move, had purchased Roberson's images and equipment from his widow.

Another individual would also be joining the traveling party of the business soon to be incorporated as "Thomas Travelogues Inc.": one Frances Ryan of Denver, Colorado. Lowell had given her some assignments: she was to learn how to type, train herself in the art of coloring slides and film and keep a journal of their travels. However, according to the mores of the time, Miss Ryan could not come along until she became Mrs. Thomas. The wedding, originally scheduled for the middle of June 1917, was to take place right before the trip. It kept getting postponed.

For Lowell, working on this scheme as he had no other, somehow had to raise the money for this combination journalism-remaking, war-effort-supporting, career-boosting and globe-gallivanting expedition, which would also serve as part of his and Fran's honeymoon. He turned, in this search for investors, to Chicago—to the distinguished and impeccably connected lawyer Silas Strawn and his clients in the meatpacking business. Lowell had earned their respect, and they had owed him a favor since he exposed Carleton Hudson, who had blackmailed some of them. However, it was not an easy project to fund.

"I am organizing a corporation and selling nothing but my own personality," Lowell half moans, half brags to Fran. The simple way to obtain financing would have been to get one or two hugely wealthy men to underwrite his corporation. Lowell obtained audiences with leaders of two giant meatpacking companies, Edward F. Swift and Jonathan Ogden Armour. They each turned him down. Lowell's spirits did what they did not often do: they sagged. The wedding was postponed until late July. But Lowell was nothing if not resilient.

He would now have to put together an investment group of a dozen or so merely very wealthy men, beginning with Strawn. He visited offices, attended lunches and made his pitch. Lowell was extraordinarily good at visiting, lunching and making pitches. In the end he assembled a group of smaller investors, including more lawyers, a banker, a doctor, the president of a steel company, the general counsel of Swift and Company and the vice president of Armour and Company. Papers filed with the state of Illinois report that Thomas Travelogues Inc. was initially capitalized at $45,000 and that its primary business was to be: "To provide, produce, conduct and furnish illustrated and other lectures and similar entertainment of all kinds pertaining to the education, amusement or edification of the public, including information on foreign travel and other subjects of general interest. . . ."

On July 27, 1917, the directors elected as president of Thomas Travelogues Inc. a manufacturer, William V. Kelley, who hailed, probably not coincidentally, from the same corner of Ohio as Lowell's family. Lowell Thomas was elected vice president. He had succeeded in forming—to put it in terminology from our time—a boutique, innovative, entrepreneurial yet well-capitalized journalism/public relations start-up. That was a rare, if not unique, phenomenon in his time.

However, as happens when dreams become businesses, Lowell's scheme quickly lost a little of its grandeur. One of his backers pointed out that a trip around the world beginning in eastern Russia would take so long that, when Lowell returned and began giving his lectures, the world might no longer be at war—negating the usefulness of those lectures in building support for the war. Lowell did hold on to the thought that this world war was not just a European story, but he agreed to sail directly for Europe.

Frances Ryan and Lowell Jackson Thomas were married in Denver on Saturday evening, August 4, 1917, in a ceremony attended by members of her family and some friends. Lowell's father, in England, and his mother and sister, in New Jersey, were unable to be there. Lowell, though thrilled about the marriage, was not all that captivated by the wedding—which, uncharacteristically, he had not stage-managed. Fran was. "Wasn't it all beautiful?" she writes in a letter to her mother the next day.[5]

((•))

In marrying Lowell Thomas, Frances Ryan, who had never before been much east of Chicago, had in essence hopped aboard—to employ an image to which Lowell was partial—a magic carpet.

From Denver, after the wedding, it was on to Colorado Springs for a night, and then, riding trains, to Chicago, where Lowell still had some business to wrap up. Next, they stopped at Niagara Falls, with all of an hour and a half—Lowell maintained a snappy pace—to gawk at the falls.

After an evening in Albany, the newlyweds took a steamship down the Hudson and had a few days in New York City, before—it was August—heading down to the Jersey shore. Princeton and Philadelphia were next, then Washington and more business and more sightseeing. All of this was accomplished, without benefit of airplane travel, in the first two weeks of their marriage.

And they moved, everywhere, in high circles. "I think more of Tommy every day," Fran writes her mother from Washington. "I didn't realize he was half so grand. . . . He has stacks and stacks of friends here among older men who seem to hero-worship him." Those "older men" included allied diplomats along with some of the top officials of the United States, from whom Lowell was still gathering endorsements for his scheme. And, of course, "Tommy" at the time was only 25 years old—just four years removed from a summer working as a ranch hand in Colorado.

By week three Fran's energy was flagging. "I am getting awfully tired trying to keep up with Tommy," she admits to her mother. "He sure works at high speed all of the time." But keeping up with Tommy led, as Fran certainly realized, to fascinating places. Twenty-five days after their wedding in Denver, they boarded, along with Harry Chase, the SS *Chicago* in New York. The ship was headed for Bordeaux. Of course, the newlyweds were regulars in the captain's quarters during the voyage. Of course, Lowell was selected to host the voyage's entertainment, designed to raise money for the troops. But there did happen to be a war going on, and German U-boats lurked in Europe's coastal waters. When they neared France, most of the passengers chose to sleep out on deck with their valuables in their pockets—to speed access to the lifeboats in case of a submarine attack.

Lowell and Fran, on their first trip to Europe, arrived in Paris in the middle of September. The fighting was just "two hours by machine [automobile] from Paris," Fran writes. But the boulevards and monuments were still lovely. The war had shuffled but not seriously diminished the city's population of interesting people, though Lowell did note early on that "two thirds of the people we see on the streets of the cities of France are in mourning." And for these two Americans from Colorado the food, while expensive, was exotic as well as inventive and often spectacular. "Tommy and I like to prowl around and see every corner," she informs her parents. "We try all kind of restaurants."[6] Lowell had married well.

Thomas—a champion at cajoling—found ways to get himself, Chase and their cameras out of the quiet city and near the front in Belgium and in

France. He sent back newspaper articles. "Lowell Thomas faculty member of Princeton University, Alaska explorer, newspaper reporter and war correspondent . . . ," the *Detroit Sunday News* explained on November 4, 1917, "went abroad recently, authorized by the United States government to interpret war conditions." However, from what little evidence of those articles I have been able to locate, it appears that interest back home was almost as much in the American role and how it was being perceived as in the war in general. This is how that article by Thomas in the *Detroit Sunday News* began: "I had long wondered just what the French people thought of our Col. Roosevelt. . . ." Another newspaper piece by Thomas, in the Philadelphia *Evening Ledger* on October 20, 1917, announced in its headline, "The Philadelphia Commission for Rehabilitating France Is Now on the Ground." There is no evidence that Thomas' work appeared in 1917 or 1918 in *Leslie's Weekly*, his original partner in all those "colossal" plans to cover the war.

By the middle of November, Lowell, Fran and Harry Chase were in Italy—sampling Turin, Milan, Genoa, Pisa, Venice, Florence and Rome. Fran saw the cities, but she did not join Thomas and Chase on their reporting trips to military areas. This was not out of timidity; Lowell explains that she was not allowed "into the war zone."[7] There, their traveling party usually consisted of Thomas, Chase and a guide supplied by the Italian War Ministry, Lieutenant Piero Tozzi—with Lowell taking notes on war factories and war damage and Harry Chase shooting sometimes exclusive film and photos of the destruction.

One night, Lowell reports, a large bomb dropped by a German airplane exploded 50 feet away from the restaurant where he and Chase were eating dinner. And while in Italy, Thomas, Chase and Tozzi undertook a particularly strenuous visit to the front, which happened to be, as Lowell explains in a letter to his mother and sister, "up on top of the Italian Alps":

> We traveled ten miles over a solid field of ice 2,500 feet thick. Dog teams pulled our supplies and equipment, but we had to make it on foot. The cold was intense. . . . We were with the Italian troops in the first line up there in the snow for several days. We could look across the valley and see the Austro-German outposts, and during one whole day we were heavily bombarded by them.

This experience was notable for two reasons. First, for what it reveals about how Lowell—and Harry—responded to such hardships and dangers (which, Lowell reveals elsewhere, were never that dire): "The Alpine troops treated us with wonderful hospitality," Lowell writes, "and we had the time of our lives." Second, it was up there with the Italian troops that Lowell Thomas got a good look at Alpine skiing and actually went "coasting" on what he still referred to as "skees." This sport became one of the great passions of his life.[8]

The pictures they shot were significant, too. Cameramen had been filming wars for perhaps 20 years when Thomas' cajoling and Thomas' and Chase's exertions brought them to the front. But much of the early footage of war, such as that of Georges Méliès, had been faked—shot in studios.[9] Lowell Thomas was in his usual position—not the first actually to film war but among the pioneers.

He and Chase had gained a remarkable perspective on this mammoth war and some its consequences. But so far they had no way of presenting the rare still and moving images they had captured, fortified by Lowell's narration, to audiences hungry for news of the war. They had the makings of what could have been compelling television news reports or movie newsreels, if it weren't for the fact that even the earliest experiments with television had yet to begin, newsreels were in their infancy in 1917 and film was still silent.

True, some companies—Pathé prominent among them—had begun screening regular news compilations in movie theaters. "A moving picture newspaper," a character in a 1913 novel called them.[10] The word "newsreel" was in use by 1916, and American movie audiences had some access to footage, interspersed with brief explanatory titles, from the European war: emperors strutting, armies marching, cannons firing—that sort of thing. But these earliest newsreels were often more cartoonish, less realistic than the war footage Thomas and Chase were producing. There is no evidence in his letters and journals that Thomas was yet aware of newsreels as a possible use for their film. Besides, his tiny corporation had no means for regularly getting his film over the then-treacherous Atlantic. The technology for gathering news footage in the early decades of the twentieth century was well ahead of the technology for transmitting, distributing and presenting it.

In order for their work to be seen and heard, Thomas and Chase would have to make it home, develop and edit their film, put together a travelogue and begin bringing it to various halls across the land. By the time all this might happen, as that one investor had feared, the war likely would have been over, and potential audiences might have been in the mood to think of something else. The business model of Thomas Travelogues Inc., in other words, was precarious, to say the least.

It is not at all clear that Thomas—buoyant as always and denied the benefit of hindsight—realized this. If he had, and if he had worried more about money, and if simply being there had not been such a large part of his motivation, he might have taken the film Chase had shot and caught the next ship back to New York. Instead, Lowell decided to extend his trip by pushing on from Europe to another part of the world suffering through the world war: the Middle East. And it was this move that ended up transforming his whole expensive expedition into an enormous success.

((•))

Lowell had been in Venice with Fran and Harry Chase when he learned that British General Edmund Allenby's forces had captured Jerusalem from the Ottoman Empire, an ally of Germany, on December 9, 1917. Lowell Thomas' success as a journalist stemmed in part from an acute sensitivity to popular tastes—aided by the fact that he often shared them. He realized how newsworthy the "liberation" of Jerusalem was and wrote a couple of cables to a British military official pleading for permission to go to Jerusalem. "From the standpoint of anyone engaged like myself in gathering material for a series of patriotic illustrated lectures in an attempt to stimulate enthusiasm [for] the war in America," Lowell explained, "the restoration of Palestine to the Christians after four hundred years of Moslem occupation was of the greatest possible importance."

His connections were strong. In those cables to that British official, Thomas invoked the American secretaries of war, state and the navy, along with a couple of ambassadors. Not surprisingly, the British agreed that Lowell Thomas, along with his cameras and Harry Chase, could travel to the Middle East.

Fran remained in Italy, as Lowell and Harry Chase made their way across the Mediterranean, which was also infested with German U-boats. As usual they were encumbered with, by Lowell's count, "two small trunks loaded with plates and films and eleven other hand pieces of baggage," which included one motion-picture camera and two still cameras.[11] They were also, as usual, encumbered with each other.

Fran often came along in those years; Harry, who had a wife of his own and a son back home, almost always came along. Lowell had no difficulty acknowledging what he brought to these expeditions:

> Chase is unique. He can grind his own lenses. . . . He can take his cameras to pieces and remove the fine particles of dust that have got into them . . . and then, in putting them together, usually he can discover some way of improving their intricate mechanism. His ability to make the fullest possible use of both his still and motion-picture cameras has made him one of the most famous cameramen in the world. But his genius does not end there. Chase can do the same things to your watch . . . , and he can effect the same magic spell over a derelict motor-car.[12]

Nonetheless, two qualities displayed by the more rough-hewn Chase could get on the nerves of the hyper-personable and socially ambitious Thomas: The first, by Lowell's account, was Chase's abiding pessimism; the second a laxness about such social graces as "thank you" and "excuse me." Lowell also complains that, despite Chase's technological wizardry and undeniable artistry, he often fell back upon a just-tell-me-what-to-do view of employee-employer relations. "You have frequently made it quite clear that you preferred to be given specific instructions rather than be asked advice," is how Lowell put it in an annoyed, undated letter to Chase that he apparently—and probably wisely—never actually sent. For the most part Harry and Lowell worked and traveled remarkably well together.[13]

Their ship docked in Egypt, headquarters of the British forces in the Middle East, on January 26, 1918.

((•))

The British were using airplanes in their campaign there, and Lowell was determined to get Chase and their motion-picture camera up in one of them. Lowell also intended to get himself into an airplane. One of the first things he did in Egypt was secure permission.

Lowell climbed into a plane first, with just a still camera. Two days later Chase and the film camera were fitted into an airplane. Then Chase filmed from the ground as a British pilot, with Lowell on board, did loops over the pyramids. "I tasted my breakfast several times," Lowell reports. While stretching to get a photo out of the front of that plane, Lowell accidentally "jammed" his foot down on a lever. "Instantly [the] machine dove straight down," he writes in his journal. The pilot yelled. Lowell lifted his foot. This was only 14 years after the first Wright brothers' flight. Once again Thomas was early . . . and fearless.

The story he was after, however, was in Palestine, not in Egypt. After engine trouble forced them to turn back once, Thomas and Chase were flown to Jaffa, not that far from Jerusalem, on February 13, 1918.

Lowell Thomas clearly was carrying an excess of cultural baggage with him to Palestine. Indeed, he prepared himself to report on "the restoration of the Holy Land to the Christians" by studying tales of the crusaders and reading the Bible.[14] But, to be fair, he was hardly alone in playing up the Christians-capture-Holy-City-from-infidels angle. For example, next to a cartoon showing a gallant crusader opening the city's gate, an editorial at the time in the New York *Evening World*, founded by Joseph Pulitzer, concluded: "Jews and Christians alike can rejoice that the ancient capital with its sacred and august associations has been recovered at last from Mohammadan rule."[15] Lowell also retained, again along with most American journalists at the time, a vulnerability to stereotypes and an eagerness to find heroes—preferably American or, since Americans were in short supply on this front, British.

Nonetheless, Lowell had become, at this young age, a thorough and alert reporter. That is demonstrated by the journals—really more reporter's notebooks—he kept while traveling around Palestine and conducting dozens of interviews. General Allenby, the hero of this tale, does not appear himself to have talked with him at this time, but Thomas captured the recollections of various brigadier generals, lieutenant generals, colonels, captains and ordinary soldiers, as well as European or American expatriates. Thomas' notebooks contain the story of the capture of Jerusalem, which ended surprisingly placidly, he notes, "without any bloodshed among the inhabitants or damage to the buildings in the city"—as first the "Brits" then the "Turks" decided not to "shell" the "Holy City."

As chronicler of this military campaign, which more often produced much bloodshed and damage, Lowell's compulsion to go everywhere and talk with everyone stood him in good stead. Here, for a quick example, is a sentence from Thomas' copious notes on Gaza (looking as it would often look again in the next hundred years): "Even a Ford couldn't get over the piles of rocks and mud bricks where houses, shop buildings and mosques had been wrecked by shells from the British artillery."

A little later in his stay in the Middle East, Lowell makes an offhanded comment in a journal that gives a sense of the number of people he had interviewed or chatted up on this reporting trip: "Every time I get on a train, go into a hotel or restaurant, I meet from one to ten people that I know."[16] With a few notable exceptions—such as the Arab mayor of Gaza—what is missing is the perspective of those who didn't patronize those hotels and restaurants: non-Westerners. That this lacuna can be found in the work of most journalists at the time—and some war correspondents today—does not make it less significant. But for a contemporary account of the capture of Jerusalem, from the point of view of those who captured it, Lowell's notebooks are hard to beat.

Once again Lowell had, in other words, performed his signature feat of prestidigitation. He was transforming himself into what he had presumptuously announced himself to be: a war correspondent. True, the products of his journalistic efforts were still skimpy or nonexistent. The reels and reels of film Harry Chase had shot in Europe and now the Middle East were not even developed, let alone being viewed. Newspaper articles with Lowell Thomas' byline remained scarce. But Thomas had seen and diligently gathered information on parts of the war other reporters had not seen. And he was about to report on—or help conjure up—perhaps the war's most intriguing figure.

The first mention in Thomas' Palestine notebook of Major T. E. Lawrence is undated but appears to have been written in Jerusalem on February 27, 1918. It records Lawrence's account of a battle in the ongoing Arab Revolt against the Ottoman Empire.[17] T. E. Lawrence's role in that uprising would become the most important news story Lowell Thomas got hold of during the First World War, and it would form the basis for perhaps the most consequential and controversial journalism of his very long career.

6.

≡≡≡≡

A Blue-Eyed, Beardless Man in Arab Robes

During the First World War Lowell Thomas was confirming—as he zipped to Europe, through Europe and then to the Middle East—that being in motion was his preferred state. And the direction he preferred for all this moving about, the direction that might best satisfy his adventure addiction, was also becoming clear: toward the increasingly exotic. From Egypt Lowell had made it to Palestine. And now he was hearing talk of a significant military campaign under way in Arabia—at the time, for a European or American, among the most exotic locales on Earth. Lowell had even spoken with a colorful Englishman, in the habit of dressing in Arab robes, reputed to be riding at the head of the Arab forces.

Arabs were among the ethnic groups using the First World War as occasion to try to gain independence from the sprawling, heterogeneous and increasingly rickety Ottoman Empire and Turkish rule. Since that empire was allied with Germany in this war, and with an eye toward postwar influence in the region, the British were enthusiastically encouraging this "Arab Revolt"—supporting it, advising it, funding it. They were primarily working with the Hashemites, Sherif Hussein bin Ali and his sons, who had dynastic claims in the western part of the Arabian Peninsula, the Hejaz. Major T. E. Lawrence first tagged along with an emissary to the Hash-emites, then became an emissary himself.

Thomas Edward Lawrence was born on August 16, 1888, in Wales to a couple hiding what at the time was a scandalous secret: they were not married to each other. Lawrence's father, Thomas Chapman, was an Irish-English gentleman and a baronet who had inherited an estate in Ireland. Chapman left that estate, Ireland, his wife and two daughters and ran off with his children's strong-willed governess. Her first name was Sarah. There is some dispute about her last name, for Lawrence's mother, too, appears to have been illegitimate. Chapman's wife would not grant him a divorce. None-theless, after they ran off, Thomas and Sarah pretended to be married and adopted the last name Lawrence. Despite or maybe because of the fact that they were "living in sin," they were quite religious. Thomas was the second of the couple's five sons.

The family moved to Oxford in 1896, in part because of the educational opportunities it offered the boys. T. E. was generally conceded to be the leader of the five brothers, and he took full advantage of those educational opportunities. Lawrence won a partial scholarship to Jesus College at Oxford and graduated with first-class honors in modern history in 1910. His specialty was the architecture of the Crusades.

Lawrence had made his first trip to the Middle East before he graduated from Oxford, traveling through what are now Lebanon and Israel alone, mostly on foot, and sleeping wherever someone would offer a bed or a piece of ground. He was often hungry. He caught malaria. He was robbed and beaten. He seems to have had a marvelous time.

Lawrence was not religious; nevertheless, he had a strong ascetic streak—a penchant for self-denial, even martyrdom. It served him well on that first trip to the Middle East, as it would later serve him well with Arab fighters in the desert. Lawrence immersed himself in Arabic and developed a love for the Arabian people and their culture, which his misfortunes and adventures only seemed to strengthen. "I will have such difficulty becoming English again," Lawrence writes in a letter to his mother.

Indeed, he managed to spend most of the years from his graduation to the outbreak of the First World War helping supervise an archeological dig at Carchemish—near the Euphrates—then part of the Ottoman Empire, now near the border between Turkey and Syria. He began wearing Arab dress. It may have been the happiest period of Lawrence's life. "The foreigners come out here always to teach, whereas they had much better to learn," Lawrence writes his family.

Aside from one unexpected and easily dismissed proposal of marriage to a longtime friend while in college, there is no evidence that Lawrence had romantic relationships with women. While at Carchemish, he formed a particularly close bond with a handsome Arab water boy, whom Lawrence once took along on a visit to Oxford. However, given the prejudices and reticence of the time, it may be impossible finally to get a clear picture of Lawrence's romantic or sexual life. (Thomas much later insisted that he "never discerned in him the slightest *indicia* of the homosexual"—which may say more about Thomas and the times than about Lawrence.) There is evidence that Lawrence later demonstrated a taste for being beaten.

After the First World War began, Lawrence entered the British Army as a second lieutenant, working on maps of the Middle East. His knowledge of Arabic and of the area won him a position in military intelligence and a quick transfer to Cairo. Lawrence—a scruffy officer, never particularly respectful of military hierarchies or procedures—began encouraging his superiors to support Arab forces in their own nationalistic rebellion against the Ottoman Empire. And he began lobbying to get closer to that rebellion.

Thomas Edward Lawrence applied for transfer within the British military to the Arab Bureau. On October 16, 1916, he landed for the first time on the Arabian Peninsula. Within a week he had been introduced to Sherif Hussein's three eldest surviving sons and was particularly impressed with one of them, Sherif—the title translates as "prince" or "ruler"—Feisal. They began talking strategy.[1]

((•))

That initial mention of Major (he had been promoted) T. E. Lawrence in one of Thomas' notebooks was an account of the effort a month earlier by Lawrence and some Arab forces to hold on to the town of Tafilah, just south of the Dead Sea, which the Arabs had captured and the "Turks" were trying to retake. Here it is in its entirety:

Maj. T. E. Lawrence

At southern end of Dead Sea, he & six Bedouins ran into outposts of a whole Turk Division, only had one machine gun & he was manning that. Held Turks off until he could send for re-enforcements. Said: "I believe I ran, yes, I'm sure I ran. But I kept count of the number of paces I ran so we had the range."

When his re-enforcements arrived he left part of his men where they were & took most of his force around behind Turk Div. Killed divisional commander, took 500 prisoners & killed all the rest.[2]

In his shows and writings, Lowell Thomas would go on to, as Ben Hecht later put it, "half invent the British hero, Lawrence of Arabia." And this is Thomas' initial sketch of that supposedly fearless, shrewd, indomitable leader of Arabs and slaughterer of Turks. It is, therefore, a significant piece of evidence.

Lowell Thomas seems to be either taking notes in these initial paragraphs on "Maj. T. E. Lawrence" or writing from notes, and given the appearance of the first person in them, they appear to be notes from an interview with Lawrence himself. In that case the story of Lawrence's holding off a whole Turkish division at Tafilah by firing a machine gun came from Lawrence. And that story is almost surely untrue. It does not appear again—even in the most hagiographic biographies of Lawrence, even in the one Thomas himself would write.

A few pages later in this notebook, Thomas returns to the subject of "Maj. T. E. Lawrence."[3] Here Thomas records a full seven pages of notes. He jots down his first description of Lawrence: "5 feet 2 inches tall. Blonde, blue sparkling eyes, fair skin—too fair even to bronze after 7 years in the Arabian desert. Barefooted, costume of Meccan Sherif." We know that at this time Lawrence, in full Arab dress, posed for photographs by Harry Chase. And these extended notes by Thomas include discussions of Lawrence's adventures that must have been based on interviews in Jerusalem with Lawrence.

One of the highlights is a brief account, this time in the first-person plural, of the capture of the town of Wejh: "We got to Wedge [sic] 230 mis. [miles] north of Medina. Captured Turks garrison." Fred D. Crawford and Joseph A. Berton have studied Thomas' notes carefully. They point out that this account of the taking of Wejh, presumably Lawrence's account, "omitted one important detail—that he and the Arabs were a couple of days late and thus missed the battle entirely." A British ship with some other Arabs on board took the town while Sherif Feisal, with whom Lawrence had been riding, delayed.[4] Did Thomas just neglect to record that fact? It seems much more likely that Lawrence neglected to mention it.

The dozens of biographers of T. E. Lawrence disagree on the extent of Lawrence's own responsibility for inflating his accomplishments and thereby helping create the legend of "Lawrence of Arabia." But it is apparent even from Thomas' initial efforts to record Lawrence's story—which would also have been Lawrence's initial brush with attention outside the military—that Lawrence inflated some of his accomplishments and therefore contributed quite a bit to that legend. There is other such evidence. If "Lawrence of Arabia" was half invented, Lowell Thomas must share credit for the invention with Lawrence himself along with some of his votaries in the British military.

And then there's the question of the other half of "Lawrence of Arabia." To what extent did this valiant British hero, who not only rode camels and blew up trains but devised brilliant strategies and helped rally and lead ragtag armies of Arab fighters, really exist? To what extent were his exploits not invented? To what extent—to put it another way—was David Lean's Academy Award–winning movie, *Lawrence of Arabia*, which presented Lawrence as troubled but undeniably gallant and spectacularly accomplished, reliable? This is the second question upon which Lawrence's biographers disagree—heatedly.

Richard Aldington, who authored by far the most controversial of the Lawrence biographies, and Arab commentators such as Suleiman Mousa focus on the distortions, exaggerations and contradictions in Lawrence's story, subtracting enough from the legend to reduce Lawrence to a mere supporting actor, a minor player in the Arab Revolt—one with a flair for self-promotion and no scruples about lying. For example, Aldington notes that the distance Lawrence later claims to have paced off while running at Tafilah—3,100 yards—would have been beyond the range of the guns his forces had deployed. And Mousa writes, based on his interviews with surviving Arab participants in the battle at Tafilah, "None of the people I spoke to recalled seeing Lawrence give an order or direct anybody to do anything." The real credit for the Arab Revolt should go, in Aldington's view, to some combination of other British officers and the Arab leaders; in Mousa's view, it should go to those Arab leaders.[5]

But is a sprinkling of inaccuracies or the comments, well after the fact, of Arabs anxious to give credit to Arabs sufficient to disprove the widely held view at the time that Lawrence played a crucial role? This is not the place to settle all the Lawrence controversies, but in their attempt to correct a tendency to exaggerate the role of this British hero, Aldington and Mousa can be accused of underplaying it.

Few would disagree that for a foreigner at that time, T. E. Lawrence was unusually sensitive to and respectful of the peoples among whom he was moving. (One hopes Thomas took a lesson here.) Lawrence was extraordinarily intelligent. His Arabic was strong. He could handle himself in the desert and on a camel. He was a mostly self-taught military strategist with a precocious appreciation for what would become known as guerrilla warfare. He was brave to the point of being foolhardy. And he did master, though not devise, a technique for attaching dynamite to the track of the Ottoman railway that ran to Medina and setting it off just when a train arrived—a very bloody and effective trick, in a very, very bloody war.

The superhero "Lawrence of Arabia," who almost single-handedly planned and led the Arab Revolt, may have been half invented by some combination of Lowell Thomas, T. E. Lawrence and Lawrence's colleagues. But Lawrence was the Englishman who did the most for the Arab Revolt, and his role in it appears to have been very important, maybe crucial. He was a hero—maybe the most important hero—of the Arab Revolt. Here, in my judgment, Ben Hecht got the math more or less right: "Lawrence of Arabia" was half real.

And this Englishman riding camels and blowing up trains with the Arabs certainly was newsworthy. Thomas continued to focus on General Allenby and Jerusalem—a decision, given interest back home in "the Holy Land," with which it would have been hard to argue at the time. Nonetheless, Lowell was becoming as skilled as anyone at sniffing out adventure, heroism and a grand tale. So when he finally arranged to meet General Allenby—over lunch in Egypt—this was the request Lowell presented to him: permission to travel "into the Arabian Desert to see something of the Bedouin army which has been fighting the Turks and at the same time attempting to create a new Arab nation." Traveling somewhere new and strange was always motivation enough for Lowell, but he knew who would be with that "Bedouin army." Indeed, Lawrence, according to Thomas' notebook, had invited him: "Wish you could come out and get a film of us blowing up trains. It's quite a sight to see one going up in the air."[6]

Yes, the photographs and film—even without a chance to observe the blowing up of trains—would be great. But Lawrence's story, as Thomas must by then have sensed, offered much more than that.

Perhaps the most successful of the early directors of fiction films, D. W. Griffith, remarked that the First World War was "too colossal to be dramatic. No one can describe it. You might as well try to describe the ocean or the Milky Way." With a tight focus on T. E. Lawrence, Lowell Thomas, who was adept at this sort of thing, had come upon a way to condense "the Great War" into something highly dramatic.[7]

((•))

There was one person upon whom many of Lawrence's biographers were in agreement: the first of his biographers.[8] In 1927 the poet and novelist Robert Graves, Lawrence's second biographer, reviled Lowell Thomas as "inaccurate and sentimental." John E. Mack's Pulitzer Prize–winning biography, published in 1976, disparaged "the ballyhooing of Lowell Thomas." In 1989 Jeremy Wilson's biography, authorized by Lawrence's family, labeled Thomas' work "distasteful." Richard Aldington needed to remove much of the blame for the Lawrence legend from Thomas in order to rest it on Lawrence, but still, in his 1955 biography, he dismissed Thomas as a "war propagandist" and credited him with a "knack" for "brisking up Lawrence's anecdotes." And Basil Liddell Hart published a lengthy biography of Lawrence in 1934 that entirely ignored Lowell Thomas, the man who had brought Hart's subject most of his renown.[9]

They were being harsh. Lowell Thomas did ballyhoo, sentimentalize and fudge some; he may have had difficulty lifting himself above the preconceptions and prejudices of his time; but he was remarkable for his ability to shine a light into a fascinating and historically important corner of the war that was being overlooked by Americans and Europeans at the time.

Thomas deserves credit, first of all, for being among the few Western journalists who found their way to the Middle East during the First World War. All the coverage of Allenby's capture of Jerusalem I have been able to find in the United States comes out of London. No other American war reporters were covering the British campaign in the Middle East prior to Thomas' arrival or while he was there. In this case Thomas was not only early but earliest. And I have seen no evidence that any other Western journalist in the Middle East during these months was reporting on the Arab Revolt, let alone following it into Arabia. "To the best of my knowledge, Lawrence didn't meet or talk to any other journalists in the Middle East during the First World War," Jeremy Wilson, Lawrence's authorized biographer, has confirmed in an interview.[10] Here Thomas was not merely first but alone.

A British officer in Arab robes riding a camel with Arab warriors may, in retrospect, seem an obvious story, but of all the thousands of reporters who covered the First World War, only one found it. Indeed, the case can be made that no other journalist in those years found a story—if the number of books based on it can be used as a standard—that good.

((•))

On March 21, 1918, Lowell Thomas and Harry Chase left Cairo for Aqaba, on the northeast fingernail of the Red Sea. They traveled on a ship, the *Ozarda*, out of Suez. Along with their usual collection of cameras, trunks and suitcases, Thomas and Chase were lugging sleeping bags, blankets and a tent, plus "tobacco for the Arabs" and "cigars for the British." Thomas was about to do something none of the other writers who undertook biographies of T. E. Lawrence would have an opportunity to do: meet him in Arabia.

The *Ozarda* steamed down the Gulf of Suez and then up the other finger of the Red Sea, the Gulf of Aqaba, on the other side of the Sinai Peninsula. (Lowell remarks that they had the unusual experience of seeing the sun rise and set over Mount Sinai exactly 12 hours apart on the same day.) On board with Thomas and Chase were, according to Lowell's notes, crowds of Egyptians, Sudanese, Somalis, Indians, Scottish troops and a few score Turkish prisoners who had been released with the understanding that, since they were Arabs, they would join the Arab Revolt. Sudanese sheep wandered the deck, while mules, originally from Peru, and donkeys from Sudan were corralled below the main deck. "No pirate ship in the . . . days of the Spanish Main," Lowell writes, "could have had as motley and picturesque a crowd aboard as we have."

The *Ozarda* anchored offshore at Aqaba on March 27, the order of disembarkation being: humans, sheep, mules, donkeys (the latter two requiring use of a sling) and then the collection of trunks, bags and cases brought by Thomas and Chase. Barges or dhows carried humans, animals and equipment to the beach. On the shore, Bedouins fired their guns with abandon. In Jerusalem Lawrence had told Lowell of the importance of Aqaba. Now Thomas, Chase and their three cameras were there.

The capture of Aqaba, on July 6, 1917, had brought the Arabs closer to the British forces in Palestine and Egypt. It made the Arabs easier to supply by sea—with, for example, sheep, mules, donkeys and reinforcements. And it positioned them to play a role in the coming drive north to Damascus. Aqaba had been well fortified against attack from the sea. After a long ride through the Arabian Desert, picking up fighters from different tribes along the way, the Arabs attacked from inland. A battle more than 50 miles northeast of Aqaba, at Abu al Lasan—where a few hundred Ottoman soldiers were killed—opened the way to the sea. The remaining Ottoman fortifications surrendered quickly after that. The Arabs, many hundreds of Turkish prisoners and Lawrence had ridden down Wadi Itm as it squeezed between potato-colored, cauliflower-textured cliffs into Aqaba.

When Thomas and Chase arrived in Aqaba, they were ushered to the British camp where they were greeted by Lieutenant Colonel (another promotion) T. E. Lawrence and seven other British officers. By all appearances Lawrence was a good host. True, he did not take Thomas and Chase and their cameras out to film him and the Arabs "blowing up trains." But Lawrence prepared a detailed, extensive and appealing itinerary for their visit. It included a meeting with Sherif Feisal and a 35-mile camel trip with Lawrence back along Wadi Itm; for that trip Lawrence specified that Lowell and Harry were expected to be "dressed as Bedouins." They were to visit the scene of the great battle, Abu al Lasan, plus some large encampments of Arab fighters. A tour of Petra, the spectacular ancient city with structures carved into often rainbow-colored cliffs, was also on the agenda.

Thomas and Chase saw their sights and shot their film. "Chase told me before we left America that it was the ambition of his life to see Petra," Lowell writes to Fran.[11] They spent some days there—dazzled, as most subsequent visitors have been. Lawrence usually was not with them; he was, after all, still fighting a war. But he and Feisal posed for a number of new photos, including one or two spurious action shots. Lawrence allowed Lowell some extended interviews—on subjects ranging from Bedouin marksmanship to whether Australia would remain under British rule to an evaluation of Britain's Mideast policy and its failings. Lawrence passed on colorful anecdotes, such as the report that when a "Turk plane came down north of here," Bedouins, after capturing the pilot, "clipped" off its wings "to keep it from flying" away like a bird.

Indeed, Lawrence and Thomas were hitting it off sufficiently well that they could contemplate collaborating on a scheme after the war. The plan was to organize an expedition for, in Lowell's typically hyperbolic phrasing, the "exploration of the largest section of the world thus far unvisited by civilized man": southwest Arabia. Lawrence, Thomas explains in his notebook, said he would gladly participate and added, "If you put up half the money, I'll furnish the other half."

What Lawrence did not do while Lowell was with him in or around Aqaba was tell a lot of heroic tales about his own actions, as he apparently had in Jerusalem. Indeed, he insisted that Auda Abu Tayi—a bold, proud, charismatic tribal leader—was the one who "captured Aqaba" and that he himself had just been "in the middle of the line of camels."

Many other British officers in Aqaba were, on the other hand, eager to talk Lawrence up. They marveled, according to Lowell's notes, at Lawrence's humility: how he refused to be saluted or made himself scarce when anyone wanted to pin a medal on him. They raved about his competence: "Colonel Lawrence is a marvel at riding a camel" and, "He always does the mine laying himself." They also emphasized, according to Lowell's notes, Lawrence's importance in the Arab Revolt: "Although Colonel Lawrence says Abu Tayi deserves all the credit for the capture of Aqaba, others who know the facts and haven't any reason to keep them back say Lawrence planned and put through the whole thing." Perhaps it was predictable that British officers would be unable to conceive of an Arab Revolt without the guiding hand of a British officer. Their testimony should have been read with suspicion, but since this was expert testimony from those in a good position to know, it couldn't have been ignored. Thomas certainly credited it.[12] The legend of Lawrence of Arabia was coming together.

((•))

A wireless found Lowell while he was in Aqaba. It read: "Please wire funds Hotel Eden Palace Genoa. Well lonesome love hurry back. Frances."[13] It was late March, Lowell had left Fran in Italy in January. She had been working for the American Red Cross in Genoa—helping resettle "trainloads" of refugees, "most of whom were old women with tiny grandchildren."[14] This wireless was as close to a "where the heck are you?" as Fran—lonely and homesick but not the cranky sort—could manage at this early stage of their marriage.

"I know you are disgusted with me for staying away so long," Lowell had written her a month earlier. But after her wireless it would take him an additional couple of months to leave the Middle East. As was becoming his habit, Lowell seemed more interested in seeing and experiencing than in racing home actually to produce the travelogues that were intended to pay back his investors and boost the war effort. He wasn't even in a great hurry to race back to Italy to see his bride.

Thomas and Chase returned to Egypt bearing information, anecdotes and some of the only photographs—and, amazingly, film—taken of Lawrence and the Arabian forces in the desert. Lowell then managed to further entertain himself with a journey up the Nile to Khartoum, across the Nubian Desert to Port Sudan and then back to Egypt via the Red Sea, with a stop in Jeddah.[15]

A British destroyer finally carried Thomas and Chase across the Mediterranean to Europe. They stopped in Macedonia and did some reporting on the war in the Balkans before landing in Italy on June 10, 1918. Italy offered Lowell a bonus: not only a reunion with his wife but with his reinvigorated father. Dr. Harry Thomas was now a major in the U.S. Army, stationed in Italy. The doctor wrangled a two-week leave, so the three of them could do some traveling and a lot of catching up.[16]

Then Lowell and Fran were off again, making their first visit to England and their second to France. On September 23 Fran sailed for home, which, since she and Lowell had established no home, still meant Denver. Back in the Middle East on October 1, 1918, British and Arab forces captured Damascus, and T. E. Lawrence entered the city either early or late—depending on which biographer you believe—and either was or was not momentarily in charge. Then Lawrence bolted—mission accomplished—for England. The Ottoman Empire surrendered on October 30, and Germany collapsed. Lowell was in France when any possibility of his morale-boosting travelogues on the war appearing during the war disappeared with the signing of the armistice, on November 11, 1918.

Lowell sent Harry Chase back home to process their reels and reels of film—a rare separation for them during these years. Lowell himself was still not finished. Indeed, one of his more daring adventures was about to begin. First he went to Strasbourg in Alsace, which with Germany's defeat was to be returned to France. Then Lowell decided to sneak into Germany itself. Germany was a vanquished, decimated and starving country at the time, a country whose leader, Kaiser Wilhelm II, had abdicated and fled, a country in the throes of a battle for power among forces that ranged from conservatives furious over the defeat to Marxists—the Spartacus League—furious over the war and the injustices of capitalism. In other words, Germany, on the verge of a second Russian Revolution, had just grown much more exotic and become the place to be for a journalist and an adventure addict.

Borders in Europe, except between the Allies, remained for the most part closed in the direct aftermath of the war. Lowell had brought a veteran journalist, Webb Waldron of *Collier's Weekly*, in on his scheme, and together they slipped from France into Switzerland—hiding in the back of an ambulance, Thomas reports.[17] Then, on December 17, 1918, Thomas and Waldron succeeded in persuading Swiss and American officials to let them cross into Germany.

Lowell's journalistic skills, honed by his intensive yearlong immersion in war reporting, served him well. Together with Waldron he traveled around the country, securing interviews on the war and its aftermath with English-speaking professors, journalists, financiers and businessmen, along with the man who played Jesus in the renowned (and reputedly anti-Semitic) Oberammergau Passion Play. Commendably, some examples of the less well-off, who at the time were doing badly indeed, were also sought out and interviewed: "We found her and her 3 small children living in 2 tiny rooms," Lowell writes in his notebook after one such interview. "She broke down & cried when we asked about her husband. . . . & she can't afford to buy meat."

Thomas reported that they had also interviewed a number of the country's top politicians, including Prince Max von Baden, the kaiser's last chancellor; a Jewish Socialist journalist, Kurt Eisner, who, remarkably, had just become the new revolutionary premier of conservative Bavaria; and Friedrich Ebert, a Social Democrat and the new German Republic's first chancellor.

Lowell was supposed to be representing *Leslie's Weekly* once again. And this time the archive for that publication does contain some reportage by Thomas—two photo spreads and one piece of writing on the situation in Strasbourg. Two extended articles Thomas wrote on Germany, including a profile of Friedrich Ebert, did appear in New York's *Evening World*. Waldron wrote a series of articles for *Collier's* based on their journey, including one about Kurt Eisner. I have found no evidence that they also managed to get an interview, as Thomas would later assert, with the storied leader of the Spartacus League, Rosa Luxemburg, shortly before she was killed by a mob. They do appear to have heard her speak. A series of articles by Thomas on this period in Germany eventually was printed by the *Globe* in New York.[18]

(((•)))

Lowell made some news of his own just before he left Germany. The following wire-service dispatch, briefly held up by military censors, appeared in newspapers around the United States:

> BERLIN. Jan. 25—[Delayed]—Lowell Thomas, formerly a professor at Princeton University, was shot below the heart and dangerously wounded at Bremen last Sunday. It was learned here today.
>
> He was saved from the wrath of a Spartacan mob which had attacked him by Webb Waldon [sic] an editorial writer for Collier's Weekly. Both had been accused of attempting to cause a split in the Spartacan organization. . . .
>
> The trouble during which Thomas was shot occurred during the national elections and developed into a battle.

"Last Sunday" would have been January 19, 1919. We have a rather complete notebook entry by Lowell Thomas for that date. It notes that it was "the first real election day in [the] history of Germany." It explains that he and Waldron boarded a French destroyer that day in Hamburg, which would take them back to France. It describes in some detail the destroyer's progress. That journal entry includes no evidence that Lowell had been in Bremen, that he had been attacked by a "Spartacan mob," that he had been shot or that he had required any medical attention.[19]

Could he have been shot earlier? If so, it is not mentioned anywhere in the surviving notebooks, nor is a hospital visit or a wound.

We know from a telegram she sent to Fran that Harriet Thomas, Lowell's mother, had been upset by these newspaper reports. Was Fran upset? In his often-fanciful late-life memoir Thomas maintains that Fran believed he had been seriously wounded, "wept" and "for the next two weeks . . . considered herself a widow."

A telegram survives that Lowell sent to Fran in Denver from New York on February 11, reporting that his ship from France back to the United States had arrived and that he was "feeling like a million dollars. . . . Stories reproduced concerning my Bremen shooting scrape," that telegram states, "exaggerated. Am nearly well." The telegram instructs Fran to "give my regards to managing editor Rocky Mountain News Times"—a combination of the names of the two Denver papers for which Lowell had worked. A story dutifully appeared in the Denver Times reporting that "Prof. Lowell J. Thomas . . . arrived in New York . . . and has completely recovered from a wound received during a riot at Bremen, Germany, according to a telegram received by his wife." Why had Lowell so cryptically instructed Fran to contact the local newspapers? And doesn't the lighthearted, conspiratorial tone of Lowell's telegram make it sound as if Fran had not been upset?

Husband and wife had their reunion in Chicago five days after he wrote that telegram. In a letter to her mother, Fran includes a hard-to-follow report on Lowell's condition, explaining that "there is hardly a scar" where the bullet presumably entered "below the rib," but that it "came out again and grazed across his back" and "left a red scar on his back"—with the words "rather bad" then interjected between "left a" and "red scar."

This is a puzzling incident. In his memoir Thomas suggests that the story that he was shot near the heart may have been the result of a wire-service reporter's either trying to "embellish" the story or confusing Lowell's "hat"—through which, he claims, a bullet did pass while he was on the street in Berlin—with his "heart." But the story placed the shooting in Bremen. And if the report of the shooting was the result of an error, why did Lowell not explain that to his wife? Why, then, did she write her mother as if there were a scar? And why did Lowell repeat the story about the Bremen shooting in later promotional material?[20]

Here's another clue: Although Lowell doesn't mention this in his surviving journals, a second young reporter who had worked in Chicago happened to show up in Berlin at the end of 1918: that master of the journalistic hoax, Ben Hecht, on assignment for the *Chicago Daily News*. The odds are that the two old friends would have crossed paths sometime before Thomas left Berlin for the last time in the middle of January 1919.[21]

And one final piece might be added to the puzzle: the fact that Floyd Gibbons, whose career path Lowell often seemed to be following, had achieved considerable attention and distinction after having been wounded covering the war. Could the story that Lowell had been shot have been a "stunt"—which he hatched himself, as a way of keeping up with Gibbons, under the influence of Hecht, presumably in cahoots with Webb Waldron and, via telegrams that were later destroyed, with Fran? Might it have been designed for publicity or for a laugh?

Although he had so successfully played the role of a veteran war correspondent for 14 months in Europe and the Middle East, it seems likely that Lowell Thomas, at the age of 26, was still making stuff up.

7.

Come with Me to the Land of History, Mystery and Romance

The Royal Opera House at Covent Garden, in London, is fronted by a stately classical portico. Inside all is a deep, plush red except for the 24-carat gold leaf decorations on the tiers of boxes and balconies. The current theater opened in 1858, during Queen Victoria's reign, and the queen was often in the audience during the opera season. Late summer remained decidedly off-season. Nonetheless, a new show opened at the Royal Opera House on August 14, 1919.

This show borrowed a set, enhanced by palms protruding from the orchestra pit, from the moonlight-on-the-Nile scene in Handel's oratorio *Joseph and His Brethren*. The performance featured Arab-inflected music initially played on an organ but soon to be performed by the band of His Majesty's Welsh Guards, themselves dressed in scarlet. Only one voice was heard during the performance: that of a 27-year-old American who did not sing but who did display a way with words and—helpfully, given his accent—a special talent for enunciation.

Every evening and in matinees on most days, Lowell Thomas walked onstage without introduction. "I would like to have you close your eyes for a moment," he would intone after a short preamble, "and try and forget that you are here in this theater, and come with me on a magic carpet out to the land of history, mystery and romance." Somewhere in front of him out in the darkened hall, Harry Chase—wearing an asbestos suit and holed up in a "big walk-in steel booth," in case the film caught fire—was madly feeding and alternating projectors. According to one surviving script, Chase managed to play 30 film segments and to cut or deftly dissolve—a specialty of his—among 285 slides, each colorized by the artist Augusta Heyder.[1] (Fran had not succeeded in taking over the colorization.)

The reviews for this pathbreaking alliance of voice, music, slides and film were ecstatic: "Unique . . . extraordinary," gushed the *Times* of London. "Perfect," concluded the *Daily Mail*. "Entrancing entertainment . . . no audience could be more enthralled," wrote the *Evening Standard*. The show played to sold-out houses. The British prime minister, David Lloyd George, and the French prime minister, George Clemenceau, came to see it. Winston Churchill appeared in the audience, as did Rudyard Kipling and George Bernard Shaw. With great fanfare, now Field Marshal Allenby— also now Lord Allenby—himself attended one performance.

The show that debuted at the Royal Opera House was initially entitled *With Allenby in Palestine, Including the Capture of Jerusalem and Liberation of Holy Arabia*. On October 27, 1919, after more than 100 performances, and as the opera was ready to return to town, the show moved to the larger Royal Albert Hall, where the color scheme was similar but the gold painted on. On one occasion Queen Mary, the wife of King George V, occupied the Royal Box there. By then the title of Thomas' show had changed to reflect the prominence it had brought one of its previously obscure subjects. It was now advertised as: *With Allenby in Palestine and Lawrence in Arabia*.[2]

((•))

Lowell Thomas required plenty of good fortune to make it from Aqaba— via Chicago and New York—to the Royal Opera House and the Royal Albert Hall. But since he presented fortune with so many opportunities, there were bound to be occasions when it came through.

Before Thomas had been able to produce any shows based on the information, photographs and film he had gathered on the First World War, he had to meet with his investors. They gathered on February 18, 1919, in Chicago. The stockholders in Thomas Travelogues Inc. had been concerned about the wound its principal asset had reportedly incurred in Germany.

They even tried, unsuccessfully, to collect on the insurance policy they had taken out on Thomas. Since the alleged shooting had occurred in what still qualified as an enemy country, it was not covered. That probably was fortuitous, since it spared Lowell the embarrassment of an insurance company's doctor poking around his supposed bullet wound. Lowell's larger concern at the time was that his financial backers would be upset that the war Lowell was ostensibly publicizing and reporting on had ended three months earlier—and he had so far produced little in the way of publicity, journalism or revenue.

Frances Thomas was herself seeing her husband there in Chicago for the first time in almost five months. She described his meeting with the investors in the same letter to her mother in which she had described his alleged wound. "Tommy appeared before the stockholders of the Thomas Travelogue company at noon," she writes. "He went fully prepared for a strafing. . . . But he said he had no trouble at all, and the men were nice as pie."[3]

Lowell could now return to New York to put together some shows on the war—if anyone still cared about the war. He made a deal to promote his lectures with the editor of a modest daily, the *Globe* in New York. (One assumes Lowell had already tried his luck with some of the city's less modest newspapers.) Ever willing to bet on himself, he hired a publicist/ manager plus someone to help him churn out articles for the *Globe* and other publications. He jumped, in other words, into this new effort with his old energy and bravado. He also acquired a questionable new claim to fame: Lowell was now being promoted—or, more likely, promoting himself—as "the man . . . who saw more of the world war than any other person."

In his memoir and various biographical sketches, Thomas talks of having produced six different shows in New York City on the First World War—including accounts of the U.S. Army's actions in France, the Italian campaign, the war in the Balkans, Allenby in Palestine, the Arab Revolt and the German Revolution. His shows were initially presented for a couple of weeks in March 1919, at the Century Theater on 62nd Street and Central Park West. Then they moved for an additional month to a long-unused theater inside what was then called the Garden, on 26th Street and Madison Avenue (also known as Madison Square).

Thomas notes that there wasn't much interest at this point in anything but the Middle East shows and the Germany story—which tended to attract partisan pro- and anti-Bolshevik crowds, and which Lowell had promoted by displaying, in a window at Lord & Taylor, a few German helmets he had brought back, one of which he was billing as "the Kaiser's helmet." Actually, there is no evidence—in the form of advertisements, reviews or notes in the journal Fran was keeping—that Thomas ever presented anything but the Middle East shows, his show on the German Revolution and one aborted effort to do something on the Western Front. Lowell certainly wasn't the sort to get too upset about this sort of thing, but all the rest of the film Chase had shot and the notes Lowell had taken over the months on the war—in France and Belgium, in Italy, in the Balkans—went mostly unused.[4]

Still, consider what Thomas had attempted and, for the most part, accomplished: He had planned, written and premiered within three weeks in New York City four different shows on the First World War and its aftermath. Each of those shows included films and dozens of slides and required Lowell to lecture for a couple of hours. The theater at the Garden turned out to be thoroughly infused with odors from the Barnum & Bailey Circus, performing in the Garden's main hall. Nonetheless, the three shows Lowell did regularly present appear to have been moderate successes.

Thomas then made a few, not entirely successful appearances at theaters outside New York City with one or another of these shows and booked more of them around the country for the fall, hoping to add revenues from a national tour to the so-far meager earnings of Thomas Travelogues.

That fall tour never happened. Instead, Percy Burton, an English impresario in New York scouting for entertainments, happened to walk into one performance of Thomas' Palestine show and saw its potential for a London audience. Good fortune? Sure. But Lowell had been experimenting with those four shows and perfecting three of them onstage night after night. He didn't plan it this way, but there had been numerous opportunities for the right person to just walk in.

Thomas and Burton hammered out a complex deal to produce a show in London combining the Palestine and Arab Revolt shows. On July 31, 1919, Lowell sailed for Europe with Fran and Harry Chase. Dale Carnagey, who was morphing from Lowell's teacher to a member of his team, also came along to help polish the script.[5]

((•))

As an American presuming to lecture the British about incidents of British heroism they themselves had overlooked, Thomas was in a ticklish position that first warm August night at the Royal Opera House at Covent Garden. But Lowell possessed an acute sensitivity to his own position, and all the verbal dexterity needed to adjust it when necessary. Before inviting his audience to "come with" him, Thomas acknowledged, according to Fran's journal, that its members might "not care to listen to this story through the nose of a yank. But," he assured them, prepared even to besmirch his compatriots in order to ingratiate, "occasionally an American can talk of something else besides himself." Thomas' next statement—a masterful play both to British vanity and to the British conviction that they were not vain—succeeded in setting the tone for his entire stay in Britain. He made "the remark," Fran writes, "that the British were so modest that they wouldn't talk about themselves, which made it necessary for someone to do it for them."[6]

Lowell had set out to fill the hero vacuum left by the First World War's sluggish and brutal trench warfare with an appreciation of "the man who freed the Holy Land, the great Field Marshal Allenby" and especially— riding camels being more dramatic than being driven around in a Rolls-Royce—with tales of "the mysterious young Englishman who freed Holy Arabia from the Turks." As the *Daily Telegraph*, in the most over-the-top of the reviews, puts it, "what is modestly and prosaically described as 'an illustrated travelogue' of the British campaigns in Palestine and Arabia is in reality an heroic epic capable of inspiring a dozen modern emulators of Homer or Plutarch."

Homer—or whoever composed the Greek epics—was, of course, an early exemplar of the don't-let-the-facts-get-in-the-way tradition, of which Thomas sometimes proved a late exemplar. And Thomas' show—as some of T. E. Lawrence's biographers would disdainfully conclude—did have weaknesses as journalism, let alone as history.

Those London audiences were, after all, being won over in part through Thomas' celebration of, as that *Daily Telegraph* review puts it, "British grit," "British resourcefulness" and British "self-abnegation." (Australian and Indian troops also come in for praise in Thomas' account.) And the elevation of one (or more) nationality or race often encourages the demotion of other nationalities or races. Thomas does on one occasion speak of the "primitive minds" of certain local peoples in the Middle East or, at his worst, disparages others as being "very much like children." He passes on

Lawrence's story about Bedouins clipping off the wings of a plane so it wouldn't fly off like a bird.

And Thomas occasionally fudges when and where. He claims to have photographed "the first Christian soldier standing on top of the Mount of Olives" or to be showing troops marching to Jerusalem, despite the fact that Thomas and Chase did not arrive in the Middle East for a month and a half after Allenby's troops had captured Jerusalem. He reroutes the journey he took to Aqaba so he can also report on his later visit to Sudan and Jeddah.

For the *Daily Telegraph* reviewer, Thomas' show was much more than just an entertainment, it was a lesson "that, superficial appearances notwithstanding, the race is no more degenerate to-day than it was when giants walked abroad in the land."[7] But the lesson was, as the *Daily Telegraph* and other London papers failed to note, sometimes misleading, especially when it came to its discussion of the short British man who in Thomas' show seemed the most giant of them all: T. E. Lawrence.

"This blue-eyed poet . . . succeeded in accomplishing what no caliph and no sultan had been able to do in over a thousand years," Lowell proclaimed. "He wiped out the centuries-old blood feuds and built up an army and drove the Turks from Holy Arabia."[8] There it was—unmodulated and unadulterated: the it-takes-a-British-man theory of history.

((•))

Overly enthusiastic, jingoistic and occasionally misleading as it may have been—and leaving Homer and Plutarch aside—Thomas did at least deserve credit for producing something much more ambitious than just "an illustrated travelogue." The *Daily Telegraph*'s review appeared in a column headed "IN FILMLAND," and the fact was that there, in Covent Garden, images and narration were working together—Lowell scripted in his cues and pauses—in a way still very rare "IN FILMLAND." (The first short sound films would not appear in theaters for another four years.)

And Harry Chase and Thomas had captured high-quality and highly original images. Where else in London was it possible, for example, to see what it looked like to fly over the pyramids? Thomas had coupled two of the new century's best new technologies—motion pictures and the airplane. "We are looking down on one of the oldest creations of man," is how he put it in his narration, "and flying a thousand feet above in the most modern."[9]

At the end of the twentieth century and the beginning of the twenty-first, it was enough to coordinate some audio with moving images or a slideshow on a CD or online to earn the designation "multimedia." But eight decades earlier Thomas had been mixing narration, music, slides and film—some of which was shot from airplanes.

And these were images and narration put to the service not just of tourist shots but of reporting on underreported or ignored battles fought in the previous year. Thomas was bringing news. He was writing an early, if not entirely reliable, draft of history. He was doing pathbreaking journalism—tech-savvy, multimedia journalism. In this sense Thomas' show actually qualifies as "something that is more colossal than anything of its kind ever tried." And Thomas' high-tech, newsy production—for which there wasn't much competition in London or anywhere else at the time—achieved what most of those multimedia efforts in the 1990s and 2000s failed to achieve: great popularity.

Ten days into their run, Fran writes in her journal that "the theatre was sold out and people were turned away. Something over two thousand dollars was taken in yesterday." After three weeks she notes that block-long ticket queues were forming a couple of hours before the show. "The queues are lengthening every night," she soon reports. More matinees were added. Then they moved to the Royal Albert Hall, "which," Fran writes, "when filled to capacity holds 13,000." And, she adds, "Tommy has filled this hall over and over again and people have been turned away." Lowell was presenting two shows a day at the Albert Hall—at 12:30 p.m. and 10:00 p.m. (leaving time for others to play the hall in the evening). Burton began planning the publicity for the one millionth customer.

After the cut of a second promoter was subtracted, Thomas and Burton had been sharing 75 percent of the net profits at the Royal Opera House at Covent Garden. Burton agreed to give Lowell 45 percent of the profits at this new venue. This was becoming a substantial sum. In his run at the Albert Hall alone, from October 27 to December 6, 1919, Lowell netted £3,644 or more than $16,000. For the first time in his life, Lowell was bringing in a lot of money. From July 1917 to March 1919, his company had spent a total of almost $39,000 on traveling expenses, film and salaries (including about $3,800 to Harry Chase, most of which was paid directly to his wife). Now Lowell was finally paying back his investors.

And Thomas was also packaging his reporting in the Middle East into magazine articles—articles focused on Lawrence, not Allenby. In September

Thomas' first piece for *Asia* magazine, back in the States, was published. Now, in suddenly Lawrence-obsessed Britain, Thomas sold a series of such articles to the *Strand Magazine*, where they would appear alongside work by H. G. Wells, P. G. Wodehouse and Arthur Conan Doyle. Thomas was paid the then-impressive sum of $2,000 for each article—"more . . . than they have paid since Conan Doyle wrote his Sherlock Holmes stories," Fran gloats.[10]

Thomas and Lawrence were the toast of the town. At least one of them was enjoying it.

((•))

Colonel T. E. Lawrence—private and reclusive by nature—had not been entirely unknown to the British public before Thomas began regaling his countrymen and women with tales of his valiant deeds. The previous year the *Times* of London had picked up a small Reuters report, itself based on a story in a French newspaper, crediting a "Colonel Lawrence as having played a part of the greatest importance in the Palestine victory . . . at the head of the cavalry force which he had formed with Bedouins and Druses."[11]

And back in London, well before Thomas opened at Covent Garden, Lawrence was being listened to on the future of the Middle East. He was asked to address a committee of the British War Cabinet. He argued vehemently for Arab independence and for giving postwar power to Sherif Hussein's sons, particularly Feisal. He wrote an article on the subject for the *Times* of London. He received an audience with King George V, at which, embarrassed by his country's lack of loyalty to the Arabs, Lawrence turned down a knighthood. And Colonel Lawrence played a significant role—as a representative of the British but also as Feisal's advisor and translator at the Paris Peace Conference, which followed the end of the First World War.

Nonetheless, before Thomas' show opened in London in August 1919 and Thomas' writings on Lawrence began appearing in America and then Britain, Lawrence had not been famous. He had not been acknowledged by the British public as a war hero. He was not being stopped on the street. He was not receiving marriage proposals from women he had never met. Now he was. He had not felt it necessary to hide. Now, thanks to Lowell Thomas, Lawrence did.

We know Lawrence was not above puffing up his own legend—even back in Jerusalem. And a sprinkling of renown, he must now have understood, would help gain his arguments attention. Nonetheless, even bargained-for fame, when it reaches this magnitude, can be overwhelming. Yet Lawrence had begun fraternizing with the young man who was remaking his life by imposing upon him this outsized fame.

A week after Lowell had first taken the stage at Covent Garden, Fran explains in her journal, "a note came from Col. Lawrence[,] the hero man[,] in which he said he had attended the 'show' a few nights previous and thanked God the house was dark during the second half. Aside from his personal history, he said he thought it an exceedingly good show." Fran by then had a sense of who could intimidate her usually poised husband. She added, "I am so glad that he was there without Tommy's knowing it."

The next day Lowell and Fran took a note to the return address on Lawrence's envelope—one block over from where they were staying on Albemarle Street and a block and a half closer to Piccadilly. The landlady "replied that about a month ago she had rented an apartment to Mr. Lawrence but to her knowledge he had not occupied it." By this point Fran, too, had fallen under the spell. "What a man of mystery he is," she gushes, "and how I'd love to meet him." They received a note back: "Apologies for the landlady—but she has had practice since you burst on an astonished London!"

Then, on August 22, the "the hero man" showed up at their apartment for lunch. "He is little and fair like a girl and extremely modest," Fran explains in a letter to her parents. "We got him talking and he stayed all afternoon. He perhaps is the greatest person I ever met." And he kept coming back. "Lawrence seems to like us," Fran writes in her journal a month later. "For the past three mornings he has come over at nine o'clock. He has a cup of coffee and sits and talks about Arabia and his Arabs until noon."

Lowell showed Lawrence the first installment of his series for *Asia*. This article was hardly evenhanded or measured in dispensing credit for the Arab victories: "Thomas Lawrence placed himself at the head of the Bedouin army of the King of the Hejaz," Thomas declared, "drove the Turks from Arabia and restored the caliphate to the descendants of the Prophet." Nonetheless, Lawrence "seemed delighted with the article in *Asia* about himself," Fran remarks. Indeed, Lawrence appeared to be supplying Thomas with material he could use in his second article for that publication.[12]

Lawrence snuck into the theater to see Thomas' show a few more times. His mother sat through the show—twice—and, Lawrence writes to Lowell, "approves of it; as she's critical, please accept this as a compliment." One of his brothers also attended. Lawrence posed in full desert regalia for some new slides Thomas wanted in order to beef up the increasingly popular Lawrence portion of his show. It was necessary to crop evidence of an English interior and garden out of those pictures, which Thomas would long deny were taken anywhere but Arabia.[13]

Lawrence ended up breakfasting with Lowell and Fran with some frequency in part because he simply enjoyed their company. Most people who encountered them felt similarly. Fran was smart, competent and gracious. Lowell was unusually quick, clever and bright, if not excessively deep. And Lowell certainly was an entertaining companion—a witty and skilled storyteller offstage as well as on. Yet he also had a genuine interest in the stories of the people he encountered—the accomplished and famous, yes, but not only celebrities: just about anyone he found himself next to in a room. That is one of the reasons Thomas proved such an effective reporter.

He certainly had proven himself an exceedingly effective lecturer. But lecturing in an entertaining fashion for a couple of hours, twice a day, in a hall known for its poor acoustics and filled with up to 13,000 people, could take something out of you. So finally, in London that fall, Dr. Harry Thomas' old fear was realized: his son *was* "overworking." Lowell writes at one point of having collapsed in his dressing room. A couple of doctors were consulted and came up with this now-dated diagnosis: "a very tired heart." Their prescription: "fresh air, lots of sleep and good food."

So Fran and Lowell moved to Wimbledon Common, about an hour by automobile out of town. Life grew quieter, the air presumably cleaner. Lowell cut back to one show a day. The couple got away for a vacation or two, apparently with the omnipresent Harry Chase. They took some horseback rides in a park, always invigorating for a pair of young people from Colorado, who had, as Fran would later put it, "ridden all our lives."[14] They went for walks. But it looks as if the one who got the most exercise was Lawrence, who on a couple of occasions, Lowell later reported, walked all the way out to Wimbledon to see the Thomases.

((•))

T. E. Lawrence, however, was growing increasingly uncomfortable with the variety of fame bestowed by this exuberant American journalist. It began to strike this Oxford-educated historian as crass and embarrassing. So Lawrence eventually commenced, in his cultured way, grumbling.

Snide comments about Thomas started showing up in Lawrence's correspondence. His earliest complaint about Thomas' lectures and writings appears in a letter to a former superior officer written in January 1920, while Thomas was still holding forth in London: "They are as rank as possible, and are making life very difficult for me." A couple of months later, Lawrence moans to the publisher, F. N. Doubleday, "You know a Mr. Lowell Thomas made me a kind of matinee idol." The next year Lawrence writes another correspondent that "the Arab war was not nearly as silly as he"— Thomas—"makes out: and I was not in charge of it, or even very prominent." In 1923, Lawrence asserts, "That poor purblind Lowell Thomas creature imagined by talking that he was doing me no harm (and making his fortune). The second possibility forced me to let him continue." Later Lawrence writes the novelist E. M. Forster of Thomas, "He is as vulgar as they make them."[15]

Jeremy Wilson, the biographer authorized by Lawrence's family, concludes that "Lawrence's remarks about Lowell Thomas seem to me to be the completely predictable reaction of an educated Edwardian Englishman to a populist American journalist of the 1920s."[16] That characterization is not entirely fair to Lowell, who was not long removed from a spot on the Princeton faculty. But it wasn't that fair, either, to Lawrence, who often seemed at war with himself and was not simply some variety of snobbish British intellectual. Part of the reason Lawrence proved such a beguiling character is that he was not simply anything. He could be shy, self-deprecating and prone to self-loathing, but also aggressive, proud and eager to call attention to himself. This British officer, after all, had liked to parade through Jerusalem in Arab dress. But this British officer also later reenlisted in the military under an assumed name as a private.

So it is not surprising that Lawrence's feelings about Lowell proved complicated and conflicted. Over the years he was rarely less than gracious with Lowell and Fran. And even when Lawrence was complaining about Thomas—in that letter to E. M. Forster, for example—he couldn't help noting that he was "disarmed by his good intentions." Lawrence would go out of his way to point out that Thomas "meant well." And even when he was calling Thomas' writings "rank," Lawrence would add, "As a matter of fact he is a very decent fellow."[17]

In time Lowell came to understand that Lawrence was not simply another larger-than-life character, someone with whom he might pal around, exchange yarns and liven up a party. He sensed that Lawrence, who was increasingly communing with literary types like E. M. Forster, Robert Graves and George Bernard Shaw, never quite accepted him as a fellow adventurer and artiste. And Thomas did eventually learn, as he put it, that Lawrence "scoffed" at his work "when talking to others."[18]

For someone like Lowell Thomas, who was the opposite of ambivalent or conflicted, these episodes of backbiting, along with Lawrence's intermittent disgust with fame, were befuddling. Private individuals with turbulent inner lives would always perplex and sometimes defeat him. Lawrence would be the most compelling subject Thomas encountered as a journalist. But Thomas, so marvelously at home on the surface, was not the one to undertake a survey of Lawrence's subterranean fissures. His grand conclusion about Lawrence's relationship to fame was nothing more insightful than, "At heart, he loved it all." Probably the best Thomas could do in his effort to make sense of Lawrence was to quote what he said was an old Turkish saying: "He had a genius for backing into the limelight."[19]

In the end, Lowell responded to Lawrence's zigzags the only way he knew how: by moving straight ahead. His sin—alas, hardly an original one for a journalist—was to craft a simplified, intelligible, sellable version of Lawrence: as a nonconformist, as a leader, as the indispensable British man, as the prize exhibit in the collection of "strong, sane men with iron nerve who are willing to take chances" Lowell had begun assembling.

What Richard Aldington sneeringly refers to as the "Lawrence lobby" would rarely pass up an opportunity to excoriate Thomas for sensationalizing and distorting the Lawrence legend. Lawrence himself privately—or not entirely privately—disassociated himself from the show, articles and book. Thus was Thomas punished for his sin.

((•))

The winter after it opened Lowell's show moved from the Royal Albert Hall to two smaller venues, Philharmonic Hall and then the Queen's Hall. Interest in it in London, while still strong, had passed its peak.[20]

One problem with the illustrated-lecture business was that such lectures had to be delivered in a particular city, in a particular hall, at a particular time, by a particular person. It was, therefore, a hard business to scale up. Lowell's attempt at a solution was to try to duplicate himself. He hired Dale Carnagey, supported by a separate advance man and a projectionist, to give his own version of the Allenby/Lawrence show in the United States and Canada. (Carnagey was still more than a decade and a half away from his great success as Dale Carnegie.) This version of the travelogue, with a Thomas facsimile, does not seem to have been a big financial success either for Thomas Travelogues Inc. or for Carnagey, who had decided to accept participation in the profits rather than a salary and then spent much of his correspondence with Lowell complaining about finances.

But Lowell, always disposed toward bigger and better, was undeterred.

On February 1, 1920, Lowell and Fran—perhaps restless in his case, certainly homesick in hers—sailed back across the Atlantic. Thomas reported once again to his stockholders in Chicago, who were taken aback by the cut his promoter, Percy Burton, had apportioned himself from the London shows.[21] Lowell did some shows in Washington, Baltimore and Philadelphia. But increasingly he seems preoccupied with business— venues and dates, percentages and salaries, deals and debts. His efforts to grow Thomas Travelogues now included sending Carnagey to Britain to try to hire and prep a couple of other lecturers—clones of a clone—to present the show on the road there.

All of this business-doing provided some early evidence that doing business was not Thomas' strongpoint. A deal Thomas had hastily made with the British War Office Committee for the use of some of their film in his show had contained restrictions, which Thomas eventually violated— costing him more than $20,000, a significant chunk of the money he had earned in London.[22]

Lowell and Fran had been living comfortably and traveling in style. Carnagey noted that, money being tight, he himself traveled third class. If this was a hint, Lowell ignored it. But the finances of Thomas Travelogues Inc. remained precarious, and there is no evidence—outside of the occasional money order forwarded to his mother and sister back home—that the success of his show had led to Lowell's accumulating any significant monies himself.[23]

By spring Lowell, Fran and Harry Chase were back in the British Isles, where audiences for his production about those two British heroes remained substantial. He gave his Allenby/Lawrence lecture with reasonable success in Liverpool, Swansea, Edinburgh, Glasgow and other large cities. Carnagey, meanwhile, was putting together his team of advance men, lecturers and projectionists to hit smaller cities. More hiring. More logistics.

The young Lowell Thomas with his mother,
the former Harriet Wagner.

Lowell Thomas, age 14.

Dr. Harry Thomas, Lowell's father, in his office in Victor, Colorado.

Lowell Thomas, while still in high school,
transporting gold from the local mines to be assayed.

Lowell Thomas, age 18, returns from college and briefly returns to the gold mines in Victor, Colorado.

The young Frances Ryan, who would be wooed by Lowell Thomas.

Image from a brochure advertising Lowell Thomas' lectures on Alaska, where he had spent only eight days. His face was probably cropped into the fur suit.

Lowell Thomas preparing to film from an airplane in Egypt during the First World War. The photo was taken by Lowell's cameraman, Harry A. Chase, who did most of the filming.

FLY WITH LESS THAN
GUNNERS COMPARTMENT.
FOR CLIMBING
...TTING OFF GROUND.
PLANE SET IN
...AL POSITION.

LIFT HER

Lowell Thomas with his equipment—camping in the Middle East during the First World War.

T. E. Lawrence and Lowell Thomas photographed by Harry Chase in Aqaba during the Arab Revolt.

[left] *Lowell Thomas needed some more images of "Lawrence of Arabia" for his wildly popular multimedia show in London, so he and T. E. Lawrence pose in an English garden, pretending they are still in Arabia. Harry Chase once again is behind the camera.*

[right] *A publicity photo of Lowell Thomas, the young journalist and adventurer, then touring the world with his show reporting on the British capture of Palestine and "Lawrence of Arabia."*

Lowell and Frances Thomas relaxing near Singapore during their tour with his show.

Lowell Thomas, Frances Thomas, Emma Chase (Harry's wife) and Harry Chase
(not visible in this photo) atop the giant elephant Primrose in Lahore.
Mrs. Chase did not enjoy the ride.

Lowell Thomas in front of
the automobile that took him
through the Khyber Pass and
into Afghanistan in 1922.

More contracts. At one point Carnagey complains that he is "almost on the verge of a nervous breakdown."[24] Lowell's correspondence at the time was very much taken up not with the travel or editorial notes that would have excited him but with the sort of business arrangements that tended to thwart him.

It must have been with some relief, therefore, that Lowell, Fran and Harry Chase escaped in June 1920 to the quiet of a series of ships. They were headed, with their various projectors and Chase's "big walk-in steel booth," to do shows in Australia. "The whole trip has been wonderful," Fran writes Lowell's family from one of those ships.

Lowell's parents and sister were doing some traveling of their own. Dr. Harry Thomas, having found himself again thanks to war work and travel, was clearly not yet ready to lose himself in a simple medical practice in the States—the business at which he had already failed. With considerable assistance from the now-global connections of his son, the doctor had secured a position on the faculty of the American University in Beirut. Harry, Harriet and Pherbia were making their way there leisurely, via Europe. So now all the members of the Thomas family—none of whom had ever left North America three years earlier—were simultaneously overseas.

Lowell began performing in Australia in August and the first half of September 1920. In Sydney both Lowell and Fran took up and quickly became enthusiasts for what was then a rich person's game, the game Lowell had pretty much ignored at Princeton: golf. This was not a sign that they themselves were becoming rich. "When you carry four or five people with you and a couple of tons of paraphernalia," Lowell complains in a long letter to, of all people, Lawrence, "the transportation ogre devours everything that you shake from the mango tree." It wasn't a particularly loud complaint—money never being Lowell's main concern, especially on a journey to somewhere new and far. "The show has done well but nothing sensational as we hoped it would," Fran reports from Sydney.

In the middle of September, Lowell, Fran, Harry Chase, a business manager they had brought over from England and the newest member of their party, Emma Chase, Harry's wife, sailed to New Zealand—with, in Fran's words, its "mountains, glaciers, geysers, hot pools, etc. etc."[25] Lowell did shows in seven cities. Then they snaked back to Australia and more shows. Lowell, always sensitive to local tastes, had changed the name of his show to *With the Anzacs* [a nickname for soldiers from Australia and New Zealand] *in Palestine and With Lawrence in Arabia*.[26] Their next destination: India and the substantial British audiences that giant colony might provide. Lowell and his team would spend almost three months enduring summer temperatures in the subcontinent's crowded, often dusty cities in the winter and spring of 1921. Lowell was, of course, smitten with the place.

((•))

Perhaps no one has considered the qualities that make for a good traveler more thoughtfully than Freya Stark. Stark, an Englishwoman, wrote memoirs—rich in description, metaphor and insight—of her journeys without a companion across Arabia in the 1930s. Here is one of her observations: "If you are wise and know the art of travel, you will . . . let yourself go on the stream of the unknown and accept whatever comes in the spirit in which the gods may offer it."[27]

Lowell Thomas was always full of plans and projects, but he also had sufficient openness and equanimity to delight in floating down "the stream of the unknown." His two main travel companions in these fruitful years, Harry Chase and Frances Thomas, were also skilled at coping and carrying on. For evidence I turn to a source to which I have mostly tried to avoid turning: Thomas' untrustworthy memoir. His account—exaggerated or not—of an incident in India atop an elephant named Primrose provides a good illustration of this talent for accepting "whatever comes." This tale also offers an example of someone who lacked that talent: Emma Chase.

As Thomas tells it, he and his wife and Chase and his wife—Thomas reports, incorrectly, that Mrs. Chase had just joined their party in India—were invited by the governor of the Punjab to tour the narrow alleys of the bazaar in Lahore atop that unusually large elephant:

Primrose swept her great trunk left and right and wrought havoc on the sidewalk stalls we passed. Nuts and fruits, baubles and beads all went flying through the air and came cascading to the ground, to be eagerly snatched up by the trail of youngsters who followed in our wake, while one of the governor's retainers ran behind to hand out copper and silver largesse to the stoic shopkeepers on our route.

There were certainly unpleasantnesses—colonial, in particular—in this situation. Sensitivity to the lives of people in lands that are being visited is unquestionably another trait good travelers ought to possess. Lowell, his wife and his cameraman may have been a bit lacking there. But they were doing a fine job, sitting atop that large elephant, of accepting whatever came. "Fran, Harry and I enjoyed the spectacle," Thomas recalls. "It was all quite gay and we were having a fine time until we noticed poor Emma." Mrs. Chase was in tears. She found, according to Thomas' account, this chaotic, exotic "spectacle" frightening, even horrifying. Emma Chase, Lowell reports, left for her home in East Orange, New Jersey, a week or so later.[28]

But the travelers pushed on—to Burma, Malaysia and Singapore. "Whatever comes" could be more dangerous then than now. Various fevers and stomach ailments were more difficult to avoid in the first half of the twentieth century than in the second half. Judging from Fran's letters, Chase seems often to have been sick, and Lowell caught a relatively mild case of Dengue fever. Thomas and Chase, when healthy, were doing some shows on this portion of the trip, but they were also by this point gathering material for what Lowell hoped would be a new production for Thomas Travelogues. The subject: South Asia.

Clearly, if Thomas Travelogues was to remain a going concern, it would require another successful show. But how could you match the "liberation" of "the Holy Land"? How could you match Lawrence in Arabia? Thomas was already trying to launch one new production: the story of Captain Ross Smith, an Australian pilot. Lowell had first encountered him when Captain Smith was flying for Allenby in Palestine. He had met him again after Captain Smith won a prize for flying from England to Australia in under 30 hours. There was some film of the flight. Thomas, by now a devoted airplane aficionado, decided that Smith telling his own war-and-adventure story would be a great draw in London. He asked Dale Carnagey, who was also enthusiastic, to work up a script and secure a booking. Captain Ross Smith played for "some weeks at London's Philharmonic Hall," Thomas reports, and "we lost quite a few quid."[29] This ship did not come in. Perhaps something on South Asia, captained by Thomas himself, might.

But Lowell had another important scheme going, as he and Fran settled for a couple of weeks into a beachfront cottage north of Singapore someone had lent them. "Tommy looks like a little boy scout," Fran writes to his parents. He wears shorts, no shoes or stockings, no collar and has his sleeves rolled up. Soon Lowell—almost as eager to play dress-up as T. E. Lawrence—was walking around in a sarong. "He has shaven off his mustache," Fran reports. "He plays like a small boy and is looking ever so much better than when we first came out." Fran learned to swim. Lowell was relaxing as much as he had relaxed in a very long time. But he was also working—on a book.[30]

The subject—but of course—would be Lawrence, and Lowell would crib extensively from the articles he had been writing on his desert hero for *Asia* and the *Strand*. The book's title he decided, rather than *Lawrence of Arabia*, would be *With Lawrence in Arabia*, which emphasized his own proximity to the events.[31]

It was not easy to question the facts in an illustrated lecture in a theater. But this book, finally published in 1924, became an easy target for many of the friendly biographers of Lawrence who followed. They could pin some of the more far-fetched aspects of the Lawrence legend on Thomas. (The main target of the unfriendly biographers would be Lawrence's own book, *Seven Pillars of Wisdom*, published in a subscription edition in 1926.)

((•))

"Everything that Mr. Lowell Thomas says about Colonel Lawrence is true," British prime minister David Lloyd George is quoted as saying in the January 1920 issue of the *Strand*, which featured the first installment of Thomas' series. The prime minister, of course, was wrong.

Lowell Thomas' writings on Lawrence and the Arab Revolt are clear, well explained and generous with historical background. His prose is well turned out and sometimes droll. But his articles for *Asia* and the *Strand*, and his book, *With Lawrence in Arabia*, lack something in balance and accuracy. And occasionally, when it came to Lowell's own role, that seems to have been intentional.

In his second article for both *Asia* and the *Strand*, for example, Thomas puts himself on a camel alongside Lawrence as he heads off on "a little dynamiting party"—one of the excursions Lawrence and a team of Arabs would take to a section of the Ottoman Empire's railroad so they could blow it up. His readers watch with Thomas as Lawrence timed the Turkish patrols, placed the dynamite, exploded the track just as the train's engine passed and, finally, calmly shot those Turkish soldiers who came after him. "Then we all ran back," Thomas writes, "climbed on our camels and swung off across the desert as fast as we could."

Thomas had ridden camels with Lawrence. He had not witnessed any engagements of any sort with the enemy or its railroad in the Middle East.

Thomas, as good reporters are supposed to do, had gathered the details of how Lawrence exploded tracks and damaged a train. But in placing himself there in his articles for both magazines, Thomas did what no reporter should do: He fabricated. He lied.

By the time this story made it into Thomas' book, it was merely misleading. In *With Lawrence in Arabia*, Thomas begins telling basically the same tale by explaining how "we" rode through the desert in a column with Lawrence. Then he writes, "Three days later the column started off . . . in the direction of the" railway. Thomas doesn't say here whether he himself was or was not with that "column." And in the book Thomas, perhaps chastened by some "scoffing" at the articles, avoids any further use of the first-person plural in describing how Lawrence went about sabotaging the railroad.

Most of the criticism of Thomas' writings, however, concerns his account of the accomplishments of Lawrence, not himself. The first *Asia* article, for example, anoints Lawrence "the real ruler of Arabia." In the book that was toned down somewhat to read, "This youth had virtually become the ruler of the Holy Land of the Mohammedans." In that *Asia* article the "capture" of Aqaba is credited "almost entirely to his"—Lawrence's— "leadership and strategical genius." In his book Thomas says more or less the same thing, though the point is weakened when he notes that "Lawrence accidentally shot his own camel through the head with his automatic" during the battle at Abu al Lasan that led up to that capture.

Did Lawrence complain to Thomas about how he was portrayed in these writings? Beyond some ironic or self-deprecating quips, there isn't evidence of that. But Lawrence was certainly complaining to others. One of his complaints was minor: he claimed that Thomas underestimated his height, which Lawrence claimed was five feet five and a half. (Jeremy Wilson says military records confirm this, though a little fudging there might have been possible.) Lowell—and some photographs may offer justification for a lower number—was unwilling to go higher than "five feet three." However, Lawrence's main line of attack was major, unfair and underhanded.

Indeed, an obsession with honor along with a capacity for deviousness was another of the contradictions T. E. Lawrence embodied. Lawrence insisted that the following statement be included in the British edition of Thomas' book: "The Publishers desire to state that Colonel Lawrence is not the source from which the facts in this volume were obtained, nor is he in any way responsible for its contents." Here, it was Lawrence who was not telling the truth. For he himself—along with, as always, his fellow British officers—had confirmed or been the source of much of the information in the book.

The admission that Lawrence had accidentally shot his own camel during a crucial battle, for example, was not in the account of that battle published in *Asia* in October 1919, but it appeared in the *Strand* in February 1920 and then in Thomas' book. Lawrence—the self-deprecating Lawrence—must have passed this embarrassing anecdote on to Thomas during one of their frequent conversations in London.

He had also passed on falsehoods. Thomas reports in his book that a very young Lawrence had met with the British military leader and diplomat Lord Kitchener before the war to protest a plan to allow Germany to control a key Turkish port. As Fred Crawford and Joseph Berton have noted, there is no evidence to indicate that such a meeting took place. Where did Thomas get it? From his own Hejaz notebook, where it is jotted down as if a direct quote from Lawrence. *With Lawrence in Arabia* similarly retails the story, also taken from Thomas' notes on an interview with Lawrence, of how "Lawrence and his men swept in from the desert" during the capture of Wejh—the battle to which Feisal and Lawrence actually arrived days late. Claire Keith, another scholar who has examined the Thomas-Lawrence relationship, has traced a handful of other similarly questionable anecdotes in Thomas' writings back to Lawrence.[*32]

The playwright George Bernard Shaw became a friend of Lawrence's, and Shaw's wife, Charlotte, grew even closer to him. She once declared in frustration, "He is such an infernal liar!" Her husband, however, concluded that Lawrence "was not a liar. He was an actor."[33] Both Shaws, in other words, were aware that Lawrence—like quite a few members of his generation, Thomas' and Hecht's generation—was not always constrained by the actual circumstances of his life. After Lawrence's death in a motorcycle accident, in 1935, Thomas supplied the following telling, if self-serving, recollection: "I frequently asked him whether certain anecdotes I had gathered were true. . . . He would laugh with glee and reply: 'History isn't made up of truth anyhow, so why worry?'"[34]

None of this stopped Lawrence—or the part of Lawrence that wanted to appear modest—from complaining about Thomas' unabashedly hagio-

---

* Claire Keith thinks Lawrence was playing with Thomas, that he was being "facetious." And Lawrence did claim at one point that he hoped to make clear the absurdity of Thomas' account by adding further absurdities. That excuse for Lawrence's misstatements seems rather far-fetched. But whatever his motivation, Lawrence certainly was not always telling the truth to Thomas.

graphic book. Basil Liddell Hart, who excluded Thomas entirely from his Lawrence biography, was among those subject to this griping about Thomas. Liddell Hart later acknowledged as much in a letter to Thomas: "T. E. was very unjust, and also ungrateful, in what he said to me and others about your book. That, regrettably, was rather a habit of his. . . . For all T. E.'s disclaimers I came to realize how much he was the source of what appeared in your book, and that his disclaimers were misleading."[35]

Thomas and Lawrence were a dangerous combination. Truth—journalistic truth, historical truth—suffered. But there is no denying that Thomas and Lawrence were also a potent combination. Two million people around the world eventually saw Thomas' show. His biography of Lawrence has appeared in at least 27 editions in English alone. And the amplified version of T. E.'s accomplishments that became "Lawrence of Arabia" helped interest the West in the Middle East at a time when its sands were releasing only a trickle of oil.

Hollywood certainly noted the drawing power of the desert hero. Two years after Thomas' show debuted in New York, Rudolph Valentino became for a time Hollywood's leading leading man by exploiting the romantic possibilities of Arab garb in his "sheik" movies. Decades later the Lawrence story itself would finally and memorably come to the screen. The publishing industry, of course, was also paying attention: Thomas' best-seller was followed by a seemingly endless parade of books that picked up or chewed over the Lawrence legend.

Thomas' show also opened two years before new countries were carved out of the old Ottoman Empire at the Cairo Conference, with the by-then-famous Lawrence helping draw some of the borders and install some of the monarchs. Feisal's brother Abdullah eventually became king of Jordan, a country—minus the West Bank—his descendants continue to rule. Feisal himself, having had a very brief reign in Syria, ended up installed, oddly, as ruler of Iraq—a precarious and short-lived monarchy. The instability of some of those countries, of course, continues to spread instability throughout the world.

"I admired the man beyond any other human being I have ever met in a lifetime of travel around the Seven Seas," Thomas wrote after Lawrence's death.[36] The Lawrence in Thomas' show and writings was simpler, greater and more admirable than the real man. But what a creation he was!

8.

≡≡≡≡

How Dull It Is to Pause

The most formidable challenge faced by most great travelers may be how to stop traveling. Ulysses is an example, though not in Homer's version of events, which succumbs to the illusion that a world-class adventurer might actually be content with something as prosaic as home.

Lowell and Fran Thomas were on a steamer from Asia back to England. With Lowell's having scored a triumph there a couple of years earlier, England would have seemed the obvious place for him to work on a new show based on their travels. They were together and, entering year five of their marriage, in a position to make a home for themselves and then populate it with a child. We know Fran was vulnerable to that dream. And Lowell tended to be vulnerable to most dreams.

It is Alfred Tennyson who best captures the difficulty Ulysses must have faced in returning to Ithaca—even as king, even with the much-sought-after Penelope waiting to share his bed and be his queen. "How dull it is to pause," his peripatetic hero announces. "I cannot rest from travel." Neither could Lowell. As soon as he arrived in England, he executed a U-turn: he left Fran behind and went back to Asia.

Tennyson's Ulysses sets off on another voyage—"to strive, to seek, to find, and not to yield."[1] A ship was also Lowell Thomas' means of escape and resistance. At the last minute he had secured permission to film a tour of India by Britain's Prince of Wales. It would be seven months before Lowell and his Penelope would see each other again.

((•))

Lowell's decision to return to India may have been justifiable, given the star power of the handsome young Prince Edward—later, and very briefly, King Edward VIII. Footage of the prince would contribute to the success of a new South Asia travelogue. But then again, Lowell never required much of an excuse to keep traveling. Harry Chase, as per normal, would be behind the cameras.

Lowell caught up to Prince Edward's tour of India a bit late, so only three weeks of the seven months he was gone were actually spent tagging along with the Prince of Wales.[2] The prince then left for Japan, but Thomas and the other members of the entourage he assembled continued their study of South Asia. "We interviewed agitators and saints, saw the Car of Juggernaut at Puri and the miraculous hand of St. Francis Xavier at Goa," one member of that traveling party later recalled. "We were blessed by the three-Breasted Goddess at Madura and drank tea with Afridi free-booters at Kus. We went everywhere from Cape Comorin, at the southern-most tip of the peninsula to Afghanistan."[3]

Yes, Afghanistan! That country was not quite the free-fire zone for warring factions and ideologies early in the twentieth century that it would be late in that century and early in the next. Nonetheless, Afghanistan then was among the hardest countries on Earth to penetrate.

Thomas and Chase arrived at the border between what was then British-ruled India and Afghanistan in the summer of 1922. That was two decades after the death of Afghanistan's longtime monarch, Amir Abdur Rahman, who had refused to let foreign companies build the railways and run the telegraph lines that would have connected his country to the rest of the world. And Thomas and Chase arrived at the border just a few years after Afghan troops had marched across it to kick off the Third Anglo-Afghan War—and after British and Indian troops, soon enough, had crossed that border in the other direction on their way to ending that war.

"Afghanistan dislikes the foreigner," Thomas would later explain. "Centuries of unpleasant experiences with invaders, coupled with the mountaineer's natural love of independence, have bred this feeling." Indeed, there is a picture of 30-year-old Lowell Thomas in a suit and pith helmet standing at the end of the Khyber Pass in front of a border guard and a sign reading, "IT IS ABSOLUTELY FORBIDDEN TO CROSS THIS BORDER INTO AFGHAN TERRITORY." Lowell, of course, had taken that as a challenge.

He had marshaled, as was his habit, some stellar recommendation letters (including one from T. E. Lawrence) and had unloosed his unparalleled persuasiveness. Thomas and Chase not only entered that "forbidden" territory, they accomplished that, given the lack of railroads, in "a brand-new, . . . six-cylinder, seven-passenger Buick," which General Motors had been inveigled into providing.

And one of the greatest of Thomas' adventures was under way. From his perspective—and in his words—Afghanistan, this "hermit realm," had it all: "very few roads . . . very few telephones . . . few electric lights . . . and . . . not . . . a single bank. Much of the territory is utterly wild and unexplored." The idea, for travelers like Thomas, is to travel in time as well as space—to get a "view of . . . life," as he put it, "without the slightest modernizing, Western touch . . . precisely as it had been for untold generations." The idea, too, for adventurers like Thomas, is to overcome obstacles, to surmount dangers. In these, Afghanistan was likewise well supplied—in the form, as Thomas tells it, of brutal desert temperatures, repeated tire-punctures, "hub-deep sand," washouts, desert storms, an earthquake and various shady and untrustworthy characters, many of whom were armed.

The chance to hobnob with one of the last of the oriental despots, Amir Amānullāh Khan—a grandson of Abdur Rahman—also added to this journey's allure. When the time came to meet the monarch, Lowell was concerned that he lacked the appropriate formal attire, which he had been unable to squeeze into the Buick already overloaded with gasoline, oil, water, spare tires and all of the photographic gear. Not a problem. Amānullāh was, as tyrants go, amiable. Following Lowell's instructions, the amir, who liked to see himself as forward-looking, dutifully posed for Chase's cameras. "You have ordered me about more than any other living man," Thomas quotes the amir as telling him. "I hope you are satisfied and have made some good pictures." The fact that, in Thomas' estimation, "no one has ever been in the land of the Afghans with a cinema camera before" was another large plus for this adventure.

A critic in the *Manchester Guardian* would later marvel at the accomplishments of Thomas and Chase in this forbidden country: "One feels that a very considerable quantity of—shall we say?—audacity must have been

required" in taking these pictures. "Indeed," he concludes, "the whole affair was one of quite remarkable audacity."[4]

((•))

The patience Lowell's wife had for all that audacity was, however, running
thin. The magic-carpet ride that was life with Lowell Thomas clearly had
its drawbacks. The travel—the compulsive journeying—was unrelenting.
And if you chose upon occasion to disembark, you might not see your husband for the better part of a year. Unlike Penelope, Fran had no home at
which to be stuck; she lived in hotels, at first in London. Like Penelope,
she shed tears.

"I am terribly terribly lonesome without you," Fran writes Lowell early
in this extended separation. But she then adds, "I must buck up and show
what stuff I'm made of. I hope that you get everything you want . . . [,] and
I know it"—the show he was researching in South Asia—"will be the greatest success London has ever seen." Fran's ranking as "the one girl in all
the world" was earned in part by such efforts at amenability and support-
iveness.

And, fortunately, Fran did not have to buck up alone: Her mother
joined her for some months touring Europe. Frances Ryan Thomas had the
pleasure of introducing Eunice Ryan to France and Italy. Then Lowell's
parents and sister tracked down his wife and mother-in-law. They were
in Vienna, where Dr. Harry Thomas—mining-town general practitioner
reincarnated as global medical expert—was engaging in his favorite activity: taking medical courses. Vienna was the place for that then. And,
perhaps due to his own struggles, Dr. Thomas would be developing a new
interest: psychology. That may have further enhanced the attractiveness
of Dr. Freud's hometown. Pherbia, meanwhile, was about to return to
the States to begin college at Ohio Wesleyan University.[5] The traveling
Thomases and Ryans convened for a Lowell-less reunion in Germany.

But Fran remained "terribly lonesome" for her husband. He was apologetic, or sort of apologetic: "This idea of being clear off on the other side
of the world from you pleases me not a bit," Lowell writes his wife. "There
may be some logic in the hackneyed assertion that it does wives and hus-
bands good to be able to view the landscape without always seeing each
other in the foreground, but fifty or one hundred miles is too great a distance to be separated, to say nothing of a thousand or ten thousand."[6]

Meanwhile, Fran watched with increasing displeasure as the number of landscapes her husband was seeing without her kept escalating.

Did Fran fear that Lowell might be entranced by the call of the various sirens one might encounter on a ship or in a foreign city? References in his scribblings to sporty blondes had mostly ceased after Lowell married. There are occasional stray mentions in his letters of a Miss or Mrs. So-And-So, but wherever he landed Lowell was ensconced in the best society—with strict rules for how its ladies, married and otherwise, behaved. And he never exhibited much interest in less proper women. No evidence survives that at this stage in his wanderings, Fran suspected philandering, or should have. Nor is there evidence, however, that Lowell ached for her sufficiently to hightail it back.

Fran clearly did feel left behind. And, yes, even she began registering complaints—quite a few of them, in fact: "Oh why did I let you go away without me?" "I've missed you so much that I cry myself to sleep many nights." "It is absolute hell. Oh! don't leave me behind again."

And money, increasingly, was an issue. "I have lived as cheaply as I possibly can," Fran informs her husband at one point. But as long as Lowell was traveling not lecturing, he was mostly spending not earning. And he still didn't travel second-class or alone. One companion speculated that the various trips involved in the production of the new travelogue had cost "a quarter of a million dollars." This was a bottom-dollar bet of majestic proportions. "We haven't money enough to live on until August," Fran moaned.

In one of her letters, Fran also hazarded a criticism of her husband's professional behavior: "Tommy dear, do remember <u>this time</u> your one bad failing." That failing was that his compulsion to travel could interfere with his drive for success. The travelogue he was working on should appear, Fran reminded him, at the perfect "<u>psychological moment</u> and that is when the Prince returns," but instead of coming back and preparing and presenting it, Lowell had been undertaking new journeys and was contemplating still more. There were even mutterings, fateful mutterings, about another forbidden land: Tibet.[7]

But Tibet would have to wait. The prodigal husband finally returned to England and Fran on September 20, 1922. In due time that new travelogue, *Through Romantic India*, was assembled—with motion pictures of the bonny Prince Edward added to intensify the romance and motion pictures of Afghanistan added to intensify the exoticness. The show was road tested in some smaller British cities, as Lowell struggled with the fact that, lacking a tale of desert heroism and Biblical reconquest, "I haven't," as he put it, "much to say." Nonetheless, with the arrival of winter, the new show took shape.

And at more or less the same time—just a few months after Lowell's return to England—a son was conceived.[8]

((•))

Meanwhile, the balance sheet of Thomas Travelogues Inc. remained vastly unbalanced, and the pockets of the newly created embryo's parents disturbingly empty. Thomas had, as was his habit, been borrowing prodigiously. He had squeezed what advances he could out of his company and its investors. He had relied on credit from various merchants and establishments as well as on loans not just from banks but from business partners. In addition, he had repeatedly and embarrassingly borrowed from friends and family, notably including his and Fran's parents. "We were broke—almost," is how Thomas sums up the situation in his memoir. Actually, they were more than just broke.

"I wish we could make enough to pay back all our debts, to buy out the Chicago stockholders and to start on our very own," Fran writes at one point. "What a happy day!" That day seemed a long way off. Since income had long been scarce, Thomas' obligations to various creditors had grown so large that he wasn't able to borrow enough from others—his usual strategy—to repay them. Ten years later, in a letter to an acquaintance, Lowell put a number on his debt at this time: £25,000, or about $125,000—a huge sum in those days. At least one of Thomas' creditors seized control of some of his projection equipment and film. And there are hints that a legal action was initiated against him back in the States.[9]

"I am trying to be cheerful and philosophical in our present hard circumstances," Fran writes in a diary on January 13, 1923, when she was (but probably would not have known she was) pregnant. Two days earlier she had transcribed this homily there: "He who is thrown down hardest bounces back higher." A bounce back would be difficult if Thomas was not able to secure a good venue for the new show in London. Even Lowell succumbed to the prevailing anxiousness, informing his parents in a letter— and this was about as close as he could come to a moan—that he was on the "edge of the precipice" financially.[10]

Through Romantic India did finally open in London on April 19, 1923—at, auspiciously, the Royal Opera House at Covent Garden, where the Allenby/Lawrence show had first "astonished" London almost four years earlier. But the show opened with, inauspiciously, only a three-week booking. The notices once again were very good: "Should be of enormous interest to the general public," *Daily Telegraph*. "At once amusing, illuminating, and dramatic," *Daily Mail*. "Lowell Thomas has the Kipling touch," *Evening Standard*. "Not only an excellent 'educational' production, but is extremely entertaining," *Times*.[11]

And people once again came—though not the crowds that had lined up to see Lawrence of Arabia. Lowell was beginning to realize, as he suggested in a letter, "that my present travelogue hadn't the financial possibilities in London just now as my previous travelogue." Lowell moved to Philharmonic Hall and switched back for a week to that "previous travelogue"—to Lawrence.[12]

Lowell Thomas Jr. was born in a "nursing home" outside London on October 6, 1923, while his father took care of business inside London. It was a very difficult birth, which probably explains why he would have no siblings. Any dreams Lowell's parents may have had of raising their son in a baronial home in England must have dissipated due to the uninspiring box office for the latest show. The boy spent his first Christmas on board a ship bound for New York with his mother, his father and their load of debt.

((•))

Between that voyage to the United States with their son and a voyage back to Europe without him two years later, Lowell and Fran still never managed to set up that elusive home. She and the baby—called "Sonny"—stayed with Lowell's parents for a while in the resort town of Asbury Park, New Jersey. That is where Dr. Harry Thomas had decided to try to make a go of another private practice.

But there were child-rearing issues in Asbury Park. "I can manage alright if I'm away from the Thomases," Fran writes her mother. "They think nurse & I are terribly cruel because we don't pick baby up every time he cries . . . but I won't have him spoiled." Fran had imbibed the latest British upper-class orthodoxy on raising a well-behaved child: don't coddle. And her Swedish nurse proved an exemplary non-coddler. But Harry and Harriet Thomas—still small-town Americans, despite their own now-extensive travels—had not surrendered the then-unfashionable notion that a crying kid ought to be comforted. Lowell, too, may have retained some such retrograde notions. He joked about "the 20th century scientific experiments that they have tried on the poor, defenseless little fellow." And when that formidable nurse left their employ for a time, Lowell suggested in a letter to Fran's parents—only somewhat ironically—that his son now had "a much better chance to develop into a regular fellow."[13]

Eventually, Fran and Lowell found places to stay in New York City—someone's temporarily vacant apartment, a hotel in Forest Hills. Fran was often alone with the baby and a nurse, however, for Lowell continued to engage in a remarkable amount of traveling.

The destination that may have made him most nervous was, once again, Chicago—for a reckoning on the finances of his corporation. He had to explain to the investors in Thomas Travelogues Inc. why revenues in the past two years had been small and intermittent while expenses were large and steady. He had to convince the shareholders that things would change. Lowell was already trying to convince Fran of that. "We'll be straightened out soon my sweetheart," he assures her, "and we are never going to let ourselves get into the bouillon"—by which he meant the soup—"again! We are going to be models of methody"—by which he meant financial responsibility.

Lowell insists to Fran that what he calls his "big ordeal"—that meeting with the shareholders, which took place at the tony Chicago Club—went well: "The gentlemen simply all agreed that the thing to do was carry on." But he does acknowledge that his investors "felt that things might be conducted on more of a business basis in the future," and that henceforth the company ought to carry on with someone besides Thomas as business manager. Indeed, he admits, the shareholders decided Thomas "should have practically nothing at all to do with the business side except to offer suggestions."[14]

So he continued his perpetual search for a business manager he could trust. But Lowell also continued handling most of his business himself, as he hustled both to erase more of the red ink on his company's books and to pay back some of what he had borrowed. Indeed, he, no one else, soon made a deal with a booking agency in Boston, Alber & Wickes, "managers of lecture celebrities"; he gathered up Harry Chase and their film, slides and projection equipment; and he hit the road in the United States and Canada—reviving the Allenby/Lawrence show and introducing *Through*

Romantic India. Meanwhile, Thomas was finishing and arranging for the U.S. publication of his Lawrence book. And he was hawking articles.

((•))

In September 1924 Lowell Thomas was invited to meet with S. S. McClure, the founder, editor and primary energy source of *McClure's Magazine*, which two decades earlier had published Lincoln Steffens' investigation of municipal corruption and Ida Tarbell's investigation of the machinations and outrages of John D. Rockefeller's Standard Oil Company—the bête noir of progressive journalists in the early twentieth century. *McClure's*, tremendously influential among such progressive politicians as Teddy Roosevelt, had helped initiate an era of reform in government and business. McClure, therefore, represented as well as anyone the most illustrious school of early twentieth-century journalism: muckraking.

This, of course, was one school to which Thomas—despite his love of TR, despite his youthful reformist leanings—had never belonged. Lowell lacked the sense of outrage required for muckraking and had no use for anti-business rhetoric. Indeed, on his most recent trip to Chicago, Lowell had met, as he usually did, with one of his mentors—N. H. Reed of the Standard Oil Company. Nor did this young lecturer, writer and journalist have any inclination toward anti-American rhetoric. Lowell was much more taken with celebrations of America such as this, which he observed on a big sign outside a Chicago business and copied for Fran: "Shirt makers to His Majesty the American Citizen." And Lowell—always drawn to people and places—was not the sort of journalist to spend hours poring over records looking for a hint of malfeasance. He had left Princeton in part to escape a life consumed with that sort of close reading.

By the time he and Thomas met, McClure's top writers and editors had left his magazine. Sam McClure acknowledged, in a phrase Lowell must have understood, that he was "worse than broke." The journalism McClure helped invent had also been in decline, as was—with Calvin Coolidge comfortably ensconced in the White House—the progressive politics it had helped inspire.

Thomas was already beginning to have a go at some elements of the people-and-places-oriented, nonpartisan, national, America-meets-the-world writing and reporting that would become the predominant strain of journalism in the United States in the twentieth century. McClure, who retained a good eye for the future, had noticed and was trying to persuade Thomas to become "a regular contributor" to what was left of his magazine. Lowell was ever alert for ways to further his reputation and, of more appositeness at the time, to make a buck. In a letter to Fran, he alludes to "all the money I owe" and suggests that "for a while I simply must fight like an Afridi brigand to pile up enough mazuma to square up with the world." Lowell didn't say "no" to much, and he was flattered by McClure's interest. But *McClure's Magazine*, at that point, didn't really have much in the way of remuneration—"mazuma"—to offer.

Besides, Lowell had come up with, and was suddenly consumed by, a new journalistic scheme—one that was global in scope, people-oriented, patriotic and seemingly capable of erasing ledgers full of debt. He informs Fran that he is "chasing rainbows as usual," before succumbing to one of the more fanciful metaphors of his career: "but this time they are rainbows flying in aeroplanes."[15]

(((•)))

The first airplane flight around the world commenced in Seattle on April 6, 1924, and concluded, about 25,000 miles later, on September 28 of that year, also in Seattle. There are good reasons why this flight is not as well known as that of Charles Lindbergh, who became the first person to fly all the way across the North Atlantic alone three years later. The around-the-world flight was completed by six fliers, not one, in three planes, not one, under the auspices of the United States military. And this flight, unlike Lindbergh's, was not nonstop; those fliers landed often along the way.

Nonetheless, this first around-the-world flight seemed like a very big deal at the time. It certainly seemed that way to Lowell Thomas, who says he witnessed the end of one of the final legs of the flight: "No matter whether they were aided by the whole blooming American fleet or not they have won for their country an honor, which will cause their own names to be remembered in history long after the names of some of our American presidents have been totally forgotten."*

Lowell foresaw travelogues, perhaps with a few teams of fliers each

---

* The names of the six around-the-world fliers are, for the record, Lowell Smith, Erik Nelson, Leigh Wade, Leslie Arnold, Henry Ogden and John Harding. Eight men had taken off on the flight—a pilot and a mechanic in each of four planes. Two of those original planes did not make it; one was replaced.

crisscrossing the country. And who better to train the airmen in public speaking, to collect and organize what film there was of their journey and, where appropriate, share the stage than Lowell Thomas? His current booking agents jumped on the idea and began talking profits in six figures, to be split three ways: one share for the airmen themselves, one share for the booking agents and one share for the fellow who was fighting like an "Afridi brigand" to resuscitate his finances.

Once it became clear that no one else had yet signed up the pilots, there was just one obstacle: the United States military—which after all had concocted, produced and financed the whole around-the-world extravaganza—had to be convinced to sanction this plan to make large profits by publicizing it. But who better to pull the strings and work the levers that might reconcile the U.S. government to his purposes than Lowell Thomas? He set off for Washington, contacted people who knew people and met with some of the people they knew. The military agreed to go along with Lowell's scheme. Contracts were signed.

In his memoir Lowell states that he joined the six around-the-world fliers for "the final four thousand miles of one of man's greatest adventures." He did not. They had flown from Boston back to Seattle as they had flown the rest of the way around the planet—without the man who dubbed himself the trip's "official historian." But Lowell did fly with various of these fliers as he, they and one or two other lecturers hired by Thomas traveled around the United States telling their story. And people did pay to see them and their film—mostly purchased from newsreel companies and edited by Thomas, one of the airmen and, of course, Harry Chase.

Lowell also foresaw—from the beginning—an authorized book on the round-the-world flight. And who better to write it than a man who had himself been all over the planet in question and who was already beginning to establish himself as a chronicler of adventures in far-off places? Thomas' *With Lawrence in Arabia* had by then made its way onto a best-seller list or two. And he was finishing a book on his Afghanistan adventure, which would be published the next year as *Beyond Khyber Pass.*

Thomas and the six airmen soon signed a contract with Houghton Mifflin Company for the story of the flight. The book, preceded by a series of syndicated newspaper articles on the flight, was published in 1925. Lowell, as usual, had not held back:

Spain had her Columbus and her Magellan; Portugal her Vasco da Gama . . . ; Holland her Hudson. . . . And now to this gallant company America has added the names of the six lieutenants of the United States Army Air Service, who were the first men to fly through the air around this terrestrial sphere.[16]

Everyone involved made money. Lowell talks in one letter of possibly clearing up to $1,000 a week, as he traveled around the country presenting the around-the-world travelogue. Lowell sent Fran checks along with detailed instructions on what to pay back to whom, when. "Of all the long trails I've trekked over," Lowell writes a judge who seems to have been involved in his crumbling finances, "this one from the valley of bankruptcy to the Pike's Peak of solvency has seemed the longest." In fact, as late as 1936 he said he was still paying back some old debts from this period. Nonetheless, while hardly becoming the paragon of financial propriety he had pledged to become, Lowell was, as promised, dragging himself out of "the bouillon." He liked to emphasize to his creditors that he would be paying them back not 50 cents on the dollar but in full.

Among those with whom Thomas presumably was now, if not square, at least reconciled, were the investors in Thomas Travelogues Inc. After eight years of losses, profits, losses and then, with the round-the-world lectures, a bit of a recovery from those losses, the company was dissolved as of December 31, 1925. The shareholders may have collected healthy dividends back when Thomas' Lawrence show was filling theaters, but upon the dissolution of the company, they were paid only about a nickel for every dollar they had invested. Nonetheless, that Thomas Travelogues Inc. had ceased carrying on must have been a relief for all concerned. Lowell and Frances Thomas were now, as she had wished, "on their very own."

And their finances were, for the moment, decent enough so that Fran— no champion of frugality herself—could start to imagine owning a house. "I just long for one," she admits to her mother. But she was quite aware of the Penelope trap. "I'm not going to have a house and live in it alone," she concludes in that letter.[17]

((•))

Meanwhile, Lowell kept concocting new plans. And he was not just scheming for himself. Fran, certainly an intelligent and competent woman in her own right, also had ambitions. "I am filled with a longing to do something all my own," Fran writes to her mother, "and not satisfied to simply be the wife of a famous man." At one point she writes disapprovingly in her journal of a European man whose "idea of a woman"—"typical of nearly all Continental men"—is that "the first essential is to be a good cook and housekeeper." So Lowell began discussing with his literary friends the possibility of Fran's publishing her diaries: "The adventures of the most travelled woman in the world" is how, with no shortage of hyperbole, he framed it.

And a new adventure began to take shape in Lowell's mind. It involved Fran, airplanes and, of course, lots of travel. Lowell and Fran would zoom around Europe via the continent's fledgling commercial airlines. (Passenger service was more developed at the time in Europe than in the United States.) Both husband and wife could then unleash their literary talents upon the experience. And some of their expenses would be covered, secretly, by the rich investor Daniel Guggenheim, who was funding academic programs and a foundation to encourage air travel and with whom Lowell had had dealings on Alaska.[18]

This time Harry Chase would not tag along. For a change—an important change—Lowell was contemplating only a book, not a new travelogue. His entourage, and this must have pleased Fran, would consist only of Fran. There was just one problem: this particular pair of adventurers and chroniclers had a two-year-old son. That did not seem to faze the boy's father all that much, since he was already away from home much of the time. But the child loomed large for Frances Ryan Thomas.

"Tommy is talking Europe again," Fran writes her mother at the end of January 1926. "I want to go too, and if I can make arrangements for Sonny I am going. I think I can fix him up at a little school. But if it is not <u>entirely</u> satisfactory of course, I can't go. We'd only be gone five weeks."

I've seen no evidence that Fran and Lowell considered leaving their son with either set of grandparents, perhaps because of those philosophical disagreements on child-rearing. Instead, they left him at a boarding school called Locust Farm near Pawling, New York. And by the beginning of February 1926 Lowell and Fran were sailing for Europe.

The school where they deposited their son took in well-off children—for the children's betterment or because, as with Lowell Thomas Jr., their parents were otherwise engaged. The place was run by a Vassar graduate, who believed, Fran explains, "that a busy child is never naughty, so she finds tasks for them all." Sonny was the youngest child there by a couple of years and at two awfully young for boarding school. His task was bringing in "two large sticks of wood" each day and placing them by the fireplace.

"I know he will have a better time than if he were cooped up in a boat or a hotel or train," Fran writes her mother. As she traveled Fran received a series of positive reports from the woman who ran the place: "All cables and letters say that he is the great favorite (being the baby), that he plays outdoors all day long. . . . He seems fond of his playmates and never mentions 'mommy' anymore." One gets the feeling, reading these cheery letters, not just that Locust Farm's proprietor is trying rather hard to calm a worried mother, but that the worried mother is trying rather hard to convince her own probably quietly disapproving mother—and herself—that she has done the right thing.

Fran and Lowell's trip managed to combine the reliable pleasures of Europe's glorious cities with the thrill of being among commercial aviation's pioneers. Fran, along with just about all of the world's population at the time, had never before been up in a plane. "Air to her," Lowell would write, "was fresh or stale, a purely impersonal medium revolving around windows and veranda, subways and promenade decks." She was initially nervous about being supported only by that air, but quickly became an air-travel aficionado—seduced by the convenience (though rides were a lot more stomach-churning then) and the views (since planes flew a lot lower then). Their trip included, by Fran's count, 35 airplane flights, and stretched from London to Moscow, from Copenhagen to Constantinople, with stops at most of the major cities in between. They flew a total, by Lowell's count, of about 25,000 miles. The trip lasted not five weeks but the better part of five months.

"I'm desperately lonesome for Junior and restless to get back," Fran writes her mother at one point. Most of her letters include such plaints. "But," she makes clear in this one, "I'm not coming without Tommy because I know how he's always getting new ideas and he might decide to take a flight to Tokyo before returning."

Lowell, for his part, would write in his memoir of having been haunted, while saying good-bye to Sonny, by "the sad look in his eyes." "Today, in light of his own fabulous adventures," he adds, "I take comfort in the hope that eventually he came to understand why we did."[19] Lowell Thomas Jr. grew up to be a reserved man with a lot of love and respect for his parents.

But I don't think he did come to understand why they left him for so long when he was so young.

Some notes that Lowell Thomas Jr. recorded toward an autobiography seem to confuse somewhat his age when he was left at Locust Farm. That may be because he was left there on other occasions. But the emotions he felt at the boarding school, whether then or later, are clear: "Mournful train whistles in the distance. Where are my Mom and Dad? When will they ever come back for me? . . . Terrible disappointment, tragic sadness when they left without me—a vivid memory that has not faded in nearly seventy years."[20]

When I interviewed Lowell Thomas Jr. more than 85 years after his first and most extended stay at Locust Farm, he said only, "It probably left a sadness."

((•))

After their return to the States in late June 1926, Fran did set about trying to transform her diaries into a book. She even sent young Sonny back for the occasional week with "his friends" at Locust Farm, so she could take lessons from someone on her writing and have time to do more of it.

But nothing came of Fran's efforts. Unlike her husband, she hadn't spent years crafting sentences. Lowell had learned to surprise, cajole, tease, defuse and, most definitely, entertain with language. In fact, his sentences, putting aside his skill in enunciating them, were the source of a large part of his indomitable charm—in person, on the stage and on the page. If Fran's journals and letters are a fair guide, while she is alert, thoughtful and clear, she does not seem to have developed her husband's knack for original and clever perspectives or phrasings, as when he writes of his wife, the air-travel virgin, "air to her was fresh or stale." This is from Fran's journal entry recounting her first airplane flight: "Below is the Channel—it looks quite calm after the bad storm of [the] night before last. There are steamers going in all directions and they look so small."[21] In the end Fran would indeed settle, with some regret, into the life of "the wife of a famous man."

That already sort-of-well-known man wanted a quiet place to work on his account of their crisscrossing of Europe by air. So Lowell and Fran began looking for someplace in the country—not a hotel, not a borrowed apartment, but an actual home of their own. It would have to be near New

York City, the locus of his business activities. It could not be too near Asbury Park, New Jersey, where Fran's in-laws lived. Lowell and Fran had been impressed by the area around Locust Farm and had decided to look for something nearby. Quaker Hill, where they ended up settling, is just 12 miles away—on the other side of Pawling, New York, in the foothills of the Berkshire Mountains.

When Lowell Thomas finally did get around to establishing a home, he did it with characteristic boldness. "What do you think?" Fran writes her parents on September 6, 1926. "We've bought a farm." They managed to produce a check for $15,000, took out a mortgage for an additional $17,000, scraped together some loose change and came up with a total of about $33,000—the equivalent of about $444,000 in today's money—to purchase Clover Brook Farm on Quaker Hill. That was not a huge amount for a 12-room white house, with dark shutters, a full basement and attic and a large porch, on 170 acres. Being in a rural area well north of New York City kept things reasonably priced. And, yes, the house did come with a working farm: 12 cows, 18 hens, turkeys (one of which they served for Thanksgiving that fall), apple, pear, cherry and plum trees, a vegetable garden, plus a friendly farm couple to take care of all of the above. Fran and Lowell also inherited and continued to employ two servants—a man from the Bahamas and his wife.

The $15,000 was taken from an $18,000 advance Lowell received that fall from Doubleday to write six more books. That was certainly more prudent than borrowing all the money, but that advance presumably should have been used to help support his family while he actually wrote those books over the years. And a house this large required furniture. Fran and Lowell soon started snapping up antiques. With servants, nurses to help with Sonny and occasional additional stays for him at Locust Farm, the rest of that advance wouldn't last long enough for Lowell to begin writing any of the Doubleday books.

Fortunately, Thomas set off on a series of lecture tours in the United States and Canada that fall, winter and spring—speaking, when the planning was good, in a different town every evening. Fees were coming in. Doing these travelogues also helped fend off the dullness a traveler like him might have experienced being stuck in one place. He was often away from his new home.

Still, it must be said that, when he finally did get around to establishing a home, Lowell Thomas did it splendidly. Quaker Hill, about 70 miles north of Times Square, is a particularly enchanting slice of northeastern American countryside. A 12-mile-long ridge (three miles of which extend across the border into Connecticut), it stands just high enough to offer long views in most directions of unpretentious eastern uplands. Grazing—this is horse as well as cow country—keeps the grasses trim. Grasslands set off the houses and color the rolling hills. The rows of trees alongside the road are stately now and must have been at least sightly then. Forests frame the farms, when they are not themselves dominating the landscape. Hidden among them is a backwoods lake.

The first of the meetinghouses that earned this ridge its name was erected in 1742, its replacement, which still stands, 22 years later. The Quakers there were early crusaders against slavery. George Washington, who for a time made his headquarters in nearby Pawling, reviewed his troops on the western slope of Quaker Hill in 1778. The land that would provide Lowell, Fran, Lowell Jr. and their employees and guests with much of their food had been farmed for 200 years; their house had been built by a member of the most prominent of the Quaker families, the Akins, in the nineteenth century. Most of the houses on Quaker Hill were, like the one Lowell and Fran bought, white, with dark shutters, and old.

Lowell could move with dazzling rapidity from enthusiasm to enthusiasm in these years. Yet somehow he was managing to furnish his life with a few involvements that would last and last. In the previous decade he had secured one of them: his marriage to Frances Ryan. Early in the next decade he would begin another: his nightly radio show. In 1926 Lowell Thomas first established a residence on Quaker Hill. That area would remain for the rest of his life his main home and headquarters, the center of many of his professional activities, as well as a gathering place for his increasingly numerous and distinguished friends—some of whom would even join Lowell in making their home there.

Indeed, Clover Brook Farm, though its new owners had never before undertaken any large-scale entertaining, quickly started filling up with guests on weekends and holidays: various friends from New York, Lowell's sister, Pherbia, and his parents from Asbury Park, members of Fran's clan she had persuaded to make the trek east. "It's just lots of fun to have heaps of company," she writes, "and we have a house that sleeps twelve."

And the guests soon began providing Lowell with some of the stimulations of travel while he stayed home. In January 1927 their home was graced by its first foreign guest: Prince William of Sweden. He was there to get pointers from Lowell before embarking on his own lecture tour.[22]

Gathering and feting interesting, distinguished, often exotic personages under his own roof proved to be an activity Lowell liked almost as much as traveling. His wit and way with a story made him an entertaining host. His sincere fascination with others—the larger their personalities the better—made him a warm host. His inability to fret about money made him a generous host. And his energy, boldness and boyish sense of fun made him a particularly effective activities director—though it would take some years for him to get the facilities on Quaker Hill up to snuff.

((•))

Thomas' book on his and Fran's most recent escapade, *European Skyways*, was published by Houghton Mifflin in 1927. In what may have been intended as a consolation prize for her inability to produce her own book, many pages of Fran's observations on flying are quoted in Thomas' book.

This was his fourth book to appear in four years. Like *With Lawrence in Arabia*, *Beyond Khyber Pass* and *The First World Flight*, this was in large part a travel and adventure book. However, the travel—confined to Europe and its fringes—was less exotic and the adventures less compelling than those in his other books. Indeed, one of Thomas' purposes was to show that the technology was maturing and commercial air flights had become safe and convenient. (His much later memoir, lacking that purpose, insists that there were plenty of "white knuckle moments" on this trip; but that version of Thomas' life generally plays up the thrills and chills.)

European Skyways turns for most of its excitement to accounts of other more perilous air flights. And like Thomas' previous books, it includes an entertainingly written, though not much more than encyclopedia-level, historical component—the history, in this case, of human flight: "The date is December 17, 1903. The scene changes from the island of Crete to a sandy stretch near the Atlantic Ocean at Kitty Hawk, North Carolina. Instead of Daedalus and Icarus we have two young bicycle mechanics."[23]

The person Lowell and Fran met while zipping around Europe who would claim the largest place in their lives was not mentioned in *European Skyways*. He would be the subject of Thomas' next book. Count Felix von

Luckner, who had raided Allied ships for Germany during the First World War, was big, brash, fearless and a champion storyteller—Lowell's kind of guy.

Lowell and Fran had first encountered—and were first dazzled by—Count Luckner at an airport in Stuttgart, Germany: "The newcomer seemed to take the whole world, including strangers, into the compass of his rollicking friendliness," Thomas later explains. "Who is that?" Thomas says he asked, and was told, "Why that's the Sea Devil."

During the First World War, Thomas was learning, Count Luckner, the Sea Devil, had commanded "a prehistoric . . . sailing ship," which had run the blockade around Germany and then sunk—pirate-like—more than a dozen Allied merchant ships. So this man, whom Thomas says they then bumped into often in their visits to European airports, was a scourge to the Allies, an enemy hero. But he was a relatively benign enemy hero, for, at least as Thomas tells it, the Sea Devil "had the unique and enviable reputation of disrupting Allied shipping without ever having taken a human life or so much as drowning a ship's cat." The crews of the ships he scuttled were taken prisoner but never harmed. So this devil had a reputation for being an angel.

He and Thomas, of course, hit it off. "At the time when Count Luckner was raiding the seas," Thomas would later write, "I had been thrown into contact with the most picturesque adventurer that the World War had brought forth—Lawrence of Arabia. Here, in the Sea Devil, was his naval counterpart. They were the two great adventurers of the two respective sides during the World War."

Count Luckner, Lowell's new buddy, soon passed through New York. In these years Luckner, like Lowell, could be relied upon to pass through just about everywhere. The Sea Devil's latest challenge to himself was to sail around the world on his modest schooner. Lowell invited him out to Clover Brook Farm. Count Luckner was the second notable to stay there. They talked—traveler to traveler, adventurer to adventurer, storyteller to storyteller, subject to author. Lowell recorded Luckner's tale, or rather tales, all of which the count would vigorously act out.

In the book Thomas' ended up writing, Felix von Luckner speaks in the first person: "By Joe, I've got a real sea yarn to tell you now. Wait a minute till I light my pipe. . . ." And Luckner did have a tale that could stand up to Lawrence's—though it must be remembered that Luckner and Thomas were, like Lawrence and Thomas, a team of skilled yarn weavers.

Count Luckner, the Sea Devil, published in 1927, became the first major book Thomas submitted to Doubleday in fulfillment of his contract. (Thomas also had a go at transforming Luckner's escapades into a film script—with the less edgy title "The Sea Eagle." The film was never made.) Thomas' Luckner book was among the year's top ten nonfiction best sellers in the United States.[24]

Actually Thomas was probably not the sole author of this book or of the others he would begin submitting to Doubleday. By then he had hired a ghostwriter—one who became another fixture in his life.

(((•)))

Prosper Buranelli was born in Texas a year before Lowell. His father was from Italy. Prosper was a short, round man—Lowell quipped that he measured "about five feet two in any direction"—with thick, wavy black hair. He was easy to pick out on the streets of New York due to the green hat, with a feather sticking out, he sported and his habit of breaking into arias from Verdi operas. Prosper, named after Shakespeare's Prospero, had come to New York in order to make it as a writer. He had secured a job at the *New York World*. In 1924 Buranelli was one of the editors of a hugely successful book, but it was just a collection of crossword puzzles, which were experiencing their initial vogue and which had fallen under Buranelli's purview at the *World*. He was also the author of three short stories that appeared in *Harper's Magazine*. His prose was about to score some larger triumphs—but those would mostly be under the name of Lowell Thomas.

Thomas, who had all those books to author for Doubleday, needed help—a partner, a sidekick more than an amanuensis. It was not that he suffered from any deficiency as a writer. Lowell simply had no desire to spend most of his time writing. He would later recall having gotten Buranelli's name from a busy friend who had enlisted Buranelli's assistance in producing a series of articles for the *World*. Lowell hired him, and he stayed hired—until Prosper's death. So Thomas' books were now really Thomas' and Buranelli's books.

Count Luckner, the Sea Devil therefore probably featured Buranelli trying to write in Thomas' voice as Thomas tried to write in Luckner's voice. Ogden Nash—about to become the champion of whimsical verse, but then an editor at Doubleday and an acquaintance of Lowell's—soon rated Prosper Buranelli, according to Nash's biographer, "the greatest ghostwriter then working."[25] He was, in other words, a talented literary ventriloquist.

Prosper worked out of Clover Brook Farm, where Lowell had set up an operation they referred to as the "book mill." In the next five years, Thomas and Buranelli produced under Thomas' name more than a dozen titles for Doubleday or other publishers. Thomas fashioned his own experiences in India into a book, but the rest of these volumes detailed someone else's heroics. The bulk—including a second volume on Luckner's adventures— took place during the First World War. However, one book reported on an American Revolutionary War hero, George Rogers Clark, another on a wildlife photographer in Africa and a third on a French trader living in the Yukon, *Kabluk of the Eskimo*.[26]

These books were generally well reviewed. Here is the *New Yorker* on *Kabluk of the Eskimo*: "As . . . an author who writes not his own words but those of another in that other's personality, Lowell Thomas brilliantly excels, as his many books of this sort bear witness." This reviewer, however, did express a qualm: "The reader may feel an insistent doubt rising in his mind . . . as to how much of it was true and how much of it was born of Lowell Thomas' imagination and writing skill. But he will go on reading just the same. It is a remarkable tale told exceedingly well."

The formula for almost all of these books? Pretty straightforward: exotic locales and Lowell's "big, strong, sane men with iron nerve"—cowboys, in essence—accomplishing something difficult. The genre? Adventure nonfiction—in an age when adventure and far-off travel were still entwined.

The style of these books? Somewhere along the path from the *Victor Record* to the *Chicago Daily Journal* to Princeton and then the lecture stage, Lowell had mastered the art of lively, vivid and often clever prose, and Prosper could manage that too. Here, from *Kabluk of the Eskimo*, describing some "loafers, worthless fellows," is one or the other of them: "They came just as debris floats and gathers in an eddy of a stream." Nonetheless, their wordings did sometimes incline, as will happen when your main selling point is drama, toward the overheated: "The men launched their lances with mighty throws." And their wordings occasionally fell back, as will happen when you are churning out a couple of books a year, upon too-familiar phrasings: "Winter came early that year."

The books' reliability? We can add to the doubts expressed in that *New Yorker* review the testimony of Louis Auguste Romanet—aka Kabluk—

himself on Thomas' account of his exploits: "What concerns the Eskimo and the Arctic was taken from my [manuscript]. What concerns myself was gathered by Mr. Thomas during my stay at his home in Pawling, NY, or drawn from his imagination in certain cases." So, no, Thomas and his accomplice, Buranelli, had still not achieved the level of reliability that would come to be demanded of a late-twentieth-century journalist or non-fiction writer.

The payoff? Thomas generally shared royalties with the individuals—starting with Luckner—whose tales he was selling. But this remarkably productive "book mill" was bringing him plenty of money.[27]

After the stock market crash of 1929, many of his friends were watching work dry up. Rose Wilder Lane, a writer with whom Lowell maintained a flirty friendship, was among them: "These days, we're all ship-wrecked mariners," she writes him, "clinging to planks in the tossing seas." At one point she complains that she doesn't have enough money to fix a broken tooth. "At the moment I'm in the Dickens of a fix," she explains to Lowell, adding, "and . . . you are not."

Lowell tried to help out those he knew who were hurting—making connections, writing introductions, offering a couple of them, Lane in particular, a role in some of his many projects: she got some of the writing work Prosper couldn't handle.[28] But Lowell was not himself hurting. Indeed, he was earning more and more, and, inevitably, spending what he made or seemed to have a shot at making. Through the end of the 1920s, in other words into the Great Depression, he lived an extravagant life, based primarily on Quaker Hill, enlivened by periodic lecture tours, funded mostly by lecture fees and book advances.

((•))

Although Prosper Buranelli started a family, which would eventually include ten kids, out in New Jersey, he mostly bunked without them up on Quaker Hill at Clover Brook Farm. One assumes this was for stimulation as well as convenience. The wide variety of guests Lowell reeled in—including those whose feats they were chronicling and an ever-denser concentration of the well known—provided the farm with diversions of a quality that would have been hard to match even in the city. And Prosper—himself a bon vivant, a wit, "a walking encyclopedia"—further boosted the entertainment level.

Lowell and Fran owned a car, a Buick—for picking people up at the Pawling railroad station, for errands, for touring the area. Fran initially shared the driving with a servant. Although Lowell did secure a driver's license and was as enthusiastic about automobiles as he was about other new technologies, there is no evidence that he ever became particularly adept at driving that Buick or any other vehicle himself. Lowell was always more suited to telling tales and hatching schemes than to prosaic matters such as where to turn and what speed to maintain.

In January 1927 Lowell and Fran had purchased an example of a slightly newer technology: a radio—Hammarlund was the make. "Mr. Chase set it up while he was here," Fran writes.

Harry Chase had, of course, been Lowell's companion on most of the greatest adventures of the first half of his life. But Lowell was no longer shooting much new film. And Chase probably was no longer eager to go out on the road as a projectionist. Instead, he brought his genius for new-fangled machines to some efforts to develop new techniques for mixing sound and film—techniques the company for which he worked proved unable to sell. Chase was left in what was, as the Depression took hold, a common bind: without "enough to pay the rent," as he puts it in a letter to Lowell. Lowell found excuses to send him some checks.

And Chase had health issues, which grew severe. In a letter to her mother some years later, Fran explains that Chase suffered from "nerve trouble" and had "lost the use of his arms and legs." Lowell had arranged for his father, Dr. Harry Thomas, to consult with Chase about his condition. To no avail. Harry Chase would die at the age of 52 in 1935.

It is fitting, perhaps, that Chase's last appearance in this narrative—this visit to Clover Brook Farm—coincides with the first appearance of radio, which would dominate the second half of Lowell's life. It is fitting that Harry Chase set up the Thomas household's first radio.[29]

9.

Having the Ear of America

T he first daily network newscast in the United States was delivered on one of the two radio networks operated by the National Broadcasting Company on, as best I can determine, June 5, 1930. It was not delivered by Lowell Thomas.

The date of this first network newscast is difficult to pin down in part because, as is often the case with such innovations, few at the time paid it much mind. The network newscast—on radio and then on television— would become arguably the most consequential source of news in the United States for most of the rest of the twentieth century. It would offer this overlarge mélange of a country a campfire to gather round every evening; it would provide a familiar voice or face to tell the latest tales not just of one ethnic group or one town but of a nation, even a world. Yet the fact that they were hearing something new—let alone that it would grow large and potent—managed to elude most who tuned in to what was, for them, just another talky radio program in the late spring of 1930. An additional reason this history seems a little fuzzy is that in its primordial forms, a *newscast*—a word that does not begin appearing regularly until the late 1930s—was hard to define.

The first commercial radio station in the United States, by some determinations, was KDKA in Pittsburgh. It began *broadcasting* (a farming term for scattering widely) on the evening of November 2, 1920—Election Day. That evening KDKA broadcast news. The election returns arrived via a telephone hookup from the newsroom of a newspaper, the *Pittsburgh Post*. Newspapers had taken a century or so to develop their own reporting systems. Because it was born with a great ability to distribute news fast and far but no innate ability to gather news, radio news had entered the world with a serious where-to-get-the-news problem. Such hookups to newspapers proved early and obvious solutions.

Less than two years later, a station owned by a newspaper—WJAG in diminutive Norfolk, Nebraska—put news on the air *daily*. So the first regular news program on the radio was local. By the late 1920s a selection of individual radio stations were devoting some minutes each day to news and weather—most taken from newspapers or from the wire services designed to feed newspapers.[1]

Nonetheless, there still wasn't much more than a light sprinkling of news on the air when Frances and Lowell Thomas purchased that Hammarlund radio in 1927. Fran doesn't report listening to any.[2] Radio schedules did feature some discussions and lectures: Thomas himself had held forth on the round-the-world flight on KDKA on March 21, 1925—giving KDKA another distinction: being the first to broadcast a whole program featuring Lowell Thomas' voice. The first comedy shows were about to debut. However, most of the day's schedule on most major stations was occupied by live, in-studio musical performances—of the sort Frances Thomas, always eager to spend an evening at a concert hall or opera house, was pleased to be able to listen to at home. And the fledgling radio networks had not yet begun to try their hand at news.

((•))

The technology for connecting one radio station to another—so that they might broadcast the same program at the same time—had first been employed in 1923 by the American Telephone & Telegraph Company, which had some experience in moving signals over wires. AT&T's *chain* of radio stations—its *network*—grew and was then sold (and AT&T's wires were leased) to the new National Broadcasting Company, which debuted in 1926. It was dubbed NBC's "Red Network."[3] And a journalist, though not the day's news, began appearing on this network: Floyd Gibbons, whose career path Thomas sometimes seemed to be following. Beginning in the summer of 1929, Gibbons hosted an NBC program one night a week called *Headline Hunter*, in which, backed by an orchestra in the studio, he regaled the audience with tales of his past reporting adventures.[4] In 1930 the Columbia Broadcasting System—still a junior network—began airing programs, featuring another renegade newspaper journalist, H. V. Kaltenborn, that did discuss current events. But he hosted two different shows, at different times, a total of no more than four evenings a week.[5] News organs thrive on regularity—on establishing themselves as a place audiences know they can turn every day for the latest. Kaltenborn's somewhat irregular efforts failed to provide that.

The first daily network newscast was presented in the East for 15 minutes at 6:45 every evening except Sunday on NBC's "Blue Network," heard on WJZ in New York City. Although this was NBC's lesser network, that was a privileged time slot because of what aired at seven on that same network on those same nights: a 15-minute "sketch"—or proto–situation comedy—featuring two white actors playing two African-American characters with some humor, some sympathy and plenty of stereotyping and condescension. *Amos 'n' Andy*, an early incursion of comedy on the radio dial, had quickly become the most popular nightly radio program in America. The show that preceded it had a chance to woo early arriving members of its audience. And that newscast did. According to the *New York Times*, it soon ranked a "close second" behind *Amos 'n' Andy* in number of listeners each night for a show on multiple nights.

The "news commentator" on that first network newscast was one of America's most renowned journalists, the man who had become a foreign correspondent, war reporter and journalistic adventurer before Lowell Thomas and who actually had been wounded during the First World War. Floyd Gibbons, the "headline hunter" himself, had now beaten Thomas to a daily news report on the radio, too.

This first network newscast had not initially been intended to be a newscast. Gibbons had been hired to host a show called the *Literary Digest Prohibition Poll*. Sponsors produced and packaged whole programs in those days. The *Literary Digest*, among the best-selling magazines in the country, specialized in quoting excerpts from articles that had appeared elsewhere. To promote itself, the publication also conducted highly influential public-opinion surveys by mailing out many millions of ballots (each with a subscription form conveniently attached).* The magazine's publisher decided he wanted a series of programs to publicize one of those polls—this one on what was, after the crumbling economy, the most pressing issue in the United States at the time: the fate of the decade-old constitutional prohibition on the sale of alcohol. The *Literary Digest* had hired Gibbons to talk up the issue, encourage responses and announce results. According to the *New York Times*, this veteran journalist was being paid an impressive $2,250 each week for his broadcasts.[6]

Gibbons also filled some of the minutes between 6:45 and *Amos 'n' Andy* with reports and comments on current events that did not have to do with that *Literary Digest* poll. As the Prohibition Poll finished up (the "wets" in the end beat the "dries"), those reports and comments began taking over the program.

On June 5, 1930, without any fanfare, the name of the show was changed to *Literary Digest Topics in Brief*, giving the United States its first network newscast. That evening's jog through the day's news by the fast-talking Gibbons ("217 words per minute," someone calculated) included reports on an eruption of Mount Vesuvius, on a military agreement between Italy and France and on one of the many ongoing efforts in the United States to repeal Prohibition—but no mention of that *Literary Digest* poll. The program solved the where-to-get-the-news problem by rewriting stories lifted primarily from newspapers and the wire services designed to feed them. The preferred source was, of course, the latest issue of the *Literary Digest*, which, Gibbons reminded his audience, was "the father and mother of this aerial blast" and "obtainable on all newsstands."[7]

With Floyd Gibbons' *Topics in Brief*, much of the United States was able to receive news at once—or, in the case of these late spring and summer 1930 broadcasts, almost at once: the newscast would be read again later each evening, by someone else, for a separate, more primitive western hookup. All that was required was some proximity to an NBC Blue Network station and a radio set.

And despite the Depression, many Americans were proceeding to out-

---

* The *Literary Digest* straw polls, thanks to the huge number of respondents they attracted, were extraordinarily accurate in predicting the result of presidential elections—until 1936, when the survey predicted that Republican Alfred Landon would defeat the incumbent in a landslide. The embarrassment of President Franklin D. Roosevelt's landslide victory that year contributed to the demise of the *Literary Digest* in 1938.

fit their living rooms with such sets. By 1930 40 percent of the families in the United States had joined the Thomases in owning radios.[8]

(((•)))

However, the host of what was said to have been the second-most-popular daily show on the radio was removed less than four months after he began doing his more general newscast. The new host was somewhat younger and substantially less well known. He would not maintain such a frantic pace on the air, being someone who, the New York *Evening World* promised, even "breathes occasionally." And the new host—also part journalist, part author, part world traveler, part adventurer; also steeped in Chicago journalism—would host this newscast for various sponsors on NBC, CBS and, initially, both for almost 46 years.[9]

A few different explanations have been offered for this decision to fix what wasn't broken—to take, in other words, the voice, style and phrasings of this very successful radio program, all of which emanated from Floyd Gibbons, and replace them with those of Lowell Thomas, who brought to the endeavor scant radio experience.

The explanation made public at the time, as reported by the *New York Times*, had to do with a switch in networks that accompanied the switch in hosts. The *Literary Digest* had decided to move the western rebroadcast of its show to the Columbia Broadcasting System's relatively strong western network. And the magazine and CBS wanted the same voice airing both. That couldn't have happened, the *Times* explains, with Gibbons at the microphone because he had an exclusive contract with NBC.

There is clearly truth in this. William Paley, the architect and president of CBS, was waking up to the importance of news for a broadcast network, and no news program—certainly neither of the on-one-day, off-the-next shows hosted on Paley's own network by H. V. Kaltenborn—drew the audiences that Gibbons' show for the *Literary Digest* drew. Paley was looking for a way of getting in on that. He did play the major role in finding Thomas and promoting him for the job. Some credit the entire Gibbons-to-Thomas switch to Paley's machinations.

But why was the *Literary Digest* willing even to consider replacing its hugely popular host? According to a couple of media historians, the problem was Gibbons' hefty salary and "brusque manner."[10] According to Thomas himself and other media historians (many of whom are relying upon Thomas' memoir), the problem was Gibbons' affection for alcohol.

An account of the change in hosts on the *Literary Digest Topics in Brief* by Ben Gross, the longtime radio columnist for New York's *Daily News*, coincides pretty well with Thomas' own version. Indeed, although it was published before Thomas' memoir, it may have been based on his version. Gross asserts that Gibbons had been engaging in "a session with drinking companions in a Long Island roadhouse" when he "had a sudden inspiration, 'On the way back to town' he said, 'let's serenade my sponsor.'" R. J. Cuddihy, publisher of the *Literary Digest*, lived on Long Island. He was a confirmed teetotaler. Prohibition was still in effect. This would not have been a good idea. Cuddihy, the story goes, set about replacing Mr. Gibbons the next day, giving William Paley his opening.

Lowell Thomas could hold an audience. He could write. As they left his mouth, words sounded their best—crisp, clear, compelling. Lowell's experience was varied and unorthodox, but radio then was a new medium with few orthodoxies and nothing resembling a career path. And Lowell had enough of a journalism background and an impressive enough academic background to be credible discussing the news. It helped that he, like Gibbons, had seen the world and embarked on many more than his share of adventures—an important draw at the time. And Thomas was never more than a social drinker. So it was not entirely surprising that Paley, by many accounts, fastened upon this radio neophyte as his candidate to take over for Gibbons. Paley arranged for Thomas to audition for Cuddihy.

The first time, Thomas simply talked for 15 minutes in front of a microphone with Paley, Cuddihy and some colleagues sitting in another room in front of a speaker. The second audition was more formal. Thomas was asked to present the day's news for this small audience right before Gibbons was to present the day's news for real on the radio.

Paley, with much at stake, corralled some CBS muckety-mucks with newspaper backgrounds to help prepare the test newscast's script. Lowell added some firepower of his own: Dale Carnagey, Ogden Nash and Prosper Buranelli. To lubricate this assemblage of eminent, if mostly novice, radio-script writers, Lowell brought down from his farm—presumably unbeknownst to Mr. R. J. Cuddihy—a few bottles of applejack, a concentrated cider. Tongues were indeed loosened, but no script was forthcoming. Instead Thomas, by his account, went off with Buranelli, purchased some newspapers—a version of Gibbons' solution to the where-to-get-the-news problem—and came up with 15 minutes worth of paragraphs on current events.[11]

The decision to replace Gibbons with Thomas was made so quickly that the weekly radio listings published on Sunday, September 28, 1930, still had Gibbons as host of the show. On Monday, September 29, 1930, however, the New York Times correctly informed its readers that at 6:45 on WJZ in New York, and therefore on the entire NBC Blue Network in the East, they could hear: "Literary Digest Topics in Brief—Lowell Thomas." The show would, as planned, be on CBS out West.

When he first sat down in front of the mike, Thomas praised and thanked the man who had previously sat there.[12] Then he introduced himself: "I am just a chap who started out as a newspaper man, with an overwhelming desire to see the whole world." Thomas certainly would bring a lot of the world to his Literary Digest show. His lead story that evening was out of Germany:

> Adolf Hitler, the German Fascist chief, is snorting fire. There are now two Mussolinis in the world, which seems to promise a rousing time. . . . This belligerent gentleman states that a cardinal policy of his now-powerful German party is the conquest of Russia. That's a tall assignment Adolf. You just ask Napoleon.

In this initial broadcast Thomas also discussed Spanish politics, which would bloody a piece of Europe before German politics bloodied much of the world.

Thomas provided another taste of broadcasts to come by succumbing that first evening to a pun and a lighthearted ribbing of politicians: "Madrid witnessed a great political meeting in a famous old bull ring there. Political meetings and bull seem to be natural together. . . ."[13]

((•))

Thomas had been given the chance to host a network newscast—when there were no others, in perhaps the most favorable timeslot in all of radio. "Like a bolt out of the blue I fell heir to what is probably the most remarkable opportunity in the whole wide world for a speaker," he effuses in a letter. Indeed, on September 29, 1930, Lowell's life—the way he earned his living, the league in which he competed, how he occupied himself, the pace at which he lived—was transformed.

Not that Lowell chained himself to a typewriter every day to produce 15 minutes worth of news. There were too many people to meet, letters to respond to and schemes to pursue. Instead Lowell immediately assigned Prosper Buranelli, already expert at writing like Lowell wrote, the task of writing like he spoke. Prosper also had an eye for the folksy, amusing stories Lowell especially liked—stories that told a story. And he was adept at making sure they could be recited in Lowell cadences—short, occasionally incomplete sentences; chatty, with frequent excursions into the present tense. The following lines are all from one evening's show—November 1, 1932:

- What weeping and wailing and gnashing of teeth there is in Reno, Nevada, today. . . .
- Today opens the hunting season in several states. . . . Farmers are hereby warned to take such means as they can to protect themselves. . . .
- . . . . It was tonight that the jobless of England proposed to present their petition to Parliament. . . .
- A marksmanship note from Chicago. . . . Each of the bullets landed, one of them in his own thigh and the other in his own ankle.
- Some four and a half years ago a German painter, an artist, came to Canada. . . .
- I assume most of you heard the important speeches delivered by Mr. Hoover and Mr. Roosevelt last night. . . .
- Now follows the tragedy of a set of false teeth. . . . [14]

With Prosper having other responsibilities in the growing Thomas journalism empire, Lowell soon brought in Louis Sherwin, a New York drama critic and columnist, to help churn out the daily scripts. Buranelli and Sherwin thereby qualify as among the first broadcast *newswriters*. They perused the local papers and the wire services each day for stories that tickled their fancies—and might also engage their boss.

News from overseas was usually a good bet, given Lowell's travels, plus the fact that Buranelli's father was Italian while Sherwin's father was German, his mother Australian and he had attended school in England.[15] So listeners to the Lowell Thomas version of *Literary Digest Topics in Brief* were fed perhaps even a steadier diet of world news than that provided by the also well-traveled and global-minded Floyd Gibbons. One early and not-atypical newscast, for instance, lined up stories from London, India, Geneva, Hungary, Argentina, Cuba and Nicaragua.[16] Often, more than half the stories would be international.

((•))

Lowell did heavily edit his scripts—eventually distinguishing himself by employing green ink. And he did have to be in the studio six nights a week to read those scripts on the air. So the cross-country lecturing had to be severely curtailed—and the bulk of the lectures he had already contracted for had to be canceled.[17] Family events outside Quaker Hill also diminished. "We'd like to visit Denver," Lowell explains to Fran's parents, "but I've got a job and as long as there is a Santa Claus named Radio I guess I better hold onto his whiskers." And as long as he was chained to a microphone in Manhattan, Lowell would no longer be able to suddenly dash off, when snow accumulated, on a skiing trip—a sport to which he was becoming and would remain addicted.

Indeed, the radio gig required that much more of his time be spent in the city. Exactly one month after he took over the *Literary Digest* shows, the *New York Times* reported that Lowell Thomas had leased an apartment on East 57th Street in Manhattan, with nine rooms on two floors. The farm would now be primarily a weekend place for him and the usual gaggle of guests. It would be primarily a weekend and summer place for his wife and son.

Sonny was seven when his father began hosting the *Literary Digest* show. The boy's weekdays were now spent studying at the small Lawrence-Smith School on East 70th Street, founded in 1914 by Clement Lawrence Smith, a Harvard graduate on a crusade to make Latin come alive. Sonny was not short of playmates in town and was not one to grumble, but his preference in this bifurcated life his family now led was clear. "Fridays were best of all days," Lowell Thomas Jr. would recall in some notes for an autobiography, "for it meant a weekend on the beloved farm. I hate NYC." Quaker Hill was where Sonny came alive.[18]

Lowell Sr., now working six days a week in the city, evinced a similar preference. "We are living altogether too fast," he writes his in-laws, "and the farm would sure look great for a stretch of about three months." Not that he could take three months or even a week at the farm, and not that

Lowell had much talent for living slow—even when he was there. "As usual he is working too hard," Fran writes her mother. Yet there were a few weekends with no guests around when, she notes, even Lowell collapsed.[19]

You wouldn't know it at Clover Brook Farm, but this was during the reign of, as Lowell put it, "Old Man Depression." Lowell watched as businesses all around him, some of which he had been doing business with, contracted or expired. "Bank failures in Asbury and the Thomases are panicky," Fran reports to her mother about her in-laws.

"We thank our lucky stars that times have been as prosperous as they have for us," Lowell writes his in-laws.[20] The radio, this ethereal Santa, was reasonably generous—quite a plus given the extended hard times the country was suffering through. Lowell was not given a weekly salary nearly as high as that of Gibbons. And his penchant for spending at least what he earned remained. Still, this was by far the largest regular paycheck he had ever received. It would grow, though not always as fast as that spending.

((•))

The audience for the *Literary Digest Topics in Brief* did not decline after Floyd Gibbons was jettisoned. To the contrary. Some of this was due to the continuing, even burgeoning popularity of the program Thomas' program preceded. A comedian friend once suggested this epitaph for Lowell, which Lowell enjoyed quoting:

HERE LIES THE BIRD

WHO WAS HEARD

BY MILLIONS OF PEOPLE—

WHO WERE WAITING TO HEAR

"AMOS 'N' ANDY."

And the audience for the *Literary Digest Topics in Brief* did not decline after the *Literary Digest* pulled out.

First, on January 1, 1932, the *Literary Digest* had ended the peculiar arrangement under which two rival networks, NBC and CBS, each carried *Literary Digest Topics in Brief* in a different part of the country. William Paley lost out. Lowell explains in a letter to his in-laws that the *Literary Digest* axed the western broadcast to cut costs in the Depression. They had also decided to eliminate the Saturday installment of the show.

Choosing which network to drop must not have been difficult. The magazine stuck with the network that could follow its show with *Amos 'n' Andy*.

This switch had two unfortunate consequences for Thomas: First, his newscast would no longer be heard in the West. The fact that CBS' western hookup was not replaced would continue to gall this man who hailed, after all, from the West. And second, Lowell himself fell victim to that cost cutting: he was forced to take a 10 percent pay cut, since he was no longer repeating his show later in the evening for the West or working Saturdays. "I will have to give a few lectures to make up the difference," he tells Fran's parents. This cut in pay did not, of course, lead to any upsurge in frugality. Later that year Lowell purchased 75 additional acres to add to what the *New York Times* was now calling his Quaker Hill "estate."

On the positive side, Lowell no longer had to stick around for that late rebroadcast or come in on Saturdays. "So he will have more time at the farm," Fran notes in her letter to her parents.

On April 6, 1932, Lowell celebrated his fortieth birthday. "He looks so young," Fran suggests.[21] Most would have agreed. A month later—shortly before Thomas was to do his show from Chicago during the Republican convention there—the *Literary Digest* made another consequential decision: the magazine would withdraw from the radio business entirely.

Lowell would need a new sponsor, which he soon found in the Sun Oil Company—Sunoco. Thomas remained on the same network, with his show aired at the same propitious time, with the same absence of western stations. Sunoco did business only in the East. The name of the show was still *Topics in Brief*, though somewhere along the way it would become known simply as *Lowell Thomas with the News*. (Program titles do not seem to have been a matter of much concern in radio journalism.) Thomas covered the same types of stories and continued to find occasions to plug his sponsor. His audience continued to grow.

That was due in part to the growth in general of radio's audience, as even more American households—83 percent of them by the end of the decade—owned sets and as people began spending larger amounts of time in their living rooms listening to them.[22]

((•))

With the rise of *broad*casting, of *mass* communication, instead of one person singing, joking or telling news to a few friends, radio's newly minted stars sang, joked or told news to millions. Instead of chitchatting with one another—about their day, about that couple down the block, about something they had read in the newspaper—people listened to Thomas talk of happenings around the world.

And with radio you didn't have to go anywhere to enjoy the comedy, the music, the news. Indeed, radio had an important place among the procession of new technologies—beginning with the printing press, the telephone and the phonograph, eventually including television, air conditioning and the personal computer—that would encourage people to spend more time inside their homes. One could hear Jascha Heifetz play the violin on the radio. One could laugh with or, alas, at *Amos 'n' Andy*. One could hear President Hoover from the White House. One could hear Lowell Thomas deliver the news. The entertainment or information available inside the home was now regularly surpassing that available on the streets, in cafés or in theaters.

Floyd Gibbons had 16 weeks; Lowell Thomas had years to insinuate himself daily into those American homes. Indeed, he had the field—the nightly network newscast—to himself through the 1932–33 radio season. Thomas was, consequently, becoming the voice of the latest, the voice that recounted and explained, the voice in the United States of news. And Thomas also had his newscast pretty much to himself. An announcer introduced his show and then repeated Thomas' name and plugged the sponsor again at the end. But otherwise Thomas did his 15 minutes mostly solo. Since the only way to record sound in those days was to cut a record, other voices—newsmakers, reporters in the field—had to come on live in order to intrude upon the communion between Thomas and his audience. That was an infrequent occurrence. And, of course, there were no images to distract from Thomas' voice.

That voice itself, of course, was large, deep, resonant and precise. It featured the careful modulations and enunciations in which his father had trained him. It employed, according to a *New York Times* article by a speech consultant, a "general American" or "Midwestern" accent—to be distinguished from a "Southern," "Eastern" or "Oxford" accent.[23] However, as was typical of the time but perhaps even more pronounced in him, Thomas' voice was crisper, with more English or mid-Atlantic flavorings, than would be found in the relaxed Midwestern accent that came to dominate American television decades later.

He opened each broadcast with a firm but affable "Good evening, everybody." Later Thomas' sendoff for each broadcast became "So long until tomorrow." Other broadcasters would have such "signature" lines: The gossip columnist Walter Winchell employed the rococo salutation "Good evening, Mr. and Mrs. America and all the ships at sea." Winchell's very popular Sunday night gossip, news and vituperation show embarked upon a long run on NBC's Blue Network in 1932. The revered broadcast journalist Edward R. Murrow would later close with a crisp "Good night and good luck," and decades later television's Walter Cronkite with the Olympian "And that's the way it is." But Thomas' open and close became as recognizable as any in the history of broadcasting. (He employed them as the titles of the two volumes of his memoir.) This was not just because he was among the first to stick to a recognizable phrase. It was because Lowell Thomas' voice was so important in American living rooms in the 1930s and 1940s.

During the 1935–36 radio season, Lowell Thomas' newscast was heard each night, according to the rating service at the time, in an average of 2.4 million homes. Of shows that appeared five nights a week, only *Amos 'n' Andy* had a higher rating that season. Figuring, conservatively, that an average of two and a half people were listening in each of those homes—and radio listening was very much a family activity in those years, especially around dinnertime—that would give the show an audience, five nights a week, of six million, at a time when the population of the United States was only 128 million, when Thomas' broadcast was not heard in the West and when a quarter of American households still did not own radios.

America's best-selling newspaper, New York's *Daily News*, sold two million copies a day at times in the 1930s, but that still could not compete with Thomas' audience—even figuring, liberally, that two and half people got their hands on each copy of that newspaper. The best-selling magazine in the United States, the *Saturday Evening Post*, was reaching a circulation of a little more than 2.7 million when Thomas went on the air. And those copies probably were each read by two or three people. But newspapers and magazines, to the extent that they can be said to have "voices," each spoke with multiple voices—those of writers, editors and publishers. And the *Saturday Evening Post* appeared only once a week. Walter Winchell, too, was on the radio only once a week, and Edward R. Murrow hosted a daily newscast for only five years.

A kind of intimacy was developing as so many Americans welcomed Lowell's voice into their living rooms after dinner each evening, year after year. He became part of their lives. It helped that he tried to leaven the grimness of the news somewhat by avoiding hysteria: "I have never tried to give my auditors the impression that the world was coming to an end," Thomas would later explain. "Most of my listeners have either been on their way to dinner, at dinner or just leaving the table. And I have always felt that it was part of my solemn responsibility not to make digestion more difficult for my fellow countrymen." It helped that he was always on the lookout for humor and was known for occasionally succumbing to giggles or even laughter himself—live, on the air, often when Prosper Buranelli had snuck a double entendre into the script.[24] "In the nine years that I have been doing this daily broadcast," he explained in 1939, "I have tried to make it a rule to end with an item of good news or nonsense." It helped, too, that a decade of lecturing had made Lowell expert at talking to, not at, large numbers of listeners. He might start a story by saying, for example: "I wonder if you saw a paragraph tucked away with today's ship news. . . ."

This relaxed, second-person, assumed familiarity inspired romantic fantasies on the part of some listeners, who were new to the experience of a friendly man's voice regularly showing up in their living rooms. One woman who wrote to him at NBC, for example, said she was trying "to ascertain whether" in his closing "So long . . ." Thomas was "saying a fare-well 'Goodbye' to me or, as I expected, 'I love you.'" There were enough of these letters so that Lowell and his secretaries developed a shorthand for them: they'd scrawl "mash" across the top and then "no reply."

A less creepy intimacy, however, developed between Thomas and the majority of his listeners. Henry Herbert Goddard was a psychologist who had helped introduce intelligence testing to America. "I of course feel very familiar with you," Goddard wrote to Thomas in 1933, "being one of the millions who carry on a conversation with you almost every evening of our lives. Of course it is a somewhat one-sided conversation. . . . But we talk to you just as though you heard. When you say 'Good evening everybody,' Mrs. Goddard always says, 'Good evening Lowell.' You see you are just a member of the family."[25]

And these listeners—members of this new kind of family—came to rely on Lowell's voice. Americans turned to Thomas as the Great Depression deepened and threw more and more of them out of work; when the baby of America's hero, Charles Lindbergh, was kidnapped; as farmlands out West turned to dust; as belligerent, bigoted, anti-democratic forces— "snorting fire"—took power in Europe. As the 1930s marched on, Thomas' show—always alert to developments overseas—featured stories from places like Rome, Berlin, Nuremberg, the Rhineland, Ethiopia, Madrid, Moscow, Shanghai, Austria, Munich, the Sudetenland, Poland and Finland.

If Germany's Adolf Hitler, Italy's Benito Mussolini, Spain's Francisco Franco, Britain's Neville Chamberlain and China's Chiang Kai-Shek were familiar to Americans by the time the fighting started in Europe and Asia, Lowell Thomas and his two newswriters could take some of the credit. Thomas had been broadening the horizons of many more Americans via radio than he had through his travelogues and books. Though this was hardly clear at the time, he had been helping prepare the citizens of the United States for their incredibly costly yet crucial role in the upcoming war.

((•))

Being the nation's most reliable source of information was, to be sure, a somewhat odd role for Lowell, given the on-again, off-again relationship with truth he had displayed at earlier stages in his career.

Thomas writes in his memoir—in one of those accounts that may have improved with the telling—that the Philadelphia commissioner of police, Smedley D. Butler, made a special trip up to New York to caution him: "My boy, you have the ear of America as no one has had it before. Why with a few words, or even an inflection of your voice, you might start a revolution." Lowell was never the most scrupulous of fellows. NBC was often castigating him for sneaking onto the air plugs for products, charitable events and his own side ventures. But, as he himself later put it, "I haven't any revolutionary tendencies."[26] And he did possess a strong sense of what would be irresponsible to say on the air; he did try to use responsibly the undeniable power his voice had been given. Lowell rose to the occasion.

For the most part, in other words, Thomas managed to shoulder this new burden—trust—without stumbling. Not only did he incite no riots or revolution; not only did he level no unforgivable insults and reveal no infuriating biases; but he was caught in no major, irredeemable falsehoods or errors. Indeed, the newsman who had invented an interview with Helen Morton, who had claimed to have dynamited Turkish train tracks with Lawrence of Arabia, who had likely pretended he had been shot after the war in Germany and who had added to his adventure books incidents "drawn from his imagination," began to demonstrate—in his journalism— an increasing reverence for the facts.

Some of this was forced upon him. When millions are listening it becomes much harder to get away with mistakes, let alone fibs or fabrications. "A lot of folks in this country are sticklers for correctness," is how Thomas put it during one of his broadcasts. "So naturally they'll jump on a fellow every time he makes an error, a slip or a bull." When the complaints were addressed to NBC and seemed legitimate, the network often passed them along—sternly. For instance, in one broadcast Lowell made some offhanded and presumably insufficiently researched remark about Washington hotels being crowded. The Hotel Association in Washington protested to someone at the network, who admonished Thomas.[27]

So with that lurking mob of letter writers out there—"trolls," they might be called today—Thomas had no choice but to become something of a stickler for correctness himself. In conversation, when appearing onstage or even in his accounts of his own life, Lowell still succumbed to the itch to embellish. But Thomas came to realize—or was forced to realize—that a newscast was no place to fiddle or fudge.

He did, however, institute a regular feature on his newscast called "Tall Stories." Thomas accepted submissions, which were, since he was always looking to sell everything at least twice, soon collected in a book: *Tall Stories: The Rise and Triumph of the Great American Whopper*. The "whopper the radio audience acclaimed as the most shameless of all," Thomas noted, was attributed to one Merle T. Sanders of Ashland, Kentucky. (And, yes, there was a person by that name in that town at the time.) It involved a very large fish with one red eye and one green eye that Mr. Sanders says he and a friend spotted lurking in a deep hole in a trout stream. This fish had an ingenious way of feeding himself:

> He would lie there and close his green eye and keep his red eye wide open. The smaller fish traveling downstream, upon seeing the red eye, would stop and wait. . . . Then the big fish would close his red eye and open his green eye. The moment the swarm of smaller fish saw the lights change they would dart forward in a wild rush. And the big fish would open his mouth and swallow hundreds of them.

"Tall Stories" became a popular feature on his show, and it demonstrated, no doubt, that Lowell had not lost his Hechtian delight in the fabulous. But this feature also indicated that he was now aware that such tales needed to be sufficiently outlandish so they would not be mistaken for news. Thomas could play his role as self-proclaimed "Exalted Giraffe of the Tall Story Club" as long as he separated it from his role as a journalist.[28]

Indeed, by the mid-1930s Lowell Thomas probably qualified as the first journalist to deserve the title that would be bestowed upon Walter Cronkite a few decades later: Most Trusted Man in America. Trust became part of his legacy. Broadcast journalists would have felt the same pressures he felt to be accurate on the air. They probably didn't require his example. But they had it—and his example was large and influential. Lowell Thomas actually deserves credit for demonstrating to the radio and television journalists who had listened to him, or who had listened to someone who had listened to him, the importance of getting the news right. And this group included just about all of America's radio and television journalists through the start of the twenty-first century.

(((•)))

Thomas also led the way toward another approach to journalism that would become deeply ingrained in American broadcast journalism. This one was less obvious and probably even more consequential. It was the notion that news on the air should be nonpartisan.

The *Literary Digest* had played a role here. It advertised itself in its own pages as providing "impartially gathered information on topics of the day" for "people who want to know both sides of every important question." So the magazine itself was an early devotee of the effort at objectivity. And it is significant that Lowell Thomas had come to radio under their sponsorship. "They wanted me to play it right down the middle," he later recalled, "which was the natural thing for me anyway."[29] It had not been natural or common for most journalists for much of the history of journalism.

After his months with the *Literary Digest* show, a radicalized Floyd Gibbons ended up campaigning for Franklin Roosevelt and later hosting an NBC program championing the work of the Roosevelt administration's National Recovery Administration. On the other side of the spectrum, CBS' Boake Carter regularly engaged in attacks on the Roosevelt administration. "I could have climbed the fence and been neutral," Carter once explained, "but . . . there's no meat in that. Meat is in argument."[30]

Thomas was prone to patriotism, nostalgia, folksiness, puns and a benign irony. He was politically alert and, with the exception of the election of 1916, a lifelong Republican—when the party was progressive and a force for reform, and then when it was not. But Thomas rarely succumbed—on or off the air—to indignation or other strong emotions. His son would later note that he had little taste for derisive gossip: "He was always on the positive side." His daughter-in-law would later observe that, even around the dinner table, he tended to avoid "anything to do with politics and controversial issues."

On the air Thomas prided himself in his ability to leave his listeners guessing as to what he personally believed. He declared himself unwilling to shove his own "half-baked conclusions down anyone's throat." He did not indulge in the "meat" of partisan argument. He was not really, as were Gibbons and Carter, a *commentator*—not, as he once noted, "a pundit." He sometimes called himself "a raconteur, a teller of the day-by-day doings of mankind." But a new word would be invented for him and the thousands who followed on radio and then television: *newscaster*.[31] And while Floyd Gibbons and Boake Carter might be sentences in a volume on the history of broadcast journalism in the United States, Lowell Thomas would be a chapter.

There are other possible places to look for the origin of the belief—more entrenched in the United States than in most other countries—that journalists should not take sides, for this notion that there was a locatable "middle" on political issues and that that's where journalists should "play it." There is evidence of it in some late nineteenth-century American newspapers.[32] Other developments in Thomas' day also made a contribution to the assumption that journalists should be unbiased—notably the federal Radio Act of 1927, which stipulated that stations must provide "equal opportunities to . . . candidates" for public office. This was a long, slow struggle, as transformations in mindsets usually are.

But given the importance of the network newscast and given the unprecedented audience Thomas attracted, the case can be made that the marriage between Lowell Thomas and the *Literary Digest* did as much to further this devotion to balance, to impartiality, in the United States as anything else. Certainly, it helped encourage most of the influential radio and then television journalists who had listened to Lowell Thomas, or who had listened to someone who had listened to Lowell Thomas, to try to "play it right down the middle."

Thomas would later state that he wanted to be remembered as "the man without a message."[33]

((•))

Thomas' new sponsor, the Sun Oil Company—with business interests that could be affected by government policies, run by the conservative Republican Pew family—may have thought it was paying for a different kind of journalism. If Thomas was to continue to practice this nonpartisan variety of journalism, he would now have to fend off his sponsor.

His resolve was rapidly put to the test. Here is a telling pair of examples: First, just two and a half months after the change in sponsors, the sales and advertising manager at Sun Oil passed on to Thomas some thoughts from Mr. J. Howard Pew—the president of the company. (The *New York Times* would later label Pew "ultraconservative in his politics, economics and religion.") Sun Oil's president wanted more stories showing that "business is better." Such stories would obviously reflect well on the current administration—the Hoover administration, a Republican administration. The letter instructed Thomas to pluck from the papers reports of "any worthwhile increase [in] employment or betterment of conditions within an industry."

Then, three years later, Pew's brother, Joseph Newton Pew Jr., another son of the founder of Sun Oil, wrote Thomas himself. This time the complaint—now that President Franklin Roosevelt and the "New Dealers" were in charge—was that there was too much news showing that the economy was improving: "I think it becomes our obvious duty, in our broadcasts, to stop all this false ballyhoo about recovery and carefully censor the news, telling the people the truth and avoiding being taken in by the false and misleading propaganda from Washington." "To Joe," Lowell once quipped, "anyone was an anarchist who was to the left of the pharaohs."

It would be cheering to be able to report that Lowell Thomas instantly rebelled against the Pews' partisan meddling. But Thomas remained more an accommodator than a crusader. Moreover, radio lacked at the time a tradition of resisting sponsor interference—especially since sponsors, or their advertising agencies, were producing the shows. As host of their program, Thomas was on the payroll of the Sun Oil Company; Sun Oil had a deal with NBC for the airtime. He and the company's management often exchanged favors. (Lowell was, for example, able to secure Harry Chase's son a position with the company.) Thomas was, for the most part, pleased with the association. He did not want to cross his bosses. And his own political leanings were decidedly Republican. But Thomas retained the notion, formed in his *Literary Digest* days, that the proper role of the radio newsman was to remain neutral.

Thomas discussed his handling of the interference by Sun Oil in his response to a complaint by one of the Pews, passed on to him near the climax of the 1932 presidential election. Whichever Pew brother it was expressed anger that Thomas had mentioned a poll showing the Democratic candidate, Franklin Delano Roosevelt, well ahead of President Herbert Hoover. Thomas insisted that the poll was reliable and unbiased, and dismissed the charge that mentioning it represented some anti-Hoover tilt on his part:

> Most of the letters of criticism that have come to me, and there haven't been a tenth as many as I've expected, have criticized me for leaning too favorably toward the Republicans. In this they were correct. If I have erred lately, I have erred on that side, knowing that you folks favored the Republican Party. But on the whole I've tried to be impartial.[34]

Actually, it is hard to see pro-Republican bias in Thomas' coverage of this election. During the presidential campaign there were 45 stories mentioning Roosevelt and 55 mentioning Hoover, but Hoover, after all, was president and therefore making news outside the campaign. The Socialist Party candidate, Norman Thomas, even received a few mentions on Lowell Thomas' newscast. The two major candidates were occasionally quoted attacking each other and responding to those attacks. Lowell himself did not attack or praise either of them.

Thomas emphasized that this apparent balance and nonpartisanship were his goals: "I have tried to make it clear many times that in these broadcasts, so far as politics is concerned, I am neutral." And Thomas, even without the support of the *Literary Digest*, was neutral—most of the time, ahead of his time, to the extent that such a thing is even possible.[35]

((•))

In 1933 the where-to-get-the-news problem—solved in the early days of radio news by borrowing from newspapers and their wire services—

suddenly was no longer solved. And Lowell Thomas had a 15-minute news-cast to fill five days a week.

Newspaper publishers had come to realize that radio—able to dissemi-nate news much farther and faster than delivery trucks and newsboys—was actually making off with their customers. Their response was not dissimilar to their response 75 years later when they were confronted with a similar threat from the Internet: they waffled.

Initially, many newspaper publishers had tried to exploit radio themselves—as a way of publicizing their papers by starting radio stations of their own, as an opportunity to attract new readers by providing radio listings. But as radio news programs—in particular one national radio newscast—began building huge audiences, that no longer seemed such a smart idea. Weren't those listings just free advertisements for Lowell Thomas and his ilk? The *New York Times* was one of the newspapers that dropped those listings for a while—in 1932. And why should newspapers permit radio newscasts to use news from their pages—or news provided by the wire services they funded—for free?

After a failed attempt to prevent the networks from relying on United Press or Associated Press reports on election night in 1932, the publish-ers finally organized themselves and did better. "Thus in the late spring of 1933 the networks and most stations"—those not owned by newspapers—"couldn't buy or beg press association news," writes Paul W. White, who was then in charge of news at CBS. Newspapers—from which Thomas and his news writers had previously, as he puts it, "swiped" news (usually with credit)—were now also off-limits. And when an As-sociated Press exclusive somehow found its way onto his show, he could be sure to receive a stern and threatening letter from them. The where-to-get-the-news problem was suddenly acute. Enter an executive named Abe A. Schechter, who had, in the haphazard way such things happen in a brand-new industry, stumbled into the role of news director at NBC. NBC had in Lowell Thomas, Schechter explained, "a million-dollar voice" without "a nickel's worth of news." Schechter set about scroung-ing some up.

Looking back on this ban on the use of wires and newspapers, Thomas later recalled, "They thought it would be the end of me. Instead, they merely put new life into what we were doing. Abe set up telephones in the hall, and after we'd read the New York papers and seen the stories we wanted, he would call" whomever was mentioned or quoted in the story "to get it direct. . . . It personalized the whole broadcast and made it stronger than ever before."

When, for example, "early in 1934 the notorious John Dillinger escaped from the jail at Crown Point, Indiana," Schechter explains, he immediately telephoned the sheriff—a woman. "This is the office of Lowell Thomas in the National Broadcasting Company," Schechter announced. And "she was thrilled when I told her that a few hours later she would be able to hear Lowell Thomas tell the story she had just told me." CBS, meanwhile, organized its own news service under Paul White.

This burst of enterprising journalism on the part of the competition was not what newspaper publishers had been trying to accomplish. They sued for peace, and eventually a Press-Radio Bureau was organized to supply the networks with news from the wire services. Still, to keep the newspapers from getting scooped, there were restrictions on when that news, and how much of it, could be broadcast. As a consequence new, unrestricted services popped up specifically to feed radio newscasts. The newspapers eventually were forced to cave in and make news from their wire services fully available—for a price—for broadcast.[36]

Radio news grew stronger.

((•))

Lowell Thomas did not have the highest-rated daily newscast on the radio every year. H. V. Kaltenborn, now airing his own daily show, sometimes nosed him out. Occasionally Murrow or even Boake Carter beat him, but their shows came and went. During the 1932–33 radio season, according to radio historian Jim Ramsburg, Thomas began a streak that has never been matched: for 13 years his newscast—competing with prime-time entertainment programs, most of which appeared only once a week—was among the top ten shows on the radio for the year *every* weeknight.[37]

And by the 1938–39 radio season, Thomas' newscast was attracting a larger audience than *Amos 'n' Andy*.[38] Tuning in to Lowell Thomas had become a ritual—often a solemn one—in all kinds of American homes:

- Doris Allen, who became an educator and politician, grew up on a farm in upstate New York. "With the advent of rural electrification, the family got a radio," a book that profiles her reports. "They listened to Lowell Thomas every evening. Politics and current events were discussed around the dinner table."

- "My father never missed that radio program," recalls Perry Edward Gross, a physician who grew up in Jeannette, Pennsylvania. His father owned a couple of grocery stores. "Lowell Thomas was his hero. My father would say that Lowell Thomas wouldn't broadcast the news if he didn't have proof. We could talk before and after the program and tell everything about our school day, but we could not talk during the program."
- "I used to listen to Lowell Thomas every evening at 6:45 before going up to Mr. Dole's to do my evening barn chores," writes Tom Shultz in a memoir about his New Hampshire childhood.
- "All conversation came to a halt at precisely 6:45 when Lowell Thomas and the news boomed from a Zenith radio that was a basic fixture in every dining room we inhabited," Burton Bernstein recalls of his well-to-do family in Boston in the 1930s. "My mother or the maid usually brought dessert in from the kitchen just as Lowell Thomas was saying, 'So long until tomorrow.'"[39]

10.

≡≡≡

The Voice of God

owell Thomas soon attracted the attention of a different but equally youthful medium, which was also beginning to dabble in journalism and trying to find its voice.

A few newsreel companies had been distributing silent footage of news events to movie theaters in the second and third decades of the twentieth century. But there aren't many such events that make a lot of sense without sound. With the exception of brief onscreen titles in these silent films, journalists were deprived of their most important tool: language.

Then, starting in the mid-1920s, the motion-picture studios began experimenting with "talkies." William Fox was among those who thought newsreels were where sound might be of most value. Fox's studio had purchased a system that enabled sound to be recorded directly onto the film. That made its system, dubbed "Movietone," easier to use outside a movie studio—i.e., at the scene of a news event—than those of some of its competitors. In 1927 Fox scored a journalistic, cinematic and commercial triumph: the studio captured the sounds as well as the sights of Charles Lindbergh taking off on his flight across the Atlantic and then being welcomed home. This was just before *The Jazz Singer*, featuring Al Jolson, demonstrated that sound was to be not just a gimmick but a necessity in all kinds of movies. Fox Movietone News soon dominated the newsreel business.

Not that this studio, or any other, had much of an idea of what sound might add to filmed news. New forms of communication do not arrive with instruction manuals. Events obviously could now be heard as well as seen: the sound of Lindbergh's plane, the noise of the crowd. Speeches were a natural: President Calvin Coolidge welcoming Lindbergh, Lindbergh thanking the president. And those early Fox Movietone newsreels reveled in any vaguely newsworthy event that featured music: a marching band at West Point, a visit by the Vatican Choir.[1]

But the idea was slow to arrive that sound might be used to allow journalists to do with moving images what they had long done in print and were beginning to do on the radio: recount, explain, comment upon. Those painfully circumscribed onscreen titles continued appearing in newsreels with sound even into the 1930s. But gradually they began being replaced by a new sound: the voice of a narrator—generally not seen in the picture, often full of facts, even pretending to omniscience, sometimes eager to share an anecdote or a chuckle.

Now, in recent decades the use of this detached narrative voice in documentaries and video journalism—"the voice of God," it is sometimes called—has often been disparaged. Its critics have dismissed it as condescending, pedantic, pretentious or artificial. They have noted how often the narrating was being done by someone white, male and disconnected from the story. Documentary filmmakers and video journalists have found clever means of abandoning narration—of letting their subjects speak for themselves, of showing, not telling. *Cinéma vérité*, as this is called, has enjoyed an extended vogue.

Nonetheless, film journalism was in significant ways handicapped before it could do more than point or say, "Look!" It was often uncommunicative—dumb—or limited to the most easily understood occurrences. Most stories cannot be told, most situations cannot be analyzed, just with sights and their sounds.

Narration began being added to newsreels in the United States in the 1930s. And Lowell Thomas had much to offer this new medium. Not only did he have a voice now as well known, thanks to his radio newscast, as that of any other American journalist. Thanks to his travelogues, he had as much expertise in speaking while film rolled—in narrating—as anyone.

In 1932, while still doing his daily radio broadcasts, Thomas was hired as the editor and narrator for a new newsreel company, American News-reel. "To the ends of the earth we are going," Thomas promised in a promo for this new enterprise, "so that you may watch with your own eyes the most fascinating spectacle on earth—the day-by-day history of you and your fel-low men." The idea was to challenge Fox Movietone and the handful of other major players in the field.

That challenge fizzled—after some fanfare but apparently without any newsreels actually being distributed. Thomas did deploy his increasingly in-demand voice as the narrator of a number of films that actually found their way to theaters in the early 1930s, ranging from short travel features for Warner Bros. and others to two full-length (sort of) nonfiction movies for Columbia, in which Lowell had a larger involvement: *The Blonde Cap-tive* ("she chose to remain with her primitive mate") and the probably even more embarrassing *Mussolini Speaks*, reporting respectfully on the Italian dictator's supposed invigoration of the Italian economy. The former had some box-office success. Thomas received the following unambiguous letter from a Columbia executive about the latter: "MUSSOLINI SPEAKS is dying everywhere in the box office. We want no more pictures like it."[2]

Lowell's film career was no threat to his radio career—yet.

((•))

In the fall of 1932, Lowell and Fran surrendered their large Manhattan apartment in favor of a suite at the new incarnation of what was arguably the city's, if not the world's, "grandest" hotel. This much larger version of the Waldorf Astoria had opened the previous year.

"Don't worry about my having my head turned because we might live at the Waldorf," Fran assures her mother. "If my head was to be turned, it would have gone over long ago." Anyway, she adds, Lowell had secured a suite at a discount because of the publicity he could bring. "It's such fun," Fran also notes, "not keeping house"—or not keeping a second house. Their little family was now holed up most school nights in three "light and airy" rooms on the twenty-fifth floor of the hotel, with a hot plate but no kitchen. There wouldn't be all that much cooking going on there anyway: when they were in the city, Lowell and Fran—sometimes together, some-times separately—were out most evenings. It was a glamorous life.

Over one not-atypical stretch of winter days in 1933, they began by at-tending "a tremendous affair" for the woman who would soon be the new

First Lady, Eleanor Roosevelt. "After hearing her speak, she rose tremendously in my admiration," Fran acknowledges to her mom. "If only she hadn't such teeth." Fran was particularly impressed that Mrs. Roosevelt "is more than an old-fashioned mother whose job is within four walls." Then it was off to Quaker Hill for a weekend of ice skating, skiing and tobogganing with guests and friends. Lowell and Fran returned to their little flat in the Waldorf in time to attend a large dinner at which President Hoover— defeated but still in office—spoke. "It was his swan song," Fran reports. Next she enjoyed a luncheon with eight of her best lady friends, followed by some rubbers of bridge, her favorite game; then more bridge the next day, along with a matinee—the new Noel Coward play.

Later that winter Fran would cruise down to the Bahamas with Lowell Jr.—just the two of them. She was also practicing on the grand piano Lowell had given her for their anniversary. Fran was an accomplished pianist. And this Denver train conductor's daughter was living the life of a rich, extremely well-connected New York socialite. And she was enjoying it. As for Lowell: He was ever busy—still managing a few out-of-town speaking gigs on the weekends on top of his weeknight radio broadcasts. But with him vim and vigor were rarely in short supply. He sailed along.

It was a good time indeed for their little family. "We are bursting with health and have such fun always," Fran exclaims in a letter to her mother early that summer.[3]

((•))

Franklin Roosevelt was another extraordinarily energetic fellow. His initial months in office—his first "thousand days"—were full of plans and bills and new federal agencies as he attempted to subdue the Depression. Lowell—anxious to get a feel for this new, dynamic administration— arranged to broadcast from Washington for a week in April 1933. This radio newsman, who on his first visit to Washington had brashly and incorrectly assumed he might meet with President Wilson, now possessed sufficient stature so that while there he was able to meet with President Roosevelt—twice.

Four months after his inauguration (which then still took place in March, not January), the new president decided to escape the Washington heat for a sojourn at his estate—Hyde Park on the Hudson River, 90 miles north of New York City. But the Northeast was experiencing a heat wave of its own: on July 31 temperatures near Hyde Park—in these days before air conditioning was common—were flirting with 100.

Given this president's propensity for making news, reporters assigned to cover him had a particular interest in keeping close tabs on him. That meant, as July became August, that almost the entire White House press corps was sweltering, along with some White House staffers, five miles down the road—in Poughkeepsie, New York, which, being more urban, felt even more airless. The heat wave had broken by the weekend, but Poughkeepsie was still unpleasant. That is when Lowell Thomas placed a call to Marvin McIntyre, the White House secretary.

According to Thomas' memoir, he said, "Mac, if some of your flock want to beat the heat for a couple of hours, come on over to Quaker Hill." Quaker Hill was 27 miles east of Poughkeepsie and, being a hill, was usually favored by a breeze. Thomas reports that the entire White House press corps, "plus FDR's four sons and his daughter, Anna," surprised him by showing up that day, Sunday, August 6, 1933. Prohibition would not be repealed until December. Nonetheless, homemade applejack flowed until it was all gone. It was only after an assault on his wine cellar, Thomas maintains, that he got the "inspiration" that everybody should head down to the field for a softball game.

At least that is how his memoir has it. Elsewhere, Lowell had written that the White House crowd had arrived with the express purpose of participating in a softball match and that the idea of challenging the White House "ménage," including those reporters becalmed in Poughkeepsie, originally came from one of his neighbors on Quaker Hill, K. C. Hogate, president of the company that owned the *Wall Street Journal*.

As the *Washington Post* told it the day after this softball showdown on Quaker Hill, the "White House White Hopes"—the press corps, fortified by some Secret Service men and those young Roosevelts—were competing against "Lowell Thomas' Saints and Sinners." As Thomas told it four decades later in his memoir, the White House team, weakened by those reporters, "many of whom hadn't done anything more athletic than climb up a barstool in years," was up against his "Debtors and Creditors," which consisted of farmers and summer people from Quaker Hill (the "Debtors") as well as townspeople and merchants from Pawling (the "Creditors").

The *Washington Post* reported the score as 23 to 8 in favor of the visiting team after seven innings, when the game was called. Thomas' memoir says the home team was ahead 10 to 0 when the game became so lopsided that they ceased keeping score "so players and their spectators alike could concentrate on having the time of their lives watching two grown men sliding into the same base, several brilliant national affairs pundits wandering together under a fly ball until it hit one of them on the head, and an overstuffed columnist swinging so vehemently at a third strike that he popped his belt and went down in a heap, entangled in his own trousers." It is true that expertise in this sport was still undeveloped: the fielders' gloves were flat and floppy, and balls often dribbled off those gloves or off the bats.

We have only Thomas' account of what transpired the next morning: President Roosevelt, he testifies, telephoned and said, "Lowell, how come I wasn't invited to your ball game." In point of fact, the president's agenda that Sunday had included a meeting with his secretary of state, who was staying at Hyde Park and reporting on a crucial international economic conference in London; a luncheon with the governor of New York; and a dinner at the home of Henry Morgenthau Jr., soon to become his secretary of the treasury. But Roosevelt seems genuinely to have regretted missing that softball game on Quaker Hill.[4]

((•))

Few technological innovations have seemed touched as much by magic as the transmission of moving images through the air into people's homes. Nonetheless, after radio and sound film had debuted, it did not require that large a leap to imagine that such a trick—"television," it was already being called—might actually be performed.

A primitive electronic system capable of accomplishing it was first demonstrated by 21-year-old Philo Farnsworth in 1927. Forty-one-year-old Lowell Thomas wrote an article entitled "A Dream of Television" in 1933, when he and news were still new to radio and film. In that piece—based on an interview with a television savant—Lowell contemplates a world in which "television sets become as numerous in the land as radio sets are now."[5]

They would, of course. And Lowell's face would be among the first to appear on them.

((•))

But first Fox Movietone News came calling. In 1934 Lowell was asked to serve as "chief commentator" for the rapidly growing newsreel producer. Movietone News—which became part of a new amalgam, Twentieth Century-Fox, in 1935—would soon have 100 cameramen on staff, stationed in 51 countries, producing films that would themselves be seen in 47 countries and translated into more than a dozen languages. Two separate sets of these newsreels were shown in theaters in the United States each week. Fox Movietone News dubbed itself—probably accurately—the "mightiest of all" newsreels.

Other Movietone News "commentators" in the United States were relegated to specialized roles: describing sports, women's fashion or "novelties," for example. Thomas introduced the entire newsreel on screen, and also served as "announcer"—a title he felt underplayed his journalistic contributions—for some of the segments. Occasionally he conducted interviews on camera. He—or, more often, Prosper Buranelli—wrote his staccato scripts. Here he reports on the use of balloons in Britain's defense against German bombers: "A plane shoots down a balloon. Burst of flame from the gas bag. The barrage balloons are effective in checking air attacks. So the Nazi pilots go after them."

Lowell Thomas was now the leading face and narrative voice of probably the leading producer of motion-picture news. For American moviegoers in the 1930s and 1940s, his would be the prototypical "voice of God."

Thomas was already well known when he joined Fox. That is one reason they hired him. A newspaper in 1937 included this headline: "Lowell Thomas Greatly Responsible for Success of New Fox Movietone News." As one newsreel historian puts it, Fox Movietone was allying itself with "the most prestigious of all the vocal hosts, the famed journalist and radio commentator Lowell Thomas."[6]

And newsreels presented Thomas with more prestige and more fame. In 1936—in a country with about 128 million men, women and children—more than 48 million tickets to movie theaters were sold each week. A newsreel would usually be part of the program. Surely 10 or 15 million people were, therefore, seeing one or both of the installments each week of Thomas' Movietone News. So that must be added to Thomas' already huge radio audience.[7] He was now the top journalist in two relatively new and increasingly dominant media—national media.

Before the 1930s daily news coverage in the United States had mostly leaned—as it did in most of the newspapers for which Lowell had worked—

toward the local. But network radio and newsreels leaned instead toward Washington and the larger world. An activist president like Franklin Roosevelt had helped increase the importance of national news; so did, of course, a depression, and so would, of course, American involvement in a second and even more bloody world war. And in the 1930s and 1940s, this nascent national journalism often looked like this small-boned, dapper man in his forties with a pencil mustache. And it often sounded like this man—trained in public speaking by Dr. Harry Thomas—who had made his way from Colorado to New York.

((•))

The rest of this book, therefore, will tell the story of a genuinely famous person—someone who had been accorded, in some ways, a new variety of fame: cozy, close, quotidian. Thomas had become, as the title of a collection of essays about him would put it, "the stranger everybody knows." Radio and movies could do that.

Individuals—Charles Dickens, Tom Thumb, Sarah Bernhardt, Abraham Lincoln—had certainly achieved fame in the United States before radio and movies. But each of these new forms of communication, let alone both together, could bring to masses of people a previously unattainable familiarity with *the person*—the voice, the face, the mannerisms—of a faraway person. Perhaps a dozen people in the United States were fully accorded this new kind of renown in the 1920s and 1930s, among them Charlie Chaplin, Jack Benny, Bing Crosby, Clark Gable, Shirley Temple and President Franklin Roosevelt.

There certainly were other well-known journalists in the United States in the 1930s: Walter Winchell; Edward R. Murrow, by the end of the decade; the newspaper publisher and media entrepreneur William Randolph Hearst; the influential columnist Walter Lippmann, of whom Frances Thomas was a big fan; Dorothy Thompson, whose weekly radio commentary was popular and, in the lead-up to war, powerful. Hearst was often in the gossip columns; Winchell was the top gossip columnist. However, it is possible—taking into account both radio and newsreels—that Lowell Thomas was the only journalist who belonged on this very short list of those who experienced this new, more intimate fame at its most intense.

And Lowell was not one of those who moaned about the wages of fame. He took pleasure in the buzz that inevitably accompanied his entrance into a room, in the individuals—usually not rich and not famous—who were thrilled to talk with him, in the opportunity to regale those people and those rooms with his stories. He had no complaint about people recognizing him and coming up to him on the street. A neighborhood kid whom Lowell brought into the film business, James Morrison, notes that while most celebrities "are very guarded" in public, "Lowell loved to share his fame."

Dallas Townsend, who would go on to a distinguished career in radio news himself, was a student taking tickets at a Columbia University football game when he saw and accosted Lowell. He received in return the special greeting Lowell reserved for, well, everybody: "He reached out his hand and grabbed mine in that powerful grip of his, and he said, 'Hello, young fellow. How are you?'" Tens of thousands of Americans could claim a memory of such a firm handshake, a "where-you-from" and, likely as not, a longer-than-expected conversation with Lowell Thomas. It was invariably a cherished memory. Decades later, Townsend referred to his version of that encounter while presenting Thomas with an award. "How can you remember a thing like that?" Lowell asked him. And Townsend replied, "Lowell, how could I forget."[8]

Being a hugely famous person also meant that his access to other major personages—the president of the United States, for example—was pretty much unlimited. Lowell, his common touch notwithstanding, very much enjoyed that too.

((•))

The failure to invite Franklin Roosevelt to Lowell's softball game was rectified the next summer. A second contest between Lowell Thomas' "Saints and Sinners" and the "White Hopes" was organized for Sunday, September 2, 1934—a year and a month after the first. The president was to host game number two, but it was not played on Roosevelt's Hyde Park estate, someone having reminded him that hosting a softball game on the Sabbath might cost votes in the Bible Belt. Instead, a diamond was laid out on a nearby golf course.

Lowell captained and coached his team while sometimes pitching or sharing catching duties with Prosper Buranelli. President Roosevelt's paralysis had not extinguished his enthusiasm for sports. He managed to manage his team from the backseat of his automobile—a convertible. Roosevelt insisted upon convertibles so he could talk to people, or in this case participate in a softball game, without having to exit awkwardly from a car.

The final score: 26 to 25, in favor of the White House squad, though in his memoir Thomas fails to acknowledge the defeat. Most of the major newspapers published an account of the game, with much of the jocularity focused on the president's decision to pull his pitcher, Rexford G. Tugwell—who, although a right-handed pitcher, was one of the most left-wing members of the administration. The *Washington Post* placed the story ("Pitcher Tugwell Yanked . . . By Roosevelt") on its front page.[9]

Lowell and his near-neighbor Franklin Roosevelt never qualified as friends; nonetheless, both seemed to take pleasure in their interactions. The president certainly was aware of Lowell's politics. And Roosevelt knew where he stood when he was on Thomas' turf: Thomas reports that FDR once acknowledged that he "can't get ten votes on Quaker Hill."[10] Lowell had four opportunities to support Franklin Roosevelt for president. He took advantage of none of them. Indeed, in the late 1930s two of the Republicans who ran against FDR—Herbert Hoover and Thomas E. Dewey—became close friends of Lowell's. Moreover, and perhaps of more significance, the president well understood the politics of Thomas' sponsors on the radio: the Sun Oil Company and the family that ran it.

Yet both President Roosevelt and Lowell Thomas enjoyed people—of all classes, politics and persuasions. They treated those they encountered with respect. And their own relationship was relaxed. It helped that they both were masters of banter and other social lubricants. Roosevelt and Thomas also shared an optimism, an ability to shrug off failure. They were easy to work for. They got things done. Oliver Wendell Holmes Jr.'s oft-quoted, if rather condescending, assessment of Roosevelt—"second-class intellect . . . first-class temperament"—could also be applied to Thomas.

Lowell's son once said of his father, "I don't think it was possible to intimidate him." Certainly FDR didn't.[11]

((•))

By the summer of 1934, Lowell had worked out a way to do some of his broadcasts from a studio he built in a barn at his summer place, Clover Brook Farm. He paid the costs of renting a line from there to New York, plus room and board for an engineer to work with him. By the summer 1935, that engineer was up on Quaker Hill on Thursdays and Fridays, giving Lowell four-day weekends in the country. His work for Fox Movie-tone News required that Lowell be in the city two evenings a week, but those summer stays would begin to fill all the remaining time.

And soon, in the winter, Lowell engineered a way to broadcast from ski areas: "He always performed his evening . . . news broadcast from wher-ever we were," recalled Ted Lamont, the son of one skiing buddy. Lamont's father used to hold up cards specifying how much of the 15 minutes were left. "My father asked Lowell if he couldn't skip a broadcast every now and then when he was on the road, to avoid the extra expense and effort of put-ting on the show away from the studio. Lowell replied that he would never do such a thing. Some of his listeners might turn the dial to another station."

These were not the first remote radio broadcasts: In fact, Floyd Gibbons had, as usual, been there first. He had managed to cover the landing of a German zeppelin live, using a "one-man radio transmitter" in 1929. But Thomas' remotes were among the earliest in radio. And one evening he even managed to broadcast his newscast from an airplane circling the then-still-new Empire State Building—with Lowell Jr. along for the ride and Fran watching from the window of the Waldorf.

When on Quaker Hill, the Thomases were invariably entertaining, of-ten on a large scale. "We fed eighty people here last week," Frances Thomas informed a food writer. Former president Herbert Hoover—perhaps the most illustrious Quaker Hill habitué—first sampled the Clover Brook cuisine on October 24, 1937. The connection was made by one of Lowell's acquaintances, Samuel F. Pryor Jr., a member of the Republican National Committee. President Hoover had been staying with Pryor at his house in Greenwich, Connecticut, and Thomas had joined them for dinner the previ-ous evening. Lowell's effort to persuade the former president to trek up to Quaker Hill for dinner the next evening undoubtedly was helped by the fact that Hoover had a major radio address to prepare. Who better to advise him?

There would be many more such dinners—often hosted by Thomas, sometimes hosted by Hoover—supplemented by lunches and fishing ex-cursions. (Prosper Buranelli became a favorite fishing companion of the former president's.) Hoover would even invite Thomas to join his own section of the alpha-males-only Bohemian Club, which held "encamp-ments" every summer in a redwood grove north of San Francisco. Every Republican president since Coolidge has frequented Bohemian Grove, where men drink, engage in arcane rituals and often—as has been much remarked upon—urinate against large trees.[12]

Sam Pryor, who would in time join the Bohemian Club himself, was also executive vice president of Pan American Airways, the largest U.S. international carrier, and a close friend of the world's most famous aviator, Charles Lindbergh. But Pryor's connection was of no use to Lowell there. Despite Lowell's intense interest in and long experience with aviation, Lindbergh was one celebrity he could not lure up to Quaker Hill. It might not have helped that Lowell was among those journalists who built audiences with coverage of the kidnapping of Lindbergh's baby in 1932 and then the trial of the man convicted in 1935 of murdering the baby. But Lindbergh, like Lawrence, was also at heart a private man with an intense and not always cheery inner life. (When his invitation to Bohemian Grove arrived, Lindbergh declined.)[13] Such individuals were sometimes put off by Thomas, a master of the outer life, and his relentless dynamism.

Nonetheless, with both the current and previous presidents of the United States putting in periodic appearances, Quaker Hill was not devoid of somebodies. And most of them had been enticed by the hill's resident radio and newsreel personality. Lowell also more or less remade the place. "The Hill was in a somnolent state," he later explained. "I didn't wake it up intentionally, but I'm full of surplus vitality."

Lowell had, to begin with, established a network of bridle paths, so those born in Colorado or otherwise familiar with horses could regularly ride them. (The distance between the New York intelligentsia and rural life was shorter then.) Lowell would always have a horse quartered at Clover Brook Farm—sometimes a "frisky" one—as would his wife. One weekend her horse "hit a groundhog hole," she explains to her mother. Fran went flying and ended up "with that high sounding ailment called *concussion*."

Lowell's next project was the softball diamond on the old golf course—upon whose base paths a selection of American notables would stumble, next to which the president of the United States would park.

Lowell installed a rope tow on one of Quaker Hill's sub-hills, so the neighborhood kids and he could ski when it snowed without having to head farther north. Those who grew up on Quaker Hill remember early-morning telephone calls from an excited Lowell reporting that the snow was deep enough for skiing or the ice in the lake thick enough to skate on. James Morrison, who grew up in Pawling, recalls a nighttime phone call from Lowell when the moon was out and the ice good. Lowell and the local kids went for a moonlit skate. "He was fun!" Morrison exclaims.

The Mizzentop Hotel had once been the area's main draw. It was now defunct and decrepit. Once it was finally torn down, much to Lowell's satisfaction, he suggested and arranged the financing for moving one of the more architecturally interesting buildings on the hill, Akin Hall, to the site, adding a Christopher Wren steeple and establishing an interdenominational church there. He set up a friend, Reverend Ralph Conover Lankler, as minister of that church. Lowell was wont to announce to his weekend guests on Saturday night, "There is golf, swimming, horseback riding, fishing, hiking or the opportunity to go to church tomorrow. We usually go to church."[14]

And the improvements he made to his own landholdings included a swimming pool, a radio studio and—oh yes—a fur farm. It is not as if Lowell had grown up herding silver foxes, fitch or mink in Victor, Colorado. In fact he knew nothing about the animals beyond their suitability for expensive coats. But what a fascinating topic of conversation! And why not? He employed a fur farmer. He lost money.[15]

((•))

"A profoundly tragic story has to be told tonight," Lowell Thomas announced at the beginning of his newscast on May 14, 1935. "It's about the serious accident to Lawrence of Arabia that happened late yesterday in England when he crashed his motorbike to avoid hitting a child." Lawrence was in a coma.

In the account of the accident Thomas presented that evening, he emphasized the pain Lawrence—"with his singular hatred for publicity and the limelight of acclaim"—had recently experienced when photographers had assaulted the small cottage in which he had been living. Lowell, though not often vulnerable to remorse, may have been feeling some guilt here, since he, more than anyone else, was responsible for Lawrence's passage from obscurity to paparazzi-attracting fame. T. E. Lawrence died on May 19.[16]

((•))

That summer the annual softball game with the president's team returned to Quaker Hill, where it would remain. It had become more of a celebrity event. President Roosevelt was there in his car, of course. At second base for Lowell's team stood Jack Dempsey—the former heavyweight champion of the world at a time when most could name the heavyweight champion. Dempsey, as the *New York Times* worded it, "proved that he was a boxer and not a baseball player." He scored none of the total of 39 runs. Lowell's team, for a change, accounted for the majority of those runs.

The contest was followed by a largely farm-to-table picnic outside Lowell's home.

((•))

Lowell, loaded with more ambition than he alone could contain, had never quite succeeded in making a writer out of his wife. He did a little better with his sister. Lowell had dispatched Pherbia Thomas on a trip around the world in 1934, ostensibly to collect material for his broadcasts. She handled herself with aplomb and secured some important interviews. Then Pherbia returned with—no surprise—a travelogue of her own. "Her illustrated lecture on Japan," explained the promotional material, "was prepared during six months of intensive travel throughout the Japanese Empire." She delivered it with mixed success (there were some equipment troubles).

Before she left, Pherbia had married Sam Guerin from Tyler, Texas, an oil man whose income seemed to decrease as the number of wells he drilled increased. Texas had not suited her, and the marriage soon ended. Then, at an alumni event for Ohio Wesleyan University, where Pherbia had been president of the student body, she met Raymond Thornburg, a businessman who had also engaged in extensive travels in Asia. They married in 1936, had one daughter, also named Pherbia, and lived the rest of their lives in Lowell's orbit on Quaker Hill, where Lowell and Pherbia's parents, of course, were always regular visitors.

Thornburg, known as "Pinky," co-founded the Pawling Rubber Corporation in 1945. Occasionally, he asked Lowell to help him out with a letter or an appearance—requests Lowell seems never to have refused. Pherbia Sr. settled into the life expected of a well-off, mid-twentieth-century wife and mother; she lectured no more.[17]

The best outlet for Lowell's excess ambitions would eventually prove to be his son.

((•))

Lowell Thomas Jr. was still too young to have a major role in the big soft-ball match on Quaker Hill in the summer of 1936. However, Franklin Roosevelt Jr., who was about to turn 22, made news by executing a triple play, with his father cheering from his convertible. Nonetheless, Lowell's team, now universally referred to in the press as the "Debtors and Cred-itors," again gained the victory. The event made the front page of the *New York Times* that year.

Softball was a relatively new sport then, first played in 1887, when a man named George Hancock from Chicago is said to have corseted a box-ing glove so that it could serve as a ball. The columnist Westbrook Pegler, in joking about why he had turned down an invitation to join Lowell's team, had dismissed the sport as "bean bag." And the *New York Times* was still informing its readers that "the game" in question was "so-called 'soft ball' with ten men to a side."

The next year Lowell himself felt called upon to defend and explain the sport—with which he was increasingly becoming associated—in a news-paper article: "To begin with the term 'softball' is a misnomer. The globule, pill, apple—call it what you will—is almost as hard as the one used in baseball. But it is larger. . . ." And, inevitably, Lowell would slap together that explanation, plus "the official playing rules" and lots of celebrity an-ecdotes and photos, into yet another quickie book—with a co-author, also inevitably, responsible for most of the slapping-together.

In 1937 Gene Tunney, another former heavyweight boxing champion, pitched without much success for Lowell's team, now renamed the "Nine Old Men"—an appellation borrowed from an insult the president's sup-porters had leveled against the Supreme Court. Westbrook Pegler, suddenly a "bean bag" aficionado himself, caught Tunney's underhand pitches. A crowd of several hundred gathered to watch this installment of the annual Roosevelt v. Thomas match—a big win for the White House side.

Lowell's "Nine Old Men" were by then also playing games for charity against other teams around the metropolitan area. In a memorable game in Oyster Bay in 1937, the best-known sports star of the era pitched and batted for Lowell's team. Against a team organized by Colonel Theodore Roosevelt, son of the former president, Babe Ruth doubled, did not homer and, in an at bat that would be treasured by softball enthusiasts, struck out.[18]

((•))

With the old Quaker Hill golf course having been sacrificed to a soft-ball diamond, Lowell—in his role of community organizer as well as golf aficionado—set about creating a new one. To design a new nine-hole golf course for Quaker Hill, he secured the most respected architect in that field, Robert Trent Jones.

A converted nineteenth-century barn became the clubhouse for that golf course and, therefore, for the Quaker Hill Country Club. It doubled as Quaker Hill's community center and featured what qualifies as one of the grandest of Lowell's creations: his "History of Civilization Fireplace." What was impressive was not the space for a fire but the 30-foot-high, 20-foot-wide wall in which it was embedded. That wall was composed of 220 foot-square cement blocks. Lowell's plan was to gradually replace the blocks with artifacts from around the world illustrating humankind's history.

He asked his friends for help assembling artifacts. He mentioned the project on the radio. He sent letters and made requests. Stuff—perhaps the ultimate souvenir collection (most of which you would be arrested for making off with today)—began to arrive: a piece of the Taj Mahal, a marble Buddha, an Inca stone, a block from the Great Wall of China, a small chunk of the Great Pyramid, a part of the ancient wall of Jericho. (This being a Lowell production, standards of verification were not high.) When he was in Moscow, Lowell wheedled a brick from the Kremlin himself.

The wall climbed in more or less chronological order, with the most recent pieces—from the Golden Gate Bridge and the Empire State Building—at the top. Some of the artifacts all the way at the bottom predated history and civilization: "flints used by cave men" and a Cro-Magnon stone lamp. One, supplied by former president Herbert Hoover, who had training in geology, predated humankind: a 500-million-year-old block of gneiss.

As an inscription for the center of the fireplace Lowell reproduced a Sanskrit proverb. It did not provide much insight into this grand monument to the world around which he loved to travel or the chutzpah that enabled Lowell to construct it. But it did capture an element of his philosophy: "He who allows his day to pass by without practicing generosity and enjoying life's pleasures is like a blacksmith's bellows—he breathes but does not live."[19]

((•))

Lowell—always with much to get accomplished—tried to use his time, as in his journalism he tried to use his experiences, for more than one purpose. He employed two secretaries, one of whom was the daughter of his mink farmer. This was the ever-protective Electra Ward, with whom Lowell formed another of those relationships that would be severed only by death (his, in this case). Lowell even played a role in her marriage to one of his engineers, Gene Nicks. The secretaries took shorthand, and one would always accompany him on the 8:30 a.m. train from Pawling into Grand Central, or while making that commute in an automobile, or in the taxis he rode from the Waldorf to NBC or to Fox Movietone News. Thus he handled his voluminous correspondence—conscientiously.

Lowell had been "raised" into a lodge of the secretive Freemasons, of whom he rarely spoke, in 1927. But he accumulated many other more public affiliations. One afternoon a week he could be found at the Dutch Treat Club, where he could simultaneously eat lunch and hobnob with New York's artistic and intellectual elite. On another afternoon he attended a luncheon with the media elite at the Advertising Club, at which Thomas for many years presided and of which Thomas, in his spare time, served as president. And he would, as much as anyone, chart the course of the Explorers Club—dear to his heart even during a period in his life when he wasn't doing much exploring.[20]

A secretary, of course, would also accompany Lowell on his trips back out to Quaker Hill, another place where he could accomplish multiple purposes: relax (if such a frenetic schedule of leisurely pursuits qualified as relaxing), enjoy himself and hang out with a cluster of accomplished and interesting folk. Lowell brought dozens and dozens of such luminaries up as his guests on weekends. Some others already summered there. And Lowell had already begun insinuating the idea of rusticating on Quaker Hill into the heads of some of the many additional distinguished and lively folk he encountered as he made his rounds in the city.

But there was trouble in paradise. Fred F. French, a builder and real estate developer, had accumulated 2,500 acres on Quaker Hill. His estate surrounded the local, 60-acre lake and encompassed a number of homes, among them French's own 30-room mansion, Hammersley Hill. That made French, who was said to have spent $1.5 million assembling this estate, the largest landowner on Quaker Hill. But Fred French, who had been hit hard by the Depression, died suddenly of a heart attack in 1936. And the word was that his wife was ready to sell. The likely buyer was, as word also had it, a developer eager to subdivide the estate into sites for rows of cheap summer cabins. That, Lowell feared, would ruin the sylvan retreat for the accomplished and interesting he was busy fashioning.

So he tried to convince his neighbors to chip in to buy the French estate. When that failed, Lowell, persuaded by his own argument that the future of Quaker Hill was at stake, decided—simply, rashly—to buy the huge French estate himself. But there was a problem here too. Lowell had continued his habit of spending what he earned . . . and then some. He had, in fact, already been investing funds—upon which he had only a tenuous hold—on land to expand his own Quaker Hill estate. Thomas lacked, consequently, anything remotely resembling the necessary cash.

He managed to finance some of the cost of the French estate, with the understanding that he would sell off the homes and some larger plots. Most or all of the down payment, a quarter of a million dollars or so, Thomas borrowed from a friendly corporation: the Pew family's Sun Oil Company.[21] So Lowell Thomas, despite all his successes, was now once again deeply in debt. And that debt was to his sponsor—a company that tried upon occasion to influence the content of his radio newscast.

((•))

Lowell Thomas Jr. had been thoroughly infected by the ski bug and had the advantage of being better at it than his father—as he was at most physical activities. In March 1939 father and son sprinted up to New Hampshire to enjoy the lingering snow.

But for Lowell the younger, now 15, this would be an excursion like most he would take with his dad. When they were in the city, this was a father who might show up in the evening with baseball tickets: the best seats, of course, and likely as not a chance to meet some of the players. But the son could also count on eight or ten of his father's best male friends— longtime or just met that day—being invited along to share the experience. "He always had to have folks with him," his son later recalled, unable to suppress some bitterness. "He couldn't be alone."[22] This time, in order to transport the crowd that would accompany him and his son on this ski trip, Lowell had secured an entire Pullman railroad car.

They were skiing Cannon Mountain, which featured a new aerial tramway—the first used for skiing in North America—along with some of the steeper slopes in the East. Lowell, and particularly Lowell Jr., handled the fast skiing well enough. "I managed to come through the entire weekend with only two spills," the father explains, "but one of those, when I got the steel edge of my ski caught, was a doozy." A young woman who had attached herself to his party, however, fell and then was hit and knocked unconscious by another out-of-control skier. Then Lowell Sr. called the ski patrol for a skier who had broken his leg. Two other unprepared and unwary members of his party took the tram up and spent the rest of the afternoon alternating skiing with falling on the way down. Another hit a tree and broke his leg. There remained, in those days, lots of room for improvement in skiing techniques, skiing equipment and understanding of who should and should not go up in trams.

Lowell always stopped to help. He did what he could. No one would ever accuse him of being unkind or inconsiderate. But he was among those who could handle others' pain. "In spite of all this," he writes Fran with only a little irony, "we had the most gorgeous weekend. The snow was as good as I ever have encountered, and those of us who didn't land in the hospital enjoyed every moment of it."[23]

((•))

"Entertaining is my particular domain," Frances Thomas would tell an interviewer for the *Christian Science Monitor* in 1941. But most of the activities were organized and led by the fellow with all that "surplus vitality." The choice of guests was mostly her husband's. Indeed, the hostess was receding further into the background behind the increasingly well-known host. The spotlight always found Tommy, as his wife persisted in calling him. Upon those nearest to him, he unintentionally but inevitably threw shade. In photos Fran looked, if not older than her years, certainly grayer and plumper than her trim, dapper husband.

"I never know how many people Tommy is going to bring home with him," she admitted to that reporter, "or whether it may be an ex-prime minister, a famous journalist or a little Boy Scout." Fran adds, "Clover Brook is often more like an inn than a private home." In her letters to her mother her amenability sometimes slipped: "There are too many around all the time. I never seem to get a moment's peace." You can feel Fran exhale on the rare weekend when she, her husband and their son are alone— or, more precisely, just with Prosper and a couple of other regulars—in their big house on Quaker Hill.

Fran's authority at Clover Brook Farm did extend to child-rearing. Lowell—not one for domestic battles and not alone with Sonny enough to have much credibility on the subject—was usually willing to leave the matter to his wife. But she remained more committed to not coddling the child—now a teenager—than he. And a decision loomed: where would Sonny go to high school? The upper-class English fashion was to send sons away to boarding school. Maybe Sonny had a chance to express his distaste for this plan on that skiing trip; for Lowell broached the subject at the end of his letter to Fran about that trip: "The more I think about Exeter, Europe and all other such ideas, the keener I am to have Sonny at home with us for the next three years. . . . just as we were with our parents."[24]

Lowell Jr. did go away to boarding school the next fall, but not far: he attended the Taft School, which had been founded in 1890, under the leadership of Horace Dutton Taft, a younger brother of President William Howard Taft. (The school lacked training in elocution—a deficiency that needed to be rectified before Lowell agreed to enroll his son.) The Taft School was located in Watertown, Connecticut, a little more than 30 miles from Quaker Hill. Lowell and Fran had compromised.

((•))

The *New Yorker* would later refer to Quaker Hill as "Lowell Thomas' hand-picked colony." He certainly did not control every house sale there, but Lowell did influence quite of few of them. And now that he owned an additional million and a half dollars worth of Quaker Hill property, paid for with borrowed money, Lowell actually became the seller on a large percentage of those sales. He needed to reduce his debt as quickly as possible by disposing of pieces of the French estate as quickly as possible. So Lowell intensified his efforts to persuade his friends and acquaintances to join him on Quaker Hill.

Quaker Hill was not Southampton or Greenwich or Newport. It was not for the idle rich. Lowell, a world-champion doer, tended to surround himself with folks who were similarly driven and accomplished. "Lowell Thomas . . . more or less sets the social and intellectual pace for the colony," the *New Yorker* added in its discussion of Quaker Hill.[25]

Not all Lowell's recruits were Protestants and internationalist Republicans. Lowell met Charles E. Murphy, for example—a well-connected and politically active Brooklyn lawyer—while trying to maneuver himself closer to the action at the Democratic National Convention in 1932. Murphy's political activities, like those of most politically active Brooklynites, were on behalf of the Democrats. Hence his presence at that convention, where he had some control over who went where. Newsman and gatekeeper hit it off.

And after Thomas bought the French properties, he talked Murphy into renting the largest of them: French's abode, Hammersley Hill. Murphy's son Tom recalls that the place was empty and they had to move their furniture out from Brooklyn for the summer. Murphy and his family purchased their own Quaker Hill home shortly thereafter. It was made of cedar logs.

And while Murphy eventually became New York City's corporation counsel and then a judge, he, unlike Thomas and others of his neighbors and Thomas' guests, was something less than a household name. Murphy made a joke of that—and of the heights some on Quaker Hill had reached— by sometimes introducing himself as a "heroic army officer, profound critic and philosopher, celebrated raconteur, gallant horseman, Olympic champion . . . unaffected by the acclaim universally showered upon him." Despite his lack of excessive profundity and gallantry, Charles Murphy was Lowell's kind of neighbor—successful, unpretentious, fun-loving.

Thomas E. Dewey, then the Manhattan district attorney, had demonstrated unprecedented zeal and effectiveness in busting and convicting racketeers. The Dewey family had previously summered in Tuxedo Park, New York, but he tired of its "manicured existence." (A form of men's evening dress was named after this tony resort.) "That Tuxedo crowd is a bunch of snobs," Dewey informed the *New Yorker*. "I want my children to grow up with farm children."

Lowell had not met him, but when he read that Dewey, his wife and two sons were now planning to summer in Connecticut, Lowell decided that ought to change. According to Dewey's biographer, Richard Norton Smith, Thomas telephoned, reminded Dewey that his political career was not in Connecticut and invited the district attorney out to Quaker Hill. The tour Lowell conducted included views of cows and pigs. Dewey was smitten. Though limited by a government salary, the prosecutor rented a 300-acre farm on Quaker Hill for two summers and then, in 1939, bought it on favorable terms—with a small down payment and the help of a hefty mortgage. "I work like a horse five days and five nights a week," he explained that year, "for the privilege of getting to the country for the weekend." Dewey added considerably to Quaker Hill's store of renown and was definitely of Thomas' political persuasion.

Thomas E. Dewey was ten years younger than Lowell, with a mustache slightly thicker than Lowell's. He took to riding horses in the morning with Lowell. He attended church most Sundays with Lowell. He soon was said to take political advice from Lowell, though Dewey publicly denied it. He clearly did not take Lowell's advice that he have an orthodontist fix "the grand canyon" between his front teeth, but he did work with Lowell on his public speaking: Smith reports that "the two men made recordings of Dewey talking, then played them back countless times"; they were working to give Dewey's voice "a more resonant timbre." Thomas Dewey was elected to the first of his three terms as governor of New York in 1942.

In 1939, according to Smith, Dewey had felt compelled to write Thomas about a "rather ugly rumor." He had heard that applicants for houses on Quaker Hill were being asked about their religion and that an ad for the houses Thomas was selling on the French estate mentioned a preference for "old American stock." Thomas responded that he had fired the realtor, who had been "not diplomatic," and that "nothing was said about demanding a pedigree of prospective purchasers." That was not quite the expression of shock and indignation one might have wanted, though—in late 1930s America—it seemed enough to satisfy Dewey.

James Morrison had worked with Thomas and was the son and brother of doctors in Pawling consulted by Lowell and his family. Thomas did "keep Jews out of the community" on Quaker Hill, Morrison acknowledges. He notes, in fairness, that there was "a difference between pre- and post–World War II attitudes toward Jews" in the United States. Before the war and its horrors, there was an easy and accepted anti-Semitism in numerous corners of American life. Many rose above it; it appears that Thomas did not. He "had a number of friends who were Jews," Morrison told Fred D. Crawford, when Crawford was researching a biography of Thomas. But these were not friends in quite the same way as Murphy or Dewey were Lowell's friends. "He worked with some for a long time, but they would never go to one another's home."

For a few decades, Jews were even scarcer on Quaker Hill than Democrats. And those African Americans who did live up there likely did not own houses and were working for those who did.[26]

On the other side of the ledger, in 1939 Thomas interviewed and championed the cause of Matthew A. Henson, who in 1909, along with Commander Robert E. Peary and four Eskimos, was said to have been the first to reach the North Pole. (Peary's claim has been questioned.) Henson was, in the terminology of the day, "a Negro," which explains why he, as Lowell writes, "remains unrecognized by any geographical body or scientific institute in the land." Thomas was trying to secure Henson the credit he deserved.

And after World War II, Thomas tried to get Lewis Strauss, a Jew and a Republican who held high government positions, admitted to the Bohemian Club, which was under attack for its various discriminatory policies.[27]

((•))

America's first television station, an experimental effort by NBC in New York, went by the rather ungainly call letters W2XBS. In 1930 the station succeeded in projecting through the air an image of Felix the Cat. Things progressed to the point where in April of 1939 W2XBS, with a transmitter atop the Empire State Building, was able to televise a speech by President Roosevelt at the opening of the New York World's Fair. Lowell Thomas appeared on camera doing the news from the World's Fair on May 3, 1939—arguably the country's first television news broadcast. Then, beginning on February 21, 1940, this embryonic television station aired what may have been America's first regular television program, at least the first seen in New York: a 15-minute nightly newscast. (It wasn't on the air every weeknight because W2XBS initially did not broadcast on Mondays.) The host of this first regular television program was Lowell Thomas.

Thomas simply presented his nightly radio broadcast while the cameras and thereby some early adopters in New York watched. His desk and microphone, along with those of his announcer, had been moved to a television studio—equipped with lights much brighter, and two cameras much larger, than those with which we are familiar. Lowell's makeup was also thicker, in order to make his features visible on this ultra-low-definition television. Nonetheless, there was Lowell himself appearing four evenings a week (or fewer if he could manage it) in people's homes as he might appear in a movie theater—except fuzzier, his thin mustache barely discernable.

As tends to happen, the experimenters with this new form of in-home communication—radio broadcasters—did not have much of an idea how to make use of what made it new: the visuals. The *New York Times* noticed:

Mr. Thomas is seen reading the script as the camera alternates from full-face to profile view. His head is down and his eyes on the script. . . .

At times his face is half hidden by the page. Not until he says, "So long until tomorrow," does he look up as if to recognize the televiewers.

Television stations were still supposed to be noncommercial. So Sun Oil presumably went unmentioned while the camera stared. That hardly mattered, given the size of the audience. In May 1940 NBC estimated that there were 3,000 television sets in the New York area.

This first regular television program was gone by August 1, 1940. NBC shut down W2XBS. The Federal Communications Commission had decided not to permit commercial broadcasting on television until broadcasters could agree upon one higher-quality television system. The shutdown was ostensibly for one month so that NBC's station could upgrade to an improved and FCC-approved technology.

Lowell continued to participate in television experiments. In May 1941 he explained global events on an experimental television broadcast into a single movie theater. This time the visuals were somewhat improved: Thomas was seen standing in front of a map.[28] And Thomas, not surprisingly, managed to "author" a book on the subject: *Magic Dials*, which found something to say on both radio and TV.

But his experience on W2XBS had left Lowell with an aversion to attempting another regular newscast on television. Indeed, even before W2XBS suspended broadcasting, Lowell's appearances on the station had grown less frequent. The problem was that TV required those unwieldy lights and cameras and therefore necessitated his presence in a studio in New York. There were other places Lowell preferred: Quaker Hill or ski areas, in particular. "The spirit of wanderlust with which I seem to have been born," he later explained, "was in full rebellion against enslavement to the TV camera."[29]

Even radio, which necessitated his being tethered to an engineer and a line back to New York, had been suppressing the more ambitious manifestations of that wanderlust. That would change.

11.

≡≡≡≡≡

Catching Up with the War

December 7, 1941, was a Sunday. So Lowell Thomas was not on the air to announce that the Japanese had attacked Pearl Harbor, finally hurtling the United States into the Second World War. He was on the air at 6:45 the next evening to report that "only a few minutes after four," President Franklin Roosevelt "signed the resolution declaring that the government and people of the United States were at war with the Japanese Empire." A few minutes later, Thomas added, "On all sides people with knowledge of naval and military matters were warning that this may turn out to be a long, hard battle. The United States and its allies seem certain to win in the long run, but the defeat of Japan and the destruction of her armed power may take time and the largest kind of effort." Germany and Italy declared war on the United States three days later.

One tiny consequence of the war was made clear by the next summer in a note from the commander in chief: "Lowell, I am afraid Hitler has ended our ball games for the duration." The war also froze the progress of television.

It had taken not a month, but almost a year, for NBC's experimental television station in New York to resume broadcasting—this time with a sharper picture and the right to air commercials. WNBT was NBC's new name for its New York television station—the most advanced of a flock of new, Federal Communications Commission–approved television stations in the United States. Thomas showed up to once again read a newscast in front of WNBT's cameras on the evening of July 1, 1941, when television returned to the air—his thin mustache now discernable on the new 525-line, less-low-definition screen. A pyramid of oilcans bearing the name Sunoco was visible behind him. An appearance on the day commercial television began in the United States was thus added to the list of Lowell Thomas' accomplishments.

But Thomas would not be a regular participant in this new round of experiments in television, which ultimately had little impact. Once the United States entered the war, five months after commercial television's debut, the need to produce weapons, radar and such for the military pretty much halted the production of new television sets. So TV's audience remained minuscule. The 22 television stations that had taken to the air in the United States in 1941 could be picked up by a total of fewer than 5,000 sets. Commercial television in the United States was essentially on hold until the end of World War II.

Lowell returned to reading his radio newscasts without makeup, without Klieg lights, without two large television cameras staring at him. So when Thomas announced President Franklin Roosevelt's signing of a declaration of war against Japan, he was on the radio—only.[1]

After Pearl Harbor—with the nation's and the world's fate perhaps as close as they have come to being at stake, with the lives of so many loved ones at risk—audiences for radio news swelled.[2] During the 1941–42 season, Lowell Thomas achieved his best ratings ever. On average 15.6 percent of the total radio households in the United States were listening to his newscast each night—more than were listening to any other show broadcast on multiple nights. Considering that in many homes at quarter to seven in the evening, finishing dinner and chatting still took precedence over turning on the radio, that is impressive. That rating made his one of the top five most-listened-to radio shows of any kind *every* weekday night. And by the 1944 presidential election, 59 percent of Americans would say they received their news primarily from radio—more than twice as many as said newspapers were their main news source. That meant that a large percentage of the population of the United States, rather than getting its news primarily from one of hundreds of newspapers with their dozens of reporters and editors, was getting it from Lowell Thomas. In 1940, according to one poll, 40 percent of Americans who said they had a favorite among all of the radio commentators would say it was Lowell Thomas.

He was now reading the news, again figuring conservatively, to about 11.4 million listeners Monday through Friday.

Walter Cronkite stated that his television newscast, which seems to have been the most-watched daily television newscast ever in America, reached an audience of 22 million Americans. That was in the 1970s and the beginning of the 1980s—when at least 95 percent of U.S. households owned television sets, when the population of the United States was more than half again as large as it was in Thomas' day. Thomas' twice-weekly newsreel audience—interest in newsreels also intensified during the war—is hard to estimate. At one point he claims that it reached 80 million, which seems impossible to justify. But even adding an audience one-fifth that size to his radio audience at the start of the war would mean that the *number* of Americans to whom Thomas was telling the news, let alone the *percentage*, was likely larger than that tuning in to Walter Cronkite decades later.

At its height in 1950, *Life*, probably America's most widely looked-at magazine, reported that its pages were turned each week by one in five Americans aged ten or older.[3] Thomas' daily radio plus twice-weekly newsreel audience at the start of the Second World War was likely closer to one-quarter of all Americans who were old enough to follow the news. The case can be made that no individual before or since has dominated American journalism as did Lowell Thomas in the late 1930s and, in particular, the early 1940s.

((•))

Not that Thomas was satisfied with his role: relaying news of the war from New York. Maybe it was a desire to relive his youth; maybe it was some macho thing; but Lowell wanted to report on the fighting himself. That is where, throughout the history of journalism, reputations were most often made.

And a few reporters had certainly been distinguishing themselves covering events leading up to, during and after the Second World War as Lowell had during and after the First World War. Dorothy Thompson, for example, managed to speak with Hitler in Germany before he came to power. "The interview was difficult," she wrote in *Cosmopolitan* in 1932, "because one cannot carry on a conversation with Adolf Hitler. In every question he seeks for a theme that will set him off . . . ; a hysterical note creeps into his voice[,] which rises sometimes almost to a scream. . . . He bangs the table." Lowell had once been the one getting, or at least saying he had gotten, exclusive interviews with movers, shakers and table-bangers in Germany.

Then, on CBS, Edward R. Murrow began demonstrating that radio—Lowell's own medium—need bow to no other in its ability to capture the drama, horror and opportunity for courage supplied by war, in this case the German bombing of Britain: "Suddenly all the lights crashed off and a blackness fell right to the ground," Murrow intoned. "It grew cold. We covered ourselves with hay. The shrapnel clicked as it hit the concrete road nearby. And still the German bombers came."

Lowell was the great anointer of World War I heroes. Now he had to watch as Ernie Pyle, reporting for the Scripps-Howard newspapers, earned acclaim by focusing on the ordinary experiences and sometimes extraordinary heroism of American soldiers and an otherwise unknown American officer: "I was at the foot of the mule trail the night they brought Captain Waskow's body down . . . ," Pyle typed reverently. "One soldier came and looked down, and he said out loud, 'God damn it.' That's all he said, and then he walked away. Another one came. He said, 'God damn it to hell anyway.' He looked down for a few last moments, and then he turned and left. . . ."

Almost a year after the war ended, John Hersey filled an entire issue of the *New Yorker* with his account of the United States' dropping the atomic bomb on Hiroshima—from the point of view of those on the ground. "He saw the flash," Hersey writes of a doctor who survived. "To him—faced away from the center and looking at his paper—it seemed a brilliant yellow. Startled, he began to rise to his feet. In that moment (he was 1,550 yards from the center), the hospital leaned behind his rising and, with a terrible ripping noise, toppled into the river."[4]

But, of course, to accomplish reporting like this you had to be there. Lowell Thomas, back in New York, had been performing a crucial service—surveying the course of the war: "We hear that the toughest of all the tough battles fought so far in the Pacific is now going on, on the island of Peleliu." Thomas was relied upon as few journalists have been before or since. But there wasn't all that much glory in that.

Thomas' bosses, in truth, did not really want their star newsman off covering the war, occasionally filing narrowly focused stories from one or another obscure place. He was more useful, as his sky-high ratings made clear, sorting out the day's developments every evening. And there are indications that the Roosevelt administration also was pleased to have the war news announced each evening by this familiar, trusted, patriotic (when it came to his country Lowell was anything but objective) and generally optimistic voice: "Good evening, everybody. This is a big day in the history of the Second World War. On this day American troops crossed the German frontier and are tonight fighting on the soil of the fatherland."[5] Thomas may have been too valuable to morale at home to put at risk near the battlefields. Ernie Pyle, after all, was hit by a bullet and killed near Okinawa toward the end of the war.

((•))

In 1940 Lowell Thomas Jr. had enrolled at Dartmouth College. In 1942 he decided to leave Dartmouth, along with a number of his fellow students, to enlist in the Army Air Forces. (This was before the air force was a separate branch of the military.) "To what avail an education if our country goes under," Sonny explained to Mom and Dad, who did not require convincing. Thus the son did something his father, for all his bravado, had never done: signed on, when he was the age for it, to actually participate in the fighting.

Even before enlisting Lowell Jr. had experienced a youth appropriate for the son of Lowell Thomas; indeed, it was a youth contrived by Lowell Thomas. Sonny's childhood had been, of course, overstuffed with rugged activities and accomplished personages, but that was hardly the end of it. At the age of 15, Lowell Jr. had assisted a Fox Movietone cameraman on a circumnavigation of South America—and then managed, yes, to deliver a lecture about the trip. "It was probably pushed along by my dad," he would acknowledge in his own memoir. At the age of 16, Sonny accompanied a mountaineer on a study of Alaskan glaciers. At the age of 17, Sonny joined an explorer on an expedition into the Canadian Rockies.

Sonny did not gripe about all this footstep following. Sonny did not rebel. He was by all accounts a highly companionable, loyal, kind, bright, competent young man. He was not, in contrast to his father, excessively outgoing or aggressive. And by forgoing imprudent introspection and remaining consistently good-natured, Lowell Jr. seems to have made sure that his father—who had difficulty with individuals with turbulent inner lives—had no difficulty with him.

A few months into Sonny's military training, his famous dad came to visit the base and gave the boys a pep talk. "The fight'nest . . . heard in these parts in some time," the local newspaper gushed. But Sonny was unable to attend his father's talk. He was in the hospital. Lowell Jr.'s contribution to his country would not, in the end, extend to combat. While learning to fly, he took sick and spent more than a year in various military hospitals with rheumatic fever. "Join the Army and get sick!" he wrote his parents. "Kind of humiliating."

Meanwhile, his tireless father was coming up with schemes for getting closer to the action. "Great news dad about your possible jaunt to North Africa," Sonny writes him in a paragraph that reveals how hard it must have been to compete with him. "I envy you! But don't get too close to enemy fire and planes. Leave at least that much for me someday." After he recovered, Sonny ended the war training French pilots in Georgia. He got nowhere near enemy fire or planes.[6]

((•))

His parents had moved their Manhattan residence from the Waldorf to a more substantial apartment in the Hampshire House on Central Park South. But Quaker Hill remained the center of their lives. And Lowell Sr. continued populating it with high achievers—mostly of a certain cast.

In the summer of 1943, he rented one of the houses he was still sitting on to the entrepreneurial minister of the Marble Collegiate Church in Manhattan, Norman Vincent Peale—a Protestant, a Republican. Peale and his wife soon borrowed enough money to buy a farm of their own up on Quaker Hill.[7] Nine years later Peale would publish his hugely successful conflation of easygoing Christianity and dogged optimism, *The Power of Positive Thinking.* Dale Carnegie's self-help blockbuster, *How to Win Friends and Influence People,* had first been published in 1936, with an introduction by Lowell Thomas. So pals of Lowell, who was relentlessly positive and a master of befriending and influencing, were responsible for the foremost self-help books of the age.

While Lowell Sr. pined on Quaker Hill for a chance to gain some proximity to action—his plan to cover the fighting in North Africa did not pan out—he convinced himself that, as he puts it in his memoir, "this wonderful place with its fine facilities could be put to use." So he marshaled some of that positive thinking and ability to influence people and brought Quaker Hill—actually, nearby Pawling—into the war effort.

Lowell found an empty boys' school, along with an unused farm, with cottages on a lake, owned by an electric company. He met in Washington with an old acquaintance, General Henry "Hap" Arnold, then heading the Army Air Forces. As a result of Lowell's efforts, early in 1944 the Army Air Forces Convalescence Center would open in Pawling—to provide soldiers just out of the hospital with physical and psychological rehabilitation. These soldiers had the added benefit of access to Lowell's horseback-riding trails, his little ski area and a Saturday-morning speaker series he arranged just for them. "There is very little 'dead time' at Pawling," a *Washington Post* article explained about the center and its new, more aggressive approach to rehabilitation. That article does not mention Lowell Thomas. But that, of course, was a very Lowell-like approach.[8]

(((•)))

In 1941—before Pearl Harbor was bombed but with the possibility looming that the United States would be pulled into the war—President Franklin Roosevelt had explained the principles for which we might have to fight: "We look forward," he said in his State of the Union address to Congress, "to a world," the "very antithesis" of that "the dictators seek to create," that would be "founded upon four essential human freedoms." They were: "freedom of speech," "freedom of worship," "freedom from want" and "freedom from fear." Some conservatives at the time found Roosevelt's "Four Freedoms"—like most of what this president did and said—infuriating.

Republican Senator Robert A. Taft, an isolationist, insisted that "war will never spread such freedoms" and moaned that such talk, which seemed to imagine a "Utopia," was "too visionary." The novelist Ayn Rand, a champion of unfettered free enterprise, wrote in 1941 that "talk about freedom (even four freedoms)" by members of the left ("pinks," she calls them) is just "an old, old trick" to hide their "subversive" purposes. Rand's sometime ally, the writer Channing Pollock, blasted Roosevelt's "preposterous and impossible 'Four Freedoms' of slaves and convicts."

And then, in a letter dated June 8, 1943, Thomas received this "caution" from his primary contact at Sun Oil, Max Leister: "Without going into any detail, I am going to ask you to refrain from making any mention of the

'Four Freedoms.'" The main attempt by the president of the United States to explain what the country was fighting for in this war could, in other words, no longer be mentioned on the country's leading newscast.

Evidence, if there had been any doubt, that this directive could be traced to J. Howard Pew, president of Sun Oil, arrived in a letter from Mr. Pew three days later. The letter was friendly, congratulating Thomas on the quality of his broadcast and its great popularity. But it also included Pew's rewrite of the "Four Freedoms" as: "Freedom of Speech, Freedom in News, Freedom of Choice, Freedom of Enterprise." Pew had, not surprisingly, excised from Roosevelt's original list "freedom from want"—which sounded "socialistic" to the right, like a global New Deal. And it certainly made sense that Pew had added "Freedom of Enterprise," given the regularity with which he decried government interference in business. But, of course, Franklin Roosevelt, not J. Howard Pew, was president of the United States.

Once again there is no evidence that Lowell rebelled against such dictates from his sponsor. The arrangement under which he broadcast was still the same: Sun Oil purchased airtime from the radio network. Thomas worked for the Sun Oil Company; indeed, he was its highest-salaried employee—at $95,645 a year in 1941, more than $30,000 more than the salary earned by each of the Pew brothers (who, of course, in addition owned large amounts of stock in the company). The Pews were his bosses. Lowell had also managed to get himself in debt to Sun Oil for a quarter of a million dollars.

Scribbled in Lowell's handwriting at the bottom of that note from Max Leister, cautioning that he no longer mention the "Four Freedoms" on the radio, is this short sentence: "I told Pros & will tell Louis." Lowell presumably had, in other words, instructed his two newswriters, Prosper Buranelli and Louis Sherwin, to honor Leister's injunction.[9]

Still, it can be reported—once again—that despite his allegiance to the Pew family, and despite their occasional attempts to fiddle with the content of his broadcast, Thomas generally kept playing it somewhere in the vicinity of "down the middle" in his newscast. Roosevelt, who was making so much news, continued to be mentioned with appropriate frequency in Thomas' newscast. His war continued to be championed. The biggest test for Thomas' own impartiality was, however, still to come: when his friend and neighbor became the Republican candidate for president.

(((•)))

Changes, meanwhile, were afoot in network radio and therefore in the arrangements under which Thomas broadcast. A new, activist chairman of the Federal Communications Commission managed to force NBC to divest itself of one of its two networks. On October 12, 1943, the FCC approved the sale of NBC's junior Blue Network—Thomas' network. The Sun Oil Company's program *Lowell Thomas with the News* was now heard, for the moment, on a network called, for the moment, just "BLUE." (It would soon be renamed the American Broadcasting Company, or ABC.)

Then, as of November 1, 1943, Lowell obtained what he had long wanted: a network called "Pacific Blue" contracted to broadcast *Lowell Thomas with the News* in the West. Sun Oil Company, since they did not do business in the West, had agreed to allow a remnant of the old Standard Oil to sponsor the program there. And—in the last of this flurry of changes—Sun Oil moved the eastern broadcast of Thomas' newscast from BLUE back to NBC. As of January 24, 1944, *Lowell Thomas with the News* would be heard in the East on NBC's formally dominant, and now only, network: what was once known as the Red Network.[10]

Thomas was in a stronger position than ever in radio: he was now heard across the country and on the top network in the East. His political significance was also about to peak, for in 1944 New York governor Thomas E. Dewey—Lowell's neighbor, friend and, in some sense, protégé—received the Republican Party's nomination for president.

((•))

Never was playing it "right down the middle" harder for Lowell Thomas than during the 1944 presidential campaign. It wasn't due only to his close friendship with the Republican candidate. Thomas faced even more than the usual pressure from the Pews, who had by this point endured 12 years of what they considered Franklin Roosevelt's anti-business, socialistic, even dictatorial presidency—and sensed that they might have to endure four years more. J. Howard Pew even offered to hire someone to replace Thomas on the air to free him to "plunge into the midst of the . . . presidential battle" at "the eleventh hour"—presumably traveling about giving speeches on behalf of Thomas E. Dewey. Lowell responded that the tiptoeing in he had been doing would probably be more effective than an all-out plunge "for a political amateur (and that's what I'd be if I jumped into it)." Pew's suggestion also would have cost Lowell the reputation for nonpartisanship he had built up over a decade and a half.

When Prosper Buranelli wrote the previous spring that he had been hearing "remarks that the broadcast has an anti-Roosevelt tone and favors Dewey," Lowell took umbrage: "We give the president fantastic publicity every day—and often 3 or 4 stories per broadcast." During the fall campaign, Thomas must have heard enough such complaints himself to feel compelled to answer on the air the "charge" that "I favor Dewey":

> The president in the White House is in such a position that any public statement he makes is news. . . . The opposition candidate on the other hand can only make campaign declarations and arguments. And people warmly in favor of the administration don't consider this news—especially in wartime. But it is news . . . and how can our Constitutional Opposition be heard if it is not considered news.

Looking through the scripts of Thomas' radio program during the fall presidential campaign in 1944, it is indeed difficult to find any sign of pro-Dewey bias. President Roosevelt, often in his role as commander in chief, is mentioned in 81 stories, Governor Dewey in only 36. And once again any attacks or responses to attacks are left to the candidates themselves. Yet when writing to the Pews or their minions, Thomas claimed to have manifested a pro-Dewey slant: "This year, for the first time . . . I have gone completely overboard, and have been the only news broadcaster with a large audience to go all out for the Republican ticket."

I'm not sure Thomas' sense that he was being fair and this statement that he was going "all out for the Republican ticket" are necessarily contradictory. Thomas saw himself as one of the only broadcasters struggling to give the Republican candidate—challenging a popular, activist, wartime incumbent—not equal time but a decent chance to be heard. In this sense he was going "all out." But on the radio Lowell certainly did not descend, as a more overtly partisan journalist might, to invective against the president or encomiums for the challenger.

Off the air—which for Thomas was something different—he clearly did "go all out." He detailed his more-than-just-neighborly support for Tom Dewey in 1944 in a letter to Sun Oil:

- "Repeatedly advised concerning speeches."
- Entertained "the press on a fair-sized scale in the country" in order to ease Dewey's problems with "newspapermen."
- "Loaned my right-hand man, Louis Sherwin, to Governor Dewey to help prepare speeches—this for nearly a year now."

Lowell's contributions to the Republican's campaign were no secret in political and journalistic circles. Occasionally they were even mentioned in the press. "The resonant, well-modulated voice in which Dewey is making his campaign speeches is no accident . . . ," wrote, for example, a gossip columnist in *Newsday* on Long Island. "Tom's Pawling neighbor, Lowell Thomas, took over and trained the Dewey voice. As a result the dulcet Dewey sounds a lot like Thomas." A news article in the *New York Post*, then a liberal newspaper, went further: "Some Pawling people are convinced," the *Post* asserted, "that Thomas, who lives two miles from Dewey's estate, is more responsible than any other person for Dewey's present political eminence."

That was the worst of it. No scandal developed over this journalist's closeness to that politician. After all, the principle that journalists should keep some distance from those they cover had not yet been established. (As late as the early 1960s, some journalists overlooked President John F. Kennedy's appetite for and questionable taste in female friends because they enjoyed being among his male friends.) Lowell, for his part, seems to have remained more concerned that the Pews might think he wasn't doing enough for Dewey than that the rest of the world might think he was doing too much.[11]

((•))

In the spring of 1945, the United States government became interested in having more journalists with large audiences examine the war in Europe. There was good reason for that: after the successful but terribly bloody Normandy landing in June 1944, after the successful but terribly bloody effort to repulse a German offensive in the Battle of the Bulge the next winter, the war seemed to be going well. It might now be looked upon by audiences at home not only with great pride but with true optimism and—the enemy's ability to inflict large numbers of casualties having declined—with less terror. Nothing regularly gathered as large an audience back home as radio.

"Hap" Arnold, head of the Army Air Forces, telephoned Lowell and asked him to join—or, according to Thomas' memoir, lead—a group of "radio news analysts" on a trip to Europe.[12] Sun Oil agreed that Thomas could contribute to his newscast from Europe while substitutes hosted back in New York.

By the beginning of April 1945, Lowell Thomas had made it to London along with a collection of seven other previously homebound radio heavyweights. He contributed his first extended report for his newscast by shortwave radio, from an underground studio in a London just about ready to resume life entirely above ground. The journalists flew on to Paris and Luxembourg. And soon some of them were flying over, and then into, western parts of Germany, which the American and British armies had recently taken. Thomas sometimes left the others behind. On his fifty-third birthday, he was flying across the Rhine.

For the first time in decades, Lowell was keeping a journal. "Well, I've at last caught up with the war," he notes, after managing to "jump from one plane to another" and penetrate deeper into Germany. Often he was scribbling sentences while inside one of those small planes: "Suddenly there's no more traffic on the autobahn. . . . Bridges are down. We see an Amer. Tank on the alert. . . . We are at the front and only a little over 100 miles from Berlin." For the first time in decades, Lowell was racing around, reporting, covering a war.

Lowell toured the destruction on the ground in Wessel: "In most of this large town every bldg. gone; cathedral, churches; 5 & 6 story bldgs.; all just heap of brick & stone & splinters. . . ." Then he saw from the air the destruction of a larger city, Cologne. "I wonder how we can make people understand what has happened," Lowell writes on that excursion. "After other wars that has always been said. But this is diff. Even the destruct. of Carthage could have been nothing compared with this. One has a feeling of wanting to shout to all men not to be so stupid, but that not a strong enuf word. Not so dumb. But that doesn't express it. Not so insane. . . ." Thomas was in philosophical mode; this was not his normal mode. "I wonder just what is the destiny of the human race."

All the while Lowell was looking for shortwave radio transmitters, so he might get his observations on the air—live; there still was no tape. Thomas managed two broadcasts from a mobile transmitter in an apple orchard outside Wiesbaden, after being driven through the black, still city, which, like most in occupied Germany, was under a seven o'clock curfew.

Lowell shared the shock of the American troops when their commander in chief, his old softball buddy, suddenly died on April 12, 1945.

Russian forces were approaching Berlin, and American forces were getting their first, dreadful look at the concentration camps, as Thomas made it on the air on April 20, 1945:

> I am broadcasting tonight from Supreme Allied Army Headquarters. The talk here today—aside from the Russian drive—has centered largely around the topic of the Nazi Murder Camps that have been liberated by the advancing First and Third Armies. General Patton was the first, I believe, to issue an order that as many German civilians, and military people too, as transportation facilities will allow, be taken through these Murder Camps. . . . and [a] British delegation is said to be on the way to Buchenwald, a huge concentration camp that I visited several days ago. In fact, I described what I saw there with my own eyes, in a broadcast from a mobile radio transmitter, and then heard afterward that the short wave signal was bad and that I had failed to get through. . . .

We don't know what Thomas said in that lost broadcast, and we don't have a journal entry in which he describes in detail his visit to Buchenwald. But it does seem odd that in this broadcast, and in some short mentions in his journals, Thomas neglects to note the religious affiliation of many of the victims of this concentration camp. In this he was not alone. Edward R. Murrow's report on Buchenwald, as the Holocaust scholar Peter Novick notes, also fails to use the words "Jew" or "Jewish." And the *New York Times*, in an otherwise thorough and revelatory piece on Buchenwald that appeared two days before Thomas' broadcast, uses more than half of its total of about 2,200 words before it identifies any victim as a "Jew." The Allies—and their journalists—had not yet begun to confront the full horror of such camps: that the Germans had not just viciously punished their opponents but had attempted to exterminate an entire people.

Here is how Thomas' on-air discussion of the Nazi camp ends:

> Apparently there are many Germans who had little knowledge of the crimes the Nazis were committing in these enormous camps, or who had closed their eyes and ears and refused to believe. As witness to this, take the burgomeister and his wife, who visited Buchenwald at Gen-

eral Patton's request, and who saw the gallows where the mass hangings had taken place daily, the torture chambers you no doubt have read or heard about by now, the furnaces, the piles of human bones, yes and the piles of dead. What is more, they saw the eighteen thousand pitiful creatures who are still in that Buchenwald camp, eighteen thousand remaining of the fifty thousand who were jammed into the place shortly before our troops got there. That burgomeister and his wife, loyal Germans, went home so overwhelmed with shame that they killed themselves.[13]

Thomas arranged for a U.S. Army Signal Corps cameraman to shoot film for him while he was at Buchenwald. The footage includes shots of Lowell walking through the camp wearing an officer's peaked cap, shots of German prisoners of war and shots of newly liberated camp survivors, as well as images, which are as disturbing as any from the war, of a truck stacked with the bodies of Holocaust victims.[14]

((•))

Lowell was now—unlike when he was covering the First World War—sufficiently established so that a large public would hear his observations. His huge audience also enjoyed his gentle mockery of military regulations: an army censor, for example, refusing to allow mention of Allied carrier pigeons having been shot down. "Why?" Lowell quips. "Because the nearest of kin haven't yet been notified."

Lowell's fame sometimes, to be sure, made life more comfortable. On at least one occasion, his bunkmate was a general. And his familiar voice and face must have helped him hitch rides on airplanes heading to particularly interesting places. In a broadcast on April 24, 1944, Thomas describes the most newsworthy of those flights, which was not at all comfortable: as the second passenger in "a single-seater fighter plane"—a P-51 Mustang—piloted by Lieutenant Colonel Karl Kraft of Clarks, Louisiana, "with me squeezed in behind Kraft. Piggyback they call it. The most cramped position so far devised by man." Accompanied by another colonel flying another Mustang, they were heading toward Berlin:

The two flying colonels wanted to go as much as I did. They had never made it all the way to Berlin. And they wanted to verify with their own eyes the reports coming in that the Russians, at last, were in Hitler's capital, blasting it to bits.

I had another reason, an unimportant reason, for wanting to get to Berlin in these closing hours of the European end of World War Two. Twenty-seven years ago, at the end of World War One, Webb Waldron— then with *Collier's*, now an editor of the *Readers Digest*— . . . and I were the first from the outside world to get to Berlin, and stay to follow the German revolution and then tell the story. . . .

The plane, with Thomas squeezed in behind Colonel Kraft, reached the Elbe:

We passed over several Nazi airfields with dozens of planes dispersed about them. But none took off to chase us . . . Following the Elbe and then the Mulde north to where the two rivers join at Dessau, we saw fires every mile or so. . . . And then from Dessau, we headed right up the Autobahn for Berlin. . . .

Potsdam and the southern side of the city seemed comparatively undamaged. The rest of it—in flames from one end to the other. We swung in over Berlin at about four thousand feet. Much too low. But we had to because of the heavy cloud layer above us. Below us an artillery duel was going on. Apparently the heavy guns on both sides going all out. Dense clouds of smoke were rolling over Berlin, concealing much of it. . . .

Thomas' radio report was one of the first on the battle for Berlin and was picked up in newspapers back home. He announced that what they were witnessing was the "bombardment and burning of the world's fourth largest city," which he called—speaking figuratively—"Hitler's smoking funeral pyre."[15] In about a week it would be that literally.

((•))

Back in London, where he was preparing to fly home, Lowell made contact with his friend Jimmy Doolittle—former Army stunt flier, leader of a daring air raid on Tokyo, now, as a lieutenant general in the Army Air Forces, undertaking various international missions for the United States during World War II. His latest would be a fact-finding trip from North Africa to

Asia and then across the Pacific to make a report in Washington. "Jimmy said that he was arranging to make this round-the-world trip in a speedy bomber," Lowell later explained. "He said that aside from himself and the crew and one member of his staff there would be room for one more—a place he would hold for me!" Lowell was exhausted after a month racing about Europe . . . but golly! The plan was for Thomas to zip back to the States and then meet up with Doolittle in North Africa to take his seat on that bomber.

"All that would be necessary," Thomas writes, "would be for me, upon arrival in America, to get the okay of General 'Hap' Arnold, the secretary of war, my radio sponsor, the heads of Fox Movietone and my wife." Oh, and it should be noted that this delineation of the tasks in front of Lowell appeared in the draft of a newspaper column. He had, just in case there might occasionally be a free moment in his day, accepted another job: a regular column on the war to be syndicated to American newspapers.

Lowell got the necessary approvals. And after two weeks in the States, he embarked, with a film camera and what would be a very busy portable typewriter, upon a trip around the world—some of which was still at war.

On May 17, 1945, via Newfoundland and the Azores, Lowell flew into Casablanca—a huge Allied air base. Then it was across North Africa in a race to meet up with Jimmy Doolittle, who was supposed to be flying down from England. Three days later Lowell was back in Cairo—from which he had set off, 27 years earlier, for Palestine and later Aqaba. But this time there was a snag: Doolittle and his plane were not there.

"At the moment it's sort of a game of tag around the world," Thomas tells his radio audience from Cairo. "Until I do fly in and find him on some Asiatic flying field, I'll be flying in any plane"—any military plane—"that can take me." Lowell later recalled that another general in Cairo bet him a magnum of champagne that he would never catch Doolittle.

On to Baghdad: but no General Doolittle. Lowell stopped in Aden; the general once again was nowhere to be found. Thomas' second broadcast was from Delhi on May 24. He did not have a rendezvous with General Doolittle to report. Finally, in Calcutta on May 28, Lowell read in the *Times of India* that the swift Lieutenant General James H. Doolittle, whom he had presumably been chasing around the world, had just landed in Washington, DC. Lowell had lost the bet, lost his ride and lost his host and guide. Actually, a book Thomas later co-wrote about Doolittle seems to indicate that the general had canceled that round-the-world trip, flown directly back to the States from London and, before heading to Washington, had been grabbing a little rest in Florida while Lowell was setting off after him.

Anyway, Lowell found himself alone in India—left to his own resources. Fortunately, those resources were formidable and were now topped off by his door-opening, ride-securing renown. So he decided to slow down some and look more closely at the last stages of the war in Asia: would a bloody invasion of Japan be necessary? And he decided to look more closely as well at Asia itself. He had never before been to China.[16]

Lowell managed some more radio broadcasts on this trip. But the bulk of the journalism he produced appeared in the series of syndicated newspaper columns reported and written mostly while Lowell flew from India "over the hump" into China, then to the Philippines, Okinawa, Hawaii and San Francisco, where the new United Nations was getting started. In the *Los Angeles Times*, at least, where I found 42 (!) of them, the columns did not appear for weeks or months after Thomas returned from his trip.

Some of these pieces were small, almost Ernie Pyle–like vignettes: the horseman from Virginia, Colonel Dan Mallon, whose job it was to buy large numbers of Chinese horses—because gasoline for trucks was in short supply; or the marine sergeant and former Virginia Tech running back who "threw himself on" a grenade to save his platoon. One column detailed having met, in China, both a British officer who had been with T. E. Lawrence when he died and a British newsman whose task it had been to tell Lawrence's mother about the fatal motorcycle accident. Thomas got two columns out of an interview with Generalissimo Chiang Kai-shek, in which the Chinese leader stated that "the Chinese Reds were not a major problem."[17]

(((•)))

Many of the syndicated newspaper columns Lowell Thomas produced were essentially travel pieces, reporting on exotic sights and customs—an old and reliable genre for him. One column focused on the Chinese belief that "nothing is more honorable and meritorious than to have aged parents and to display filial piety toward them." Lowell, he reports, had gained respect when speaking with a group in China by noting that his father, "although more than three-score and ten, was still a practicing physician and surgeon," and that both his parents "were still alive."

However, at the end of the next year, Lowell's mother, Harriet M.

Thomas, passed away in Asbury Park, New Jersey, at the age of 77. She died "after a long illness"—as the tiny obituaries in the *New York Times* and *Los Angeles Times* put it. That was, in those days, often a euphemism for cancer.

"Some of my most vivid memories of my mother have religious overtones," Lowell would explain in a letter years later. "After Sunday School, we would hear the minister deliver his sermon. Also every Wednesday evening she would drag me out to prayer meeting. . . . While all this exposure didn't make a 'fundamentalist' out of me, I so admired my mother that I have always had a special regard for all clergymen, missionaries, evangelists and so on."[18] It would soon become clear that this regard extended to Buddhists.

((•))

Lowell's wartime newspaper column was soon permanently retired, and he eased back, for the moment, into Quaker Hill, winter skiing, large-scale entertaining, New York City, unceasing speaking engagements, Fox Movietone, NBC, Sun Oil—his routine.

However, that jam-packed schedule concealed a rather large and, for Lowell, familiar problem: he had once again fallen hugely in debt. In successfully saving Quaker Hill from tacky overdevelopment, Lowell had, in purchasing the vast French holdings himself, undertaken a huge real-estate speculation—one well beyond his means. And his bet had gone bad. Yes, he had sold some homes to various interesting people. But he was not recouping enough by selling land or houses to make much of a dent in the debt he had assumed in buying those lands and houses—especially given the short supply during wartime of construction materials and construction labor, with which he might have engaged in some non-tacky development of his own.

Lowell and Fran finally decided to move themselves into the grand, 30-room unsold French estate, Hammersley Hill; no sense letting it sit empty. They would bid adieu to their beloved Clover Brook Farm. But this was just rearranging the furniture on what had become a financial *Titanic*.

Rescue arrived in the person of a short, chubby man, who would become another member of Lowell's burgeoning associates-for-life club: Frank Smith. Smith, Lowell's new business manager and future partner, had been raised in Jellico, Tennessee, when the distance between such places and New York City remained vast. But his father was a banker, and the young man eventually graduated from Harvard's Graduate School of Business Administration. The distance between Harvard and Wall Street was small. Still, Smith shied away from finance and chose to enter a then relatively new, relatively entrepreneurial business: broadcasting. Lowell met Smith during the war, when Smith's contribution was producing special programming for the war effort and among Lowell's manifold contributions was appearing in one of Smith's programs.

They hit it off. And Lowell's new lawyer—Gerald Dickler, who would become another Lowell lifer—suggested that Smith might just be the financial wizard Lowell had long been searching for: someone who might resuscitate and then stabilize his finances. Lowell offered. Smith—"Smitty," he called him—accepted, and soon established himself as a full-fledged, first-circle friend of Lowell by acquiring a place of his own on Quaker Hill and being invited to join the golf foursome that included Lowell and Tom Dewey.

"It is my considered opinion that no man in the annals of humankind, who had so little interest in gambling, strong drink or fancy women, has ever managed to unload as much money as has LT," Frank Smith concluded. For example, Lowell, or "LT" as his associates increasingly called him, had supplemented the nine-hole Robert Trent Jones–designed golf course on Quaker Hill with 21 holes on his own Hammersley Hill estate, which would include, just for fun, the longest hole in the world: 830 yards, par 7.5. Smith, consequently, had insisted on one condition before agreeing to work with Lowell: the great newsman and Pawling potentate had to agree that he would not write a check without Smith's approval. That was a large concession for a sophisticated and proud man. That was the key to making the whole thing work. And it worked magnificently.

With Lowell's checkbook (more or less) under lock and key, Smith could get around to dealing with the damage produced when it had roamed free. This was a client, after all, who did have a hefty annual income to go along with his debt. Smith's charge was to release Lowell from the shackles of Sun Oil, his main creditor, and the Pew brothers.

Once again, it would be cheering to think that Lowell's gripe with Sun Oil had to do with the political pressure the Pews sometimes put on him and his broadcasts. It may have been, but that is not how Lowell told the story. "They wanted me to sign up with Sun for life," Lowell maintains in his memoir. "I just couldn't do it. Life was such a long time." As employer-employee relations go, a request for a lifetime contract does not seem that huge an irritant. Couldn't Thomas and the Pews have agreed, by way of a compromise, to take it a decade at a time?

Whatever had inspired this break with Sun Oil—and it may just have been a search for higher compensation—Smith deftly managed to accomplish it. He secured a new sponsor for *Lowell Thomas with the News*: Procter & Gamble, an enormous but innocuous and politically quiescent household-products company. Smith arranged that Procter & Gamble would employ Lowell on sufficiently favorable terms—with sufficient money up front—so that Lowell could rapidly repay his debt to Sun Oil.

And this change of sponsorships necessitated a change of radio networks: Smith shifted Thomas' western broadcast back to CBS in 1946. Then, on September 29, 1947, *Lowell Thomas and the News* (at about this time the show's title exchanged a preposition for a conjunction) began being carried by CBS throughout the United States. Lowell Thomas would now be heard on the chief rival of NBC, his home for 17 years. This divorce left NBC, according to one trade magazine, "considerably steamed."[19]

((•))

After Edward R. Murrow had returned from covering the war in Europe and supervising CBS' coverage of that war, the longtime leader of CBS, William Paley, made Murrow a vice president of CBS News. And once Lowell Thomas began his migration to CBS, he invited Murrow and his family out to spend some time on Quaker Hill. Murrow declined. He felt it inappropriate to socialize with someone he would be supervising—albeit very, very loosely. Murrow's refusal may also have reflected their differences.

Ed Murrow and Lowell Thomas both hailed from the West and had both achieved outsized success in radio journalism by great displays of energy and talent. Murrow's view of journalism, however, was different from Thomas': He brought to his work an alertness to injustice, even a commitment to social justice. He would later call attention, for instance, to the exploitation of migrant farmworkers in United States.

Thomas was certainly a caring person. Charities found him free with his time and his money. He was sensitive to the plight of individuals, such as the elderly rich women preyed upon by the grifter he had exposed in Chicago, Carleton Hudson Betts. But given Lowell's trust in capitalism and America, he wasn't disposed to look into, or even look for, systematic flaws.

It is hard to find any Murrow-like crusades in Thomas' travelogues, books or newscasts. "Lowell wasn't a real journalist to Ed," Frank Stanton, who became president of CBS, later explained. In Murrow's view, with which Stanton said he disagreed, Thomas "was just a storyteller."

Murrow was serious, occasionally somber. He could usually be found with a cigarette in one hand and, when out in company, a scotch and water in the other. Frequently he was engaging in social situations, but Murrow could also be distracted and prickly. He was a demanding boss. Yet his co-workers at CBS News mostly loved and respected him. Despite the fact that he later did a gossipy show on CBS television called *Person to Person*—a series of celebrity interviews shot inside the subjects' homes—Murrow was seen at CBS News and elsewhere in broadcast journalism as epitomizing that which was most noble in broadcast journalism. Thomas was easy to work for, well liked by his colleagues and well loved by his audience. But he was not generally seen as that. He was once the subject of an installment of *Person to Person*—and had the largest home of any of the celebrities the show visited.

In the end, Ed Murrow proved uncomfortable as an executive, and by 1947 he had surrendered the position. Instead, he undertook his own nightly CBS radio newscast—on at 7:45 p.m., an hour after Thomas'. The next time Lowell invited him out to Quaker Hill, Murrow accepted. He, his wife and their young son ended up spending a month in a cottage belonging to Thomas. "I shall always embarrass you with my gratitude for the month we spent on Quaker Hill . . . ," he warned Lowell. "It was, in all respects, ideal."

Murrow enjoyed the golf and played often in that foursome with Thomas, Dewey and Frank Smith. And Murrow, who had grown up on a farm in Washington State, fell hard for Quaker Hill's agrarian charms. He was taken, in particular, with one rural-looking house made out of cedar logs. In 1948, on a train out of New York City, Murrow and his wife, Janet, met Charles Murphy, the man who owned that house. "By the time we reached Washington," as Janet Murrow tells the story, "I knew we had bought the house." (Murphy's family soon purchased another house on Quaker Hill.)

To a colleague at CBS Murrow wisecracked that he was "surrounded" on Quaker Hill "by reactionary Republicans." He advised his wife not to "get into any political discussion with the people there." Murrow himself didn't socialize much and mastered the art of avoiding the subject. "Though

Dewey and I are friends and neighbors," he explained, "we have a strictly arms'-length relationship when it comes to politics."

Still, Murrow loved Quaker Hill. And he could be there more during the summer because he could borrow Lowell's studio for his own radio newscast. Seven years later—looking for a tax shelter—the Murrows traded up to a 281-acre spread there: Glen Arden Farm. The actual farming was done by a farmer, who leased the land. But Murrow relaxed by clearing brush or moving dirt. He bought a bulldozer. Upon nearing his farm, Janet Murrow reported, "You could see him start to unwind."[20]

((•))

When the war ended, Lowell Thomas Jr. returned to and graduated from Dartmouth. Then, in 1948, he was recalled into the military to fly with Stuart Symington, first secretary of the air force, on a trip around the world, which included a chance to observe the test of an atomic bomb at Bikini Atoll in the Pacific. Presumably Lowell Sr.'s influence had helped gain his son this opportunity. Presumably Lowell, as resistant as he may have been to remorse, had been regretting his failure to fulfill what he called, in one of the World War II journals, "my ½ way promise to Sonny to remember this was his war."

Father and son, however, still had a large adventure—perhaps the most audacious of either of their lives—in front of them.

((•))

Lowell had one more opportunity to root for, but not tilt his newscast toward, Thomas Dewey in a presidential election. In 1948, running against Harry Truman, the Republican was heavily favored.

Eric Sevareid remembers broadcasting the election returns with Ed Murrow and some others on CBS on November 2, 1948. "Lowell was there wearing that white Stetson of his, which he kept on all evening, absolutely certain that his close friend and neighbor, Tom Dewey, was going to be the next president . . . ," Sevareid later recalled. "As the returns went on, Lowell's smile slowly faded and his head slowly drooped and that hat went down over his eyes. And late, late in the evening, when it was clear that Dewey wasn't going to make it, I think he fell either into a deep sleep or into a depression, but he was immobile. And that I never forgot."[21]

12.

The Very Roof of the World

With all of Lowell's adventures in wild and out-of-the-way places, with all of the risks he took, the only time he was ever seriously injured was when he was thrown by a pony. That was on the way down from Tibet.

(((•)))

Tibet covers a swatch of the Himalayas and the world's broadest and highest plateau. It sits "on the very roof of the world," as Lowell put it—north of India, Nepal and Bhutan, and south of China. For decades Lowell had ached to visit. No surprise there. Lowell's ardor for Tibet had been fanned by the fact that this country was as hard to get into as any on Earth. Tibet neither employed nor was visited by any airplanes, railroads or automobiles. (The thirteenth Dalai Lama had once been presented with some motorcars, which had arrived in boxes and eventually broke down.) The only way in was by caravan—up the Himalayas. But that wasn't the largest obstacle: Tibet's government almost never allowed in visitors.

"Forbidden Tibet!" Lowell writes in the first of a series of articles he would contribute to *Collier's* magazine. "Westerners have called it that for centuries. . . . Only a few have been able to penetrate that sealed and silent land. And fewer still have been allowed to visit its fabulous capital, the sacred city of Lhasa."

In 1904 a British expedition—looking for trade rights and trying to counter Russian influence—had fought its way into Lhasa. The British fired machine guns at Tibetans armed with swords and muzzle-loading rifles. From the withdrawal of that expedition through the end of World War II, fewer than 75 Westerners—and only five Americans—had made it that far, according to a British expert on the subject, Roger Croston.[1]

But as Mao Zedong's Communists were driving Chiang Kai-Shek's Nationalists out of mainland China, Mao's forces had begun showing an interest in also "liberating" Tibet. They subscribed to the position that Tibet was an "outer province" of China. Isolation, hence, was no longer looking like such a surefire strategy in Lhasa.

Tibetan leaders had therefore come to the conclusion that a visitor or two—say from the United States, the world's current superpower—might be useful in developing sympathy and support for their sparsely populated and poorly defended country. An envoy of the Tibetan government, Tsepon Wangchuk Deden Shakabpa, had an acquaintance in New York—one of the last of those five Americans who had visited Lhasa: Ilya Andreyevich Tolstoy, a grandson of the novelist, who had been sent to Tibet during the war as an emissary of President Roosevelt. Shakabpa sought Tolstoy's advice on whom the Dalai Lama's government might invite. Ilya Tolstoy was a member of the Explorers Club as, of course, was Lowell Thomas.

And Lowell, in 1949, was facing an unfamiliar circumstance: time off. The new sponsor of his radio newscast, Procter & Gamble, put its programs on hiatus in the summer. There was no doubt how Lowell wanted to spend his first real vacation in 19 years: he wanted to travel. Finally, he could go wherever he wanted without worrying about hiring substitutes and arranging to get on the air somehow along the way. And there was no doubt where he wanted to go.

As Lowell tells the story, he dashed off a letter to "an old friend," Loy Henderson, the new U.S. ambassador to India. "Now that you are in Hindustan, a land of miracles," Lowell wrote, "how about performing a miracle? How about arranging for me, my son and three other Americans to visit Tibet?" But Lowell fails to mention that this, like most miracles, was accomplished through some earthly machinations, involving Henderson and Shakabpa, whom Ilya Tolstoy may have convinced that no one could better publicize his nation's plight in the United States than the country's best-known journalist. So, sure enough, Lowell received a midnight telephone call from the State Department reporting that a radio message had come from Tibet via India inviting him and his son—but no other Americans—to visit Lhasa . . . immediately.

These machinations took time, however—two weeks of Lowell's summer vacation were already gone. And the preparations and the travel— from India up to Tibet and back, without the benefit of propellers or engines—would also take time, more than the six weeks he had left. Therefore Thomas would, after all, have to obtain permission from his sponsor and line up substitute hosts. He did, promising to be heard occasionally on his newscast when it resumed in September through the use of a brand-new technology: a battery-powered tape recorder. Thomas, always pushing his son's career, would have him record reports for airing on his father's newscast too.

Lowell Thomas Jr. was finishing up an adventure of his own in eastern Iran at the time. On July 14, 1949, Sonny received this telegram from his father: "The miracle has happened. Meet me in Calcutta."[2]

((•))

Lowell Thomas Jr. made it to Calcutta before his father and, with guidance from American consular and embassy officials in India, began organizing and outfitting their caravan. He purchased, he later explained, "saddles and bridles, army cots and sleeping bags, mosquito netting, flashlights, a portable table, two portable chairs, and a canvas bath (which we never used)," plus "a complete kitchen" and "eight cases of food, each case weighing sixty-five pounds." Their diet would be heavy on crackers, jam and canned meats. Sonny had brought with him "a portable Primus cooker"— which they would use even in Tibetan houses that had a stove, "since we did not particularly relish the peculiar and penetrating flavor of food prepared over a yak-dung fire."

We should note here—as this will become something of a coming-of-age story—how effectively Sonny performed, at age 25, in provisioning this expedition, in an often-chaotic city in a Third World country he was visiting for the first time. We should also note that it seems to have been assumed— by his father, by Sonny himself—that he would handle this task competently, maybe even more competently than would have his more hyper, more easily distracted father. Looking back Lowell Jr. did admit to one mistake: he purchased a medical kit but acknowledged that "in my frantic hurry I failed to give this matter adequate attention." It included "no sedatives or splints."

Lowell Sr., meanwhile, flew in from New York with warm ski outfits and "rubberized" naval "rain suits." Suydam Cutting—who was, with his wife, one of the other Americans to have visited Lhasa—had advised him that Tibetans preferred coins to bills, so the Thomases filled a trunk with bags of Indian coins. They also brought along that audio recording equipment and six cameras. When they were all packed, Sonny counted "thirty-seven boxes and pieces of luggage."

On July 31 the two Lowells left Calcutta by train for Siliguri—at the foot of a section of the Himalayas topped by Kanchenjunga, the world's third-tallest mountain. John Roberts, a young photographer who had been working with Sonny in Iran, joined them for the first part of the trip—until they got into Tibet. Their next stop: Sikkim, an Indian state jutting out between Nepal and Bhutan and sharing a border with Tibet. They and their stuff proceeded to Gangtok, Sikkim's capital, by truck through the Teesta Valley, where a large landslide in front of them, loosed by monsoon rains, delayed them for a day.

Gangtok, a city clinging to the side of a deep gorge, is where the caravan mustered. The Thomases and Roberts were joined by "six baggage-carrying coolies, nine pack mules and four riding ponies," plus a head-bearer, a cook, an interpreter and one "swarthy Sikkimese, who, for a fat fee and ten percent of the salaries" of everybody else, organized the whole thing. The first order of business was hiring carpenters to rebuild all their boxes, and make some new ones—three of them for the bags of coins. The original cases and that trunk had proven too heavy for the mules. From Gangtok Lowell Sr. dispatched to New York his first tape recordings—plus some by his son—for his newscast.

((•))

On August 5, 1949, the caravan set off for Tibet, following an ancient trade route—a branch of the Silk Road. "The pack animals, with bells tinkling from their necks and the heavily laden coolies on foot," Lowell Sr. writes, "followed us . . . up the mountain through the bamboo forest." Actually, the *Collier's* articles from which this description is taken are credited to

"Lowell Thomas with Lowell Thomas Jr." The book recounting their journey to Tibet, *Out of This World*, shares numerous paragraphs and wordings with those magazine articles, including the phrase "the pack animals, with bells tinkling from their necks." But that book is ascribed just to Lowell Thomas Jr.

This next passage, as with most of the quotations in this section, is from Lowell Jr.'s book:

> From Gangtok to the Tibetan capital is usually a trip of twenty-one days. In our eagerness to reach Lhasa, we expected to speed things up and trim five or six days off the schedule. But we reckoned without the mules. No one can drive a mule faster than the critter is willing to move.

One of Lowell Sr.'s *Collier's* articles adds: "In a popular ballad the lyrics describe a mule train moving forward at a brisk 'clippity-clop, clippity-clop.' Obviously, the tunesmiths got their inspiration from mules in some region other than Central Asia." And the whole set of overburdened, adagio pack animals in their caravan needed to be exchanged every few days. And it proved wise to halt that caravan each afternoon at a bungalow built for travelers or in a village rather than risk being caught at nightfall in the often-uninhabited lands in between. And this was hard traveling—even if you were often catching a ride on a mule or pony, especially if you were, as was one of the three Americans, in your late fifties.

The first plague was rain: the monsoon brought Sikkim's jungles on the southern slopes of the Himalayas some particularly heavy rains. Clouds loitered above, below and around them. Tiny leeches dropped from trees onto the various mammals below. And the humans, ponies and recalcitrant mules, many bearing heavy loads, were all the while ascending—8,000 feet, 10,000 feet. At one point the Americans decided it was better to walk than to fret about the footing of a distracted four-legged beast of burden on those narrow trails over impossibly deep chasms.

"I can't help thinking," Lowell Jr. remarked to his father at one point, "what might happen if a landslide like the one we met back in the Teesta Valley suddenly caught us here."

"Let's talk about a more pleasant subject," Lowell Sr. replied. Few were better at turning a conversation in a positive direction. As Sonny notes about his father: "He has a way of extracting the utmost pleasure from his experiences." And there was, in fact, much in which a resilient, positive-thinking traveler might take pleasure as their caravan climbed through and then out of Sikkim's rain forests: In a travelers' bungalow the Americans had the opportunity "to stretch out before a crackling log fire and dry our dripping clothes." According to a journal Sonny kept during the trip—in the form of unsent letters to his girlfriend back home—he and "Dad" admired "multitudes of stunning wild flowers," including "360 varieties of orchids" (in *Collier's* his father, underplaying for once, makes it 350 varieties); and they stopped at another bungalow that sat in "a valley of Rhododendron" overlooking Tsomgo Lake—"a long, black sheet of water." Altitude: 12,310 feet above sea level.*

The caravan's cuisine had been improved significantly by some local produce the head-bearer had managed to scrounge: "a slew of tiny tomatoes, potatoes, string beans and eggs, along with twenty-four loves of bread." Sonny, while not the ebullient personality his father was, had been raised not to whine, to make do—to pronounce glasses half-full. After one satisfying meal, Lowell Jr. asks in his journal, "What more could one ask for, anyplace?" And, like his dad, Sonny never outgrew a boyish enthrallment with adventure.

It was still raining but colder as they neared Nathu La (in Tibetan *la* means *pass*), and crossed from India into Tibet—"that highest and most remote of all countries," as Lowell puts it—at more than 14,000 feet. The border, Sonny reports in a tape recorded for his father's newscast, was guarded only by "three bushy-tailed" yaks.

After traveling downhill several miles past the border, the two Lowells and Roberts stopped at a bungalow. "We were . . . inside Tibet at last!" Lowell Jr. exults.

((•))

Tibet's geography greatly contributed to its allure for his father. While Lowell Sr. regularly fell for cities and farmlands, deserts and jungles, having grown up at an elevation of almost 10,000 feet, he most adored mountains. Every city in Tibet rests at a higher altitude than Victor, Colorado—a couple are almost half again higher. Indeed, many Tibetans

---

* The altitudes recorded by Lowell Thomas Jr. and Lowell Sr. tend to be a couple of hundred feet higher than those I have found and am using.

make their homes at altitudes that exceed that of the tallest peak in the Rockies.

Tibet's strangeness, from the point of view of a twentieth-century American, was also beguiling. Not only had Tibet succeeded, halfway through that century, in abstaining from all forms of steam-, gas- or oil-powered transportation; Tibet was—thanks to steep and narrow trails—almost entirely devoid of wheels. Goods and humans were moved upon the backs of ponies, mules, donkeys, horses, yaks and humans. Tibet had one telegraph/telephone line, one electrical generator, a small number of light bulbs and a few battery-operated radios. No newspapers, modern hospitals, central heating or sewage systems were to be found.

And it wasn't just that the country lacked the wealth or wherewithal to keep up. Here is how Lowell explained the Tibetan attitude in *Collier's*: "They think that they alone, of all the peoples on earth, are not slaves to the gadgets and whirring wheels of the industrial age," he reports. "They want no part of it." This was, to switch to a more contemporary vocabulary, a country run by technophobes—almost entirely unplugged. How intriguing for a technophile!

And, in a further antique touch, the country was ruled by—or by the advisors to—a teenaged demigod. After various signs and tests, and while only a toddler, Lhamo Dhondrub, the fifth child in a farming family, had been recognized as the fourteenth incarnation of the Dalai Lama—the "Great Ocean," a living Buddha. Perhaps no place on Earth provided a better opportunity for time travel than this antimodern theocracy.

Lowell was among the multitudes in the West then taken with the myth of a premodern "Shangri-La" in the East. That hidden valley of happiness in the Himalayas was first imagined in James Hilton's 1933 novel *Lost Horizon*, which had been made into a film in 1937. The novel and, therefore, this myth were heavily influenced by and associated with Tibet—adding to its allure.

The three Americans drank some scotch to celebrate their first night in Tibet. They wrote some notes, then—exhausted and feeling the altitude—were asleep in their bungalow by 7:30. For security, father and son often slept next to their boxes full of bags of coins. But tastes, they soon learned, had changed in Tibet. The locals now preferred to be paid for their products and services in light, easy-to-carry bills—and accepted coins only at a discount.

The next morning John Roberts, lacking an invitation from the Tibetan government, turned back—accompanied, as Sonny puts it in his journal, by a "cook, coolie and mule." He was carrying with him additional tape recordings for Lowell's newscasts.[3]

((•))

In these years almost one-quarter of the male population of Tibet entered monasteries. And it did not take long for the two Lowells to be reminded that they had trekked into the most religious country on Earth. Mahayana Buddhism—the (relatively) less austere variety—is said to have been introduced to Tibet (relatively) late: in the seventh century. It took. Indeed, Buddhism became as strong there as anywhere in the world. But it also was transformed somewhat by exposure to the old local religion—an "indigenous animistic faith," as the writer and China scholar Orville Schell puts it, "centered on . . . propitiating myriad spirits, deities, demons and demigods whom Tibetans imagined to inhabit every part of the natural landscape."

As soon as the Thomas caravan had crossed the border, it had passed prayer flags, fluttering from long poles, and then a prayer wheel. Tibet's Buddhists believed that each time a written prayer moved it was re-sent. About six miles after their caravan entered Tibet, it passed its first monastery. This one was occupied by "red-hat monks," known for sometimes *not* practicing celibacy.

In fact, this religious country had, as the Thomases would learn, some ideas of its own on sexuality. Various forms of adultery were worked into hospitality rituals or festivals. Polygamy was practiced by those who could afford it. And a form of polyandry—brothers sharing a wife—was not uncommon among the less well-off. And the less well-off, as the Thomases saw, were exceedingly poor. The gap between them and the country's nobility was vast enough to fire up any Communist agitator.

The first Tibetan city the caravan entered was Yatung, which sits in a valley so deep that the sun can find its way in for only part of the day. The first government official they encountered was, as Lowell Sr. writes, wearing "a full-length blue robe wound with a red sash. His dark pigtail was coiled atop his head, and from his left ear dangled a four-inch pendant of turquoise, pearl and gold." As this official, from whom they needed to secure some sort of visa, approached, "he stuck out his tongue and hissed"—a gesture of welcome in Tibet. And then his servants arrived with the gifts:

One carried a tray piled with eggs—a hundred or more of them—some fresh, some ancient. . . . The next servant had a large shoulder of yak for us, all butchered and dressed. The third held a big bowl of yak butter. All these were much appreciated, especially by our servants who used the rancid yak butter for their all-important yak-butter tea, the national drink of Tibet.

At age 57, with more than three decades of far-and-wide travel behind him, Lowell Sr. had developed a somewhat warmer, less judgmental attitude toward other cultures and peoples. The condescension and ugly stereotyping that had occasionally slipped out on Lowell's early journeys—describing someone as possessing "that sickly oriental smile," for example—were mostly gone.

This new, more enlightened, mid-twentieth-century Lowell Thomas was still a little too bemused by such unfamiliar ceremonies and foodstuffs—those ancient eggs, for example—to meet twenty-first-century multicultural standards. He later describes this particular gift as "A heaping platter of eggs, which we discover were freshly laid, long years ago." And Thomas continued to employ terms like "coolie," which we have learned to reject as derogatory. Still he had always displayed an extraordinary eagerness to see, and usually to try, unfamiliar practices from foreign cultures. And in Tibet he seemed not only to engage with but to honor the local traditions.

Scarves were waved and then presented by way of greeting, so Lowell stocked up on, and then waved and presented, scarves. Demons in the ground or water had to be subdued or driven away or counteracted or satisfied. So the Thomases—raised to respect religion—joined in protective prayers or evasive behaviors, or they contributed a handful of their vast supply of coins to buying the demons off. And they drank the ubiquitous tea—rancid yak-butter and all. "You can imagine the smell of that tea," Lowell would later remark, "a smell that pervades the entire country and it tastes even more so. But you can get used to it—we did."

Lowell Sr. was not particularly tough even on a group of Communists they encountered.

There is no evidence that a distaste for Communism—or a desire to serve as a witness to its expansionism—had motivated Lowell's decision to visit Tibet. As a well-off Republican, working for the Pew family, he had obviously been no fan of the Soviets, of their sympathizers or, for that matter, of Socialists. But he came to Tibet as he went most places: for the experience, not the politics. In Yatung the two Lowells met some people from China who, given the rise in tensions, were being expelled from Tibet. Lowell Sr. notes that they might have been—and here he does succumb to an epithet—"Reds." Yet he is not unsympathetic toward these displaced people. "They were being expelled and they told us frankly how unhappy they were about it," he reports in *Collier's*.

After he came to know the Tibetans and then watched what Mao and his troops would do to their land, anti-Communism would become a major cause for him.

The Thomases ceremoniously bestowed upon that official in Yatung—who had welcomed them with a few servant-loads of presents—a gift of their own: a gold-plated mechanical pencil that could write in four colors. They received the visa—written on a two-foot-by-three-foot piece of parchment. "The wishes of the two Americans are to be fulfilled at a moment's notice . . . ," the document stipulated, "as Americans are very good friends of Tibet." And they moved on with an even larger caravan—now powered by 21 Tibetan mules, in addition to some ponies, and protected by a one-man military escort, "with a rifle slung over his shoulder."[4]

((•))

They were climbing again—trying to move faster now. "The rock and snow summit" of another huge peak, Jomolhari, was occasionally visible, as Lowell Jr. writes, "through a hole in the clouds" to their right. "How would you like to take off down those slopes on your skis?" Lowell Sr. asked his son at one point. Their caravan crossed a second pass, this one at more than 15,000 feet. The summit of the highest mountain in the 48 contiguous states, Mount Whitney, reaches about 14,500 feet.

"What a contrast between the south and the north side of that Himalayan wall!" Lowell Sr. writes. "Jungle on one; barren mountains and bleak plateau on the other." The rugged terrain here was all sand, dirt and stone, but hardly monochromatic. It displayed half-a-dozen shades of brown. Sometimes—on that "bleak plateau"—they spotted the "black yak-hair tents" used by shepherds or the "thick-walled stone and mud-brick buildings" of a village, "with prayer flags flapping in the stiff wind." For lunch along the trail the Americans ate cheese, crackers and chocolate; the locals a ball of dough kneaded out of barley flour and water. Barley, which can handle the altitude, was Tibet's principal crop and foodstuff. Their caravan changed mules and ponies once again, this time "taking on a few unruly yaks."

The local official who formally welcomed them to Gyantse—Tibet's third-largest city—was also, as was then common in Tibet, a monk. He appeared "in a golden silk gown brocaded with dragons, a two-story golden hat shaped a little like a lampshade, and adorned with elaborate turquoise and gold jewelry. . . . His little fingernail was an inch long." He would have the American father and son as guests in his city for an extra two days because Lowell Thomas Jr. was not feeling well. An Indian medic in town diagnosed—perhaps a bit hastily—malaria and prescribed quinine. Sonny quickly recovered.

And the caravan moved on, "winding upward through a deep gorge," as Lowell Jr. explains in his book. "All around us were barren mountains. No trees or flowers grew at this high altitude." There were no more travelers' bungalows beyond Gyantse. It was necessary to obtain rooms every night in a house. Such abodes, inevitably in Tibet, would have dirt floors and devote rooms on their ground floors to the animals. The plumbing, Lowell Sr. explains, would consist of "a slit in the floor over the manure pile downstairs." Occasionally the two Americans found fresher air by braving the harsh winds and pitching a tent on the roof.

Three days after leaving Gyantse, the caravan climbed up to a pass called Karo La—between a couple of glaciers at about 16,500 feet. After that they surmounted one more pass—almost that high—before making a steep descent to the wide river that would become the Brahmaputra and help fill the Bay of Bengal. Yak-skin boats—light enough so a man could carry them upstream on his back—transported them and their boxes down that river to within a couple of days of Lhasa.

Their trip from Gangtok to Lhasa not only was accomplished no faster than the expected 21 days; it took three days more.[5]

((•))

On September 1, 1949, in Lhasa, father and son, according to the latter's journal, "rose sleepily" at 7:00 a.m.—"it having been a comparatively late evening for us, . . . with a fine dinner and conversation." They shaved, ate breakfast and then organized some presents: "a stunning tiger's head inlaid with gold and silver, a Swiss alarm clock and one of those real thin raincoats that can be carried in a pocket." At 8:30 they traveled by horse and mule to Norbulingka, the summer palace.

The two Lowells strolled through the flower gardens, then sat down on cushions in a courtyard and were offered tea and crackers. A group of about a hundred monks stared at these pink-skinned Americans curiously. On the roof a few monks blew impossibly long trumpets. On the other side of the courtyard, a monk climbed a ladder and struck a gong several times. At that moment a line formed at a doorway. The Thomases joined it along with monks, common people and others from their caravan. Their gifts, carried by their servants, were taken at the door.

They entered the room and saw the young Dalai Lama sitting on cushions, bareheaded and wearing a red robe.

It was customary to wait three days before receiving the Dalai Lama's blessing. In the interim the Thomases attended a dance festival and met with Shakabpa, who was back from some travels. Lowell also recorded a radio broadcast, which was sent by courier to India, from which it would be forwarded to New York and rushed onto the air—five weeks later.

"When Dad came before the Dalai Lama's throne," Sonny writes in his journal, "he unfolded his scarf." The two Lowells had been well briefed. On that scarf one of the Dalai Lama's top assistants placed "various religious offerings— . . . a symbol of the earth, one of the spirit, one of the mind." The Dalai Lama took each of the offerings. Then Lowell presented him with the scarf itself, which was accepted by one of the Dalai Lama's servants. "Dad bowed so the Dalai Lama might touch his head with his fingers, thus bestowing his blessing." (Women and "common folk" were touched only with a red tassel.) When it was Lowell Jr.'s turn, he mistakenly tried to give the scarf to the Dalai Lama himself, but the monk intercepted it, preventing a breach of protocol.

The Thomases took seats on cushions on the floor of that throne room, and then they noticed something interesting: "His Holiness," Sonny notes in his journal, "smiled at us and kept glancing down at us, obviously as curious over these two white men from a far-off nation, the most powerful and modern in the world, as other Tibetans." At that moment the awe-inspiring Dalai Lama himself seemed "a little awed." "Being a boy of 15, I'm sure he was," Lowell Jr. concludes. (The Dalai Lama was actually only 14.) In a recent interview, the Dalai Lama himself recalled this meeting in 1949: "I was very much impressed with Lowell Thomas. His voice," the Dalai Lama said, deepening his own voice, "a very strong voice. And," he added, laughing, "quite a big nose."

Lowell Sr. seemed a little awed, too—if not by the young religious leader, then by the depth and splendor of the traditions that surrounded him. This remained a more open Lowell, a more respectful Lowell. "A backward, undeveloped country?" he would ask in the movie they would make of their trip. "Ah, not at all. We found that it has its own special civilization. It has its own rich culture."

Twenty-seven years earlier, Lowell Thomas and Harry Chase had been able to photograph and film the amir of Afghanistan. Now the Thomases were given the opportunity to photograph and film—this time in color— the young man slated to become the spiritual and political leader of Tibet. The Dalai Lama posed on a throne of cushions wearing a gold, conical crown. He sat on a chair among opulent chrysanthemums. He stood with Lowell Sr.—Lowell Jr. took most of the pictures—and some of his much older advisors, who were wearing robes no different from his. Sometimes the Dalai Lama displayed the awkwardness of a young man who had not yet grown into his body.

In their writings the Thomases consistently describe the Dalai Lama as "bright-eyed and smiling." Lowell Sr. adds in *Collier's* that "he seemed human, kind, gentle-mannered and handled his duties with surprising self-aplomb for one so young." It doesn't seem as if the young man did much more in their presence than smile and handle his duties. Lowell admits that they "spoke only a few words to him directly."

They had spoken many more words that day—before the photo session— with the adult who was currently running the country: the regent, Tokra. Some of those words would prove to have political significance.[6]

((•))

Lowell Thomas' radio broadcasts recorded in Tibet mostly concerned themselves with local color and customs: "About that yak roast we're about to have, the *chokidar* is making signs that it's all ready. . . ." He has little to say about politics—even with Tibet about to become another flashpoint in the intensifying Cold War.

But was Thomas in Tibet on some sort of secret mission for the United States government? The Soviets claimed that he was. *New Times*, a weekly published in multiple languages to publicize the Soviet Union's positions, "charged," according to an Associated Press report, "that American authorities employed Lowell Thomas, radio commentator," in an American and

British plan to "turn Tibet away from China and into their colony and a war base."

Certainly, with Communist troops gathering at the border and the Cold War heating up, Tibet was a country in which the United States had an interest. It was also true that Thomas was hardly the sort to refuse to help his country. Nor was he short on connections to the U.S. government: Lowell had been a classmate at Princeton of Allen Dulles, who would soon become director of the new Central Intelligence Agency. Moreover, Thomas had obtained permission to visit Tibet with the assistance of Ilya Tolstoy, another old U.S. intelligence hand, and of the State Department, which also helped with his preparations for the trip.

Once they arrived in Lhasa, Lowell Thomas and his son were certainly consulted and feted as if they were representing the United States. "During our eleven days in the capital of Tibet late last summer," Thomas Sr. writes in *Collier's*, "our hosts kept us on a continual merry-go-round of interviews, parties and sight-seeing."

The city of Lhasa is dominated by the ancient red, white and gold Potala—the Dalai Lama's winter residence. Lowell anoints it "the combined Vatican and St. Peter's of the Buddhist world." The Potala has entered as impressive a partnership with a hillside as has any structure on Earth. It mounts that hill tier-by-tier, chapel-by-chapel, palace-by-palace until it is 300 feet above the city and 12,140 feet above sea level. The two Lowells were given extensive tours of the Potala, as well as of a couple of monasteries. They were presented to the Dalai Lama's family. They met with all of the country's top leaders and were entertained by some of them.

Both Thomases would later eagerly inform the U.S. government of what they had seen and heard in Tibet. And in the pronouncements he as well as his son would make after their trip, Thomas—assuming as much of a public political role as he ever had—did his best to build support for the Tibetan government's efforts to resist a Communist invasion.

Nonetheless, it is difficult to believe Thomas was functioning in Tibet as some sort of government agent—secret or otherwise. His own response to the charge, in his memoir, is self-deprecating, droll, dismissive and fairly believable:

> For what a secret agent I was. Not only did I neglect to consult with anyone in Washington about the trip—not even my old classmate Allen Dulles—I even forgot to take a letter or a gift to the Dalai Lama

from President Truman, the most common courtesy. And, of course, considering my regular broadcasts and the news coverage we got, the entire affair was conducted with all the secrecy of a World Series.

This effort to present Thomas as some sort of spy or emissary trying to accomplish some sort of U.S. government purpose has additional weaknesses: The first is that the U.S. government didn't seem to have much of a purpose in Tibet at the time. The Truman administration decided it was not willing to go to war to keep the Chinese Communists out of this rather small and severely isolated country. South Korea, for which the United States *would* shortly go to war, had a population five times larger. Furthermore, this was a territory with which the United States did not have separate diplomatic relations.

And all concerned must have realized that the Tibetans themselves—with an army outfitted with surplus from World War I—were not capable of holding off Mao's People's Liberation Army, whether or not an American showed up to buck them up. Were U.S. officials glad to have a witness in Tibet to publicize an upcoming Communist outrage? Perhaps. But this witness would also call attention to America's failure to come to the rescue.

The final weakness in the argument that Lowell Thomas was in Tibet to accomplish something for the U.S. government is that he did an awfully ineffective job of representing the position of the U.S. government. Lowell Thomas Jr.'s journal paraphrases one crucial part of the conversation his father and he had with Tokra, the regent, as follows: "We talked of furthering U.S.-Tibetan relations, how Am[erica] felt regarding freedom, that we were interested in helping any freedom-loving peoples keep their independence."

This last statement is not repeated in the *Collier's* articles or in Lowell Jr.'s book—for good reason. Given the weight that might be placed on their statements, the Thomases had no business implying to the head of the Tibetan government that the United States would help protect Tibet's independence. The Thomases left Tibet's top foreign-policy officials with similar falsely raised hopes: "Dad said he thought we'd help as a nation," Lowell Jr. reports in that journal.

Hugh E. Richardson—a British diplomat and veteran Tibet hand, then representing India in Lhasa—concluded, rather scathingly, that Thomas "appeared to know nothing of American policy toward Tibet and to be unaware that the State Department consider[ed] Tibet as part of China."[7]

((•))

While in the "forbidden city," the Thomases spent time too—as one does when in a place where other foreigners are rare—with what few other foreigners there were. Richardson was one. Reginald Fox, an Englishman with a talent for operating a shortwave radio, was another. He had made himself useful to the country's leaders by bringing them up-to-date news of the outside world—the increasingly threatening outside world.

Shortwave radio also made it possible to contact outsiders. And one evening Fox asked Lowell Jr., who enjoyed watching him operate the radio, if there was anyone back home to whom he wanted to get a message. Sonny and a young woman his age had begun talking marriage but had not yet discussed their plans with their parents. Not that their parents were likely to object: Mary Taylor Pryor, known as Tay, was the daughter of Sam Pryor of Connecticut, executive vice president of Pan Am Airways and Sonny's father's fellow aviation enthusiast, fellow Protestant, fellow Republican, sometime travel companion and longtime friend. Lowell Jr. later recalled asking Fox to send Tay something along the lines of: "Hello from Tibet. Hope you will join me on the next trip."

Fox sent that message over the air, hoping that some shortwave-radio enthusiast in the United States would hear it and telephone its intended recipient. One did. But lots of others heard too—including someone who passed the news on to Walter Winchell for his gossip column. For in those days a young man asking a young woman to accompany him on a trip was akin to proposing marriage.

Reginald Fox was probably also responsible for helping Lowell Sr., who was still taping accounts of their journey for much later broadcast, to do better than that. While in Lhasa, Lowell Thomas managed to appear on his CBS newscast live via shortwave radio. But it was past time for him to return to New York and resume hosting that newscast. The only way out of Lhasa, though, was the arduous route the two Lowells had followed in.

((•))

Their return caravan departed on September 10, 1949. In a recorded broadcast, Lowell reported that another traveler they overtook early on the return trip saw the gray beard he was growing and said, "You are too aged for this, aren't you?"

After five days they had made it past Karo La—the highest point of their journey—and were hopeful of reaching New York early in October. The two Americans were riding ahead of the train of pack mules, as they often did. They stopped for a brief rest—probably just after they had entered an open plain above which one of Karo La's glaciers hovered. Then Lowell Thomas Sr. attempted to remount a pony without having someone hold its bridle.

Lowell was flung through the air, landing on a pile of rocks. Sonny's father was seriously injured, barely conscious and struggling for breath in the thin air at about 15,000 feet above sea level.

There comes a time in most close parent-child relationships, if both live long enough, when the child has to take care of the parent. Lowell Thomas had always been guiding his son, showing him the ropes, making connections for him, even drawing up plans for his career. He did this to an extent most fathers—even the most concerned fathers—did not. For example, sometime during this period Lowell Sr. laid out on note cards nine different, though overlapping, possible career paths Lowell Jr. might follow—plans *A* through *I*. He made sure to provide some extra note cards in case the young man wanted to sketch out some additional alternatives himself.

But now the father was lying, in great pain, on the ground in a country without an X-ray machine, let alone an ambulance or a helicopter, a country that believed in folk remedies, not doctors. They were more than four miles from Ralung, the nearest village; two days' ride from Gyantse, the nearest city; and two weeks' ride from a thoroughfare that might be negotiated by an automobile. His father was unable to do anything for himself. It was up to Sonny to get him out.

He sent their translator to Ralung for assistance. Then their caravan caught up. "We wrapped Dad in a sleeping bag and lifted him onto an army cot. But our first-aid kit contained no morphine. I had nothing to relieve his agony." Sonny and some villagers carried the cot to Ralung, as darkness fell, and it grew cold. Then he and they lifted his father up to the sleeping quarters of a house. "The shock and exposure brought on high fever and frequent fainting," Lowell Jr. recalls. "It was a long gasping night of agony and worry in just about the most out-of-the-way spot you can find on this planet."

Sonny's task the next morning was to find a doctor; this country of about four million people had, he states, a total of four doctors, only one of whom had actually finished medical school. But Sonny had been sick in Gyantse and had been treated by an Indian army medic there. Ralung was on the country's lone telegraph/telephone line. Sonny hiked to that rare thing, a telephone, and managed to connect with that medic—not a med-school graduate—who rushed out to help them, accomplishing the two-day journey in one very long day. The medic did what he could to make it possible for Lowell to be moved.

"It sometimes took ten Tibetans to carry Dad's stretcher over the steep rocky trails, which skirted chasms and swift streams, moving at a snail's pace to keep him from plunging into the river far below," Lowell Jr. writes. "Strapped to the stretcher, with his leg in a splint, Dad roasted when the sun was out and nearly froze when it ducked behind the clouds and the cold winds blew up. The first night . . . we had to borrow Tibetan tents, sleeping out in the cold." On the third day the Thomases and their caravan made it to Gyantse, where they spent ten somewhat more comfortable days.

There was a primitive telegraph station in Gyantse. Word of Lowell's accident found its way back to the States and into newspapers, under head-lines such as this from the *Boston Globe*: "Lowell Thomas Hurt So Badly in Tibet He Cannot Be Moved." These stories were credited to Thomas' office, and they had gained a bit in drama. First, the accident was said to have "occurred in a 17-thousand-foot-high Himalayan pass." The account in Lowell Thomas Jr.'s book makes clear that it happened on the descent from Karo La. And second, the animal that threw Lowell had been up-graded to a horse. Indeed, the pony had grown into a horse, too, in that book and in the *Collier's* articles. By the time Lowell wrote his memoir, it was a "high-spirited, half-broken" horse.

It does not seem likely that it was a horse. Otherwise on their journeys to and from Lhasa, the Thomases were astride only mules or ponies. Full-size horses would have been too large for the narrow, twisting trails. And the first account of the accident actually based on an interview with Lowell Sr.—a *New York Times* story datelined Calcutta on October 10—states that he had been "thrown by a half-wild pony." Acknowledging that the perpetrator was a pony—the "half-wild," too, seems likely an embellishment—may have seemed, in the end, too embarrassing. And this was in truth a tough pack animal, not the type of pony who gives rides to little children in parks. Lowell—who was indeed a highly competent horseman, riding at high altitude, in the midst of a grueling trip—certainly had nothing to be ashamed of, whatever the size of the animal that threw him.

That headline's claim that Lowell "Cannot Be Moved" was not that far from the truth. But he had to be moved. September was ending; the deep snows were coming; and the Americans had to leave Gyantse now or wait for the next summer. Lowell Jr. helped fashion a wooden sedan chair, which would be carried "in teams of four." He reorganized the caravan, and they set off, with the father being carried and the son in charge, through and eventually out of Tibet. The chair bearers chanted a prayer and sang the same song—with lyrics that translate as, "O Lord Buddha, lighten our load"—over and over. The man being borne, a representative of the modern world and therefore of variety, tried to teach them some new songs. Sometimes the turns were so sharp that it was necessary for him to get out and limp along himself. It took about 11 days to reach Gangtok, in India.

The U.S. ambassador to India had sent a rescue team to join them for the final stretch. Sonny, while grateful, seemed to find that a bit superfluous; for, as he writes, "we had just about done our own rescuing." Let us not underestimate the toughness Lowell Sr. displayed on the trip down from Tibet: his ability to handle severe pain, his good humor and optimism, his refusal to whine. But he might not have survived without such a competent and resourceful son. "For he it was," the father later wrote about his son, "who pulled me through and brought me out."

The embassy had a plane waiting at Siliguri to fly the Thomases to Calcutta. (*New Times*, that Soviet magazine, saw this as further proof of the importance of their trip to "the intrigues of the imperialist powers in Tibet.") The two Lowells then quickly found a flight to London, where they reunited with Fran. The family soon arrived in New York.

In a hospital there it was determined that Lowell Thomas' leg had been broken in eight places just below the hip. "His right femur, which had begun to knit improperly during the month since the accident, was rebroken," Lowell Jr. reports, "and properly set."

Lowell Senior was on crutches through the spring, but was skiing again on a glacier in Alaska in August.[8]

((•))

Meanwhile, it fell to Lowell Thomas Jr. to visit Washington and present a letter from the Dalai Lama to President Harry Truman. That he did, with little obvious effect on U.S. foreign policy. Lowell Thomas' radio broadcasts from Tibet, "because," Orville Schell explains, "they represented the first voices ever to be heard from Tibet, had an enormous impact on listeners when they aired back in the United States." But they did not stir the sort of public outcry that might have changed government policy.

Publicly and in meetings with Secretary of State Dean Acheson, Lowell Thomas called for arming the Tibetans and training them in guerrilla warfare. And the United States would make some mostly unsuccessful efforts to funnel arms to Tibetans through India. But the Truman administration was more interested in the use of Tibet as a propaganda weapon against the Chinese Communists than in a military effort that could actually keep them out or, later, kick them out. In January 1950 President Truman made it clear that "the U.S. Government will not pursue a course which will lead to involvement in the civil conflict in China." By then Chinese Communists troops were near the border of what they considered to be their "outer province."[9]

Those troops entered Tibet in October of 1950—a year after the Thomases exited. "The Tibetans feel," Thomas explained on the air, "that since they've been getting no aid whatever from the West, the only thing they can do is to negotiate with the Chinese Communists." By May 1951 the Tibetan government had capitulated, with little bloodshed, and accepted Chinese rule. The Dalai Lama—who had fled to Yatung, near Sikkim— returned to Lhasa, but then left his homeland for good in 1959.

Lowell Thomas Jr.'s book on their journey to Tibet was published in November 1950, and he soon began using their film of Tibet in a successful travelogue based on the trip. Among the 4,000 people who turned out for his show in Pasadena was one who had never been to that part of the world but was responsible for much of the interest in it: James Hilton, author of *Lost Horizon*. The two Thomases then weaved their exclusive film into a feature-length movie on Tibet and their journey, *Out of This World*, which opened in 1954.

Both would remain active supporters of Tibetan independence for the rest of their lives. Lowell Thomas Sr. formed the American Emergency Committee for Tibetan Refugees—an energetic and successful relief organization. Although they met the Dalai Lama on other occasions, he would remember with special fondness their first visit. When Lowell Thomas Jr.'s daughter, Anne Thomas Donaghy, herself was introduced to the Dalai Lama, he declared, "Now I have met three generations of Thomases!"[10]

13.

▬▬▬▬▬
▬▬▬▬▬
▬▬▬▬▬

An Entirely New Form of Entertainment

On May 20, 1950, more than 2,000 people squeezed into an Episcopal church in Greenwich, Connecticut, as Lowell Thomas Jr. did in fact marry Mary "Tay" Pryor. "Outside the church a crowd of onlookers just stood and watched the people coming in," according to one radio commentator. The guests including the governor of New York, the mayor of New York, two United States senators and one Supreme Court justice. Nine hundred people were invited to the reception that followed at the home of Sam Pryor Jr. and his wife on Long Island Sound. The wedding was covered not only by the New York newspapers but in *Vogue*. As his best man Sonny made an interesting choice: his father—who walked down the aisle "without crutches or cane for the first time since his accident in Tibet."[1]

His leg mostly healed, his son increasingly established, his finances under control and his reputation as a reporter burnished in the last year of the war and in Tibet, Lowell Thomas Sr. was about to undertake a few additional ambitious schemes. One would even prove an undeniable success. They all were spurred by a major change in the media landscape.

This was the moment when the elephant—television—finally began

making itself comfortable in American living rooms. Now that U.S. factories no longer had to concentrate on war materials, Americans began purchasing TV sets in large numbers. Television would invade two-thirds of
American homes by 1955. But, as would happen again with the invasion of
the Internet a half-century later, it was hard to grasp at the time the extent
of the damage the upstart would inflict upon older media—including older
news media.

Movies took an early and large hit. In 1948, 90 million movie tickets
were sold each week; five years later only about half that number were being sold. No need to find your way to a theater and pay for admission when
you could be well-entertained any evening for free at home. Feature films
did manage to survive the onslaught—in significantly reduced numbers.
However, as television introduced nightly newscasts, interest in twice-weekly
news updates in theaters plummeted. Fox Movietone News continued producing some newsreels into the early 1960s, but Lowell Thomas ended his
17-year relationship with the company in 1952.[2]

Thomas stayed with radio. Thomas always stayed with radio. And this
now old medium actually benefited from a couple of postwar developments: The first was the tape recorder, with which Lowell had experi-
mented in Tibet and which slowly began allowing voices from outside the
studio regularly to be heard on radio newscasts. (Initially, the taped voice
most likely to appear on Thomas' newscast was that of his son.) The growing
amount of time Americans were spending in automobiles after the war
also helped—since those cars were increasingly outfitted with radios.

However—when the audience's eyes were not focused on something
else, like the road—television had an obvious advantage over radio. And
TV news was in the process of figuring out that its ability to transmit images might be employed for more than just showing newscasters' faces.
First the network newscasts contracted with newsreel companies for film
of news events; then, with Don Hewitt of CBS in the lead, they began
shooting their own news film.

Having written about television's potential as early as 1933, Thomas
may have suspected that being America's foremost radio newscaster would
eventually no longer mean being America's foremost newscaster. And his
alertness to new technologies had not entirely deserted him: at the time
of his son's wedding, he was attempting to help movies compete with television through a company that vastly improved the impact of the film

shown in movie theaters. Four years later Lowell Thomas would become the major shareholder in a television station. A few years after that, he would launch his own TV show.

Nonetheless, Thomas frequently made clear that he had no interest in sliding over to host CBS' new television newscast.* He offered his usual explanation: an unwillingness to be chained to a New York City studio. He was also wont, as defenders of older media often are, to see something mystical being lost in the transition from one medium to another: "On radio you are accepted as a disembodied voice and given the authority of outer space," Lowell once opined. On television, his point was, that mystery and excitement were lost: "There's no fun looking at the same person night after night." The more tangible fact that radio journalism remained at the time the senior and more prestigious form of broadcast journalism undoubtedly also played a role in Thomas' inclination to stay put. And radio still paid better than TV: Lowell was making $502,300 a year for the work he did on CBS in 1949. Accounting for inflation, it would be decades before any TV newscaster made the equivalent.

Douglas Edwards, a lesser star, was the CBS newsman who did agree to sit each evening under the hot lights, encased in makeup, in front of the big cameras. But he had to be talked into leaving radio news for this new and untested medium. Edwards recalled CBS Television president Frank Stanton saying, "Doug, I guarantee if you do this TV broadcast you'll soon be as well known as Lowell Thomas."[3]

((•))

Harry G. Thomas, Lowell's father, died on May 6, 1952, at the age of 82. He had outlived his wife by five years and had continued, to recall Tennyson's wording, "to strive, to seek, to find, and not to yield"—practicing medicine into his seventies. Moreover, when he was 81 Dr. Thomas had enrolled in yet another course—this time in creative writing at New York University. And—during this same period, mixing studying and teaching as his son once did—Dr. Thomas taught courses there, in pathology and psychology.[4]

---

* Few understood it at the time, but Thomas probably was the wrong type for a daily program on TV anyway: too slicked-back, clipped and aggressive; too much the sort who seems to jump out of the screen at you; too "hot," in Marshall McLuhan's idiosyncratic use of these words, for a "cool" medium.

(((•)))

American politics was roiled in the early 1950s by allegations that a number of individuals who flirted with Communism were lurking within U.S.
institutions. These allegations were occasionally true, often outdated or
unsubstantiated, sometimes fabricated and probably nobody's business
anyway. They were leveled, many of the loudest and phoniest of them, by
Wisconsin Senator Joseph R. McCarthy. Those charges posed a stern test
for the nonpartisan, just-report-what-each-side-says form of journalism
Thomas saw himself as representing on his 15-minute CBS Radio newscast. Shouldn't accusations made by a United States senator, of whatever political persuasion, be reported? Someone disposed to playing it
"right down the middle" would, of course, also report any contrary statements from the responsible—i.e., credentialed—opposition. But as an anti-
Communist hysteria swelled in the United States, there weren't many
mainstream politicians brave enough to take on Senator McCarthy. And if
reporters themselves began challenging him, wouldn't that be taking sides?

Thomas was hardly the only journalist whose handling of this dilemma
proved, in retrospect, inadequate. On December 16, 1950, to pick one example, the *New York Times* published an Associated Press story under the
headline "FEDERAL VIGILANCE ON PERVERTS ASKED." No statements were
included in the article questioning assertions by some senators, including
Joseph McCarthy, that the State Department had mishandled "ninety-one
cases of homosexuality among its employees" by *merely* firing them—not
permanently blacklisting them. And, of course, nowhere in the article was
the use of the term "perverts" questioned.

Thomas' position on the political spectrum—even post–Sun Oil—and
his deep sympathy with Tibet probably made him more susceptible than
some other journalists to paranoia about hidden Communists. He frequently
denigrated Communists on the air as "Reds" and had been known to dis-
miss those sympathetic with them as "Pinks."

On April 10, 1950, the United States Supreme Court refused to over-
turn the contempt of Congress conviction of two Hollywood writers, John
Howard Lawson and Dalton Trumbo, for, as Thomas worded it, refusing
"to answer the sixty-four dollar question, 'Are you a Communist?'" In its
report on the court's action, the *New York Times* did manage to acknowledge, in paragraph eight, that there was a civil liberties issue here: "In

appealing their convictions, Lawson and Trumbo argued that the Constitution guaranteed them protection against revealing their private beliefs and associations." In his necessarily much shorter account the previous evening of the Supreme Court's action, Thomas did not find room to note that there might be a reason why Americans might resist being asked by their government about their political beliefs. Indeed, he did not find room here for any statement of Lawson and Trumbo's position. He just "impartially" recounted the court's action.[5]

Thomas, to his credit, did help one of the journalists victimized by the paranoia Senator McCarthy and others fanned. Cliff Carpenter, who had been the voice of Terry in the popular radio show *Terry and the Pirates*, had stood up for a victim of the blacklist and had been rewarded by himself being blacklisted. Carpenter had a place on Quaker Hill. He and Lowell were friends. Lowell found him some work and was ready to lend his name to Carpenter's projects.[6]

The most consequential journalistic investigation of the tactics and errors of Senator Joseph McCarthy came four years after the Lawson and Trumbo case—not in a newspaper or on the radio, but in the new medium: TV. This investigation was led by Lowell's colleague and neighbor Edward R. Murrow and Murrow's producer, Fred W. Friendly. They devoted their CBS Television program, *See It Now*, to it. And it may have been crucial that, while the senator was given equal time to respond in a subsequent show, Murrow otherwise made no attempt at impartiality. He presented the evidence and drew his own conclusions: "The line between investigating and persecuting is a very fine one, and the junior senator from Wisconsin has stepped over it repeatedly," Murrow declared on camera. "We must not confuse dissent with disloyalty. . . . We are not descended from fearful men, not from men who feared to write, to speak, to associate and to defend causes that were at the moment unpopular."[7]

American journalism eventually began to learn from its failures in covering Senator McCarthy's wild charges and similar falsehoods from, for example, government officials during the Vietnam War. Mere "he said, she said" journalism did not work well when some "he" in authority was exaggerating or lying and "she" was either too unimportant or too cowed to contradict him. And who was to say both sides were equally deserving of being heard? At some point journalists had to take on responsibility for trying to determine whether what "he" or "she" said was correct. And they would begin to—but slowly, over half-a-dozen decades.[8]

Thomas himself does not seem to have learned much from Senator McCarthy's exploitation of "impartial" journalists' reluctance to check and evaluate a public figure's statements—or from the success Murrow had when he did. He had been near the front lines in the struggle against partisanship in journalism. He would not—an older man now—be a participant in the slow counterrevolution: the struggle to persuade reporters to produce a wiser, less stenographic journalism.

But Thomas was about to help command an insurgency that would reshape another medium—in part in response to television.

((•))

On September 30, 1952, at the Broadway Theater in New York, filmgoers saw a familiar face, with an even better-known voice, appear on a standard motion-picture screen. Lowell Thomas was shown in black and white sitting at a desk as he announced: "You are about to see the first public exhibition of an entirely new form of entertainment. We call it Cinerama." Thomas then outlined the history of film up to that point. When he was finished, he stood up. "Ladies and gentlemen," he proclaimed, "this is Cinerama." At that moment the theater's curtains opened much farther to reveal a giant, 51-foot-wide screen.

Those staring at that amazing screen immediately found themselves looking out from the front of a roller coaster as it plunged, in full color, almost straight down—giving "some viewers," *Variety* quipped, "mal-de-Cinerama." That was followed by a potpourri of dazzling sights and sounds, which included a dance from the opera *Aida*, views of the canals of Venice, plus, as a finale, shots of the United States taken from the nose of a low-flying airplane. "People sat back in spellbound wonder," Bosley Crowther wrote in his review in the *New York Times*. "It was really as though most of them were seeing motion pictures for the first time."

Lowell Thomas was not just serving as an announcer or celebrity pitchman here. True, he had not been involved in the earliest development of Cinerama. Fred Waller invented this (imperfect) blending together of images shot by three different cameras on a super-wide, arced screen. The curvature of the screen was intended to involve even the audience's peripheral vision in the experience. Another inventor, Hazard Reeves, had added similarly spectacular seven-channel sound—"stereophonic sound," they dubbed it. At the shifting collection of companies that owned the process, owned the specialized theaters where it was shown or produced the movies themselves, these two inventors gained and lost influence, along with a Rockefeller; various movie executives; Lowell's business manager, Frank Smith; and an aggressive showman, Mike Todd.

Lowell had been invited to see a demonstration of the technique out on Long Island in 1950. He describes himself as having been "stunned" when "they threw their huge picture on their Oyster Bay screen and hit me with all of that stereophonic sound." For the next seven years, Lowell Thomas was prominent among those determining what Cinerama would be. His name was above the title on *This Is Cinerama*, on which he was credited, with Todd, as executive producer.

In the next few years, only 17 or so movie theaters in the United States were equipped to show Cinerama films, yet *This Is Cinerama* managed to be seen by more than eight million people. Indeed, Cinerama, the Imax of its time, appeared to have solved the problem then being faced by feature films: the experience it delivered could not be imitated, "with present television standards," as one excited film executive put it, "in the homes." Thomas, the entrepreneur, was helping run—not for the first time but now at the age of 60—a high-tech start-up. And Thomas, the showman, had scored another triumph in yet another medium. *This Is Cinerama* smashed box-office records in a number of the cities in which it was shown.

In his review of that first Cinerama movie, Bosley Crowther had cautioned that "something more than a program of sensations will be expected . . . before long," from this new form of film. A story, Crowther meant. But Lowell was not convinced one was necessary. (And early Cinerama had the distinct disadvantage—for a love story, say—of not being able to accomplish a close-up.) Lowell did leak word of a possible Lawrence of Arabia Cinerama film—with John Wayne playing the diminutive Oxford-educated historian and Arabist. No shortage of narrative potential—not to mention ironies—there, but, alas, nothing came of it.

So with Thomas at or near the helm, Cinerama stuck with travel pictures, occasionally assisted by some gosh-let's-go-see-for-ourselves dialogue. "Lowell Thomas told *Variety*," as that publication reported in its lively patois, "that he thinks the triple-camera threat medium could continue indefinitely sans plot." Indeed, Lowell believed Cinerama could resuscitate another endangered species of entertainment—one particularly close to his heart: the adventure travelogue.

Thomas next produced and hosted for Cinerama a classic Lowell

Thomas extravaganza: *Seven Wonders of the World*, which featured, along with the Pyramids and the Sphinx, a collection of marvels and oddities (lots more than seven) in Israel, Rome, Saudi Arabia, Africa, India, Japan and—Lowell never being one to slight the homeland—the United States. (Hitching one's wagon to Lowell certainly provided some interesting opportunities: Prosper Buranelli was credited as lead writer on this film, along with the next Cinerama extravaganza.) *Seven Wonders of the World* played in New York and other places for a year and a half beginning in 1956 but earned less than three-quarters as much as *This Is Cinerama*.

There is a limit to how many times you can see "motion pictures for the first time." Thomas' third Cinerama film—*Search for Paradise*, released in 1957—featured visits to India and Nepal. This time critics proved less thrilled by the spectacle and began tiring of the act of "the principle principal." *Variety* accused "Producer Thomas" of having "overstarred himself." He had conceived the project and was often on screen as well as "being in on script, narration" and even "song lyrics." In the *Times*, Bosley Crowther revealed himself to be fed up with "Mr. Thomas' tasteless type of travelogue."

Lowell's taste and propensity for featuring himself were not the only explanations for the troubles of his later Cinerama efforts. His beloved travel films were definitely showing signs of having outlived their time. Increasingly it was possible for middle-class Americans to see the canals of Venice and even the Pyramids themselves. Increasingly, they were taking their own travel pictures, often on cheap Kodak "Brownie" cameras. And increasingly they were having difficulty convincing even friends and relatives to sit through all the slides and 8mm films with which they returned.

Search for Paradise earned only 52 percent of what *This Is Cinerama* took in, and these films were expensive to make and show. Meanwhile—Cinerama having indeed shown the way to a larger-screened future—other film companies had begun challenging it with mostly less impressive but also less expensive one-projector versions of wide-screen cinema—usually featuring full-bodied stories. Mike Todd, having been forced out at Cinerama, had launched such a movie format of his own, Todd-AO, employing extra-large, 70mm film. "Cinerama outa one hole," Todd called it. His film *Around the World in Eighty Days*, with a prologue by Edward R. Murrow and a tale borrowed from Jules Verne, won the Academy Award for best picture in 1957.

Cinerama theaters, meanwhile, began closing. Efforts continued to be made to keep the format afloat. None of those efforts included a new film by Lowell Thomas, though he kept firing off proposals.[9]

Clearly, just hosting his radio show—without the newsreels, without feature films to produce—was not enough for him, even though Lowell was nearing retirement age. "He was always busy," his son later observed. "He had a hard time just taking it easy."[10] So Lowell Sr. turned to television. He had found additional possibilities in that new medium for what he was now calling—the term *travelogue* sounding a bit hoary—"expedition films."

((•))

First, though, he bought a television station.

Lowell Thomas' entry into broadcast station ownership—which would make him very rich—actually began with a phone call from New York governor Thomas Dewey to Frank Stanton, the president of CBS, as Walt Hawver explains in his history of the company these liaisons spawned. The subject: WROW-TV in Albany, New York, which was then owned by the chairman of New York's Republican Committee and some other friends of the governor. It was a weak, UHF station—too weak and unimportant to command more than a limited affiliation with the then-junior television network, ABC. Dewey's friends were, consequently, losing money. The governor wanted Stanton to help them by letting the station affiliate with CBS. The network president suggested that Dewey talk to Frank Smith, his neighbor on Quaker Hill. And then Stanton came up with a plan.

If Smith agreed to buy WROW-TV and its sister radio station, getting the governor's friends off the hook, Stanton said Smith could get the Federal Communications Commission to allow him to move the station to an unused VHF channel, Channel 10, which had been allocated to a small, nearby town. This would make WROW-TV an Albany powerhouse— worthy of carrying CBS' programming. Stanton even suggested changing its name to WTEN.

Smith realized he was being given an opportunity to buy a sow's ear with a reasonable shot at becoming a silk purse. Together with three of his neighbors on Quaker Hill, Thomas prominent among them, he purchased most of Hudson Valley Broadcasting, which owned WROW-AM-TV, at full price: $298,000 plus the assumption of almost $400,000 in debt.[11]

Hudson Valley Broadcasting was now very much a Quaker Hill enter-

Lowell Thomas, Frances Thomas and their son,
Lowell Thomas Jr., known as Sonny.

The Thomas family—Lowell, Fran and Sonny—skiing in Lake Placid, New York.

Lowell Thomas, raised in Colorado, was a skilled horseman. And horseback riding was one of the main activities at the farm he purchased on Quaker Hill, near Pawling, New York.

In 1930 Lowell Thomas took over as host of what was then the only network radio newscast in the United States. With his radio and newsreel work over the next two decades, Thomas would become perhaps as dominant a presence in journalism in the United States as any individual has ever been.

Former president Herbert Hoover became a regular guest of the Thomases at Clover Brook Farm on Quaker Hill after his defeat in the 1932 election.

Lowell Thomas about to go for a swim after one of the yearly softball games he organized on Quaker Hill against a team managed by President Franklin Roosevelt.

One of Lowell's favorite photos of his wife, Frances Thomas.

Lowell Thomas Jr. with his father in 1937.

Lowell Thomas Jr. and Sr.—active, as usual.

In what was perhaps the first regular television newscast in the United States—perhaps the first regular television program of any kind—Lowell Thomas simulcasts his radio show from a TV studio for NBC's experimental New York television station in 1940.

The caravan in which Lowell Thomas and his son traveled up the Himalayas and into Tibet in 1949.

Lowell Thomas photographing the Dalai Lama, then 14, in Lhasa. Thomas and his son were among only a handful of Americans allowed into Tibet in the decades before the Chinese Communists invaded.

*Lowell Thomas with the Dalai Lama's family
in front of the Potala in Lhasa in 1949.*

*Lowell Thomas posing with members of a tribe in New Guinea during
the filming of his 1950s television program,* High Adventure with Lowell Thomas.

From left: the distinguished broadcast journalist Edward R. Murrow, the three-time governor of New York and two-time Republican presidential candidate Thomas Dewey, the golfer Gene Sarazen, Lowell Thomas and the golfer Sam Snead. Murrow and Dewey bought farms on Quaker Hill. Lowell is standing on tiptoes.

Lowell Thomas and his second wife, the former Marianna Munn.

prise. Indeed, it was at a party at Lowell's house that Frank Smith ran into the man whose contributions to the development of this enterprise would prove as large as his own. Thomas Murphy—the son of Hill stalwart Charlie Murphy—was 29 at the time and a graduate, like Smith, of what was now called the Harvard Business School. The young man had a good job— as a brand manager at Lever Brothers, a soap and detergent company. But Smith had something to say to him. "He explained he had just taken over a TV station that was about to go broke," Murphy recalls, "and he needed someone to run it 'who is a salesman, with advertising experience, the kind of background you have. Let me know if you have any suggestions.'" Murphy did—a couple of friends. But later he remembered that his father had passed up a great opportunity by neglecting to mention his own name when presented with a similar request.

Charlie Murphy passed a message on to Smith: his son would himself like the job. Thus Tom Murphy became general manager of tiny WROW-AM-TV. It took three years and losses to the stockholders larger than their initial investment, but the TV station did become CBS affiliate WTEN. In 1957 Frank Smith gave all the tiny company's employees, including young Tom Murphy, an opportunity to buy 100 shares in the company for $575. Some thought the offer was "utter nonsense." Murphy was among those who bought the stock.

And then—such was the television business in the United States in the second half of the twentieth century—the money started rolling in. By 1959 the company, now known as Capital Cities Television Corporation, also owned TV stations in Stockton, California, and Durham, North Carolina, as well as radio stations and a television station in Providence, Rhode Island. The next year Frank Smith moved Tom Murphy from Albany to New York City and made him executive vice president of Capital Cities.

If Lowell Thomas seems mostly absent from this tale of the foundation of a wildly successful business, it is because he was mostly absent from the running of Capital Cities. He was, as *Forbes* put it, the "godfather," not the "father," of Capital Cites. Thomas attended—or at least put in an appearance at—board meetings. He lent his name. And that name was a huge help. "When you're a small company starting out," Tom Murphy would later explain, "one of the greatest things that can happen to you is to be able to say, 'Well, our major stockholder is Lowell Thomas.'"

Thomas was certainly consulted. He gave Smith and Murphy the benefit of his business acumen, such as it was. And, as Capital Cities went public, Lowell, while remaining the largest shareholder in the company, began selling off some of his stock holdings—at a huge profit. In 1963 Thomas sold $1.4 million of his stock, but his remaining investment in the company was still worth $12.5 million.[12]

((•))

Tay Thomas had gotten the first taste of what it meant to be Lowell Thomas' daughter-in-law just a year after she married his son. Her new husband, then almost 28, had decided to spend a year studying at Princeton's Woodrow Wilson School of Public and International Affairs, which had recently begun offering a graduate professional program. (This, for the record, was in accordance with "Plan E" on the note cards Lowell Sr. had used to sketch out possible futures for his son.) Tay was then shocked when her father-in-law telephoned to say that *he* had found a place for *them* to live in Princeton—a room, with kitchen privileges, in someone's house yet.

Tay did not protest. "I was a quiet person," she explained in a 2012 interview. "I couldn't stand up for myself very well." Besides, families like this in the 1950s were not known for their eagerness to talk everything out. Rather, Tay recalled, "we found a tiny little house on our own—perfect for our first years. We moved there instead. He never said anything."[13] In fact, Lowell and his daughter-in-law rarely exchanged angry words about anything.

Nonetheless, Tay Thomas was beginning to realize that it would not be easy to build a life of her own near the irresistible force that was Lowell Thomas.

((•))

Lowell felt he still had something to prove "concerning the fabulous potential," as he put it, of "the nonfiction field." So he began looking for a way—short of having to show up in a New York studio every evening—of transferring some of what he had been doing for Cinerama's huge screen to television's then-tiny screen. His solution was to design his own nonfiction (well, mostly nonfiction) television show. It was Thomas' most wholehearted assault upon television and, like many of his productions, mixed journalism, travel, storytelling, geography, anthropology and derring-do. Thomas would, in other words, produce and air "expedition films."

In 1954 Thomas' newscast on CBS radio had switched sponsors once again: to Delco car batteries, a subsidiary of General Motors. Delco also agreed to sponsor and fund—mounting such expeditions was expensive—Lowell's television offensive. CBS Television agreed to put it on the air. The plan was for seven one-hour specials to be televised about once a month beginning in fall 1957.

Thomas' camera crews set off for New Guinea, Nepal, Venezuela, the Arctic and Central Africa. Eight hundred pounds of rice a day had to be secured to feed the five hundred native spearmen who were hired, Lowell reported, to help hunt down an allegedly marauding tiger in Nepal. Sixty loincloths had to be shipped to New Guinea to protect the sensibilities of CBS viewers because, as the executive producer of the series, Gil Ralston, put it, "they normally wear less than that down there." (CBS *would* allow some shots of topless female natives—long a staple of the genre.) There were snafus: A crew above the Arctic Circle, Lowell reported, had been expecting a package of all-weather boots. Instead, they received "salt tablets and mosquito-bite lotion." The boots showed up in "steaming" New Guinea.

His TV show would be entitled *High Adventure with Lowell Thomas*. But Lowell insisted on apologizing for the name just about every time he mentioned it—including in his introduction to the first installment. It had been just a "working title," he explained, and remained something of an embarrassment to him because it implied that his experiences were more adventurous than other people's. "According to my notion," he asserted on that first show, "you and you, in fact all of us, live lives full of adventure. . . . A great surgeon has high adventure nearly every day in the operating room. Teaching children and seeing the change in them from week to week," he asserts, is high adventure. ". . . Oh yes, and what could be more thrilling than making love to that girl next door. Yes, to my way of thinking all of life is high adventure."

At age 65, Lowell, however, was still seeking—as he had at, among other ages, 23, 24, 25, 30, 52 and 57; as he would into his seventies and eighties—the form of adventure that came from traveling to places that were distant, exotic and perhaps a touch dangerous. A total of more than one million miles, Lowell asserted, were traveled to produce those first seven *High Adventure* shows, many of them by him. (His and his son's Tibet footage was reused for one edition of the new show.)

The ratings for this new show were strong. These were travel films, to be sure, but they featured excursions to parts of the world very, very few members of the swelling hordes of American travelers, with their Kodak cameras, could get near. The reviews were not always strong.

"The program included some interesting and informative footage," *New York Times* television critic Jack Gould acknowledges about the first installment of *High Adventure*, aired in November 1957, which featured a journey up the May River in New Guinea. But Gould—echoed by some other reviewers—criticizes a number of aspects of this initial program:

- An overemphasis on "the glamour" of Thomas' "role as explorer," with "repeated close-ups of the commentator standing on the deck of his well-provisioned river boat." (In at least one later show the commentator criticized for dominating the screen was Lowell Thomas Jr.)
- A tendency to sink into the clichés of "the old-fashioned, picturesque travelogue," thereby limiting the show to a "superficial" account of the "culture of the natives."
- The addition of a "contrived note of suspense"—waiting, for instance, after an Australian official forced the return of a kidnapped girl, to see whether a group of "headhunters would retaliate," a threat which "never rang true." Campbell Ewald in *Variety* complains that "Thomas, in his narration . . . , constantly warned of approaching cannibals out to do their stuff but the viewer saw comparatively tame natives, sometimes bewildered, sometimes friendly."
- Finally and of most concern, the contrivances extended, Gould suggests, to staging scenes: "With presumably all of the jungle to scan the camera luckily happened to be in the right spot for a close-up when the first headhunter emerged from the bush," he notes, and adds, "Many . . . scenes betrayed pre-arrangement."

A critic in the *New York Herald Tribune*, Sid Bakal, is kinder to that first *High Adventure* show: "On the whole the program was an arresting and laudable documentary." But by episode three, on native tribes in Africa, Bakal too is complaining of "bare morsels that never probed beneath the surface" and "a lack of spontaneity or some segments obviously contrived for the cameras."

High Adventure returned for a second and final season of four installments in October 1958. Richard F. Shepard, writing in the *Times*, praises one of those shows—showing scientists studying a solar eclipse on the island of Pukapuka—as "a fascinating hodgepodge of scientific mission, native island life, adventurous frogmen and a number of other aspects." But then Shepard adds: "The material on hand was so attractive that it is hard to appreciate the reason for the obvious staging of scenes and incidents."

The bad notices must have hurt. And Thomas may even have learned from them—at least by the very last *High Adventure* installment, which was broadcast in March 1959. In his review of this account of a journey in a "creaky old Arab dhow bound from the Persian Gulf to Zanzibar," Shepard locates "no obvious staging of incidents such as have marked other shows in the series."[14]

These 11 *High Adventure* shows, whatever their limitations, helped secure Lowell Thomas' reputation as, to quote one newspaper, one of the world's greatest travelers. And, since they were rebroadcast on American television a number of times in the 1960s, they made another couple of generations—not just the Kerouac generation but the early *Lonely Planet* generation—aware not only of his reputation but of some of the remotest parts of the world and of the possibility that they too might go there.

((•))

Lowell Thomas would make another notable television appearance in the fall of 1959. Not only did he not stage anything for this one. He did not know about this star turn of his on network television in advance. It would prove memorable.

This Is Your Life, among the numerous 1950s migrants from radio to television, specialized in surprising guests, many of them—like the Reverend Billy Graham, Casey Stengel or Ronald Reagan—well-known. Then it would tell, on camera, the story of their lives. Important personages from earlier stages in the life in question—say, a beloved former teacher—were flown in to flesh out the tale, as well as elicit, on the part of the person undergoing the surprise, astonishment and, if all went well, tears. *This Is Your Life*, as its critics noted, leaned toward the sentimental. (In this, too, it had company in 1950s television.) The show earned high ratings in each of its nine years on NBC-TV. It was broadcast live.

Lowell Thomas had been invited to serve as toastmaster at a sports banquet at the Astor Hotel on the evening of September 30, 1959—for the purpose of being ambushed. The whole television apparatus—including the host of *This Is Your Life*, Ralph Edwards—was secreted behind the curtain on a stage in back of the ballroom. Edwards would later describe what followed after the curtain opened as the "worst evening" he ever had hosting the show.

One would have thought that Lowell—given his comfort and satisfaction with his own celebrity—would have been delighted by this opportunity to have his life displayed on national television. He was not. "I . . . went up to him and said, 'Tonight, Lowell Thomas, this is your life!'" Edwards recalled. "He said"—on camera—"'This is a sinister conspiracy.' The show went downhill from there. As I took him up toward the stage, I said to him, 'You're going to enjoy this.' He said, 'I doubt it very much.' And he didn't."

Lowell's sister, Pherbia, was on hand to rhapsodize about her brother's Colorado childhood. "Father insisted that Lowell know every geographical formation in the Cripple Creek area," she explained. To which her brother responded, on camera: "I knew all the saloons in the mining area." An old actress friend, Beulah Bondi, was brought out to say, "I happened to be there on the night that your very first radio contract happened. Do you remember?" To which Lowell replied, "No, I don't." When any factual errors cropped up in Edwards' account of his life, Lowell (Lowell!) insisted on correcting them. Prosper Buranelli was among the old acquaintances who came out to descant upon aspects of the great man's life. Once he got going, Lowell interjected: "Prosper, you've had too many drinks." To which Buranelli, having noted how the show was progressing, responded, "Haven't had enough."

Eventually Lowell, not used to being second banana, began taking over the program—devoting so much time to plugging his former teacher Mabel Barbee Lee's memoir, when she was brought out, that there wasn't time enough for Count Felix von Luckner, who had been flown in from Europe. Nor was there room to fit in all the show's commercials.

On his radio show the next evening, an apologetic Thomas chalked up his rude behavior to surprise. "Who wouldn't be startled—being greeted by such an array of old friends," he explained. "Perhaps I should have been in tears, but I was too flabbergasted." Thomas supplied another explanation for his rebellion against *This Is Your Life* to the *Daily News*: "I had always heard that it was a maudlin tear-jerker, so I subconsciously resolved that there would be no tears." Both of these explanations seem insufficient, however, to explain Lowell's obvious irritation, even anger. Did he have some personal secret he was afraid might come out on TV that evening?

(This was the theory later held by Lowell's second wife, Marianna.) Perhaps it is most likely that Lowell—beginning to show signs of cantankerousness in his late sixties—simply didn't like others taking control of his evening, let alone taking control of the story of his life.

After the show ended—and he had made sure a separate television appearance for Count Luckner would be arranged—Lowell's normal good cheer and graciousness reasserted itself. Ralph Edwards, for his part, brightened once he realized Thomas' obstinacy made for compelling television. "The rating kept going up during the show as people called their friends to tune in," Edwards later noted. It became the best-known installment of *This Is Your Life*, featured on the show's (many) retrospectives. Indeed, Thomas and Edwards ended up becoming pals.

Not everyone, however, wanted to see Thomas kiss and make up. John Lardner, writing in the *New Yorker*, found Thomas' not-exactly-characteristic refusal to go along with the schmaltz exemplary: "He resisted his tormentors fiercely," Lardner stated. "In short, few things in his long career became him like his last adventure."[15]

Lowell must have enjoyed this testament to his backbone in a highbrow magazine. But he must have flinched at those final two words. In the next two decades, his wife would get sick—so he took her on adventures; he would suffer a heart attack—and then go on more adventures. There could be no thought of a "last adventure" as long as Lowell Thomas was still ambulatory.

14.

~~~~~~~~~~~~~~~

To Strive, To Seek, To Find, and Not to Yield

Lowell Thomas remained trim all his life. He was not prone to excessive drinking. He did not smoke. He was physically active—remarkably so. However, many men in Lowell's post-farm, pre-gym generation proved much more devoted than he to the pleasures of overeating, alcohol, smoking and filling a soft chair. Many of Lowell's friends and associates did not live to see their seventies.

Prosper Buranelli—Lowell's sidekick, collaborator and top assistant—had a talent for all these vices. And Prosper favored a particularly strong Turkish cigarette, Murad. Prosper Buranelli died in his sleep of a heart attack on June 19, 1960. He was 68 and had worked with Thomas for half his life.

Prosper, the obituaries reported, was survived by his wife, who lived in Tenafly, New Jersey, and their nine children. (A tenth child had been killed in the war.) But Buranelli had not lived with his family in that house in Tenafly, which Lowell had selected and purchased for them. "He'd take a cab out and visit maybe every year or eight months," recalls his son Bernard "Buddy" Buranelli, the second-youngest of the brood. "He took an interest in the older children. I would go to the office in New York maybe once every six months and maybe we would have lunch. I didn't have any kind of relationship with him."

The newspapers, not surprisingly, failed to mention Prosper's two additional children by a "showgirl" in New York. "He had a real way with women," Buddy Buranelli notes.

The obituary in the *New York Times* gave Prosper's address as a hotel in New York, but on weekends and during the summer he had continued to reside in Lowell's Hammersley Hill estate on Quaker Hill, where his conversation delighted the collection of the accomplished with whom Lowell surrounded himself. In fact that is where Prosper died—after an evening spent, the newspapers reported, with Thomas E. Dewey, Edward R. Murrow, Norman Vincent Peale and Lowell Thomas.[1]

((•))

Lowell Thomas Jr., his wife, Tay, and their two young children moved to Anchorage, Alaska, in the summer of 1960. Sonny and Tay made an effort to return to Quaker Hill for holidays. And Lowell Sr., whose enthusiasm for the wilds of Alaska had never faded, tried to make it up there whenever he could, preferably with Fran. But still, their only child, their daughter-in-law and their two grandchildren were now more than 4,000 miles away.

And this distance between Lowell Jr.'s family and his parents was not just an unfortunate side effect of his and Tay's own passion for Alaska; it was one purpose of the move. Lowell Sr. was well-meaning. He certainly cared. But he was, as Tay put it, "a dynamic man." And he could—even with the best of intentions—become overbearing. Tay felt his interference on large matters—presuming to select the house in which she and her husband would live in Princeton was an example. And she felt it on more routine matters. When she wanted to go skiing with her husband, for instance, her father-in-law would insist on coming along and insist on a difficult trail. "I wasn't such a good skier," Tay explained. "I said 'sorry' and went my own way." Tay saw herself as caught in a "triangle"—competing with her husband's father for her husband's time and for control of their lives.

Lowell Sr. did not seem to notice. This world-class extrovert was once again having difficulty understanding and connecting with a quiet, inner-directed person. "I think he was puzzled by my feelings," she explained. "He couldn't see the relationship between him and me and Lowell, and the terrible pressures he put on Lowell."

Indeed, as Lowell Thomas Jr. enrolled for graduate work at Princeton and began to establish himself as a traveler, lecturer, filmmaker and adventure-book writer, it had become obvious that a ski trail was not the only trail he was following his father down. "It wasn't what Lowell wanted to do," Tay concluded, "it was what [his father] wanted him to do. . . . He wanted to mold him to follow him."

Lowell Jr. eventually saw this. "For many, many years my life was programmed very intensely," he later told a reporter. "Dad helped and encouraged me, and I learned from him. But as a kid, being Lowell Thomas Jr. was a real pain in the neck."

In 1954 Lowell Jr. and Tay had begun a journey to and around Africa and the Middle East in a single-engine plane he piloted and she navigated. That trip resulted in a series of *National Geographic* articles and his second book, Tay's first: *Our Flight to Adventure*. In 1957 and 1958 Lowell Jr. produced two shows on Alaska for his father's *High Adventure* series—often flying around the state with Tay and their young daughter, Anne.

After the birth of their son—named David Lowell Thomas (not Lowell Thomas III)—they settled in Alaska. "I needed to get going on my own," Lowell Jr. himself has acknowledged, ". . . out of my father's shadow. He cast such a big one."[2]

((•))

Interest in T. E. Lawrence, which had never really faded, grew even more intense in the United States and around the world at the end of 1962—more than 27 years after Lawrence's death, more than 43 years after Lowell's show on him had opened in London. That's when the movie *Lawrence of Arabia* debuted.

"I loathe the notion of being celluloided," Lawrence himself had groused when becoming the subject of a film first became a possibility. Yet Lawrence—at war with himself as always—sold the rights to *Revolt in the Desert*, the abridged version of his desert memoir, to the British movie producer Alexander Korda. Korda, occasionally consulting with Lowell Thomas, made many attempts to bring together a script, a director, actors, a location and government clearance, but always in the end failed. Others tried and failed too—including Thomas himself, with his John Wayne–Cinerama brainchild.

But then the hottest duo in moviedom, producer Sam Spiegel and director David Lean—fresh from a huge artistic and commercial success in 1957 with *The Bridge on the River Kwai*—turned to Lawrence's story. Spiegel scooped up the rights to many of the Lawrence biographies, most definitely including the first. Michael Wilson—a blacklisted screenwriter—wrote, uncredited, the first two drafts of the screenplay. In the second of those drafts, Wilson gave such a large role to a character known as "Lowell Thomas" that Spiegel negotiated with Kirk Douglas, then one of Hollywood's top stars, about the role. That draft opened with Thomas and one of his London shows, and "throughout the second half of the screenplay," Thomas was presented—fancifully—as being with Lawrence: "filming his entry into Jerusalem and Damascus."

In the final draft of the screenplay—written by a British playwright, Robert Bolt—the role of the American reporter, now named Jackson Bentley, shrank. A respected supporting actor, Arthur Kennedy, ended up playing him in the film as a gruff, hard-bitten, middle-aged Chicago journalist, wielding a large flash camera—in other words as nothing like Thomas, who was, his appearance on *This Is Your Life* notwithstanding, preternaturally smooth and charming.

It took Thomas some months to catch up with Spiegel and Lean's blockbuster. On his radio show, after he finally viewed *Lawrence of Arabia*, Thomas professed to being unconcerned with the treatment of the character based on him, though he did note "that not one single incident or action by the man playing this role is accurate."

Errors in the film's portrayal of Lawrence, Thomas insisted, bothered him more: "Actually, you can get about as much accurate information on Lawrence of Arabia by seeing *Mutiny on the Bounty* or *Ben Hur*," he told his radio audience. "That's how much the story has been distorted." Thomas' example, however, is just that Lawrence was very short but the actor who played him, Peter O'Toole, was "a six foot Irishman." "It's grotesque," he concludes. (John Wayne, it must be noted, was two inches taller than O'Toole.) But the root problem with the film, in Thomas' view—and that of Lawrence's younger brother Arnold, with whom Lowell was in contact—seems to have been a surfeit of intractability and angst in the movie's protagonist and an insufficiency of heroism.[3]

Lawrence of Arabia won seven Academy Awards, including best picture.

((•))

"Tho' much is taken, much abides," Tennyson writes of the aging Ulysses. In the television era Thomas' radio newscast was no longer the campfire around which the most Americans sat. He was reluctant to admit it, but Cinerama, along with the better part of his film and television career, was also behind him. But Lowell remained professionally active well past the age of 70—unusually active. Like Tennyson's Ulysses, in other words, he was still striving, seeking, finding; still not yielding.

This modern-day, long-in-the-tooth argonaut did not always strive, however, in a manner befitting a Greek hero. In one of the more widely known photographs of him, Lowell is standing with a group of celebrities— from left: Edward R. Murrow, Thomas Dewey and the golfers Gene Sarazen and Sam Snead. Murrow and Snead were on the tall side, Sarazen short. Dewey was about Lowell's height: five feet eight. But Clay Johnson, director of the Garst Museum near Lowell's birthplace in Ohio, points out something interesting, even revealing, in that photograph. Lowell is standing between the two golfers. He was undoubtedly the one who had brought together these eminent men. The gathering likely is taking place on Quaker Hill—on his territory. Yet if you look closely at his shoes, you can see that Lowell is standing on tiptoes.

((•))

Lowell continued to race around the planet—and tell everyone about it. Indeed, as he entered his seventies, his reputation as one of the world's foremost travelers was as strong as it had ever been. "Long before jetliners shrunk the world," President Lyndon Johnson quipped, "Lowell Thomas had it in his pocket." His ability to pick up and go—go far—did in fact abide, even as age intensified the discomforts of places other than home.

Indeed, if there was an impediment to Lowell's continued adventuring, it was not his advanced years but the Earth's. With just about two-thirds of the twentieth century complete, the planet was running short on under-explored (from a Western perspective) lands. Hence Antarctica (which had been underexplored from anything but a penguin's perspective). Research posts were just starting to be established there. And this was also, significantly, the only one of the seven continents upon which Lowell Thomas had never set foot.*

---

* A five-mile-long range of mountains in Antarctica had, however, been named the Lowell Thomas Mountains in the late 1940s by Finn Ronne's Antarctic Research Expedition; Thomas had been a supporter of the expedition.

In November 1962 Lowell flew into McMurdo Sound in Antarctica from Christchurch, New Zealand, with General Jimmy Doolittle and a handful of politicians and other journalists.

Routes that airplanes had not previously flown were also growing scarce at this stage in the history of air travel. When, in 1968, Lowell Thomas and Lowell Thomas Jr. published a book called *Famous First Flights That Changed History*, 14 of the 16 flights they celebrated had been made before 1940—including those of the Wright brothers, Charles Lindbergh and, of course, that first round-the-world flight. Lowell Jr. had tagged along on one of the two recent flights: the first longitudinal circumnavigation of the planet—over both poles—in 1965. Lowell Sr. was on board the other recent, though less impressive, "first flight": a 4,700-mile, 14-and-a-half-hour non-stop hop from Cape Town, South Africa, to McMurdo Sound in Antarctica in the fall of 1963.[4] So this septuagenarian had not only been on board for a "first flight" but had made it to Antarctica twice in less than a year.

((•))

Age may not have been tying Thomas down, but it was exacting a price. In a letter written to New York's Cardinal Spellman in December 1963, Lowell reported "a near collapse" in Michigan after "making three speeches in one day." This was after he had "just come in from jumping all those meridians between the South Pole and Detroit." In that letter Lowell made sure to write, "At any rate they say it wasn't heart, and have given me a clean bill of health, told me to resume work, get on with my skiing and even go on another expedition if I have one up my sleeve."

But it was heart. Lowell may have been too vain to acknowledge it, but the *New York Times* reported that he had been diagnosed as having suffered a mild heart attack.[5]

((•))

Lowell Thomas Jr. was flying his plane from Anchorage to Fairbanks during the Great Alaska Earthquake—the second-largest ever recorded anywhere—on March 27, 1964. His wife, Tay, was home in Anchorage cooking dinner for their two children, Anne, who was eight, and David, two years younger.

She heard the rumble and rushed outside with the kids. "Within a few seconds the entire house started to fall apart . . . ," Tay recalled in a *National*

Geographic article she wrote on the experience. "Now the earth began breaking up and buckling all about us. A great crack started to open in the snow between Anne and me, and I quickly pulled her across it toward me. . . . Then our whole lawn broke up into chunks of dirt, rock, snow and ice." Tay and the two children rode one such "wildly bucking" slab down from the high bluff above an inlet upon which their house had stood. They were eventually pulled back up—shivering but unharmed—by neighbors. Two children had died in the house next door.[6]

((•))

Edward R. Murrow was 16 years younger than Lowell Thomas. "They didn't hang out together on a weekly basis," notes Murrow's son Casey, who spent much of his childhood on Quaker Hill. But Murrow and Thomas had developed a friendship built not so much upon their parallel professional lives as around Quaker Hill. "They would play golf together," Casey Murrow recalls. "They would undoubtedly sidle up to the bar at the Country Club. They would see each other at times at Lowell's [radio] studio [on Quaker Hill] . . . , which he also used as sort of an office." And Murrow had begun addressing Lowell as "Tommy."

Ed Murrow died of lung cancer on Quaker Hill on April 27, 1965. "He was only fifty-seven," Lowell told his radio audience the next evening. "My neighbor, friend and a great, great guy."

Murrow's ashes were scattered upon Glen Arden Farm on Quaker Hill.[7]

((•))

A tone of deep caring had begun appearing in Lowell's letters to Fran:

- "Rome is dismal in Nov. but doubly dismal without you," he writes in 1958, and then refers to an article suggesting that people should not put off engaging in activities that please them. "Most of my work I enjoy, but I would like to do what you would enjoy the most. I love you my darling."
- "Everybody here asks for you—and I miss you, Fran Dearest," he notes from one ski resort. "Life is too dull without you to put zip into everything."
- "Hello My Darling:—I miss you! I miss you!" he writes from Tahiti

while en route—and it was a long route—to Antarctica for the first time. "I keep thinking of you and how I really did not want to leave you in LA—especially after that much too noisy dinner party where we couldn't even talk to each other."

- "Golly I wish I were with you!" he writes from Europe on one of many ski trips and on one of the rather large subset of those trips—in these days before snowmaking was well established—when it was not possible to ski. "I'm lonesome, bored and fed up."[8]

Perhaps these effusions owed something to guilt. He was so often away. But surely they were motivated in large part by love. Indeed, Lowell's correspondence with his wife bespeaks an intimacy—an ability, in particular, to admit to feeling down—that is in evidence in his letters to his parents when he was young but nowhere else in his correspondence or writings. Lowell's emotions in these letters may also have been intensified by the sense that the woman who inspired them was fading.

Frances Thomas' health problems had begun to be mentioned in Lowell's correspondence as early as 1953, when he writes their son, "Mother hasn't been at all well for five months." The next year she broke her leg. In 1959 she had her appendix and gallbladder removed. The diagnosis was phlebitis in 1964. Lowell, nonetheless, took her around the world the next winter: "to the big game country in East Africa, where she had long wanted to go . . . a few stops in Europe, Arabia, India, Malaysia, the Far East and a final three days with Sonny and his family in Alaska."

Fran broke her shoulder early in 1969. That spring she began having dizzy spells. Lowell's characteristic response to those maladies was another trip that summer. "She came through our round-the-world journey in grand style," he writes in a letter. But then in the fall, he reports, "she took [a] fall on a staircase at home" and broke her shoulder again.[9]

((•))

Lowell traveled during this period with another woman. This caused some talk. She was quite young—18 or 19—and quite comely, with hair teased and sprayed in place in early-1960s fashion. Moreover, Christl Thalhammer was of the type who had turned Lowell's head as a youth and, according to his son and daughter-in-law, still got his attention: "He was captivated by charming, blond ladies," is how Tay Thomas put it.

Christl was the daughter of an Austrian man who had played a large role in bringing Alpine skiing to the United States, Kurt Thalhammer, and his wife, Hilde. The parents returned to Austria. The young woman stayed on for a while, "to do something about her English," Lowell explains in a letter to a friend. "I was supposed to keep my eye on her." He "took her on a ski jaunt through New England, and also the West." He took her with him on a long journey to New Guinea, where he was doing some filming for a short-lived BBC television series on global oddities: *The World of Lowell Thomas*. He even secured a contract for her to write a book on their travels (undoubtedly helped by him or one of Prosper's replacements): *Adventures with the New Guinea Headhunters*, by Christl (they did not use her last name), "Introduction by Lowell Thomas." Doubleday published it in 1965.

In her book Christl writes as if she is infatuated with her renowned benefactor and guide: "Like most men who love the outdoors, Mr. Marco Polo seems to be bursting with energy, which he must control. His deep blue eyes look at the world with never-failing interest; his mind is so restless with ideas that they seem to fly from him like sparks." (If there was a ghostwriter on this passage, one hopes it was not Lowell himself.) And Lowell can barely hide his infatuation with Christl. At one point he writes her at length—under the heading "Taken to the Cleaners" or "The Saga of the Beautiful Blonde's Missing Pants"—about his quest to recover a pair of ski pants she had left at a Manhattan dry cleaner, which one Christl could not recall. And Lowell, after their great journey together, did his best to persuade Christl to transfer from the Sorbonne in Paris, where she was then studying, to the much-nearer McGill University in Montreal—not far, he assures her, from some first-rate ski slopes and where, he assures her, he has "a great many . . . friends."

Did this man in his early seventies, with an increasingly infirm wife, actually have an affair with a woman in her late teens? His son and daughter-in-law insist Lowell was not a womanizer. Theirs may not be the most persuasive testimony on this subject, but in this conclusion, at least in this instance, they were not alone. And it probably was more likely—especially given Lowell's friendship with Christl's parents and the openness with which they moved around together—that this old man was merely engaging in a flirtation with this young woman. But Lowell—in his incessant striving—certainly was not above showing his cute blond friend off as they traveled.[10]

((•))

Frank Smith's wife had died in 1965. He had experienced some heart trouble of his own, which he did not mention to his coworkers. He remarried.

Meanwhile Capital Cities, the company he ran, had been adding properties: TV stations in Buffalo and Michigan, a radio station in the New York market and then one in Los Angeles. That LA station was "the kind of station that in those days was just right for Capital Cities," the executive who found it for Smith later explained: "a good property whose commercial time had not been well sold."

Twelve days after that purchase Smith was driving with his new wife back to New York. They stopped at a motel in Maryland. That night— August 6, 1966—Frank Smith died of a heart attack.

The man who had finally gotten Lowell Thomas out of debt, and then created the company from which Lowell was making his fortune, was only 56.[11]

((•))

Marianna Munn Krickenbarger had raised four children on a farm in Ohio—near Lowell's parents' hometowns. Her husband, Harold Krickenbarger, she later reported, "always called me 'mommy' instead of my name" and "never said either 'thank you' or 'I'm sorry.'" It was becoming clear that this was not the life she wanted for herself.

Marianna met Lowell Thomas, by her account, on the day she had begun protesting the Vietnam War. This was somewhat ironic, since Lowell, ever an anti-Communist, was a staunch supporter of American involvement in Vietnam. He had even participated in a prowar film, *No Substitute for Victory*, hosted by one of America's leading hawks, John Wayne. But Lowell was passing through Ohio. Marianna, a handsome woman who was not a blonde, handed him an antiwar pamphlet.

Lowell "was attracted to me from the beginning," Marianna writes in a letter to Fred D. Crawford, who was then researching a biography of Thomas. "He always felt there was something 'mystical' about my being from the place where he was born." Marianna Munn obtained a divorce and moved to New York City in 1968. She was 40. Lowell found her a job helping fundraise for the Spafford Children's Center in Jerusalem, a charity with which he had a long association.

"At first, because I was asking for help for my peace organization and then stepping into the work he offered me," she wrote to Crawford, "when he made advances I naively thought he might be 'testing me' to see if I were a solid person with whom to be associated. So at first I resisted." Then she didn't resist. "I am ashamed," she explained, "that the 'relationship' developed well before his wife died." In another letter to Crawford, she is candid in her comments about that relationship:

> Shall I tell you that once, when we were courting, he retrieved me from the airport and held one long, passionate kiss the entire ride from La-Guardia into Manhattan? . . . He WAS a great lover! And a great gentleman. No matter where we were, on any spot on earth, he never failed to open a door for me. He never took a bite to eat until I began. He was tough but <u>never</u> crude. How many women get to know that?

There is one more reference in a letter from Marianna to her amorous experiences with the aged Lowell Thomas. "In those days," she writes, "I was also very sensual, and we had a remarkable sex life."[12]

((•))

The transition from Frank Smith to Tom Murphy as chairman of the board and chief executive officer of Capital Cities went smoothly. And Murphy, well trained by Smith, did not wait long before he started buying stations—stations that propelled the company into a higher league. The number of AM, FM and TV stations one company could own was strictly limited by the Federal Communications Commission. Smith had brought Capital Cities up against that limit. So to add stronger television stations—in Houston, Philadelphia and New Haven—Murphy had to sell weaker ones. Then Murphy made Capital Cities into a media—not just a broadcast—company by purchasing Fairchild Publications, which owned *Women's Wear Daily.* "They will buy only if the price and property are right," Warren E. Buffett, a fan and a friend of Murphy's, would later tell the *New York Times.* "It's like watching Ted Williams hit."

As for Lowell? "He was an exciting guy to be around, bigger than life," Murphy explains in an interview. However, while it continued to increase the value of his stock, Thomas was not a major player in any of Capital Cities' buying and selling. "Lowell would come to our board meetings. He wouldn't sit down but would tell us a story about where he was just about to go—which would be fascinating. Then he'd look at me, say, 'Tom whatever you decide is alright with me' and leave." Murphy adds: "He was always giving the impression that he was in perpetual motion."[13]

$$((\bullet))$$

Thomas once framed his goal thusly: "To know more about this globe than anyone else ever has." He had a claim to that distinction.

As a rule he brought back from his travels stories, not particularly profound insights. "My life has been one of motion, not thought," Lowell conceded in 1970.[14]

$$((\bullet))$$

"I was certainly distressed to learn," Lowell Thomas Jr. wrote his father's majordomo, Electra Nicks, in the spring of 1971, "that mother has had another fall and is back in the hospital." This time Frances Thomas had broken her pelvis. "She has reached the stage where it's important to have someone with her whenever she walks about the house or goes anywhere," Lowell Sr. explains in a letter in September of that year. Nonetheless, he was still contemplating taking Fran on trips "to some of her favorite spots" in Europe. By January 1972 she had to use a walker or be held up, but Lowell wanted to take her, along with Electra, on a tour of South America. Fran certainly was eager to visit their son's family in Anchorage. And at a point when speaking was becoming difficult for her and, as Lowell explains in a letter, "she has reached the stage where only the most fundamental reactions emerge," Lowell quotes his wife as exclaiming, "More trips!"

Exactly what ailed Frances Thomas is not clear in the surviving correspondence. There was talk then of "hardening of the arteries." The best guess later among those who knew her was Parkinson's disease. Maybe the concussion she received after being thrown by a horse had been more significant than they realized. Or perhaps it was Alzheimer's. "Fran has been in a sorta twilight world for just over two years," Lowell acknowledges in a letter to a friend in August 1973. And he admitted that month, in a nostalgic letter to an old friend from Colorado, that "the doctor says there is no hope for improvement."[15]

$$((\bullet))$$

Thomas E. Dewey died of a heart attack in Miami on March 16, 1971. He was 68. His wife had died eight months earlier.

Dewey's biographer, Richard Norton Smith, tells a story about what followed that illustrates, as he puts it, the fact that Lowell Thomas "could be smothering in his embrace." Shortly after his father's death, Dewey's eldest son received a call from Lowell announcing that, in Smith's telling, he would conduct a memorial service up on Quaker Hill for the governor and his wife, and that they would both then be permanently buried on an attractive plot of land, with a long view, which Lowell had chosen, on the Hill.

Thomas E. Dewey Jr. responded that his parents would be interred in a mausoleum they had designed together in a Pawling cemetery—down the hill. And that Lowell would be invited to the memorial service, which would be held there in a couple of months on what would have been their wedding anniversary.

Smith's version of Lowell's reply to Dewey's son, which he must have gotten from Tom Dewey Jr. himself, sounds uncharacteristically blunt and ungracious for Lowell: "But you can't do this to me. I've already got both Javits and Nelson coming."[16] (Jacob Javits was then one of New York's senators and Nelson Rockefeller its governor.) Lowell's annoyance in seeing his well-worked plans thwarted was characteristic. And as he aged he hid his annoyance less well.

((•))

A 15-minute, one-man newscast had no real place in the hurried world of after-television, before-NPR radio—which was now designed for quick listening on transistor, clock or car radios. CBS had reduced *Lowell Thomas and the News* to ten minutes as of September 28, 1958. As of June 3, 1974, the network cut that newscast to five minutes. And two of those five minutes had to be devoted to commercials.

Its host was not pleased. "Human interest, adventure, colorful stories from around the globe have been my specialty," Thomas later explained. "And the present radio format allows only enough time for headlines."[17]

((•))

Presidents all found occasions to welcome Lowell Thomas to the White House, and Thomas was close with most of the Republican presidents.

Now in his eighties, he was not all that impressed by the Watergate scandal, which forced one of them, Richard Nixon, from office. "I've known President Nixon a long time," Thomas told a reporter for the *Hartford Courant* in August 1974, two weeks after the president resigned, "and I've never seen a sordid side to him. But then again I haven't been opposing him in political combat." Lowell added: "The Nixons have visited us here."[18]

And, of course, investigative journalism—of the sort that had helped expose Nixon's extralegal efforts—was not Lowell's journalism.

((•))

Lowell Thomas Jr. had embarked on a political career in Alaska. He had lost two races for Congress and pulled out of another one, before being elected to the state senate—all without his father's assistance. "LT Jr. hasn't asked my opinion on this!" Lowell Sr. wrote an acquaintance. ". . . He makes his own decisions. In the last campaign he wouldn't even take a nickel from me."

Then, in 1974, Lowell Thomas Jr., at the age of 51, was elected lieutenant governor of Alaska. He ran always as a Republican, but in 1974 Lowell Jr. had been part of a ticket, with Jay Hammond, in the Republican primary and then the general election, that emphasized defending the state's natural resources. The family moved to Juneau.

In 1977 the lieutenant governor, following a visit to South Africa, made a highly objectionable statement in support of the white government there and then appeared, shockingly, to come out against interracial marriage. There were calls for him to resign. Lowell Jr. quickly apologized. He noted that he had "intervened with prison authorities only last year to enable a black prisoner and his white fiancé to marry." And, significantly, the lieutenant governor attributed the sentiments he had blurted out to "a prejudice rooted in my childhood that, frankly, I was not even aware of."

This probably was a reference to some of the insensitivities toward and biases against people from other backgrounds that his father had displayed and taken too long to shuck. That is the impression of Lowell Jr.'s daughter, Anne Thomas Donaghy. "Dad absorbed many attitudes from his father without questioning," she explains. "But he has always rooted for the underdog." Those whom I've been able to contact who knew Lowell Thomas Jr. in those days in Alaska insist they saw no sign of intolerance or discrimination in his work or behavior there. The late Governor

Hammond's wife Bella, is, as she explains, "half Eskimo." "I've never known Lowell Jr. to be racist about anything," she states.

Lowell Thomas Jr. served one term as lieutenant governor, did not run for re-election—in part because of his discomfort with the uproar his statements had created—and returned to Anchorage. "That was the end of my career in elective politics, and I was content with that," he later explained. After moving back, Lowell Jr. returned to his first love, flying. He ran a business as a bush pilot—among the small group licensed to land on Mount McKinley.[19]

((•))

Frances Ryan Thomas died on February 16, 1975, at the age of 81. She was buried in that attractive plot, with a great view, Lowell had selected near the Country Club on Quaker Hill.

No cause of death was mentioned in the UPI obituary that was picked up by most of the newspapers. It described her as a "prominent world traveler, hostess and wife of newscaster Lowell Thomas Sr."

Her passing "left a great void in my life," Lowell noted.[20] But she had been mostly gone for years.

((•))

Upon Fran's death, Lowell donated his huge mansion on Quaker Hill—Hammersley Hill, the biggest piece of the old French estate—to Denver University, from which she had graduated and he had received two of his degrees. He also bestowed upon them a collection of his memorabilia.

Lowell was none too pleased when the university, instead of making use of the estate or selling it as a conference center, soon sold it—for less than he thought they might have gotten—to the brash film producer Dino De Laurentiis. "Hammersley Hill is the key to a glorious area . . . ," Lowell complained in an angry letter to the university's chancellor. "And now it falls into the hands of some character from Hollywood who hasn't been introduced to me and of whom I hadn't even heard." In another slight, Lowell's memorabilia were never displayed at Denver University. However, the money from the sale of his mansion was used to help establish the Lowell Thomas Law Center on its campus.

With Hammersley Hill gone, Lowell set about building his third residence on Quaker Hill. He had picked out a 40-acre site that sat atop a rise, giving it an even better view than the rest of Quaker Hill—a "five-state view," Lowell liked to say—and he began work there on a three-story, 15-room Georgian brick home. One day Cliff Carpenter hopped over the chain to take a peek and rated the unfinished structure "presidential—Jovian" and the view "unbearably exhilarating."[21] It was called Main Top.

((•))

On May 14, 1976, at the age of 84, Lowell Thomas left his radio show. This was big news, the program then being the longest-running network news show in the history of American radio—the longest-running broadcast of any kind, Lowell insisted. Thomas had been doing his newscast on NBC and CBS, on just NBC and then on just CBS, for almost 46 years. (Paul Harvey—a more opinionated, less accomplished broadcaster—would pass him in the first decade of the next century.)

"As you may have heard I'll be off radio for awhile," Thomas told his audience. "But there's nothing in the rumor that I'm retiring, nothing. On the contrary, I'll probably be busier and more involved than ever." His plans included, he informed the newspapers, working on the PBS television series *Lowell Thomas Remembers*, which employed film from old Fox Movietone newsreels, and finishing two more books: a biography of General Jimmy Doolittle and the second volume of his memoir. "I'll be off on a brief vacation," those listening to that last newscast heard him say, "perhaps doing some glacier skiing in the mountains of British Columbia and Alaska."

"Instead of my usual, 'So long until tomorrow'," is how Lowell concluded that final broadcast, ". . . tonight it will simply be, 'Here's to you. So long.'"

Then, in a further demonstration that he was not the retiring sort, in 1979 Lowell began work upon a series of short pieces for radio: *The Best Years*, which, using the example of eminent people, tried to make the case for old age.[22]

((•))

Waiting for Lowell Thomas to have some free time was not a particularly satisfying way to spend your own time. It was not just those remnants of radio and television work that continued to occupy him even in his eighties;

Lowell was also regularly dashing off to give talks and add to his bulky collection of honorary degrees and keys to cities. And Marianna Munn had spent nine (mostly) lonely years in New York City (mostly) waiting for dribs and drabs of Lowell Thomas' time.

So Marianna, who had had enough, decided to move to Texas, where some of her children were living. Lowell, she says, asked her to stay in New York. "Not once dreaming he might be amenable to the idea," Marianna recalled in an account she penned of her life with Lowell, "I wrote him a letter stating he would have to marry me to keep me there. When he decided we should then be married, I was awed. . . . . . amazed. . . . . . thrilled!"

However, as she explains, the wedding planning was rather one-sided. "Excitedly I told him I wished to have as my bridesmaid a dear friend from Greenville, Ohio, an elegant widow. But . . . he emitted a horrified, 'Oh no!' and instructed me that he had already asked someone else to be my bridesmaid"—someone Marianna had never met. "As a second choice, he offered me his lovely daughter-in-law Tay," although she was not exactly a supporter of the marriage.

Marianna had other complaints. By her account, Lowell's secretary, Electra Nicks, kept phoning him, crying, and phoned his friends "saying she would break up this marriage." And then Lowell himself—in an age that was less comfortable with divorce—changed the facts of his new wife's life in announcing their marriage: he told the papers she was a widow— although her ex, Harold Krickenbarger Sr., was still very much alive. And Lowell omitted all mention of her children.

Marianna Munn and Lowell Thomas were married on January 5, 1977—he was 84, she 49. The wedding took place on Maui, where Lowell Thomas Jr. and Tay Thomas had built a second home. Lowell Sr. returned the honor his son had paid him by asking Sonny to serve as his best man.

Five days later, Lowell was to receive the Medal of Freedom Award from President Gerald Ford. He flew to Washington for the ceremony not with his new wife, Marianna reports, but with Electra.[23]

((•))

Marianna did accompany her new husband on their honeymoon—"probably the longest and most unusual honeymoon in history," Lowell, in a burst of superlatives impressive even for him, told the *New York Times*. "By his calculation, it lasted nine months and spanned 70,000 miles," the *Times* reports. (That would have been equivalent to almost three circumnavigations of the globe, and elsewhere he upped the distance covered to 100,000 miles.) Their trip was something of a greatest-hits tour for Lowell—with visits to, among many, many other places, Jordan, where they met King Hussein (thanks to Lowell's Lawrence connection); Afghanistan; and Tibet.[24]

Tibet was the best-publicized stop. The newlyweds had made it there as part of a party led by George H. W. Bush, who had served by then as chief of the U.S. Liaison Office in the People's Republic of China and director of Central Intelligence. Bush, traveling as a guest of the Chinese government, had brought along a distinguished group of dignitaries and friends, including his wife, Barbara.

Lowell and Marianna tagged along on the tour, which included a boat trip down the Yangtze River. Then, at Lowell's urging, their guides agreed to let the whole party visit Tibet. When they arrived in Lhasa, many of those in Bush's troop were felled by the altitude. Not the honeymooner. "Lowell, at eighty-seven years of age, seems to be in better shape than any of us," Barbara Bush noted in her diary. (She had added, however, a couple of years to his age.) Indeed, while Lowell had recently had a pacemaker implanted to correct an irregular heartbeat, at one point earlier in their tour Barbara had spotted him jogging—albeit "in *very* slow motion." The Americans jocularly suggested to their guides in Tibet that Lowell and Marianna wanted to consummate their marriage at 14,000 feet.

In her memoirs, Barbara Bush ranked Lowell as "the most interesting member of the delegation." At one point, Barbara writes, "George invited Lowell to tell us about his first trip with his son, Lowell Junior to Tibet." It became a long story. ("After eighty," Thomas was wont to say, "everything reminds you of something.") The Bushes had no complaint: "He took us around the world, dropping famous names as he went. We were fascinated."

This visit to Tibet came after the Cultural Revolution—a violent, bloody attempt to eradicate any hints of resistance to Mao Zedong and his radical brand of Communism in China; indeed, the visit was evidence that more moderate forces were now in control. But the damage that had been done to Tibetan culture during the Cultural Revolution had been horrifying—most monasteries and many other religious sites had been destroyed, monks had been jailed or forced to de-robe and marry.*

When Lowell asked their hosts about the Tibetan officials he had met with in 1949, Lowell was told—according to James Lilley, another member of the party—"They are gone" or "They are no longer here" or "They have disappeared." Lilley reports that they saw no monks in Lhasa in 1977. Thomas' conclusion: "It's a feeble imitation of the Tibet I knew."[25]

((•))

Tom Murphy had also been buying newspapers for Capital Cities—none too huge, most eventually requiring staff cutbacks if they were to meet the company's high profit expectations. There were, consequently, battles with some strong labor unions. The ugliest of them occurred in 1978, when Murphy purchased, cheap, the Wilkes-Barre *Times Leader* in Pennsylvania. The resulting strike led to the unions' starting a competing newspaper that lasted for years. This time Tom Murphy appeared to have swung and missed.

But Capital Cities remained a tremendously successful company. And, although Thomas had continually been selling off stock in it and diversifying his holdings, as of 1976 he still owned more than $8.5 million of Capital Cities stock.[26]

((•))

Walter Cronkite, Norman Mailer and Tom Wolfe were among those who distinguished themselves reporting on the American space program, particularly the landing on the moon. A younger Lowell Thomas would have joined them with a quick book at least. It was his kind of story.

And even an older Lowell Thomas saw it as his kind of adventure. In fact, at the age of 85 Lowell claimed to be number two on the list of civilians who might be sent into space—right after the head of NASA.

"What I'd really like to do is get outside our own solar system, where there would be a possibility of visiting a planet that might be inhabited,"

---

* Many monasteries have since been rebuilt under Chinese control and the monks have returned, though not in nearly the same numbers.

he told a reporter for the *New York Times*. But he added—"wistfully," the *Times* reported—"I don't think that will happen in my time."[27]

((•))

The new Mrs. Lowell Thomas, as she was happy to call herself, was never all that comfortable on Quaker Hill. Neither Lowell nor Fran had been born to money, but they had hobnobbed with the accomplished and well-off for many decades. Marianna, a bright woman who had spent much of her life on an Ohio farm, had been thrust rather abruptly into this society—presuming to take the place of the beloved previous Mrs. Thomas. She was seen by some as a usurper, as a gold digger and as a little bit out of control.

It did not help that Marianna leaned toward a mystical spirituality in a neighborhood that mostly confined itself to genteel Protestantism. It did not help that Marianna, concerned about supporting herself after Lowell's death, eventually asked him for an increase in her trust fund, which she considered modest and inadequate. Nor did it help that—when Lowell was away—she had taken to driving herself down from patrician Quaker Hill to plebeian Pawling: for a salad at the local pharmacy, an ice cream cone dipped in chocolate, and then a chat and a scotch with a friend at an antique shop. The rumor on the Hill was that Mrs. Lowell Thomas was frequenting a bar.

Lowell in his eighties was not the easiest man to live with: He had trouble, as did many men of his generation, discussing emotions (though he had seemed to manage this well enough with his first wife). He insisted that matters be handled his way—even if they involved others' lives. Lowell, for instance, set the TV rules in their house: Marianna said only the evening news was permitted. He could get angry—and as he aged, this, too, he hid less well. "When Lowell discovered I was hanging out with 'commoners' and having a drink as well he was furious," she writes.

"Then why did we all stay close to him?" Marianna asks herself in a letter to Crawford. "We stayed on because, . . . aside from a black temper occasionally, he was warm, utterly charming, affectionate . . . and he made life more exciting for us than anyone else on earth." She also raved about his "generosity in helping others." And Lowell's second wife added an additional compliment: "Only once in my fifteen year association with him did he ever say anything unkind about ANYONE." And even that was hardly nasty. "He stated simply that 'I just don't care much for him.'"[28]

((•))

Lowell's sister Pherbia, 12 years younger than he, died on November 24, 1980. Her husband, Pinky Thornburg, who was Lowell's age, survived her by two months.[29]

((•))

Walter Cronkite was among those who had succeeded in fending off Lowell's urgings that he get a place on Quaker Hill. "To hell with that!" James Morrison recalls Cronkite proclaiming when they were working on a film together. "Lowell's a control freak. I didn't want him running my life."

There was one other subject upon which Lowell could be rather insistent: "this problem of skiing," Walter Cronkite called it. "Every time you saw him," Cronkite explained, "he said, 'You ought to be on skis. You're the kind of guy that'd really love skiing.' Well, I tried to pacify Lowell by saying I tried it, but I was really lying."

Lowell's evangelism was often more successful. President Gerald Ford, an avid and skilled skier, numbered himself among those who were first motivated to try the sport by Lowell's many on-air panegyrics.

Richard Moulton interviewed and skied with Lowell for a documentary he was producing, *Legends of American Skiing*. Lowell was 88 at the time.[30]

((•))

David Lowell Thomas had an opportunity to ski with his grandfather at some of the world's best ski resorts and sometimes with some of the world's best skiers. He had an opportunity to attend ballgames with his grandfather—often ending up on the field, once being handed a baseball signed by Yogi Berra. As a teenager he found all this intimidating.

His grandfather, prodigious letter writer that he was, also barraged him with quick notes and newspaper clippings—often harboring suggestions on a career path. Dave found this more than intimidating. He found it oppressive.

Lowell sent his grandson a package after he graduated from college. Dave Thomas did not even open it until recently, almost 30 years later. It had contained the stopwatch CBS gave each of its longtime employees when they retired, along with a request that the young man call to discuss his career plans.[31]

((•))

By his late eighties Thomas had published, by his count, 54 books. Usually they were entertaining. Many sold well. Often they garnered respectful reviews. At least one—*With Lawrence in Arabia*—qualified as pathbreaking. None of them—certainly neither of the two volumes of his memoir—stands as a particularly distinguished piece of writing or research.

Many journalists—hypnotized by the back-and-forth of their time—fail to produce work that is lasting. But Lowell, despite an impressive facility with sentences and a nose for a good tale, had other shortcomings as a litterateur. High among them were his contentment with quick, popular success and his tendency to hand over much of the responsibility for achieving that success to others. Nor did it help that Lowell's energies were perpetually scattered.

"All my life I've had this bad habit," Thomas sometimes told interviewers. "I can never settle down to doing just one thing at a time." That was what is called today a "humble brag," intended, in part, to call attention to his many and varied accomplishments. But it was also an acknowledgment.[32]

((•))

James Morrison had had the pleasure of spending time with Lowell since Morrison was a kid. "I loved being around him," Morrison adds. "You'd say something; he'd pick up on it and run with it."

Near the end of Lowell's life, Morrison watched him deliver a high school commencement address in Colorado Springs. Morrison, as he told Fred Crawford, was apprehensive. The "acoustics were horrible," and this was a very old man. Lowell, Morrison recalled, stood at the front edge of the stage and asked, "Can everybody hear me?" Then he "spoke extemporaneously for an hour and a half, and was absolutely masterful."

At about that time, Tom Brokaw, then host of the *Today* show, interviewed Lowell Thomas at his home on Quaker Hill. "He appeared in a Tibetan coat with his dog at his side, arranged the camera location and practically asked the questions," Brokaw remembers. "The consummate showman and producer to the end."[33]

((•))

On August 27, 1981, Lowell Thomas, age 89, insisted, according to his wife, in engaging her in a tennis game full of "crazy exertion." "Was he trying to prove his youth?" she later wondered.

The next day Richard Moulton and a camera crew showed up on Quaker Hill to interview another "legend" of American skiing: Austrian-born Toni Matt. After Matt had severely injured his leg, Lowell found him a job running the golf course on Quaker Hill. They were filming Matt for Moulton's documentary, but Lowell not only set up the shot—in front of his "History of Civilization Fireplace"—he conducted the interview with Matt himself.

"Lowell then asked, 'Is that a wrap?'" Moulton recalls. "The lights were turned off. And as he slid off the stool he'd been sitting on, all of a sudden this impresario became a little old man."

Then Lowell drove off. His chauffeur had admitted to Moulton that he never knew where they were going next. This time it proved to be a Capital Cities board meeting in Manhattan. Lowell made it back to Quaker Hill for the night.

Marianna reports that she and her husband followed their normal routine that evening—reading in separate bedrooms. (They both leaned toward biographies.) Then, she says, she walked, as was her habit, into his room, crawled into the bed, and they went to sleep. The next morning, Marianna explains, she left the room early, and when she returned at about 8:00 a.m., on August 29, 1981, Lowell was dead. The obituaries *would* give a cause of death: a heart attack.

The lengthy *New York Times* obituary the next day emphasized Thomas' work for newsreels and, in particular, radio. T. E. Lawrence was not mentioned until the fourteenth paragraph. In that article the *Times* quoted former president Herbert Hoover as expressing a preference that, if he were to be reincarnated, it be as Lowell Thomas. The newspaper also passed on Thomas' own calculation that his voice "probably has been heard by more people than any other voice in history." And that obituary included this description: "Handsome, tall and slim, Mr. Thomas looked the romantic role in which he so often cast himself."

Standing on tiptoes had paid off.

((•))

Lowell Thomas had outlived most of the notables he had met and often befriended, but one former president, Gerald Ford, and one future president, then–vice president George H. W. Bush, were among the 800 people who attended his funeral at St. Bartholomew's Episcopal Church in New York City. The Reverend Norman Vincent Peale presided.

What tensions there were that day surrounded his widow. Marianna Thomas was upset that before the service she was not invited into the room where Reverend Peale, Lowell Thomas Jr., Tay Thomas and their children were waiting.[34]

A small cemetery had been laid out near the Quaker Hill Country Club. But Lowell's grave is not in it. He and his first wife, Frances Ryan Thomas, lie alone in an area outside that graveyard, below an attractive boulder with the name "Thomas" affixed to it. The lush, neatly mowed grass above and around them, the nearby woods, the long view, represent Quaker Hill—his Quaker Hill—at its most attractive.

He Loved the Face of the Earth

Two days after Lowell Thomas died, CBS ran a special prime-time report on his life—hosted by Walter Cronkite, featuring a few other CBS News correspondents and interspersed with clips of Thomas himself. "He was that man-about-the-world that every adventurous boy wants to be when he grows up," Cronkite declared at the beginning. "He crammed a couple of centuries worth of living into those four-score years and nine."

Eric Sevareid, who had been a commentator on Cronkite's newscast, expanded upon that theme: "Let me say first, Walter, that . . . it's almost hard to feel grief at Lowell's death, because he won, you know. He accomplished life in such an absolutely full and joyous and complete way. And I think we all envied that quality in the man." Sevareid added, "He just loved the face of the earth."

That Lowell had an exceptional life was impossible to dispute. The significance of his work was harder for these CBS newsmen to pin down. "As a journalist," Sevareid concluded, "he was kind of a wandering minstrel in prose. He didn't care who took care of the country's macroeconomics or geopolitics as long as he could tell its stories." From Sevareid's perspective

Thomas had become, in other words, something of an anachronism. "He loved stories about people. And that's almost a kind of journalism that's gone, I'm afraid. We're all too damn serious."

But one important journalistic stricture Thomas helped introduce was not only not gone but was well established in the United States in 1981, particularly in broadcast news: the commitment, as Cronkite put it, "not to confuse opinions with hard news or to be drawn into taking sides." On the air that evening, Cronkite connected this commitment with Thomas. Looked at this way, Lowell Thomas was not out of place in journalism in the second half of the twentieth century; indeed, he was among the first to sail down what became the mainstream.

That was one reason Douglas Edwards, another veteran CBS newsman, could publicly proclaim on behalf of his fellow broadcast journalists a few weeks later: "Lowell Thomas was truly the granddaddy of us all."[1]

((•))

Four years after the death of the man who was long its largest shareholder, Capital Cities essentially bought ABC, one of the country's foremost media companies. This acquisition would repeatedly be described as "the minnow swallowing the whale."

Tom Murphy had sought out his friend Leonard Goldenson, who had long been running ABC. Goldenson was 80. "I said Leonard I've got an idea, but I don't want you to throw me out of the thirty-ninth floor window," Murphy recalls. "I said I'd like to merge Capital Cities with ABC." Goldenson, Murphy says, was enthusiastic as long as Murphy agreed to run the company. They roped in another pal, Warren Buffett, as what Murphy calls "a 400 pound gorilla." Buffett's large stake would ensure no other bidders entered the fray.

By 1993 those hundred shares in Capital Cities that Frank Smith had made available to company employees in 1957 for $575 would have been worth, Walt Hawver estimates, half a million dollars.

Then, in 1995, Capital Cities/ABC—some sliver of which still belonged to Lowell Thomas' heirs and the trust he had set up for them—was sold to the Walt Disney Company for $19 billion.[2]

((•))

Five years after Thomas died, a story in the *Chicago Tribune* began with a then-shocking thought: "The day may not be far, alas, when some otherwise informed adult . . . wonders, 'Who is Lowell Thomas?'"[3]

According to Google Books, every year from 1935 to 1945 Lowell Thomas' name had been mentioned in a larger percentage of books published in American English than that of either Charles Lindbergh, F. Scott Fitzgerald or Fred Astaire—contemporaries who had risen to prominence at about the same time. This is but a rough measure of significance and renown, but it can be used to make a point: journalists can accrue considerable fame; still, that fame, like much that is connected with news, is fleeting. Journalists—unlike novelists or filmmakers—rarely produce work of interest to future generations. History textbooks pay most of them—mere messengers—little mind. So, once they are no longer regularly in the public eye and the audiences to which they had told the news age, they quickly begin to be forgotten. Indeed, by the year 2000 Lowell Thomas was being mentioned in Google's huge selection of books less than one-fourth as often as Lindbergh, Fitzgerald or Astaire.

Journalists today—none of whom are as well-known as Lowell Thomas was in his heyday—can look forward to a similarly precipitous drop in name recognition. Walter Cronkite and Tom Brokaw have already begun experiencing it.[4]

A half-dozen institutions in the United States—including one in Pawling, one on Quaker Hill and one in Poughkeepsie—display Lowell Thomas memorabilia. The Garst Museum in Greenville, Ohio, is prominent among them. Indeed, the small house in Woodington, Ohio, in which he was born was moved to the museum's grounds in 1987. As recently as 2011 the sign in front of the Garst Museum trumpeted its extensive exhibits on the two notable personages who hailed from that area: Annie Oakley and Lowell Thomas.[5] Now the sign mentions only one of them—the female sharpshooter.

The museum in Victor, Colorado, was named after the town's favorite son in 1981. It includes rooms full of displays on Thomas and his family. But the museum's president, Ruth Zalewski, estimates that 99 percent of the visitors to the Victor Lowell Thomas Museum now have no idea who Lowell Thomas was.[6]

"I have often expressed regret that eminent people are so quickly forgotten," Lowell wrote in a letter a year before he died.[7] He was, ostensibly, talking about someone else.

((•))

The variety of journalism practiced by Lowell Thomas, along with most of his professional "grandchildren," is in many ways no longer, in the twenty-first century, our journalism. It is not just that the newsreel is long gone and the travelogue—the "expedition film," if you will—is just about extinct. It isn't just that radio—overshadowed for half a century by television—is now being nudged out of whatever niches it continues to occupy by something more specialized and idiosyncratic: the podcast.

There has been a larger change. With the arrival of the first cable networks in the 1970s and 1980s, the World Wide Web in the 1990s and then smartphones and social media in the next two decades, the United States has left the era when a few national news outlets could amass mammoth audiences. No regular form of nonfiction now seems able to. That is why the national stature Thomas and then Cronkite and Tom Brokaw achieved as hosts of network newscasts has not since been equaled. A country that, before Lowell, had been divided geographically is increasingly divided, after Lowell, by cable network, website or Twitter feed.

And this new, more fragmented media environment has also altered what we ask from journalism. Americans have no less need to have their attention directed overseas than they did in Lowell's day. Storytelling, too, continues to have a place in journalism: it is difficult to imagine humans without a hankering for a good tale. Getting the facts right remains crucial. And fairness certainly retains value in this new, wilder news world.

Nonetheless, now that news from everywhere seems just a few clicks away, the skill of our journalists, the best of them, is no longer measured by their ability to tread "right down the middle" or discourse authoritatively on any and all topics. Barraged by an excess of reports, we are increasingly looking for an original point of view, a salient insight. That requires expertise. Having a personal relationship with the king of Jordan does not always help. Academic training in economics, one of the sciences, Middle Eastern studies or another specialized field seems to.

Many such distinct and searching takes on current events will come from individuals in other countries, not just Americans who visit those countries. Some are already emanating from groups or individuals to whom the old network newscasts paid little mind. We have a right to hope that these perspectives might collectively produce a fuller and more diverse picture of the world than could be obtained from Thomas' news-casts, newsreels or travelogues.

And given all we now know about messengers and their limitations, we have a right to expect a journalism that proclaims less and suggests more.[8]

After the Vietnam War and a few equally unsuccessful Mideast wars, the can-do, American-cowboy worldview is also looking old. The politics of the twenty-first century, like its journalism, is to a large extent being developed in reaction to that of Lowell Thomas—that quintessential twentieth-century American.

((•))

The way Lowell lived his life was in one important respect also an artifact of his century: a time when the world's most far-off places could be reached but were not yet tamed by guidebooks. However, another quality with which Lowell was oversupplied—blazing, unquenchable ambition—seems to flare up in individuals here and there in most centuries, and it shows no sign of being extinguished anytime soon.

There has been and likely will remain a touch of the tragic about those who, like Lowell, seem unable to stop trying to impress—who, as he had put it in a burst of self-awareness when he was 23, are always "trying to do things that would make people say nice things about me." The problem is, of course, that many who are supposed to be wowed manage somehow not to be; that stratospheric trajectories, too, eventually peak; and that great success in some areas inevitably is accompanied by failings in others—even for those who manage to squeeze a couple of centuries' worth of living into one lifetime.

Lowell would not want to exit on such a melancholy or philosophical note. And he would certainly demand the last word.

"Looking back . . . ," he told a reporter when he was 80, "I'd say it was rather silly to try to do so many things—except it's been so much fun!"[9]

Acknowledgments

About a decade ago Richard Moulton came to interview me for a documentary he was contemplating on Lowell Thomas. As a journalism and media historian, I was certainly aware of Thomas' significance: the major figure in the salad days of both radio news and newsreels, one of the makers of modern journalism. And I was old enough to have seen reruns of the television program *High Adventure with Lowell Thomas*. But I knew little of the rest of his life.

I ended up working with Rick Moulton on a plan for a documentary, and I learned—about Thomas' discovery of T. E. Lawrence, about his journey to Tibet, about his role in Cinerama, about his softball games against a team managed by President Franklin Roosevelt, about his incessant and intrepid travels. Eric Sevareid's characterization of Thomas, which I came upon in Rick's notes, stuck with me: "He just loved the face of the earth." I had done some traveling myself and fancied myself carrying a similar torch.

Rick ended up inviting me to pitch in on a Web site about Lowell Thomas and T. E. Lawrence, cliohistory.org/thomas-lawrence/. That led to this biography. My first thanks, therefore, go to Rick Moulton—for the introduction to Lowell, for his abiding knowledge of all things Lowell and for his friendship.

Another great benefit of the chance to contribute to that Web site was the opportunity to work with the wonderful Lola Van Wagenen, director of the Clio Visualizing History Web site. And Rick is now finally producing and directing, and I am writing, that documentary on Lowell Thomas. That project has introduced me to an extraordinary cinematographer and traveler, David Wright, its co-producer. Anne Thomas Donaghy, Lowell's granddaughter and executive producer of the documentary, has also been a great pleasure to get to know and a tremendous help on the book: supplying materials she has found in her father's home in Alaska, checking facts, even copyediting chapters. Thanks, too, to our Tibet teammates, the indomitable Jo Keller, and another Lowell-level traveler, Jakob Urban.

Lowell Thomas was too rich a subject for a biography to have been so long overlooked. And I had, indeed, a predecessor in this endeavor: Fred D. Crawford, an English professor at Central Michigan University, who came to Thomas via Lawrence and who came to Lawrence via George Bernard Shaw. Professor Crawford died in 1999, just short of his fifty-second birthday, after many years of research on Thomas and having drafted a few of the 58 chapters he planned to include in his biography. His widow, MaryAnn Krajnik Crawford, donated his papers to Marist College. My researchers and I have consulted Professor Crawford's impressive files, correspondence and interviews, along with his outline, which we used as a timeline. I have not yet allowed myself to read the chapters he drafted. But it has been an honor to follow in his footsteps.

The Lowell Thomas Trust—noting the conspicuous absence of a biography—has encouraged and supported my work on this book, though its representatives at the law firm Wilk Auslander have not been shown any of the chapters and have understood from the beginning that I was committed to a "warts and all" portrait. I am grateful for the support there of Thomas R. Amlicke, Leslie Steinau and the indefatigable Ten Lin Lee Wyatt.

An impressive series of students have worked as researchers on this project—all but one undergraduates, all but one from New York University. Daniel Moritz-Rabson and I embarked upon the investigation together, learned together and mastered the train schedule to Poughkeepsie together. Jordan Scharan then stepped in with her characteristic energy and intelligence. Kulsoom Khan, a graduate of our masters program, helped me take Lowell's story into the second half of the twentieth century. Nicholas Chhoeun, from Marist, capably took over the research in the archive there. Tommy Collison made a brief but characteristically impressive appearance. Melvis Acosta saw the project to its end, and proved an ace fact-checker as well as an enterprising researcher.

I have had the great benefit of the extensive Lowell Thomas expertise possessed by John Ansley, head of archives and special collections at Marist's Cannavino Library. I rarely left his office without a couple of new leads. John has completed his own important study of Thomas' trip to and engagement with Tibet. Gregory Wiedeman, who organized the Fred Crawford papers at Marist, gave me direction when I first started out on this journey. Thanks, too, to Nancy Decker and Ann Sandri at the Marist archives.

Lowell's own generation was gone when I embarked upon this project. Yet I managed to talk to quite a few people who grew up around him or met him later in his life—beginning with his son, Lowell Thomas Jr., who passed away right after I handed in this manuscript, and his daughter-in-law, Mary "Tay" Thomas, who died two years earlier. I also got a sense of what it was like to be in a room or on a ski slope with Lowell Thomas from Thomas Murphy, James Morrison, William Morrison, Eileen Morrison, Anne Thomas Donaghy, David Thomas, Thomas R. Amlicke, Jim Fowler, Richard Moulton and Casey Murrow. Although they did not all end up being quoted in this book, all of these people were gracious and useful in helping me understand Lowell Thomas. I gained, too, from the insights of Roger Cranston, Jeremy Wilson, Bernard Beranelli, Joseph A. Berton, Margaret MacMillan, Tom Brokaw, Colin Vaines, Neil Brand and Giovanna Dell'Orto. (Many of these interviews were organized by Richard Moulton.) Thanks too to Mona Campbell, Ruth Zalewski, Jeff Campbell, Brad Poulson and Mark Perdew in Victor, Colorado; and to Clay Johnson and Phyllis Crick in Darke County, Ohio. Tanzy Coffin researched Thomas' real-estate transactions on Quaker Hill for me.

I am particularly grateful to my agent, Jessica Papin, and my wise editor, Elisabeth Dyssegaard. Thomas Studwell read and improved many of these chapters.

I have had the pleasure of acknowledging my debt to my wife, Esther Davidowitz, in a number of books by now. She contributed more than usual to this one. While between jobs, she pitched in on the research and the interviews. And—this hasn't changed—she was my first reader on all these chapters. I have also thanked our children—Lauren, Seth and Noah Stephens-Davidowitz—before. But as their own careers progress, their insights become even more searching, their suggestions even more valuable.

My son-in-law Mark Osmond is an important new addition to the family editorial board.

There's one more individual I must mention. Lowell Thomas, whom I never met, was nevertheless great good company over these years. It has indeed been fun.

Notes

A Note on Sources

Almost all the letters, most of the radio scripts and a number of the newspaper clippings, pamphlets, brochures and unpublished manuscripts the author consulted or cited can be found in in the Lowell Thomas Papers at Marist College in Poughkeepsie, New York. Indexes to these materials, and access to those that have been digitalized, are available online at: http://library .marist.edu/archives/LTP/LTP.xml.

The author has also made considerable use of the Fred Crawford papers at Marist College: http://library.marist.edu/archives/crawfordPapers/FredCrawfordPapers.xml. Crawford, who was working on his own biography of Lowell Thomas when he died, organized some of the material in the Thomas Papers and added his own interviews and correspondence with many who had known Thomas.

1. Lowell Thomas, in A. W. Lawrence, ed., *T. E. Lawrence by His Friends* (New York: McGraw-Hill, 1963), 167.

Prologue: The Messenger

1. United States war correspondents were required to wear some sort of uniform during the First World War; James L. Gilbert, *World War I and the Origins of U.S. Military Intelligence* (Lanham, MD: Scarecrow Press, 2012), 78. Lowell Thomas journal, Palestine; Lowell Thomas, *With Lawrence in Arabia* (New York: P. F. Collier & Son, 1924), 3–5. For Thomas' boots, see the entry for December 17, 1918, in Lowell Thomas' first German journal.
2. Scott Anderson, *Lawrence in Arabia: War, Deceit, Imperial Folly and the Making of the Modern Middle East* (New York: Doubleday, 2013).

1. A Portrait of the Journalist as a Young Cowboy

1. Doris Kearns Goodwin, *The Bully Pulpit: Theodore Roosevelt, William Howard Taft, and the Golden Age of Journalism* (New York: Simon and Schuster, 2013).
2. Harry G. Thomas, "Cripple Creek at the Turn of the Century," Draft No. 1, May 25, 1954. This chapter from the draft of a never-completed, unpublished memoir by Lowell

Thomas' father seems the best source of information about the family in these early years and is the source for much information in this chapter. I have also made use of the transcripts of a 1951 interview with Dr. Harry G. Thomas by Dick Roelofs, reel 1, reel 2, reel 12.

3. Susan C. Lawrence, "Iowa Physicians: Legitimacy, Institutions and the Practice of Medicine, Part Two: Putting Science into Practice, 1887–1928," *The Annals of Iowa*, 62, Winter 2004. The memoir referred to here and elsewhere in this chapter is Lowell Thomas' *Good Evening Everybody* (New York: William Morrow, 1976), 19–78. When I attribute information or a quote to Thomas, it is from this memoir. As I note, Thomas' recollections in this book are often unreliable, perhaps occasionally even mendacious. However, for these early years of Lowell Thomas' life, for which letters and other sources are scarce, his recollections are often the only source of information about events. I have tried to use them carefully and skeptically.

4. The first name of Harry Thomas' brother, C. D. Thomas, seems to have been Carrel. Harry calls him Carl in his attempt at a memoir. Lowell refers to him as Corrie. Harry says he is a younger brother and should know, though the only records I can find list C. D. Thomas as having been born before Harry.

5. Thomas, *Good Evening Everybody*, 51.

6. Harriet Thomas to Lowell Thomas, October 10, 1915; Thomas, *Good Evening Everybody*, 30, 49–50.

7. This route is now known as Gold Camp Road.

8. Thomas, *Good Evening Everybody*, 31.

9. Lowell Thomas to Mr. Green, April 21, 1972.

10. Mabel Barbee Lee, *Cripple Creek Days* (Lincoln, NE: University of Nebraska Press, 1984), 239.

11. Ben Hecht, *Gaily, Gaily* (New York: Doubleday, 1963), 190.

12. Thomas, *Good Evening Everybody*, 47–48.

13. Thomas, *Good Evening Everybody*, 61.

14. Lee, *Cripple Creek Days*, 239.

15. Thomas, *Good Evening Everybody*, 64–68.

16. Harriet Thomas to Lowell Thomas, January 10, 1916.

17. Charles Dickens, *American Notes for General Circulation*, in *The Works of Charles Dickens*, Vol. 13 (London: Chapman & Hall, and Bradbury and Evans, 1866), 432–433.

18. See Mitchell Stephens, *A History of News* (New York: Oxford University Press, 2007), 26, 54–55.

19. H. L. Mencken, *Newspaper Days: Mencken's Autobiography: 1899–1906* (New York: Alfred A. Knopf, 1941), xiii–xiv.

20. Mitchell Stephens, *Beyond News: The Future of Journalism* (New York: Columbia University Press, 2014), 55.

21. Thomas, *Good Evening Everybody*, 73, 74, 76, 77–78.

2. Two Scoops in Chicago

1. "A look at the formation of ASNE," http://asne.org/content.asp?pl=24&sl=83&contentid=83, accessed June 9, 2014. "Canons of Journalism—ASNE—Code of Ethics—1922," http://www.scribd.com/doc/19499595/Canons-of-Journalism-ASNE-Code-of-Ethics-1922, accessed June 9, 2014.

2. Ben Hecht, *Child of the Century* (New York: Simon and Schuster, 1954), 126–127; William MacAdams, *Ben Hecht* (New York: Barricade Books, 1990), 14.

3. Ben Hecht, *Gaily, Gaily* (New York: Doubleday, 1963), 201.

4. Wayne Klott, *Chicago Journalism: A History* (Jefferson, NC: McFarland & Company, 2009), 88.

5. By one account 27 people were killed in the city's newspaper wars from 1910 to 1912—the year before Thomas arrived; Klott, 89, 92.

6. Edith Abbott, "Recent Statistics Relating to Crime in Chicago," *Journal of Criminal Law and Criminology* 13: 3 (1923), 329–358; "Chicago Leads World in Number of Murders," *Chicago Herald*, September 17, 1914; Jeffrey S. Adler, "'It Is His First Offense. We Might As Well Let Him Go': Homicide and Criminal Justice in Chicago, 1875–1920," *Journal of Social History*, Fall 2006, 5–24; Jeffrey S. Adler, "Shoot to Kill: The Use of Deadly Force by the Chicago Police, 1875–1920," *Journal of Interdisciplinary History*, XXXVIII: 2 (Autumn 2007), 233–254; "A Reporter's Diary," Lowell Thomas, journal, January 26, 1915.

7. Hecht, *Gaily, Gaily*, 183–187.

8. "Selected Chicago Daily Newspapers" and "Selected Chicago Daily Newspapers, Foreign Language," *Encyclopedia of Chicago*, http://www.encyclopedia.chicagohistory.org/pages /2474.html, http://www.encyclopedia.chicagohistory.org/pages/11525.html; Gaston B. Perilli, "The Foreign Press," in University of Washington, Department of Journalism, *Supplemental Lectures in Journalism* (Seattle: University of Washington, 1914), 116; Lowell Thomas, *Good Evening Everybody* (New York: William Morrow, 1976), 78.

9. "Newspaper Makers at Work: Richard J. Finnegan," *Editor and Publisher* 52, July 24, 1919, 17.

10. Hecht, *Gaily, Gaily*, 5.

11. Doug Fetherling, *The Five Lives of Ben Hecht* (Toronto: Lester and Orpen, 1977), 21.

12. Hecht, *Gaily, Gaily*, 4, 163; Fetherling, 20.

13. Ben Hecht, *Letters From Bohemia* (New York: Doubleday, 1964), 187.

14. Hecht, *Gaily, Gaily*, 186; Edward J. Veasey to "Fellow Students," Chicago-Kent Law School, undated.

15. Thomas, *Good Evening Everybody*, 79.

16. Various papers collected by Fred D. Crawford on Chicago-Kent Law School; Lowell Thomas to Frances Ryan, November 27, 1913.

17. Hecht, *Gaily, Gaily*, 5.

18. Thomas, *Good Evening Everybody*, 81; Hecht, *Gaily, Gaily*, 13–14.

19. Irving E. Fang, *Those Radio Commentators* (Ames, IA: Iowa State University Press, 1977), 47; David Randall, *The Great Reporters* (London: Pluto Press, 2005), 166.

20. Hecht, *Gaily, Gaily*, 183; Lowell Thomas, "A Reporter's Diary," journal, January 6, April 2, 1915.

21. "HELEN MORTON HAS 32 GUARDS," *Chicago Evening American*, July 7, 1914; Thomas, 98–99.

22. Mitchell Stephens, *A History of News* (New York: Oxford University Press, 2007), 239–240.

23. MacAdams, 16. See also Hecht, *Child of the Century*, 134–135.

24. Martin J. Hutchens to Lowell J. Thomas, November 24, 1915.

25. Hecht, *Gaily, Gaily*, 190.

26. Lowell Thomas journal, May 7, 1915.

27. Thomas, *Good Evening Everybody*, 87–88.

28. Lowell Thomas journal, June 20, 1915.

29. Herbert Asbury, *The Gangs of Chicago* (New York: Thunder's Mouth Press, 2002), 292–311.

30. Thomas, *Good Evening Everybody*, 103.

31. Thomas, 89–90. The meeting with Paul Chamberlain is mentioned in "A Reporter's Diary," Lowell Thomas, journal, March 27, 1915; however, there is no mention of any discussion of Frances Ryan in that entry.

32. The amount of this swindle is given as $200,000 in "Carleton Hudson Once in Tombs as Forger," *Chicago Daily Journal*, December 3, 1914. This number is based on "Rich Chicagoan Is Seized as Fugitive from Here in 1895," *New York World*, December 4, 1914.

33. Thomas, 84–88; *The Virginia Enterprise* (Virginia, St. Louis County, MN), October 16, 1914; *Chronicling America: Historic American Newspapers*, Library of Congress, http://chroniclingamerica.loc.gov/lccn/sn90059180/1914-10-16/ed-1/seq-6/; "Rich Chicagoan Is Seized as Fugitive from Here in 1895," *New York World*, December 4, 1914.

34. "Carleton Hudson Once in Tombs as Forger," *Chicago Daily Journal*, December 3, 1914.

35. "Arrested After 20 Years," *Logansport Pharos-Tribune* (Logansport, Indiana), June 13, 1916.

36. "Thomas Runs Criminal to Cover in East; Former Editor of Victor Record Effects Capture of Notorious Crook," *Cripple Creek Times*, December 6, 1914; Pythias Runon, "Lowell Thomas Uncovers Scoop of Year in Chicago by His Bulldog Tenacity," *The Scoop*, April 17, 1915; Paul Crissey, "Story of the Carleton Hudson Scoop," *The Quill*, January 1915.

37. "Rich Chicagoan Is Seized as Fugitive from Here in 1895," *New York World*, December 4, 1914; Thomas, 86; "Carleton Hudson Once in Tombs as Forger," *Chicago Daily Journal*, December 3, 1914.

38. Thomas, *Good Evening Everybody*, 86.

39. Lowell Thomas, "A Reporter's Diary," journal, April 17, 1915; Lowell Thomas journal, May 1, 1915.

40. Lowell Thomas to Dan Batchelor, undated; Dan C. Batchelor to Lowell J. Thomas, undated; Lowell Thomas, "A Reporter's Diary," journal.

41. Lowell Thomas, "A Reporter's Diary," journal, January 19, March 18, 1915.

3. See America First

1. Lowell Thomas to Frances Ryan, January 16, 1916.

2. Lowell Thomas journal, May 3–5, 1915.

3. Lowell Thomas, *Good Evening Everybody* (New York: William Morrow, 1976), 87.

4. Lowell Thomas, "This Will Be in Answer to Five or Six of Your Questions: How I Met My Wife, and So On," undated and unpublished.

5. Lowell Thomas to Frances Ryan, undated, probably winter 1913–14; Lowell Thomas to Frances Ryan, November 29, 1913; Lowell Thomas postcard to Frances Ryan, July 1913.

6. In a letter to Fran a little more than two months later, Lowell, in what he describes as a "morose" mood, backtracks. He tries to maintain that he was not "proposing" that evening back in May, since he was not worthy enough "to make a 'proposition' to anyone"; Lowell Thomas to Frances Ryan, July 11, 1915.

7. Lowell Thomas journal, May 5, 13, 1915.

8. Lowell Thomas to Frances Ryan, December 20, 1916.

9. Jennifer Lynn Peterson, "'The Nation's First Playground': Travel Films and the American West, 1895–1920," in Jeffrey Ruoff, ed., *Virtual Voyages: Cinema and Travel* (Durham: Duke University Press: 2006), 81–82; Marguerite S. Shaffer, "'See America First': Re-Envisioning Nation and Region through Western Tourism," *Pacific Historical Review* 65: 4 (November, 1996), 559–581.

10. "Lowell Thomas Will Tell East about This District," *Cripple Creek Times*, May 8, 1915; "Springs Undiscovered Says Eastern Writer, Feature Men Propose to Spread Its Fame," *Colorado Springs Gazette*, May 12, 1915; "Denver Boy May Go to Front as War Correspondent; Has Made an Exceptional Record," *Denver Express*, May 6, 1915; Lowell Thomas journal, May 5–12, 1915.

11. Lowell Thomas journal, May 11–20, 1915.

12. I owe my introduction to this piece of popular culture to Ariela Fryman.

13. Lowell Thomas journal, May 21–29, 1915.

14. Lowell Thomas journal, June 15 and July 5, 1915; Lowell Thomas to Frances Ryan, from

the Sol Duc Hot Springs Hotel, June 16, 1915; Lowell Thomas postcard to Frances Ryan, July 7, 1915.

15. Lowell Thomas to Frances Ryan, from the Barbara Worth Hotel, May 27, 1915; Lowell Thomas journal, May 25, 1915.

16. Lowell Thomas, *Good Evening Everybody*, 92; Lowell Thomas journal, June 14, 1915.

17. Lowell Thomas journal, June 19, 1915; Thomas, 92.

18. Lowell Thomas, "LT re: Alaska"; Lowell Thomas to Frances Ryan, March 12, 1916; see also Lowell Thomas, *Beyond Khyber Pass* (New York: Century Co., 1925), 42.

19. Lowell Thomas journal, June 11, 20, 1915.

20. Lowell Thomas journal, June 20, 21; July 2, 1915.

21. Some of the earliest photographs of Alaska had been taken in 1886; Ian Frazier, "Alaska Through New Eyes," *New York Review of Books*, March 14, 2015; http://www.nybooks.com /blogs/gallery/2015/mar/14/alaska-new-eyes/.

22. Lowell Thomas journal, June 21, 27, 1915.

23. *Weekly Star*, June 25, 1915.

24. Lowell Thomas journal, June 22–July 4, 1915; Letters from Lowell Thomas to Frances Ryan, July 6, 1916.

25. Lowell Thomas journal, July 14, 1915.

26. Some pieces that discuss places Thomas visited appear in the *Chicago Daily Journal* as advertisements, credited to the Rock Island Travel Bureau; see June 25, 1915. For another example of a possible Lowell Thomas article on Colorado, see "Health and Joys in the Great West," *New York Times*, December 25, 1915, 8 (though this discusses winter travel to Colorado Springs and Lowell was there in May), http://timesmachine.nytimes.com/timesmachine /1915/12/26/104235697.html. For Mount Rainier and the Pacific Northwest, this seems the best bet to have been Lowell's: "Mount Rainier Crowns Wonder Park," New York *Sun*, August 8, 1915, http://chroniclingamerica.loc.gov/lccn/sn83030272/1915-08-08/ed-1/seq -59/#date1=1915&index=10&rows=20&words=MOUNT+Mount+RAINIER+Rainier&se archType=basic&sequence=0&state=&date2=1915&proxtext=Mount+Rainier&y=11&x =13&dateFilterType=yearRange&page=2. But see also "Mount Rainier: Icy Octopus," which appeared in, for example, *Beaver Herald* (Oklahoma), October 14, 1915, http:// chroniclingamerica.loc.gov/lccn/sn93066071/1915-10-14/ed-1/seq-2/#date1=1915&sort =relevance&rows=20&words=Mount+MOUNT+Rainier+RAINIER&searchType =basic&sequence=0&index=3&state=&date2=1915&proxtext=Mount+Rainier&y=11& x=13&dateFilterType=yearRange&page=1; and the *Dakota County Herald* (Nebraska), September 16, 1915, http://chroniclingamerica.loc.gov/lccn/2010270500/1915-09-16/ed-1 /seq-3/#date1=1836&index=3&rows=20&words=FROZEN+octopus&searchType=basic &sequence=0&state=&date2=1922&proxtext=%22frozen+octopus%22&y=11&x =16&dateFilterType=yearRange&page=1. See also the similar "Flowers Bloom in Midst of Snow," *Greenville Journal*, August 10, 1916, http://chroniclingamerica.loc.gov/lccn /sn83035565/1916-08-10/ed-1/seq-7/#date1=1836&index=8&rows=20&words =frozen+octopus&searchType=basic&sequence=0&state=&date2=1922&proxtext =%22frozen+octopus%22&y=11&x=16&dateFilterType=yearRange&page=1.

27. See H. G. Thomas to Lowell Thomas, October 17, 1915; Lowell Thomas journal, September 24, 1915.

28. Lowell Thomas journal, July 15–August 24, 1915.

4. Too Good to Be True

1. Lowell Thomas journal, August 30, 31, 1915.

2. "Sunset of Riley's Career Still Far Distant," *New York Times Magazine*, September 12, 1915, http://query.nytimes.com/mem/archive-free/pdf?res=9D0DE0DC153BE233A25751 C1A96F9C946496D6CF.

3. Lowell Thomas journal, September 1, 7–11, 13, 16, October 16, December 11, 1915. Lowell Thomas to Frances Ryan, undated but written December 31, 1915, January 20, 1916.

4. Lowell Thomas journal, September 19, 22, 23, 28, 1915, May 6, 1916; Lowell Thomas to Frances Ryan, September 26, December 7, 1915. See Winston & Strawn LLP's account of its first 150 years, 2003. The printed version of this history is more definitive on Strawn's contributions to Thomas' education than the first draft.

5. Lowell Thomas journal, August 24, 30, 1915; September 29, 31, 1915; Lowell Thomas to Frances Ryan, January 9, 1916.

6. Lowell Thomas journal, October 8, November 27, 1915.

7. Lowell Thomas to Frances Ryan, May 28, 1916.

8. H. G. Thomas to Lowell Thomas, October 17, 1915.

9. Harriet Thomas to Lowell Thomas, January 12, 1916.

10. H. G. Thomas to Lowell Thomas, November 10, 1915.

11. Harriet Thomas to Lowell Thomas, October 24, 1915; Harriet Thomas to Lowell Thomas, November 1, 1915; Harriet Thomas to Lowell Thomas, January 12, 1916; Lowell Thomas journal, October 30, 1915; Lowell Thomas to Frances Ryan, October 26, 1915.

12. Martin J. Hutchens to Lowell Thomas, November 24, 1915; Lowell Thomas to Paul Crissey, undated but about December 1, 1915; Lowell Thomas to Dan Batchelor, December 1, 1915; Lowell Thomas to Martin J. Hutchens, November 30, 1915; Dan Batchelor to Lowell Thomas, January 11, 1916.

13. Harriet Thomas to Lowell Thomas, December 3, 1915.

14. Lowell Thomas to Frances Ryan, December 7, 16, 18, 1915; January 9, 1916; telegram from Lowell Thomas to Frances Ryan, December 11, 1915; Frances Ryan to Lowell Thomas, December 20, 1915; Harold "Nook" Vinacke to Lowell Thomas, misdated December 3, probably written either at the end of December 1915 or the beginning of January 1916; Harriet Thomas to Lowell Thomas, January 25, 1916.

15. James E. Lathrop, membership secretary YMCA of Baltimore, February 7, 1916; "'ALASKA,' UNCLE SAM'S PARADISE: Y.M.C.A Lecture Upon Territory Brings New Facts to Light," *Reading News-Times*, January 5, 1916; Harriet Thomas to Lowell Thomas, February 15, 1916; Lowell Thomas to Robert Sterling Yard, March 20, 1917; Lowell Thomas to Frances Ryan, March 12, 1916.

16. Harriet Thomas to Lowell Thomas, March 14, April 27, 1916.

17. Lowell Thomas to Frances Ryan, April 5, 1916; transcript of 1951 interview by Dick Roelofs with Dr. Harry G. Thomas, reel 20.

18. Jeffrey Ruoff, ed., *Virtual Voyages: Cinema and Travel* (Durham: Duke University Press: 2006), 2–4.

19. Lowell Thomas to Frances Ryan, December 26, 1915.

20. See Frits Anderson, "Eighteenth Century Travelogues as Models for 'Rethinking Europe,'" *European Review* 15, 1 (2007), 115–124; Jennifer Lynn Peterson, "'The Nation's First Playground': Travel Films and the American West, 1895–1920," in Jeffrey Ruoff, ed., *Virtual Voyages: Cinema and Travel* (Durham: Duke University Press: 2006), 92–96; Hamid Naficy, "Lured by the East," in Ruoff, 129–131.

21. Lowell Thomas, "Alaska—Uncle Sam's Polar Paradise," unpublished.

22. Or sort of prove it—the photo was taken in Dawson City, technically south of the Arctic Circle; see Lowell Thomas journal, June 26, 1915.

23. While on board a steamship, someone who said he used to be Jim Christie's pal repeated to Lowell this fairly well-known tale about Christie; see Lowell Thomas journal, June 27, 1915.

24. Unpublished lecture script, Lowell Thomas, "Alaska: Uncle Sam's Polar Paradise"; Lowell Thomas to Frances Ryan, May 6, 1916; Lowell Thomas to Robert Sterling Yard, March 20, 1917.

25. Lowell Thomas to Frances Ryan, May 6, 8, 9, 14,15, 19, 22, December 8, 1916; March 3,

1917; Harriet Thomas to Lowell Thomas, May 11, 1916; Lowell Thomas journal, November 21, 1915.

26. Lowell Thomas to Frances Ryan, May 1, 23, 26, June 5, 15, 24, 1916.

27. http://www.burtonholmesarchive.com/?page_id=14.

28. Erik Barnouw, *Documentary: A History of the Non-Fiction Film*, second revised edition (Oxford: Oxford University Press, 1993), 31–42; Richard Koszarski, *An Evening's Entertainment: The Age of the Silent Feature Picture, 1915–1928* (University of California Press, Berkeley: 1994), 241–244.

29. Lowell Thomas, *Good Evening Everybody* (New York: William Morrow, 1976), 100; http://www.filmnotes.net/galleries/moviecameras/movie-cameras-d-f/; Lowell Thomas to Frances Ryan, June 2, 1916.

30. Taku is one of the small number of glaciers that are still advancing—pushing silt and outwash into the inlet in front of it. As a result the glacier's face no longer hangs over tidewater into which it can spawn icebergs, and the cruise ships and ferries that have replaced those steamships can't even get close enough to view this giant glacier. Lowell Thomas to A. F. Zipf, Traffic Manager, White Pass & Yukon Route, October 17, 1916; Lowell Thomas to Frances Ryan, June 23, 25, July 6 (fourth letter), 13, August 20, 30, September 10, 17, 1916.

31. Lowell Thomas, "Foreword," in John Sherman Long, with Grace Doering McCord, *McCord of Alaska* (Cleveland: Dillon/Liederbach, 1975), 13–14.

32. Lowell Thomas to Frances Ryan, October 4, 1916.

33. Frances Thomas, "When Mrs. Lowell Thomas Was a 'School Marm' on the Jackass Ranch Near Castle Rock," undated and unpublished; Lowell Thomas to Frances Ryan, November 15, December 5, 17, 18, 20, 22, 1916; January 1, 3, 1917.

34. *New York Tribune*, January 13, 1917.

35. Lowell Thomas to Frances Ryan, November 4, 1916, January 12, 17, 19, 24, February 23, March 3, April 22, May 4, 1917; Stanley Johnson, "Lowell Thomas Marks 80th Year, Finds Life Still and Adventure," *Los Angeles Times*, April 7, 1972; Lowell Thomas journal, "Malta, Egypt and Palestine."

5. Something More Colossal Than Anything of Its Kind Ever Tried

1. Lowell Thomas to Dean Andrew F. West, December 1, 1919.

2. Registration Card, June 5, 1917. He also mentioned his sister, though she was past the cut-off age, 12, for a sibling to qualify as a dependent.

3. Frances Thomas journal, begins August 4, 1917.

4. Lowell Thomas to Frances Ryan, July 4, 1917.

5. Lowell Thomas to Frances Ryan, May 4, 7, 8, 24, 31, June 2, 3, 25, July 2, 4, 7, 9, 15, 16, 17, 24, 27, 1917; Frances Thomas to Eunice Ryan, August 5, 14, 1917; Fred D. Crawford to Marianna Thomas, July 8, 1998. A third member of Thomas' traveling party, when he left to cover the First World War, was Dr. Louis B. Blan, who was supposed to work as an additional publicist and writer, but the relationship did not work out.

6. Frances Thomas to Eunice Ryan, August 9, 17, 24, October 1, 1917; Lowell Thomas to Harriet Thomas, October 28, 1917.

7. Thomas had by then stopped traveling with the fourth member of their original party, Dr. Louis B. Blan; Lowell Thomas, "Malta, Egypt and Palestine" journal.

8. Lowell Thomas to Harriet and Pherbia Thomas, November 24, December 3, 26, 1917; Lowell Thomas, Italy journal, 1917; Lowell Thomas, *Good Evening Everybody* (New York: William Morrow, 1976), 120–121.

9. Mike Dash, "The Early History of Faking War on Film," Smithsonian.com, November 19, 2012; http://www.smithsonianmag.com/history/the-early-history-of-faking-war-on-film-133838317/#ITc2bYAY7ukGT2H2.99.

10. Richard Koszarski, *An Evening's Entertainment: The Age of the Silent Feature Picture, 1915-1928, History of the American Cinema*, Vol. 3 (Berkeley: University of California Press, 1994), 167.

11. Thomas had formally to break with Louis B. Blan, with whom he was no longer traveling and who had angered some officials in Italy with some revolutionary-sounding statements, in order to get permission to travel to the Middle East; Lowell Thomas journal, "Malta, Egypt and Palestine."

12. Lowell Thomas, *Beyond Khyber Pass* (New York: Century Co., 1925), 58.

13. Lowell Thomas to Harry Chase, draft, undated: http://library.marist.edu/archives /lttravelogues/Harry%20Chase/Chaseletter/chaseletter.html.

14. Lowell Thomas journal, "Malta, Egypt and Palestine."

15. "Jerusalem Recovered," *Evening World*, December 11, 1917.

16. This is from an untitled Lowell Thomas journal that covers his progress from Egypt to Arabia.

17. Lowell Thomas journal, "Palestine"; Fred D. Crawford and Joseph A. Berton, "How Well Did Lowell Thomas Know Lawrence of Arabia," *English Literature in Transition, 1880– 1920* 39: 3, 1996, 299–318. There is, as my researcher Daniel Moritz-Rabson noted, one earlier reference in one of Lowell's notebooks to an expert on horse hospitals by the name of Major Lawrence. This is part of a list of possible sources Thomas jotted down just before he left Egypt for Palestine in February 1918. It is possible that this was the same Major Lawrence, though if T. E. Lawrence ever did have anything to say about horse hospitals, Lowell did not record it. Lowell Thomas journal, "Palestine"; Crawford and Berton, "How Well Did Lowell Thomas Know Lawrence of Arabia," 299–318.

6. A Blue-Eyed, Beardless Man in Arab Robes

1. This account of Lawrence's early life is closely based on the one I wrote, "Lowell Thomas and Lawrence of Arabia: Making a Legend, Making History," for the Web site Clio Visualizing History, which I worked on with Lola Van Wagenen and Richard Moulton, http:// www.cliohistory.org/thomas-lawrence/lawrence/youth/. My account there made use primarily of two of the Lawrence biographies, John E. Mack, *A Prince of Our Disorder: The Life of T. E. Lawrence* (Cambridge, MA: Harvard University Press, 1998), and Jeremy Wilson, *Lawrence: The Authorized Biography of T. E. Lawrence* (New York: Collier Books, 1992). Lowell Thomas, in A. W. Lawrence, ed., *T. E. Lawrence by His Friends* (New York: McGraw-Hill, 1963), 172.

2. Lowell Thomas journal, "Palestine."

3. One of these entries is entitled "Major T. E. Lawrence, 'King of the Hejaz.'" There is some chance that title is being bestowed upon Sherif Hussein, who is discussed in the fourth paragraph of this entry and who was about to declare himself king. If it is being bestowed upon Lawrence it is, of course, an example of legend building—by Thomas and whoever suggested it to him, perhaps Colonel Ronald Storrs, the military governor of Jerusalem.

4. Fred D. Crawford and Joseph A. Berton, "How Well Did Lowell Thomas Know Lawrence of Arabia," *English Literature in Transition, 1880-1920* 39: 3, 1996, 299–318; see Wilson, *Lawrence*, 140–141. Richard Aldington presents a characteristically cynical, even farcical, account of the capture of Wejh; Richard Aldington, *Lawrence of Arabia* (Harmondsworth, Middlesex, England: Penguin Books, 1971), 204–209.

5. Suleiman Mousa, *T. E. Lawrence: An Arab View* (London: Oxford University Press, 1966). Richard Aldington's assault on this national hero was so controversial that a 1971 edition of his book published in Great Britain features quotes on the back cover from newspapers attacking it: "'There is a passion behind this book which strangely puts one in mind of a personal vendetta'—*Guardian*"; Richard Aldington, *Lawrence of Arabia*

(Harmondsworth, Middlesex, England: Penguin Books, 1971). Aldington's biography of Lawrence was first published in 1955. Fred D. Crawford's book, *Richard Aldington and Lawrence of Arabia* (Carbondale: Southern Illinois University Press, 1998) is the best account of Aldington, his book and the resulting ruckus. Crawford is generally impressed with Aldington's research but suspicious of his vehemence: "When Aldington became convinced that TEL was a vainglorious liar who had fabricated his own legend at the expense of the real heroes of the Great War, he could view TEL only with loathing and express his antipathy only in the most forceful terms"; Crawford, 12. For the argument against Lawrence's importance at Tafilah, see Aldington, 253–256, Mousa, 132–143. For the argument for Lawrence's importance at Tafilah, see Michael Korda, *Hero: The Life and Legend of Lawrence of Arabia* (New York: Harper Perennial, 2010), 365; B. H. Liddell Hart, *Lawrence of Arabia* (Boston: Da Capo Press, 1935), https://books.google.com /books?id=Ch2cJTVZDnUC&pg=PT4&lpg=PT4&dq=Lawrence+of+Arabia,+de+capo+ press&source=bl&ots=XlaCDckPzh&sig=C_HW0ZOPy8YWOyLUolX0EOHSn50&hl =en&sa=X&ved=0ahUKEwjA2PfM5qHOAhWEmh4KHZosBPoQ6AEIOjAF#v =snippet&q=Tafila&f=false.

6. The citations from Thomas here are all from the Lowell Thomas journal, "Palestine." A different, fuller description of the lunch with Allenby is in Lowell Thomas' Jerusalem journal. It does not mention the request to travel into the Arabian Desert. Fred Crawford and Joseph Berton write, "Nothing in Thomas' 'Palestine' diary suggests that he recognized how important the Lawrence story would become later"; Crawford and Berton, "How Well Did Lowell Thomas Know Lawrence of Arabia." My reading, instead, is that the importance of the Lawrence story was gradually dawning upon Thomas during his stay in the Middle East, and then as he worked on his travelogues after the war.

7. Cited, Mike Dash, "The Early History of Faking War on Film," Smithsonian.com, November 19, 2012, http://www.smithsonianmag.com/history/the-early-history-of-faking-war -on-film-133838317/#ITc2bYAY7ukGT2H2.99.

8. T. E. Lawrence's biographers, who are so often dismissive of Lowell Thomas' errors about Lawrence, often themselves get aspects of Thomas' own story wrong: Jeremy Wilson, for example, is among many of these biographers who claim that, before coming to the Middle East, Thomas had found "the Western Front . . . offered little material to suit his purpose"; Jeremy Wilson, 224. In his journals, however, Thomas was, to the contrary, quite excited by what he was seeing in Europe. Suleiman Mousa has Thomas being "sent . . . abroad as a war correspondent" by those in the United States who were "encouraging their Government to join the war on the side of the Allies"; Mousa, 263; of course, the United States had already entered the war. Michael Korda makes Thomas the "inventor of the travelogue" and reports that Woodrow Wilson had sent Thomas to Europe to "make a film"; Michael Korda, *Hero: The Life and Legend of Lawrence of Arabia* (New York: Harper Perennial, 2010), 353. Some of these and other errors are due, to be sure, to too-heavy reliance upon Thomas' own writings, particularly his book on Lawrence and his memoir, which are considerably less reliable than his journals; Lowell Thomas, *With Lawrence in Arabia* (New York: P. F. Collier & Son, 1924); Lowell Thomas, *Good Evening Everybody* (New York: William Morrow, 1976).

9. Robert Graves, *Lawrence and the Arabian Adventure* (New York: Doubleday, Doran & Company, 1928), 1; Mack, 178; Jeremy Wilson, 624; Aldington, 135, 160; Liddell Hart, *T. E. Lawrence: In Arabia and After* (London: Jonathan Cape, 1935). Suleiman Mousa speaks, somewhat awkwardly, in the English translation of his book at least, of Thomas' "publicity stunts" on behalf of Lawrence; Mousa, 235. Adrian Greaves' more recent biography also manages to leave Thomas out; Adrian Greaves, *Lawrence of Arabia* (London: Weidenfeld & Nicolson, 2007). Michael Korda is somewhat kinder to Thomas in his biography of Lawrence—the most recent as this is written. However, even Korda includes

a characterization of Thomas: "an inspired huckster in the tradition of P. T. Barnum"; Thomas, of course, saw himself instead as a "war correspondent"; Korda, 386.

10. These conclusions are based on a search of the Library of Congress' "Chronicling America" online database of 1,587 digitalized U.S. newspapers, which include many major papers such as the *New-York Tribune, The Sun* and the *Evening World*. I have also searched the *New York Times* archive. Before or while Thomas was in the Middle East, the *New York Times* did print two dispatches from W. T. Massey, who is described as "official correspondent of London newspapers with the Egyptian Expeditionary Force." One was attributed to a "British correspondent with the Palestine army" and appears entirely within quotations marks; "BEERSHEBA TAKEN IN NIGHT CHARGE," November 5, 1917. The other, which postdated the capture of Jerusalem, is labeled a "Special Cable to The New York Times"; "SCALED PRECIPICES TO WIN JERICHO," February 26, 1918. The *New York Times* appears to have arranged for rights to Massey's reports in September of 1918—months after Thomas had moved on—and the newspaper published a handful of articles on events leading up to and following the capture of Damascus by him; see, for example, "TURKS OUTWITTED BY GEN. ALLENBY," September 23, 1918. Massey would write three books on the British campaign in the Middle East. He does not mention T. E. Lawrence in the first two of these books; W. T. Massey, *The Desert Campaigns* (New York: G. P. Putnam's and Sons, 1918) and W. T. Massey, *How Jerusalem Was Won* (New York: Charles Scribner's Sons, 1920; this was probably not the first edition of this book). The third volume was first published after Thomas had made Lawrence famous and does mention Lawrence; W. T. Massey, *Allenby's Final Triumph* (London: Constable and Company, 1920). The next chapter will mention a *Times* of London story based on a Reuters report that actually mentions Lawrence but only near the end of the Middle East campaign, long after Thomas had moved on; "British Colonel with the Arabs," *Times* of London, September 25, 1918. Interview with Jeremy Wilson, outside of Oxford, October 2015.

11. Lowell Thomas to Frances Ryan, April 8, 1918.

12. The citations from Thomas here or his quotes from others are from the Lowell Thomas journal "Hejaz."

13. Cited, Lowell Thomas journal, "Hejaz."

14. Frances Thomas, Journal notes, 1917–1918.

15. In the script for his Allenby/Lawrence show, this trip is incorrectly said to have been taken on the way to Aqaba; The Lowell Thomas Travelogues, "With Allenby in Palestine and Lawrence in Arabia." The error is also repeated in his memoir; Thomas, *Good Evening Everybody*, 143–147.

16. Lowell Thomas to Frances Thomas, February 25, April 19, 1918; Lowell Thomas to Harriet Thomas, April 29, May 5, and June 16, 1918.

17. Thomas, *Good Evening Everybody*, 167–169.

18. Thomas' claims are in promotional material for Thomas' series, "SEVEN MOST TIMELY AND IMPORTANT ARTICLES"; and in Thomas, *Good Evening Everybody*, 181–183. Except for the interview with Prince Max von Baden, evidence is lacking in Thomas' notebooks of any interviews with German leaders, including the two Thomas or Waldron wrote about. It is possible that there were other notebooks that have not survived. And some dates in early January 1919 are indeed not covered in Thomas' journals. Or perhaps the interviews were very brief or were stitched together from other sources; Lowell Thomas, German journals. Lowell Thomas, "Americans in Recovered Alsace," *Leslie's Weekly*, January 25, 1919; Lowell Thomas, "Four Years of Agony in Strasbourg," *Leslie's Weekly*, February 15, 1919; Lowell Thomas, "Switzerland Welcomes U.S. Prisoners," *Leslie's Weekly*, February 15, 1919; Webb Waldron, "The Battle of Berlin," *Collier's*, March 29, 1919; Webb Waldron, "The Journalist Who Made a Revolution," *Collier's*, April 5, 1919; Webb Waldron, "'Not Blood, but

Blossoms!'" *Collier's*, April 12, 1919; Webb Waldron, "From Munich to Oberammergau," *Collier's*, May 17, 1919; Lowell Thomas, "'Give Germany Food and End Bolshevism,' Says President Ebert," *Evening World*, May 2, 1919; Lowell Thomas, "A Berlin Journalist's Story of the German Revolution," *Evening World*, April 30, 1919; see the *Globe and Commercial Advertiser*, February 14 to April 2, 1919.

19. Judging from the newspapers in which this dispatch appeared, it seems to be from United Press. The Lowell Thomas archive at Marist has clippings from a handful of newspapers reporting the shooting and Thomas' recovery, but the papers they are from and the dates when they appeared are not recorded. A few note that Thomas had been "a Denver newspaper man" or on the "staff of the Denver Times"—a sign they were Denver papers. I have located versions of the dispatch on the front pages of both the *Seattle Star* and the *Washington Times* on January 28, 1919. *Leslie's Weekly*, calling Thomas "a LESLIE'S Staff Correspondent," also picked up this dispatch. One Denver newspaper, probably after having spoken with Fran, added four paragraphs about Lowell and their travels in Europe.

20. Telegram from Lowell Thomas to Frances Thomas, February 11, 1919; telegram from Harriet Thomas to Frances Thomas, January 28, 1919; Frances Thomas to Eunice Ryan, February 1919; Thomas, *Good Evening Everybody*, 184; "Eye-Witness Will Tell Story of Hun Revolt," *New York Globe*, February 24, 1919.

21. According to Doug Fetherling, Hecht arrived in Berlin on December 30, 1918; Doug Fetherling, *The Five Lives of Ben Hecht* (Toronto: Lester and Orpen, 1977), 26; see also William MacAdams, *Ben Hecht* (New York: Barricade Books, 1990), 46–47. Thomas seems to have been covering events in Berlin at least by January 11, 1919, and to have left Berlin for the last time on about January 16; Lowell Thomas, German journals.

7. Come with Me to the Land of History, Mystery and Romance

1. The Lowell Thomas Travelogues, *With Allenby in Palestine and Lawrence in Arabia*. As Claire Keith has noted, references to the Irish in this script indicate that it was used on a later tour outside London. Keith has counted the film segments and slides; Claire Keith, "The Lowell Thomas Papers, Part I: the General Collection," *The Journal of the T. E. Lawrence Society* VII: 2, Spring 1998.

2. See advertisements in the *Times* of London, August 18 and October 9, 1919; "Mr. Lowell Thomas at the Albert Hall," *Times* of London, October 22, 1919; Frances Thomas journal, October 1919. See also Keith, "The Lowell Thomas Papers, Part I: the General Collection," 20.

3. Frances Thomas to Eunice Ryan, February 1919.

4. Thomas had sold some of the film he had purchased from others in Germany to Pathé, the fledgling newsreel company.

5. Lowell Thomas, *Good Evening Everybody* (New York: William Morrow, 1976), 193–199; Frances Thomas journal, March 2 to August 14, 1919; *Sun*, March 7, 1919; advertisement, Mr. Lowell Thomas, "The German Revolution"; Lowell Thomas, "Palestine," tape 7; Kevin Brownlow, *The War, the West, and the Wilderness* (New York: Alfred A. Knopf, 1979), 441–451; the *Globe and Commercial Advertiser*, February 14 to April 2, 1919. A show entitled *From Hoboken to the Rhine* ran for three days in Madison Square Garden.

6. Frances Thomas journal, August 14, 1919.

7. Alder Anderson, "History in Pictures," *Daily Telegraph*, October 2, 1919.

8. I have edited this quote from the travelogue to leave out Thomas' distracting claim that Lawrence was "of Gaelic ancestry." Lawrence's father had lived and owned an estate in Ireland but apparently did not consider himself of Irish origins. Lawrence and his brothers were raised in England. However, as noted above, the surviving copy of the script I am using, The Lowell Thomas Travelogues, *With Allenby in Palestine and Lawrence in Arabia*,

was probably intended for an Irish audience, and Thomas would have jumped on any way to connect Lawrence to Ireland.

9. Keith, "The Lowell Thomas Papers, Part I: the General Collection," 23.
10. Percy Burton to Lowell Thomas, August 14 and October 22, 1919; Frances Thomas journal, October 1919; "Statement of Account for the Season at the Royal Albert Hall," http:// library.marist.edu/archives/LTP/digitizedContents/Box%20502/1.25.2.4.1.502.10.pdf; "Thomas Travelogues Inc.: Statement of Expenditures Containing Complete Cost of Obtaining Materials for Present Production," http://library.marist.edu/archives/LTP /digitizedContents/Box%20502/1.25.2.4.1.502.11.pdf.
11. "British Colonel with the Arabs," *Times* of London, September 25, 1918.
12. Frances Thomas journal, September 25, 1919; Lowell Thomas, "Thomas Lawrence, Prince of Mecca," *Asia*, 19, September 1919, 819–829.
13. Cited, Keith, "The Lowell Thomas Papers, Part II: 1918–1923"; Crawford and Berton, "How Well Did Lowell Thomas Know Lawrence of Arabia."
14. Betty Shannon, "Mrs. Lowell Thomas Discusses Her Many-Sided Job as Wife, Homemaker," *Christian Science Monitor*, January 28, 1941.
15. T. E. Lawrence to Sir Archibald Murray, January 10, 1920, in Malcolm Brown, ed., *The Letters of T. E. Lawrence* (Oxford: Oxford University Press, 1991), 171–173; see also http:// telawrence.com/page/37. T. E. Lawrence to F. N. Doubleday, March 20, 1920; http://www .telstudies.org/writings/letters/1919-20/200320_f_n_doubleday.shtml; T. E. Lawrence to Edmund Blunden, in Malcolm Brown, ed., *The Letters of T. E. Lawrence*, 243; T. E. Lawrence to Fareedah El Akle, in Malcolm Brown, ed., *The Letters of T. E. Lawrence*, 183. T. E. Lawrence to E. M. Forster, June 17, 1925, in Malcolm Brown, ed., *The Letters of T. E. Lawrence*, 282–284. See also Claire Keith, "The Lowell Thomas Papers, Part II: 1918–1923," *The Journal of the T. E. Lawrence Society* VIII: 2, Spring 1999; Fred D. Crawford and Joseph A. Berton, "How Well Did Lowell Thomas Know Lawrence of Arabia," *English Literature in Transition, 1880–1920* 39: 3, 1996, 299–318; Keith, "The Lowell Thomas Papers, Part I: the General Collection."
16. Cited Claire Keith, "The Lowell Thomas Papers, Part II: 1918–1923," *The Journal of the T. E. Lawrence Society* VIII: 2, Spring 1999. Wilson gave a more nuanced view of Lawrence's reaction to Thomas—noting to whom he was writing, for example—in our interview with Jeremy Wilson, outside Oxford, in October 2015.
17. T. E. Lawrence to E. M. Forster, June 17, 1925, in Malcolm Brown, ed., *The Letters of T. E. Lawrence*, 282–284; T. E. Lawrence to Ralph H. Isham, August 10, 1927; T. E. Lawrence to Sir Archibald Murray, January 10, 1920, in Malcolm Brown, ed., *The Letters of T. E. Lawrence*, 171–173. See also Crawford and Berton, "How Well Did Lowell Thomas Know Lawrence of Arabia"; and Jeremy Wilson, *Lawrence of Arabia*, 289.
18. The citations in this section are from Crawford and Berton, "How Well Did Lowell Thomas Know Lawrence of Arabia."
19. Lowell Thomas, in A. W. Lawrence, ed., *T. E. Lawrence by His Friends* (New York: McGraw-Hill, 1963), 173. See also Jeremy Wilson, "Some Thoughts on Lawrence and Lowell Thomas," *Journal of the T. E. Lawrence Society*, 4:1, Autumn 1994, 76–80.
20. Frances Thomas journal, October; Frances Thomas to Harriet Thomas, December 9, 23, 1919; Lowell Thomas to Percy Burton, June 11, 1920; Keith, "The Lowell Thomas Papers, Part II: 1918–1923"; Lowell Thomas to Harry Chase, undated and perhaps unsent, http:// library.marist.edu/archives/lttravelogues/Harry%20Chase/Chaseletter/chaseletter.html.
21. Frances Thomas to Harriet Thomas, January 18, 1920; Lowell Thomas to Percy Burton, June 11, 1920.
22. See Keith, "The Lowell Thomas Papers, Part I: the General Collection," 23.
23. Frances Thomas to Harriet Thomas, December 9, 1920; Dale Carnagey to Lowell Thomas, undated, probably mid-May 1920.

24. Dale Carnagey to Lowell Thomas, November 10, 1920.

25. Frances Thomas to Harriet Thomas, July 25, September 17, October 28, 1920; Lowell Thomas to T. E. Lawrence, December 25, 1921.

26. "LOWELL THOMAS," *Otago Daily Times*, Issue 18077, October, 27, 1920; http://paperspast .natlib.govt.nz/cgi-bin/paperspast?a=d&d=ODT19201027.2.71.

27. Freya Stark, *Baghdad Sketches*, http://www.goodreads.com/author/quotes/62875.Freya _Stark.

28. Thomas, *Good Evening Everybody*, 231–32. We do have a contemporary account of this wild elephant ride in Lahore in one of Fran's letters. It notes that Primrose's name derives from a "pinky blue" tattoo. It assumes that Primrose was male. It does not mention Emma Chase as one of those riding the elephant through the market. But elsewhere Fran acknowledges that Mrs. Chase "was awfully unhappy in India" and "left for home"; Frances Thomas journal, May 22, 1921; Frances Thomas to Harriet Thomas, March 14 and May 26, 1921.

29. Thomas, *Good Evening Everybody*, 221–222; Dale Carnagey to Lowell Thomas, October 28, and November 12, 1920.

30. Frances Thomas to Harriet Thomas, May 26, June 2, 1921.

31. Lowell Thomas, *With Lawrence in Arabia* (New York: P. F. Collier & Son, 1924).

32. The citations in this section are from Crawford and Berton, "How Well Did Lowell Thomas Know Lawrence of Arabia"; Keith, "The Lowell Thomas Papers, Part II: 1918– 1923"; Lowell Thomas, "Thomas Lawrence, Prince of Mecca," *Asia*, September 1919; Lowell Thomas, "With Lawrence and Feisal in Arabia," *Asia*, October 1919; Lowell Thomas, "The Uncrowned King of Arabia, *Strand Magazine*, 59, 349, January 1920; 59, 350, February 1920; Thomas, *With Lawrence in Arabia*. I have leaned here on the analyses of Fred D. Crawford and Joseph A. Berton, as well as those of Claire Keith.

33. David Fromkin, "The importance of T. E. Lawrence," *New Criterion* Vol. 10, September 1991, 86. This passage is cited on the Web site *Lowell Thomas and Lawrence of Arabia: Making a Legend, Making History*, Clio Visualizing History; http://www.cliohistory.org /thomas-lawrence/lawrence/perspectives/fromkin/.

34. Lowell Thomas, in Lawrence, ed., *T. E. Lawrence by His Friends*, 171–172.

35. Cited, Crawford and Berton, "How Well Did Lowell Thomas Know Lawrence of Arabia."

36. Lowell Thomas, in A. W. Lawrence, ed., *T. E. Lawrence by His Friends*, 163.

8. How Dull It Is to Pause

1. Alfred, Lord Tennyson, *Ulysses* (Poetry Foundation), http://www.poetryfoundation.org /poem/174659. The connection between Lowell Thomas and Tennyson's *Ulysses* was made by John Lardner in "The Air: Travel," *New Yorker*, October 24, 1959.

2. Francis Yeats-Brown to Lowell Thomas, July 11, 12, 20, 1922. Lowell Thomas to A. W. Parsons, April 23, 1922.

3. Francis Yeats-Brown, "He Tells the World," in Norman R. Bowen, ed., *Lowell Thomas: The Stranger Everyone Knows* (Garden City, NY: Doubleday & Company, 1968), 46–52; Thomas, *Beyond Khyber Pass*, 49–51; Lowell Thomas to Frances Thomas, July 16, 1922.

4. Thomas, *Beyond Khyber Pass*, 113, 115–120, 127, 203–204, 210–211, 216, 218; Lowell Thomas to Frances Thomas, July 14, 19, 25, 1922; A. L. C., "A Camera in Kabul," *Manchester Guardian*, January 11, 1927.

5. Transcript of 1951 interview by Dick Roelofs with Dr. Harry G. Thomas, reel 17; Lowell Thomas to H. G. Thomas, October 11, 1922.

6. Lowell Thomas to Frances Thomas, April 5, 1922.

7. Frances Thomas to Lowell Thomas, February 18, 22, 25, 28, March 1, 10, 28, April 27, May 4, 1922; Francis Yeats-Brown to Lowell Thomas, July 11, 1922; Yeats-Brown, "He Tells the World," 51.

8. Lowell Thomas to Percy Burton, November 21, December 2, 1922.

9. Lowell Thomas, *Good Evening Everybody* (New York: William Morrow, 1976), 257; Frances Thomas to Lowell Thomas, March 28, 1922; Lowell Thomas to "Mr. Shelton," February 2, 1925; Lowell Thomas to "Judge Schaaf," February 2, 1925; Lowell Thomas to "Willie," September 22, 1936. For an accounting of lingering debts *after* the money started to flow in once again, see Lowell Thomas to Frances Thomas, March 14, 1925.

10. Frances Thomas Daylogue, January 11, 13, 1923; Lowell Thomas to Harry Thomas, January 5, 1923.

11. *Times* of London, April 20, 25, 1923.

12. Lowell Thomas to Percy Burton, April 26, 1923; Percy Burton to Lowell Thomas, undated but probably August 1923.

13. Frances Thomas to Eunice Ryan, January 28, 1924; Lowell Thomas to Eunice Ryan, March 15, 1924. Anne Thomas Donaghy has been particularly insightful on the cultural background behind her grandmother's parenting and her father's upbringing.

14. Lowell Thomas to Frances Thomas, January 29, 1924, undated, January or February 1924, February 12, 1924.

15. Lowell Thomas to Frances Thomas, January 31, September 11, 1924.

16. Lowell Thomas to "Mr. Shelton," February 2, 1925; *The American Magazine*, Vol. 98, 1924; Lowell Thomas to Frances Thomas, September 18, 1924; Lieutenant Lowell Smith to Lowell Thomas, August 1925; Lowell Thomas, *The First World Flight* (Boston and New York: Houghton Mifflin, 1925), xvii–xix, 1–3.

17. Lowell Thomas to Frances Thomas, March 14, 16, 1925; Lowell Thomas to "Judge Schaaf," February 2, 1925; Lowell Thomas to "Willie," September 22, 1936. An "Affidavit of Withdrawal," saying Thomas Travelogues Inc. "discontinued business in Illinois" as of December 31, 1925, was filed in Illinois on June 23, 1926. See "Thomas Travelogues, Inc., Preferred Stockholders, October 1, 1925," http://library.marist.edu/archives/LTP /digitizedContents/Box%20502/1.25.2.4.1.502.15.pdf. Frances Thomas to Eunice Ryan, January 31, 1926.

18. Frances Thomas to Eunice Ryan, undated, 1926, http://library.marist.edu/archives/LTP /digitizedContents/Box%20317/1.10.7.1.317.3.pdf; Frances Thomas journal, Europe 1926, http://library.marist.edu/archives/LTP/digitizedContents/Box%20271/1.10.2.7.271.4.pdf.

19. Frances Thomas to Eunice Ryan, January 31, 1926. Dates on the rest of Frances Thomas' letters to Eunice Ryan in winter, spring and summer of 1926 are unclear in the online archive, found at these three sites: http://library.marist.edu/archives/LTP/digitizedContents /Box%20317/1.10.7.1.317.2.pdf; http://library.marist.edu/archives/LTP/digitizedContents /Box%20317/1.10.7.1.317.3.pdf; http://library.marist.edu/archives/LTP/digitizedConte nts/Box%20317/1.10.7.1.317.4.pdf. Thomas, *Good Evening Everybody*, 269–270.

20. Lowell Thomas Jr., "Locust Farm Years," "Autobiographical Draft," Lowell Thomas Archive, Marist College. Thanks to John Ansley for forwarding this draft. Frances Thomas to Eunice Ryan, September 1, 1929, http://library.marist.edu/archives/LTP/digitizedContents /Box%20317/1.10.7.1.317.7.pdf.

21. Frances Thomas journal, Europe 1926, http://library.marist.edu/archives/LTP/digitized Contents/Box%20271/1.10.2.7.271.4.pdf.

22. Thomas, *Good Evening Everybody*, 262, 277; Frances Thomas to Eunice Ryan, September 6, 13, November 14, 19, 1926; Richard Norton Smith, *Thomas E. Dewey and His Times* (New York: Simon and Schuster, 1982), 318; Joseph E. Persico, *Edward R. Murrow: An American Original* (New York: McGraw Hill, 1988), 266; Rev. Ralph Conover Lankler, *Lowell Thomas of Quaker Hill* (Pawling, NY: The Historical Society of Quaker Hill and Pawling, 1990); Rev. Warren H. Wilson, *Quaker Hill in the Eighteenth Century* (Quaker Hill, NY: Quaker Hill Conference Association, 1970); "Prince William to Put in Week Seeing New York," *New York Herald Tribune*, undated, 1927.

23. Thomas, *Good Evening Everybody*, 269–276; Lowell Thomas, *European Skyways* (New York: Houghton Mifflin, 1927), 23.

24. S. T. Williamson, "Two German War Heroes Who Were Sportsmen," *New York Times*, December 25, 1927; on the next page in the *Times* is a review of Thomas' *European Skyways*. Michael Korda, *Making the List: A Cultural History of the American Bestseller, 1900–1999* (New York: Barnes & Noble Publishing, 2001), 52, https://books.google.com/books?id =isnf42j5rRUC&pg=PA35&lpg=PA35&dq=best+seller+lists+1924+nonfiction&source =bl&ots=yNOpxuYoD3&sig=zKk4skDpR3QJmeYQzcXk8Mglilw&hl=en&sa=X &ved=0CEIQ6AEwBmoVChMIsqj5uI-FxgIVWH-SCh2_WQCB#v=snippet&q =%22Lowell%20Thomas'&f=false. There is evidence, however, of one fatality: a British seaman aboard the Horngarth died after a stray bullet hit a steam pipe and caused an explosion—an incident not mentioned in Thomas' book, http://www.statemaster.com /encyclopedia/Felix-von-Luckner.

25. Prosper Buranelli, "The Lost Lip," *Harper's Magazine*, January 1921; Prosper Buranelli, "Si Vendetta," *Harper's Magazine*, October 1922; Prosper Buranelli, "Bright Snowflakes," *Harper's Magazine*, November 1923; Thomas, *Good Evening Everybody*, 278–282; David Stuart, *The Life and Rhymes of Ogden Nash: A Biography* (Lanham, MD: Madison Books, 2000), 17–20, 30, https://books.google.com/books?id=MWsYAgAAQBAJ&pg=PA17&lpg=PA17&dq =prosper+buranelli&source=bl&ots=6QQo5pDO9L&sig=5W8iey5KKrrp4W_VTpaYy 1uu02s&hl=en&sa=X&ei=-OmEVajON4GdNquFg4gP&ved=0CCwQ6AEwBDgK#v =onepage&q=prosper%20buranelli&f=false; Frederick Lewis Allen, *Only Yesterday: An Informal History of the 1920s* (Open Road Media, e-book, 2015), 165, https://books.google .com/books?id=vYS8BwAAQBAJ&q=Prosper#v=snippet&q=Prosper&f=false.

26. A list of most of Thomas' books during this period:
    - *Raiders of the Deep* (1928)—a very successful account of German submarines—or U-boats—during the war.
    - *The Sea Devil's Foc's'le* (1929)—Luckner revisited.
    - *Woodfill of the Regulars. A True Story of Adventure from the Arctic to the Argonne* (1929)—an American military hero.
    - *The Hero of Vincennes: The Story of George Rogers Clark* (1929)—on the frontier during the American Revolution.
    - *The Wreck of the Dumaru: A Story of Cannibalism in an Open Boat* (1930)—the struggle for survival in 1918 after a U.S. steamship was destroyed by lightning. A. W. S. writing in the *New Yorker*: "Your conscientious but chicken-hearted reviewer read the story avidly—for it is really swell—up to the point where the men in the lifeboat began to get dangerously hungry. There are some things I would rather not know about."
    - *Lauterbach of the China Sea: The Escapes and Adventures of a Sea-Going Falstaff* (1930)—another swashbuckling German sea captain, also written in the first person.
    - *India: Land of the Black Pagoda* (1930)—Lowell's own adventures on the subcontinent and the only one of these books honestly related in the first person (though undoubtedly partly written by Buranelli).
    - *Rolling Stone: The Life and Adventures of Arthur Ra* (1931)—the wildlife photographer Arthur Radclyffe Dugmore in Africa and elsewhere.
    - *This Side of Hell: Dan Edwards, Adventurer* (1932)—an American World War I hero.
    - *Kabluk of the Eskimo* (1932)—the adventures of a French trader, Louis Auguste Romanet, in northern Canada.

    In preparing this list, I began with an outline by Fred D. Crawford, which in turn is based on lists in the Lowell Thomas Archive. C. Campbell to Lowell Thomas, December 22, 1948; Robert F. DeGraff to Lowell Thomas, May 28, 1931.

27. A. W. S., "Recent Books," *New Yorker*, September 20, 1930; "Among the Eskimos," *New York Times*, March 6, 1932; Lowell Thomas, *Kabluk of the Eskimo* (Boston: Little, Brown,

1932), 10, 142, http://babel.hathitrust.org/cgi/pt?id=mdp.39015010846981;view=1up;seq
=28; cited, "Biography of Louis Auguste Romanet," University of Alberta, http://archives
.library.ualberta.ca/FindingAids/LouisRomanet/LouisRomanet.html.

28. Rose Wilder Lane to Lowell Thomas, August 14, 1931.

29. Frances Thomas to Eunice Ryan, undated, probably early 1925, http://library.marist.edu
/archives/LTP/digitizedContents/Box%20317/1.10.7.1.317.4.pdf, Frances Thomas to
Eunice Ryan, January 10, 1927, November 12, 1935, http://library.marist.edu/archives
/LTP/digitizedContents/Box%20318/1.10.7.1.318.7.pdf, page 1; "HARRY ALONZO CHASE:
Prominent Photographer Took Pictures Along Allied Front," *New York Times*, Novem-
ber 12, 1935; Harry Chase to Lowell Thomas, April 20, 1933, June 22, 1935.

9. Having the Ear of America

1. See Jim Cox, *Radio Journalism in America: Telling the News in the Golden Age and Beyond*
    (Jefferson, NC: McFarland & Company, 2013), 12, 17, 85. Mitchell Stephens, "Radio:
    From Dots and Dashes to Rock and Larry King," *New York Times*, November 20, 1995;
    Mitchell Stephens, *Beyond News: The Future of Journalism* (New York: Columbia Univer-
    sity Press: 2014), 56; Erik Barnouw, *A Tower in Babel: A History of Radio Broadcasting in
    the United States*, Vol. I (New York: Oxford University Press, 1966), 61–70. Barnouw also
    makes a case for some early stirrings in Detroit. A program called *Time Newscasting*,
    probably sponsored by *Time* magazine, is mentioned in *New York Times* radio listings on
    October 14 and December 2, 1928. The word "newscast" is used in connection with radio
    advertising in the *Times* on July 6, 1936, but more frequent uses begin on December 11,
    1938.

2. Frances Thomas to Eunice Ryan, January 10, 1927, http://library.marist.edu/archives/LTP
    /digitizedContents/Box%20317/1.10.7.1.31, page 1.7.6.pdf, page 1.

3. Daniel J Czitrom, *Media and the American Mind* (Chapel Hill: University of North Caro-
    lina Press, 1982), 75–78. Jim Cox, *American Radio Networks* (Jefferson, NC: McFarland &
    Company, 2009), 12, 20–23; Barnouw, *A Tower in Babel*, 191.

4. John Dunning, *On the Air: The Encyclopedia of Old-Time Radio* (New York: Oxford
    University Press, 1998), 495–496. Jim Cox and others place Lowell Thomas on *Headline
    Hunter*, but I can find no evidence that Thomas appeared on the show, let alone cohosted
    it; Cox, *Radio Journalism in America*, 22; the same claim is made in Anthony Slide, *Great
    Radio Personalities* (New York: Dover Publications, 1982), 98.

5. See, for example, the radio listings in the *New York Times* for September 21, 1930.

6. George Engles, "The Public Casts Votes for Favorite Programs," *New York Times*, September
    21, 1930; "Listening In," *New York Times*, June 1, 1930.

7. *Literary Digest Topics in Brief*, with Floyd Gibbons, June 5, 1930. The Gibbons papers are
    at the University of Maine; thanks to Desirée Butterfield-Nagy there.

8. Bruce Lenthall, *Radio's America: The Great Depression and the Rise of Modern Mass Cul-
    ture* (Chicago: University of Chicago Press, 2008), 12.

9. Cited, "Boxing the Compass with Lowell Thomas," *Literary Digest*, October 25, 1930; Cox,
    Radio Journalism in America, 88.

10. Orrin E. Dunlap Jr., "Listening In," *New York Times*, October 12, 1930; Emery, Michael,
    Edwin Emery and Nancy L. Roberts, *The Press and America: An Interpretive History of
    the Mass Media, 9th Edition* (Hoboken, NJ: John Wiley & Sons, 2004), 319; cited and see
    also Cox, *Radio Journalism in America*, 22.

11. Lowell Thomas, *Good Evening Everybody* (New York: William Morrow, 1976), 307–311; Ben
    Gross, *I Looked and I Listened: Informal Recollections of Radio and TV* (New York: Ran-
    dom House, 1954), 164–65; Edward Bliss Jr., *Now the News: The Story of Broadcast Jour-
    nalism* (New York: Columbia University Press, 1991), 27–28; David Stuart, *The Life and
    Rhymes of Ogden Nash: A Biography* (Lanham, MD: Madison Books, 2000), 43, https://

books.google.com/books?id=MWsYAgAAQBAJ&pg=PA17&lpg=PA17&dq
=prosper+buranelli&source=bl&ots=6QQo5pDO9L&sig=5W8iey5KKrrp4W
_VTpaYy1uu02s&hl=en&sa=X&ei=-.

12. Actually, Thomas complains in his memoir that in his final broadcast Gibbons underplayed his journalistic credentials and made it appear that "he was to be succeeded by a
professor." Ben Gross echoes Thomas' allegation. But this charge is not supported by Gibbons' script for his final broadcast. Gibbons remained a major personage on NBC's networks, including on the coverage of the 1932 political conventions. Thomas, *Good Evening
Everybody*, 310–311; Gross, *I Looked and I Listened*, 165; *Literary Digest Topics in Brief*, with
Floyd Gibbons, September 27, 1930.

13. Lowell Thomas, *Literary Digest Topics in Brief*, September 29, 1930.

14. Lowell Thomas, *Literary Digest Topics in Brief*, November 1, 1932.

15. Irving E. Fang, *Those Radio Commentators!* (Ames: Iowa State University Press, 1977), 73;
Edward Bliss Jr. and John M. Patterson, *Writing News for Broadcast*, Second Edition (New
York: Columbia University Press, 1978), 12–14. Louis Sherwin was born Hugo Louis Sher-
win Görlitz; Sherwin was his mother's maiden and stage name. Amy Sherwin was a re-
nowned soprano; Dixie Hines, Harry Prescott Hanaford, eds., *Who's Who in Music and
Drama* (New York: H. P. Hanaford, 1914), 280.

16. Lowell Thomas, *Literary Digest Topics in Brief*, January 20, 1931, http://library.marist.edu
/archives/LTP/Textual%20Materials/transcripts/427.97.pdf.

17. The various lecture bureaus that had booked his travelogues were beside themselves: "It
is a ghastly business," the manager of one stated when the number of dates he would have
to cancel became clear; Lowell Thomas to Mr. Mathews, undated; O. B. Stephenson to
Lowell Thomas, October 2, 15, November 3, 1930; R. E. Barnette to Lowell Thomas,
April 2, 1931.

18. Lowell Thomas to Eunice Ryan, December 14, 1932; "APARTMENT LEASES," *New York
Times*, October 29, 1930; Harvard College Class of 1897, *Twenty-fifth Anniversary Report,
1897–1922* (Cambridge, MA: Riverside Press, 1922), 500–501; "Making Latin Alive," *New
York Times*, March 13, 1921; "School Loses Tax Suit," *New York Times*, May 24, 1939;
"School Building Bid In; Lawrence-Smith Property Goes to New York Trust Company,"
New York Times, March 17, 1939; "Boys' Schools Combined; Lawrence-Smith Joins
Browning in East 62d Street Building," *New York Times*, January 30, 1939; Lowell
Thomas Jr., "Some Reflections on My Past Worth Nothing," undated. After unsuccessfully
suing New York City to preserve its tax-exempt status, the Lawrence-Smith School would
be merged into another preparatory school in 1939, but that was well after Lowell
Thomas Jr. had left for the Taft School.

19. Frances Thomas to Eunice Ryan, March 31, 1932, http://library.marist.edu/archives/LTP
/digitizedContents/Box%20317/1.10.7.1.317.9.pdf, page 53.

20. Frances Thomas to Eunice Ryan, undated, probably early 1930s, http://library.marist.edu
/archives/LTP/digitizedContents/Box%20317/1.10.7.1.317.9.pdf, page 11; Frances Thomas
to Eunice Ryan, March 3, 1932, http://library.marist.edu/archives/LTP/digitizedContents
/Box%20317/1.10.7.1.317.9.pdf, page 63; Lowell Thomas to Eunice Ryan, December 26,
1931, December 14, 1932; Rose Wilder Lane to Lowell Thomas, August 14, 1931.

21. Thomas, *Good Evening Everybody*, 323; Cox has the date wrong on the *Literary Digest*
dropping CBS, Cox, *Radio Journalism in America*, 88; Lowell Thomas to Daniel Tuthill,
April 24, 1936; Lowell Thomas to Eunice Ryan, December 26, 1931; Frances Thomas to
Eunice Ryan, December 28, 1931, http://library.marist.edu/archives/LTP/digitized
Contents/Box%20317/1.10.7.1.317.9.pdf, page 18; Frances Thomas to Eunice Ryan,
April 6, 1932, http://library.marist.edu/archives/LTP/digitizedContents/Box%20317/1
.10.7.1.317.9.pdf, page 71; "Lowell Thomas Adds to Estate," *New York Times*, June 25,
1932.

22. Lenthall, *Radio's America: The Great Depression and the Rise of Modern Mass Culture*, 12.

23. Dr. James Bender, "Ninety Million Speak 'General America,'" *New York Times*, August 27, 1944.

24. Lowell Thomas to Federal Communications Commission, 1960; "When News Wasn't Completely Grim—Lowell Thomas," 1946, http://crooksandliars.com/gordonskene/when -news-wasnt-completely-grim-lowell.

25. Lowell Thomas, *Literary Digest Topics in Brief*, October 3, 1930; Corella to Lowell Thomas, October 4, 1934; cited in Lionel Crocker, "Lowell Thomas," *Quarterly Journal of Speech* 28: 3, 1942; Henry Herbert Goddard to Lowell Thomas, January 23, 1933, in Leila Zenderland, "Contextualizing Documents, Data and Controversies: Working with the Henry Herbert Goddard Papers," in David B. Baker, *Thick Description and Fine Texture: Studies in the History of Psychology* (Akron, OH: University of Akron Press, 2003), 84–85.

26. Thomas, *Good Evening Everybody*, 312. Thomas gives a less colorful version of Butler's admonition in a letter to M. H. Leister of Sun Oil on October 27, 1944. See Charles E. Phelps to Lowell Thomas, February 15, 1936, and John F. Royal to Lowell Thomas, January 22, 1937.

27. Lowell Thomas, *Literary Digest Topics in Brief*, June 10, 1932; Mr. Labin of NBC to Lowell Thomas, January 14, 1935.

28. Lowell Thomas, "My Favorite Whoppers," intended for publication in *Cosmopolitan*, undated but probably late 1932.

29. Tom Tiede, "The Lowell Thomas Story Goes On and On," *Argus-Press*, July 12, 1973.

30. Fang, *Those Radio Commentators!*, 59–61; cited, Irving E. Fang, "Boake Carter, Radio Commentator," *Journal of Popular Culture* 12: 2, 1978, http://onlinelibrary.wiley.com/doi /10.1111/j.0022-840.1979.1202_341.x/abstract.

31. Interview with Lowell Thomas Jr. and Mary Taylor Thomas, Anchorage, Alaska, November 14, 2012; cited in Lionel Crocker, "Lowell Thomas," *Quarterly Journal of Speech* 28: 3, 1942; Lowell Thomas to M. H. Leister, October 27, 1944.

32. David Paul Nord, "Benjamin Franklin and Journalism," in David Waldstreicher, ed., *A Companion to Benjamin Franklin* (New York: John Wiley & Sons, 2011); Mitchell Stephens, *Beyond News: The Future of Journalism* (New York: Columbia University Press, 2015), 31–54; Interview with Whitelaw Reid, in F. Wingate, ed., *Views and Interviews of Journalists* (New York: F. B. Patterson, 1875), 25–40; Whitelaw Reid, "Journalism as a Career," University of the City of New York, 1872, in *American and English Studies, Volume II* (New York: Charles Scribner's Sons, 1913), http://www.ebooksread.com/authors -eng/whitelaw-reid/american-and-english-studies-volume-2-die/page-14-american-and -english-studies-volume-2-die.shtml; David T. Z. Mindich, *Just the Facts* (New York: New York University Press, 1998).

33. "It's a Wonderful World: Thomas," *Newsday*, October 4, 1951.

34. M. H. Leister to Lowell Thomas, August 23, 1932; Kevin Kruse, *One Nation Under God: How Corporate America Invented Christian America* (New York: Basic Books, 2015), 15–16; J. Howard Pew to William Radford Coyle, August 8, 1934; Joseph Newton Pew Jr. to Lowell Thomas, April 25, 1935; Ray Henle, interview with Lowell Thomas, October 7, 1969; Michael C. Jensen, "The Pews of Philadelphia," *New York Times*, October 10, 1971; "Ann" to Lowell Thomas (about Harry R. Chase), undated; Lowell Thomas to M. H. Leister, November 2, 1932.

35. Lowell Thomas, *Topics in Brief*, November 3, 1932; cited, Edward Bliss Jr., *Now the News: The Story of Broadcast Journalism* (New York: Columbia University Press, 1991), 108. For the role of advertisers in general in radio programming, see Czitrom, *Media and the American Mind*, 79–86.

36. Bliss, *Now the News*, 39–44; Paul W. White, *News On the Air* (New York: Harcourt, Brace & Company, 1947), 30–42; Thomas, *Good Evening Everybody*, 313; Jackson S. Elliott, as-

sistant general manager, the Associated Press, to Lowell Thomas, February 4, 1933; John Dunning, *On the Air: The Encyclopedia of Old-Time Radio* (New York: Oxford University Press, 1998), 486. Abe Schechter's accounts are cited in White, 37–38. Thomas' speech is cited in Bliss, *Now the News*, 42.

37. Ramsburg, *Network Radio Ratings*, 21, 38, 48–54; Ramsburg does not have separate ratings each night of the week for Thomas' show; he uses the average rating. I have seen claims that Thomas' audience reached 20 million in the 1930s, but I have not been able to find numbers to justify these claims; Dan D. Nimmo and Chevelle Newsome, *Political Commentators in the United States in the 20th Century* (Westport, CT: Greenwood Press, 1997), 253; Douglas B. Craig, *Fireside Politics: Radio and Political Culture in the United States, 1920–1940* (Baltimore: Johns Hopkins University Press, 2000), 13; Fang, *Those Radio Commentators!*, 72; David E. Sumner, *The Magazine Century: American Magazines Since 1900* (New York: Peter Lang, 2010), 77; William Whitworth, "An Accident of Casting," in Thomas Fensch, ed., *Television News Anchors* (Woodlands, TX: New Century Books, 2001), 63.

38. Jim Ramsburg, *Network Radio Ratings, 1932–1953* (Jefferson, NC: McFarland & Company, 2012), 78.

39. Helen Engel and Marilynn Smiley, eds. *Remarkable Women in New York State History* (Charleston, SC: The History Press, 2013), 12; Perry Edward Gross and William Clifford Roberts, "Perry Edward Gross, MD: A Conversation with the Editor," *Baylor University Medical Proceedings*, July 2008; Tom Shultz, *A 1940s Monadnock Childhood* (Charleston, SC: The History Press, 2011), 86; Burton Bernstein, "Personal History: the Bernstein Family, Part I," *New Yorker*, March 22, 1982.

10. The Voice of God

1. Douglas Gomery and Clara Pafort-Overduin, *Movie History: A Survey*, Second Edition (New York: Routledge, 2011), 137–141; James Deaville, "Sounding the World: The Role of Music and Sound in Early 'Talking' Newsreels," in Holly Rogers, ed., *Music and Sound in Documentary Film* (New York: Routledge, 2014), 41–55. For errors on divining the uses of new forms of communication, see Mitchell Stephens, *the rise of the image the fall of the word* (New York: Oxford University Press, 1998), 42–45.

2. *The Film Daily*, January 24, February 18, March 2, 8, 9, 29, April 26, May 5, June 6, July 9, August 4, September 7, October 13, 14, 1932, January 28, February 3, March 1, 1933; Raymond Fielding, *The American Newsreel: A Complete History, 1911–1967* (Jefferson, NC: McFarland & Company, 2006), 111; American Newsreel to Lowell Thomas, February 23, 1932; Jack Cohn to Lowell Thomas, April 26, 1933.

3. Frances Thomas to Eunice Ryan, August 23, October 4, 25, 1932, http://library.marist.edu /archives/LTP/digitizedContents/Box%20318/1.10.7.1.318.1.pdf, pages 51, 61, 75; Frances Thomas to Eunice Ryan, February 15, 1933, http://library.marist.edu/archives/LTP /digitizedContents/Box%20318/1.10.7.1.318.2.pdf, page 11; Frances Ryan to Eunice Ryan, June 23, 1933, http://library.marist.edu/archives/LTP/digitizedContents/Box%20318/1.10 .7.1.318.3.pdf, page 11. "Hoovers Go to Camp Today: Party of New Yorkers Will Accompany the President to Virginia," *New York Times*, August 1, 1930.

4. Ernest K. Lindley, "Roosevelt Toils In 101 Heat He Hoped to Avoid," *New York Herald Tribune*, August 1, 1933; "Miscellaneous Brief Reviews," *New York Times*, August 6, 1933; Lowell Thomas, *Good Evening Everybody* (New York: William Morrow, 1976), 332–343; Lowell Thomas, "The Sport of 15,000,000: That's Softball," *New York Herald Tribune*, September 5, 1937; Lawrence Sullivan, "With Roosevelt at Hyde Park," *Washington Post*, August 9, 1933; Westbrook Pegler, "Fair Enough: Pegler Refused Bean-Bag Offer," *Atlanta Constitution*, September 12, 1934; Ernest K. Lindley, "Hull Completes Policy Review With Roosevelt," *New York Herald Tribune*, August 7, 1933.

5. Lowell Thomas, "A Dream of Television," dated 'August 15, 1933?' This article appears to have been written for a magazine, the *Commentator*, which did not yet exist. The *Commentator* was another of Lowell's schemes: a publication designed to exploit the popularity of the new radio commentators. Thomas would have the title editor. The magazine began publication in 1937 and survived until Pearl Harbor; Ronald Lora and William Henry Longton, eds, *The Conservative Press in Twentieth-Century America* (Westport, CT: Greenwood Press, 1999), 273–279.

6. *Milwaukee Sentinel*, August 27, 1935; "Battle of Britain Continues with Mounting Fury," undated, Movietone News, https://www.youtube.com/watch?v=p_d_CTtPjGY; Fielding, *The American Newsreel*, 113–116; Raymond Fielding, *The March of Time, 1935–1951* (New York: Oxford University Press, 1978), 33; Gomery and Pafort-Overduin, *Movie History*, 150; Lowell Thomas to Truman Talley, October 24, 1934; Thomas Doherty, *Hollywood and Hitler, 1933–1939* (New York: Columbia University Press, 2013), 79.

7. Irving E. Fang, *Those Radio Commentators!* (Ames, IA: Iowa State University Press, 1977), 75; Lary May, "Making the American Way: Moderne Theatres, Audiences, and the Film Industry 1929–1945," *Prospects* 12, 1987.

8. Interview with James Morrison, July 15, 2016; "Remembering Lowell Thomas, with Walter Cronkite," in George Plimpton, ed., *As Told at the Explorers Club* (Guilford, CT: Lyons Press, 2005), 431–445.

9. "Ball Team Coached By Roosevelt," *New York Times*, September 3, 1934; Ernest K. Lindley, "Roosevelt's Baseball Team Wins As He Benches Pitcher Tugwell," *New York Herald Tribune*, September 3, 1934; Leon H. Dure Jr., "Pitcher Tugwell Yanked Out of Ballgame by Roosevelt," *Washington Post*, September 3, 1934.

10. Thomas, *Good Evening Everybody*, 338.

11. See Christopher Swan, "Lowell Thomas: These Are The Good Old Days," *Christian Science Monitor*, November 26, 1980, http://www.csmonitor.com/1980/1126/112652.html; interview with Lowell Thomas Jr., Anchorage, Alaska, November 12, 2012.

12. Grace Turner, "Front Page for Food: Lowell Thomas," *New York Herald Tribune*, September 27, 1936; Spencer Howard, Herbert Hoover Presidential Library-Museum, to Kulsoom Khan, one of the author's research assistants, October 13, 2015; President Hoover's calendar, October 24, 1937; Lowell Thomas to Herbert Hoover, October 27, 1937; Herbert Hoover to Lowell Thomas, October 28, 1937; "Hoover, Former President, Prepared Radio Address at Lowell Thomas' Home," *Poughkeepsie Sunday Courier*, October 31, 1937; Julian Sancton, "A Guide to the Bohemian Grove," *Vanity Fair*, May 2009, http://www.vanityfair.com/culture/2009/05/bohemian-grove-guide200905. In an interview with Ray Henle, on October 7, 1969, Thomas insisted that he first met Herbert Hoover in London during World War I.

13. Charles Lindbergh to Samuel F. Pryor Jr., April 20, 1972, http://www.pbagalleries.com/view-auctions/catalog/id/147/lot/40247/?url=%2Fview-auctions%2Fcatalog%2Fid%2F147%3Fcat%3D11%2C17.

14. See Lowell Thomas to Charles E. Phelps, May 24, 1935; "Tiny Broadcaster Tested," *New York Times*, August 4, 1929; Ted Lamont, *The Happiness of the Pursuit: Felicitous Episodes Along the Way* (Lanham, MD: Hamilton Books, 2006), 15; Wolcott Gibbs and John Bainbridge, "Profiles: Thomas E. Dewey, St. George and the Dragon," *New Yorker*, May 25, 1940; Marylin Bender, "Quaker Hill, Where Lowell Thomas Is Patriarch of the Quiet Celebrities," *New York Times*, November 10, 1968; Herbert Warren Wind, "Profiles: Robert Trent Jones," *New Yorker*, August 4, 1951; interview with James Morrison, July 15, 2016; Frances Thomas to Eunice Ryan, July 19, 1932, http://library.marist.edu/archives/LTP/digitizedContents/Box%20318/1.10.7.1.318.1.pdf, page 8; May 5, 1933, http://library.marist.edu/archives/LTP/digitizedContents/Box%20318/1.10.7.1.318.2.pdf, page 65. Ralph Conover Lankler, *Lowell Thomas of Quaker Hill* (Pawling, NY: The Historical Society of Quaker Hill and Pawling, 1990).

15. Lowell Thomas to C. C. Avard, December 13, 1939; Hurdman and Cranstoun, certified public accountants, to Lowell Thomas, October 29, 1943.

16. Jeremy Wilson, *Lawrence: The Authorized Biography of T. E. Lawrence* (New York: Collier Books, 1992), 403; John E. Mack, *A Prince of Our Disorder: The Life of T. E. Lawrence* (Cambridge, MA: Harvard University Press, 1998), 409. See also Frances Thomas to Eunice Ryan, May 21, 1935, http://library.marist.edu/archives/LTP/digitizedContents /Box%20318/1.10.7.1.318.5.pdf, page 10; and Lowell Thomas, in A. W. Lawrence, ed., *T. E. Lawrence by His Friends* (New York: McGraw-Hill, 1963).

17. Pherbia Thomas Guerin to Lowell Thomas, July 5, 1932; Lowell Thomas to Ellery Walter, January 30, 1934; Monica H. Grey of Alber and Wickes to Lowell Thomas, February 14, 1938; "Pherbia Thomas Thornburg," *Poughkeepsie Journal*, November 25, 1980; "Pherbia Thomas Thornburg," *Pawling News-Chronicle*, November 26, 1980; "S. Raymond Thornburg," draft of obituary, January 1981.

18. Charles W. Hurd, "ROOSEVELT CHEERS HIS TIGERS IN VAIN," *New York Times*, September 22, 1935; Grace Turner, "Front Page for Food: Lowell Thomas," *New York Herald Tribune*, September 27, 1936; Charles W. Hurd, "PRESIDENT'S TEAM LOSES DESPITE AID," *New York Times*, August 17, 1936; Westbrook Pegler, "Fair Enough: Pegler Refused Bean-Bag Offer," *Atlanta Constitution*, September 12, 1934; Lowell Thomas, "The Sport of 15,000,000: That's Softball," *New York Herald Tribune*, September 5, 1937; Lowell Thomas and Ten Shane, *Softball, So What?* (New York: Frederick A. Stokes, 1940); "White House Ten Routs Softball's All-Stars, 21 to 10," *Washington Post*, September 20, 1937; "NINE OLD MEN WIN BEHIND BABE RUTH: As a Softballer He's Not So Good," *Daily Boston Globe*, October 18, 1937.

19. James R. Hansen, *A Difficult Par: Robert Trent Jones Sr. and the Making of Modern Golf* (New York: Gotham Books, 2014), e-book; "Sidelines," *New York Herald Tribune*, October 27, 1940; Lowell Thomas, "Fabulous Fireplace," *Los Angeles Times*, June 11, 1950; Alex Pizzati, "'So Long, Until Tomorrow': Lowell Thomas and the 'History of Civilization' Fireplace," Penn Museum, March 2006, http://www.penn.museum/sites/expedition/so -long-until-tomorrow-lowell-thomas-and-the-history-of-civilization-fireplace/; "Lowell Thomas Fireplace Book," uncredited, undated explication of the "History of Civilization Fireplace."

20. Jeffrey L. Kuntz, "Good Evening, Everybody," *The Northern Light*, February 2015; "Lowell Thomas Runs Himself as Super One-Man Industry," *Christian Science Monitor*, December 6, 1938.

21. "2,100 Acres Bought By Lowell Thomas," *New York Times*, November 1, 1937; "Lowell Thomas to Try Hand at Real Estate," *New York Herald Tribune*, July 14, 1938.

22. Interview with Lowell Thomas Jr., Anchorage, Alaska, November 12, 2012.

23. Lowell Thomas to Frances Thomas, March 20, 1939.

24. Betty Shannon, "Mrs. Lowell Thomas Discusses Her Many-Sided Job as Wife, Homemaker," *Christian Science Monitor*, January 28, 1941; Lowell Thomas to Frances Thomas, March 20, 1939; Frances Thomas journal, 1938; Frances Thomas to Eunice Ryan, July 21, 1933, http://library.marist.edu/archives/LTP/digitizedContents/Box%20318/1.10.7.1.318.3 .pdf, page 38, January 22, 1934, http://library.marist.edu/archives/LTP/digitizedContents /Box%20318/1.10.7.1.318.4.pdf, page 10, undated, http://library.marist.edu/archives/LTP /digitizedContents/Box%20317/1.10.7.1.317.9.pdf, page 39, July 3, 1935, http://library .marist.edu/archives/LTP/digitizedContents/Box%20318/1.10.7.1.318.6.pdf, page 27.

25. Joseph E. Persico, *Edward R. Murrow: An American Original* (New York: McGraw Hill, 1988), 266–269; Wolcott Gibbs and John Bainbridge, "Profile: St. George and the Dragon, Thomas Dewey," *New Yorker*, May 25, 1940.

26. Interview with Thomas Murphy, August 17, 2015; "Dewey Acquires Estate in Roosevelt's County," *New York Times*, October 17, 1939; Wolcott Gibbs and John Bainbridge, "Profile:

St. George and the Dragon, Thomas Dewey," *New Yorker*, May 25, 1940; Lindesay Parrott, "DEWEY IS MORE ACTIVE IN THE POLITICAL ARENA," *New York Times*, August 6, 1939; Richard Norton Smith, *Thomas E. Dewey and His Times* (New York: Simon and Schuster, 1982), 296, 317–322; Leo Egan, "DEWEY WELCOMED BY HIS HOME FOLK," *New York Times*, June 27, 1948; Fred D. Crawford interview with James Morrison, June 18, 1991; interview with James Morrison, July 15, 2016; interview with John A. Brockway, May 23, 2016.

27.   Lowell Thomas, "First At The Pole," *This Week, New York Herald Tribune*, April 2, 1939; Fred D. Crawford to Marianna Thomas, April 16, 1995; Dan Morain, "Bohemian Club Unyielding: Bastion of the Powerful Clings to Male Mystique," *Los Angeles Times*, May 26, 1987, http://articles.latimes.com/1987-05-26/news/mn-2818_1_bohemian-club.

28.   "VISITORS TAKE PART IN TV SHOW," *New York Times*, May 4, 1939; Lowell Thomas is first listed as doing the news on television on January 2 and January 3, 1940 ("Telecasts for the Week," *New York Times*, January 2, 1940), but he does not even appear to have been doing his radio newscast on that date (*Lowell Thomas with the News*, January 2, 1940); and in his memoir Thomas states that he first simulcast on television on February 21, 1940, and that is when his radio script mentions that he is also on television; Lowell Thomas, *So Long Until Tomorrow* (New York: William Murrow, 1977), 21; "Notes on Television," *New York Times*, May 5, 1940; "News Around the Studios," *New York Times*, February 25, 1940; Mike Conway, *The Origins of Television News in America: The Visualizers of CBS in the 1940s* (New York: Peter Lang, 2009), 59, 80, 133; Edward Bliss Jr., *Now the News: The Story of Broadcast Journalism* (New York: Columbia University Press, 1991), 218–219; Danielle Sarver Coombs and Bob Batchelor, eds., *We Are What We Sell: How Advertising Shapes American Life . . . and Always Has*, Vol. I (Santa Barbara: Praeger, 2014), 193–195; "TELEVISION SHOW GIVEN IN THEATRE: 1,400 in Audience Here Witness First Public Program on Large-Size Screen," *New York Times*, May 10, 1941.

29.   Thomas, *So Long Until Tomorrow*, 19.

11. Catching Up with the War

1.   *Lowell Thomas with the News*, December 8, 1941; Lowell Thomas, *So Long Until Tomorrow* (New York: William Murrow, 1977), 20; "Notes on Television," *New York Times*, May 5, 1940; "News Around the Studios," *New York Times*, February 25, 1940; Mike Conway, *The Origins of Television News in America: The Visualizers of CBS in the 1940s* (New York: Peter Lang, 2009), 59, 80, 133; Edward Bliss Jr., *Now the News: The Story of Broadcast Journalism* (New York: Columbia University Press, 1991), 218–219; Danielle Sarver Coombs and Bob Batchelor, eds., *We Are What We Sell: How Advertising Shapes American Life . . . and Always Has*, Vol. I (Santa Barbara: Praeger, 2014), 193–195; T. R. Kennedy Jr., "Welding Sight to Radio's Sound: New York Will Have Three Stations on the Air by Tuesday," *New York Times*, June 29, 1941; "Television Starts Today," *New York Times*, July 1, 1941; "Advertising News and Notes, *New York Times*, July 2, 1941; Ron Simon, "The First Crazy Day of TV," Paley Center, June 28, 2011, http://www.paleycenter.org/b-simon-the-first-crazy-day-of-tv; *Lowell Thomas with the News*, December 8, 1941 .

2.   For wars and the audience for journalism, see Mitchell Stephens, *A History of News*, Third Edition (New York: Oxford University Press, 2007), 138.

3.   Jim Ramsburg, *Network Radio Ratings, 1932–1953* (Jefferson, NC: McFarland & Company, 2012), 103–107; Michael A. Davis, *Politics as Usual: Thomas Dewey, Franklin Roosevelt, and the Wartime Presidential Campaign of 1944* (DeKalb: Northern Illinois University Press, 2014),192; Susan J. Douglas, *Listening In: Radio and the American Imagination* (Minneapolis: University of Minnesota Press, 2004), 174, http://ezproxy.library.nyu.edu:2054/lib/nyulibrary/reader.action?docID=10159601#; William Whitworth, "An Accident of Casting," in Thomas Fensch, ed., *Television News Anchors* (Woodlands, TX: New Century Books, 2001), 63. The Cronkite statement is in the dedication of his autobiogra-

phy, Walter Cronkite, *A Reporter's Life* (New York: Ballantine Books, 1997). Lowell
Thomas to M. H. Leister, October 27, 1944, Theodore Peterson, *Magazines in the Twentieth Century* (Urbana: University of Illinois Press, 1956), 52, http://library.brown.edu/cds
/mjp/pdf/mojp000046.pdf.

4. Dorothy Thompson, "I Saw Hitler!" *Cosmopolitan*, March 1932, http://isites.harvard.edu
    /fs/docs/icb.topic1292219.files/Week%205/I%20Saw%20Hitler!.pdf; Ernie Pyle, "The
    Death of Captain Waskow," January 10, 1944, http://mediaschool.indiana.edu/erniepyle
    /1944/01/10/the-death-of-captain-waskow/; cited in Mitchell Stephens, *Broadcast News*,
    Fourth Edition (Belmont, CA: 2005), 46; John Hersey, "Hiroshima," *New Yorker*, August 31,
    1946, http://www.newyorker.com/magazine/1946/08/31/hiroshima?intcid=mod-most
    -popular.

5. *Lowell Thomas with the News*, September 11, 18, 1944.

6. Lowell Thomas Jr. with Lew Freedman, *Flight to Adventure, Alaska and Beyond* (Portland,
    OR, 2013), 40; Lowell Thomas Junior to Lowell and Frances Thomas, undated, January 24,
    February 7, March 31, April 3, 1943; Dr. Charles C. Lund to Lowell Thomas, June 16, 1947.

7. Arthur Gordon, *Norman Vincent Peale: Minister to Millions* (Englewood Cliffs, NJ:
    Prentice-Hall, 1958), 205–206; Clarence Westphal, *Norman Vincent Peale, Christian
    Crusader* (Minneapolis: Denison, 1964), 92.

8. Betty Shannon, "Mrs. Lowell Thomas Discusses Her Many-Sided Job as Wife, Home-
    maker," *Christian Science Monitor*, January 28, 1941; Thomas, *So Long Until Tomorrow*,
    20–24; Dorothy Barclay, "Air Casualties Cured at Pawling," *New York Times*, May 21, 1944;
    Marquis W. Childs, "Washington Calling," *Washington Post*, December 18, 1944.

9. Radio address: Robert A. Taft, "Russia and the Four Freedoms," June 25, 1941, in *The
    Papers of Robert A. Taft*, Clarence E. Wunderlin, ed., Vol. 2 (Kent, OH: Kent State Univer-
    sity Press, 2001); Ayn Rand to DeWitt Emery, October 4, 1941, in *Letters of Ayn Rand*,
    Michael S. Berliner, ed. (New York: Plume, 1997); cited, Kevin Kruse, *One Nation Under
    God: How Corporate America Invented Christian America* (New York: Basic Books, 2015),
    15; Jeffrey A. Engel, ed., *The Four Freedoms: Franklin D. Roosevelt and the Evolution of an
    American Idea* (New York: Oxford University Press, 2015), 134; M. H. Leister to Lowell
    Thomas, June 8, 1943; J. Howard Pew to Lowell Thomas, June 11, 1943; "Sun Oil Paid
    $95,645 to Lowell Thomas in '41," *Wall Street Journal*, July 9, 1942.

10. Erik Barnouw, *The Golden Web, A History of Broadcasting in the United States, Volume
    II—1933–1953* (New York: Oxford University Press, 1968), 171, 180, 187–190; Advertise-
    ment: "Standard Oil Sponsors Lowell Thomas Five Nights a Week on Pacific Blue,"
    Broadcasting, November 1, 1943; "Sunoco Reported Moving Lowell Thomas to NBC,"
    Broadcasting, October 25, 1943; Jack Gould, "Radio Row: One Thing and Another," *New
    York Times*, January 9, 1944.

11. Lowell Thomas to J. Howard Pew, November 2, 1944; "Under the Heading of Pro-
    Roosevelt and Anti-Dewey," memo sent to Sun Oil during the 1944 presidential cam-
    paign; Lowell Thomas to M. H. Leister, October 27, 1944; Prosper Buranelli to Lowell
    Thomas, March 1, 1944, with handwritten response by Lowell Thomas on bottom; Lowell
    Thomas, "A Neighbor Talks About Tom Dewey," Walter Winchell's column, "The Man on
    Broadway," August 18, 1944; Deborah Lane, "Heads & Tales," *Newsday*, October 5, 1944;
    "The Champ Defends His Title," *Atlanta Constitution*, September 25, 1944; Dexter Teed,
    "Pawling Folks'll Vote for Dewey," *New York Post*, July 10, 1944. The story Thomas aired
    that may have received the most complaints from Democrats concerned a fight that
    erupted at the Statler Hotel in Washington after President Roosevelt spoke to a Teamsters
    Union meeting there. The Teamsters were accused of attacking a couple of navy men who
    had failed to profess support for the president. A couple of wordings in Thomas' script
    verge on the hyperbolic or melodramatic, neither new embarrassments for Thomas, but
    otherwise the initial account Lowell broadcast, which he said was based on that of the

United Press, was not substantially different from that the *New York Times* printed from the Associated Press. There's not a lot of support here for on-air anti-Roosevelt bias; *Lowell Thomas with the News*, October 2, 3, 17, 1944; "NAVY OFFICER SAYS TEAMSTERS HIT HIM: Midway Veteran Charges Six Attacked Him and Friend Night of Roosevelt Speech," *New York Times*, October 3, 1944. For allegations against Thomas on the story, most not substantiated and including numerous factual errors, see Benjamin Davison, "Softball and Hard Rhetoric: Lowell Thomas and Hudson Valley Political Culture, 1933–1945," *Hudson River Valley Review* 28: 2, Spring 2012, http://www.hudsonrivervalley.org/review /pdfs/hrvr_28pt2_full.pdf; Davison seems not to have consulted the scripts in question.

12. Thomas, *So Long Until Tomorrow*, 34–35; "EIGHT RADIO NEWSMEN ON ETO ASSIGNMENT," *Variety*, April 4, 1945; "Bill Henry, By the War," *Los Angeles Times*, April 7, 1945; "Newsmen Touring European Fronts," *Broadcasting*, April 9, 1945.

13. Lowell Thomas, World War II Journal, #1, April 4–14, 1944; #2, April 14–20, 1944; *Lowell Thomas with the News*, April 20, 1945; Peter Novick, *The Holocaust in American Life* (New York: Houghton Mifflin, 1999), 63–66; Joseph E. Persico, *Edward R. Murrow: An American Original* (New York: McGraw Hill, 1988), 227–231; Gene Currivan, "Nazi Death Factory Shocks Germans on Forced Tour," *New York Times*, April 18, 1945; Laurel Leff, *Buried By the Times* (New York: Cambridge University Press, 2005), 220–222, 308–314.

14. "Newsreel Pictures Tell Shocking Story of the Nazi Murder Mills," *Variety*, May 2, 1945; "Nazi Atrocities: Pictorial Proof of German Bestiality," Fox Movietone, narrated by Ed Thorgersen, http://www.ushmm.org/online/film/display/detail.php?file_num=902; Lowell Thomas and Dick Ham, "The Liberation of Buchenwald," April 1945, the Lowell Thomas Collection, http://www.ushmm.org/online/film/display/detail.php?file_num =1054.

15. Lowell Thomas, World War II Journal, #2, April 14–20, 1944; #3 April 20–May 8, 1944. *Lowell Thomas with the News*, April 24, 1945; "BERLIN, EXCEPT POSTSDAM, AFIRE: LOWELL THOMAS," *Chicago Daily Tribune*, April 25, 1945; "LOWELL THOMAS SEES BERLIN FROM PLANE," *New York Times*, April 25, 1945.

16. Lowell Thomas, "Flying Around the World," draft of newspaper column; *Lowell Thomas with the News*, Cairo broadcast, May 21, 1945; Thomas, *So Long Until Tomorrow*, 47–87; "Doolittle Heads Home; Pacific Job Foreseen," *Washington Post*, May 15, 1945; Lowell Thomas and Edward Jablonski, *Doolittle: A Biography* (New York: Doubleday & Company, 1976), 303–304.

17. Lowell Thomas, "Chiang Kai-Shek," *Los Angeles Times*, July 25, 1945; Lowell Thomas, "The Last Play," *Los Angeles Times*, July 28, 1945.

18. Lowell Thomas, "I Gain Great Face," *Los Angeles Times*, August 11, 1945; "Lowell Thomas Kin Dies," *Los Angeles Times*, December 29, 1946; "Lowell Thomas' Mother Dies," *New York Times*, December 29, 1946; transcript of 1951 interview by Dick Roelofs with Dr. Harry G. Thomas, reel 17; Dr. Thomas said his wife had cancer but died of "apoplexy." Lowell Thomas to Mr. Green, April 21, 1972.

19. Walt Hawver, *Capital Cities/ABC: The Early Years, 1954–1986, How the Minnow Came to Swallow the Whale* (Radnor, PA: Chilton Books, 1994), 9–10; interview with Thomas Murphy, August 17, 2015; Thomas, *So Long Until Tomorrow*, 92–93, 106–107, 130–134; "Lowell Thomas in Shift to CBS for P&G," *The Billboard*, November 2, 1946; "Lowell Thomas," *Variety*, October 1, 1947.

20. Joseph E. Persico, *Edward R. Murrow: An American Original* (New York: McGraw Hill, 1988), 266–269, 355–358, 499; A. M. Sperber, *Murrow: His Life and Times* (New York: Freundlich Books, 1986), 324; Alexander Kendrick, *Prime Time: The Life of Edward R. Murrow* (Boston: Little, Brown, 1969), 308, 313, 363–364; Edward R. Murrow to Lowell Thomas, May 24, 1957; interview with Casey Murrow, Vermont, August 19, 2015.

21. "Remembering Lowell Thomas, with Walter Cronkite," in George Plimpton, ed., *As Told at the Explorers Club* (Guilford, CT: Lyons Press, 2005), 431–445.

12. The Very Roof of the World

1. Patricia Cronin Marcello, *The Dalai Lama: A Biography* (Westport, CN: Greenwood Press, 2003), 14–20; Richard Worth, *Dalai Lama (Tenzin Gyasto)* (New York: Chelsea House, 2004), 4–7; Thomas Laird, *The Story of Tibet: Conversations with the Dalai Lama* (New York: Grove Press, 2006); Lowell Thomas Jr., *Out of This World: Across the Himalayas to Forbidden Tibet* (New York: The Greystone Press, 1950, Kindle edition); Rosemary Jones Tung, *A Portrait of Lost Tibet* (Berkeley: University of California Press, 1980), 89; Lezlee Brown Halper and Stefan Halper, *Tibet: An Unfinished Story* (New York: Oxford University Press, 2014, Kindle edition); Peter Bishop, "Not Only a Shangri-la: Images of Tibet in Western Literature," in Thierry Dodin and Heinz Rather, eds., *Imagining Tibet: Perceptions, Projections, and Fantasies*, (Boston: Wisdom Publications, 2001), 208–209; Orville Schell, *Virtual Tibet* (New York: Metropolitan Books, 2000), 241–248; Lowell Thomas with Lowell Thomas Jr., "Out of This World: Journey to Lhasa," *Collier's*, February 11, 1950; interview with Roger Croston, October 11, 2015.

2. Lowell Thomas Jr., *Out of This World*; John Kenneth Knaus, *Orphans of the Cold War: America and the Tibetan Struggle for Survival* (New York: Public Affairs, 1999), 34, 42–45; Lezlee Brown Halper and Stefan Halper, *Tibet: An Unfinished Story* (New York: Oxford University Press, 2014, Kindle edition); Tsepon W. D. Shakabpa, *Tibet: A Political History* (New Haven: Yale University Press, 1967), 298; George N. Patterson, *Requiem for Tibet* (London: Aurum Press, 1990), 98; interview with Roger Croston, October 11, 2015; Schell, *Virtual Tibet*, 264–265.

3. Lowell Thomas Jr., *Out of This World*; Lowell Thomas with Lowell Thomas Jr., "Out of This World: Journey to Lhasa," *Collier's*, February 11, 1950, February 18, 1950; Lowell Thomas Jr., Tibet journal; Lowell Thomas Jr. radio broadcast, "This time from Tibet. . . ." The song "Mule Train" was a hit in the 1940s for Frankie Lane and Bing Crosby, then sung by Gene Autry in a movie of the same name.

4. Schell, *Virtual Tibet*, 18–22; Lowell Thomas Jr., *Out of This World*; Lowell Thomas with Lowell Thomas Jr., "Out of This World: Journey to Lhasa," *Collier's*, February 11, 18, March 4, 1950, February 18, 1950; Lowell Thomas Jr., Tibet journal; from the movie *Out of This World*, a travelogue by Lowell Thomas and Lowell Thomas Jr., presented by Theodore R. Kupferman, 1954.

5. Lowell Thomas Jr. in his book states that "we halted for the night at a village seven miles from Lhasa, impatient as we were to reach our destination after toiling for twenty-three days over the rugged Himalayas"; so they actually entered Lhasa on the 24th day. This jibes with my calculation: They left Gangtok on August 5 and arrived in Lhasa on August 29, three days before the blessing by the Dalai Lama, which took place the day before Lowell Jr.'s journal entry dated September 2. Lowell Thomas Jr., *Out of This World*; Lowell Thomas with Lowell Thomas Jr., "Out of This World: Journey to Lhasa," *Collier's*, February 18, 1950; Lowell Thomas Jr., Tibet journal.

6. Lowell Thomas Jr., *Out of This World*; Lowell Thomas with Lowell Thomas Jr., "Out of This World: Journey to Lhasa," *Collier's*, March 4, 1950; Lowell Thomas Jr., Tibet journal; the movie *Out of This World*, a travelogue by Lowell Thomas and Lowell Thomas Jr., presented by Theodore R. Kupferman, 1954; "Lowell Thomas Becomes First Person in History to Speak to Outside World From Lhasa, Tibet," CBS News press release, October 7, 1949; Marcello, *The Dalai Lama: A Biography*, 52; interview with the Dalai Lama by Anne Thomas Donaghy and David Wright, October 31, 2016.

7. "Reds See West Plot on Tibet," *Wilkes-Barre Record*, November 30, 1949 (this is an Associated Press story, which appeared in newspapers around the country); *New Times* did indeed connect "a certain Lowell Thomas" with what it called "American imperialist

interference in Tibetan affairs"; T. Yershov, "Imperialist Intrigue in Tibet," *New Times*, number 49, November 30, 1949. Lowell Thomas, *So Long Until Tomorrow: From Quaker Hill to Kathmandu* (New York: William Morrow and Company, 1977), 142; Lowell Thomas Jr., Tibet journal; Lowell Thomas Jr., *Out of This World*; Lowell Thomas with Lowell Thomas Jr., "Out of This World: Journey to Lhasa," *Collier's*, March 4, 1950; Lowell Thomas, Tibet broadcast, #5; Knaus, *Orphans of the Cold War*, 42–43; Alastair Lamb, *Tibet, China & India, 1914–1950: A History of Imperial Diplomacy* (Hertingford-bury: Roxford Books, 1989), 516; Halper and Halper, *Tibet: An Unfinished Story*, 75–77; A. Tom Grunfeld, *The Making of Modern Tibet*, revised edition (Abingdon, Oxon: Routledge, 2015), 103–105, 165; Thomas Laird, *Into Tibet: The CIAs First Atomic Spy and His Secret Expedition to Tibet* (New York: Grove Press, 2002).

8.   Lowell Thomas Jr., Tibet journal; Lowell Thomas Jr., *Out of This World*; Lowell Thomas with Lowell Thomas Jr., "Out of This World: Journey to Lhasa," *Collier's*, March 18, 1950; "Lowell Thomas Hurt So Badly in Tibet He Cannot Be Moved," *Daily Boston Globe*, September 24, 1949; Lowell Thomas, "High Adventure"; Robert Trumbull, "Tibet Fears Told by Thomas," *New York Times*, October 10, 1949.

9.   Patterson, *Requiem for Tibet*, 98; Knaus, *Orphans of the Cold War*, 43; Richard H. Rovere, "Letter from Washington," *New Yorker*, November 2, 1950; Lowell Thomas Jr., *Out of This World*; Lowell Thomas with Lowell Thomas Jr., "Out of This World: Journey to Lhasa," *Collier's*, March 18, 1950; Lezlee Brown Halper and Stefan Halper, *Tibet: An Unfinished Story* (New York: Oxford University Press, 2014, Kindle edition); Laird, *Into Tibet: The CIAs First Atomic Spy and His Secret Expedition to Tibet*.

10.   Lowell Thomas broadcast, July 7, 1950; conversation with Anne Thomas Doughty, 2015.

13. An Entirely New Form of Entertainment

1.   Broadcast by Jack Zaiman, *Needle Club*, WDRC, May 22, 1950; "LOWELL THOMAS JR. WEDS MARY PRYOR," *New York Times*, May 21, 1950; "People and Ideas: The Thomas-Pryor Wedding," *Vogue*, July 1, 1950; G. Lynn Sumner, "Wedding of the Year," May 24, 1950.

2.   John Belton, "Glorious Technicolor, Breathtaking Cinemascope and Stereophonic Sound," in Steve Neale, ed., *The Classical Hollywood Reader* (New York: Routledge, 2012), 356; Mitchell Stephens, "History of Television," https://www.nyu.edu/classes/stephens/History%20of%20Television%20page.htm; U.S. Department of Commerce, "Housing and Construction Reports: Housing Characteristics," series H-121, number 1, September 26, 1955; Walter C. van Buren, "The American Newsreel Lives On!" draft of article based on interview with Lowell Thomas.

3.   Richard F. Shepard, "FAR FROM BROADWAY: 'High Adventure with Lowell Thomas' Looks High and Low for New Fare," *New York Times*, November 10, 1957; Les Brown, "Notes: The Fall Season Yields a Couple of Surprises," *New York Times*, October 17, 1976; Gary Paul Gates, *Air Time: The Inside Story of CBS News* (New York: Berkley, 1979), 58.

4.   Transcript of 1951 interview by Dick Roelofs with Dr. Harry G. Thomas, reel 2, reel 17.

5.   When, two months later, Lawson and Trumbo were going to prison, Thomas did add some "balance" by reporting that they "spoke bitterly, saying they are victims of what they call 'the bi-partisan pro-war policies of the Truman administration.'" But was this the best criticism of the case against the two screenwriters? Thomas did not quote their assertion, which the *Times* mentioned in its headline the next day, that "the government itself is guilty of wholesale violations of the Bill of Rights." *Lowell Thomas and the News*, October 29, 1947; April 10, June 4, 29, 1950; March 9, June 9, 1954. "FEDERAL VIGILANCE ON PERVERTS ASKED," *New York Times*, December 16, 1950; Lewis Wood, "FILM WRITERS LOSE CONTEMPT APPEAL," *New York Times*, April 11, 1950; "Lawson and Trumbo, Film Writers, Are Committed to Jail for Contempt: Before Starting 1-Year Sentences, They Say Bill of Rights Is Violated," *New York Times*, June 10, 1950.

6. Scott Feinberg, "Blacklisted: Cliff Carpenter & Jean Rouverol," *Hollywood Reporter*, November 17, 2012, http://www.hollywoodreporter.com/news/blacklisted-cliff-carpenter-jean-rouverol-391764; Lowell Thomas to Cliff Carpenter, March 17, 1978; Clifford A. Carpenter to Lowell Thomas, February 3, 1980.

7. Jack Gould, "Television in Review: Murrow vs. McCarthy," *New York Times*, March 9, 1954; W. H. Lawrence, "EXCHANGE BITTER: Counsel Is Near Tears as Crowd Applauds Him at Finish," *New York Times*, June 10, 1954.

8. Mitchell Stephens, *Beyond News: The Future of Journalism* (New York: Columbia University Press, 2014), 50, 86–88.

9. Bosley Crowther, "LOOKING AT CINERAMA," *New York Times*, October 5, 1952; Greg Kimble, "The Thrill of Cinerama," *American Cinematographer*, September 2002, 83, 9, 82–96; Belton, "Glorious Technicolor, Breathtaking Cinemascope and Stereophonic Sound," 358–360; Tino Balio, ed., *Hollywood in the Age of Television* (Boston: Unwin Hyman, 1990), 25, 190–194; Louther S. Horne, "SPOKESMAN CALLS MOVIES UNBOWED," *New York Times*, September 13, 1952; Hy Hollinger, "Cinerama Still Makes History," *Variety*, September 29, 1954; "CINERAMA'S $1,771,500 FOR FIRST YEAR IN L.A.," *Variety*, May 5, 1954; "'Cinerama' in 21st Week, 350,000 Draw, Breaking All Known Det. Records," *Variety*, August 12, 1953; "'CINERAMA' TO START 109TH WEEK TODAY," *New York Times*, October 26,1954; "Pictures: Lawrence of Arabia, 'Paint Your Wagon' Due Next for Cinerama," *Variety*, January 14, 1953; "Lowell Thomas Opines Film Travelogues Will Continue Via Cinerama," *Variety*, September 3, 1958; "Film Review: "Search for Paradise," *Variety*, September 25, 1957; Gerald Dickler to Milton Lyons, June 10, 1959; "Film Review: '7 Wonders of the World,'" *Variety*, April 11, 1956; Bosley Crowther, "CINERAMA TOURISM: 'Search for Paradise,' Another Travelogue," *New York Times*, September 29, 1957; "All-Time Top Gross Films," *Variety*, January 10, 1962; Fred D. Crawford interview with James Morrison, June 18, 1991; Alan D. Kattelle, "The Evolution of Amateur Motion Picture Equipment, 1895–1965," *Journal of Film and Video* 38: 3–4, Summer–Fall 1986; "'Paradise' in 31-Week N.Y. Powder," *Variety*, March 26, 1958; "An Interview with Mike Todd Jr.," 1995, 70mm.com, http://www.in70mm.com/news/2004/todd_jr/interview/index.htm; "Cinerama," Lowell Thomas, circa 1962; Lowell Thomas to Bernard Smith, October 6, 1960. Cinerama did have one more real success, a fiction film in 1962: *How the West Was Won*.

10. Interview with Lowell Thomas Jr., Anchorage, Alaska, November 12, 2012.

11. "Lowell Thomas, Associates Seek to Buy WROW-AM-TV," *Broadcasting*, October 18, 1954; "WTRI Protests Thomas' WROW Buy; Claims CBS 'Tie-in' Was Withheld," *Variety*, December 8, 1954; Walt Hawver, *Capital Cities/ABC: The Early Years, 1954–1986* (New York: Capital Cities/ABC, 1994), 10–16.

12. Interview with Thomas Murphy, February 5, 2013; Hawver, *Capital Cities/ABC*, 16–52; Frank. M. Smith, "Memorandum for the Board of Directors Meeting," 1955 and 1956; "Hudson Valley Broadcast Co. Buys KOVR (TV) for $3.5 Million," *Broadcasting*, September 9, 1957; "Capital Cities TV Puts 52,000 Shares on the Block," *Broadcasting*, December 23, 1957; "From Cripple Creek to Capital Cities," *Forbes*, October 1, 1976; Jack O'Brian, "Lowell's in the High Brackets," *New York Journal-American*, August 6, 1963.

13. Interview with Lowell Thomas Jr. and Mary "Tay" Thomas, Anchorage, Alaska, November 12, 14, 2012.

14. Jack Gould, "TV: Superficial Journey: Lowell Thomas Presents First of His New Series—A Trip to New Guinea," *New York Times*, November 13, 1957; Sid Bakal, "TV REVIEW: High Adventure," *New York Herald Tribune*, November 13, 1957; Sid Bakal, "TV REVIEW: High Adventure," *New York Herald Tribune*, January 23, 1958; Campbell Ewald, "HIGH ADVENTURE WITH LOWELL THOMAS," *Variety*, November 20, 1957; Richard F. Shepard, "Lowell Thomas on a Trip to Puka Puka," *New York Times*, January 20, 1959; Richard F.

Shepard, "Lowell Thomas Offers Last 'High Adventure,' *New York Times*, March 28, 1959.

15. *This Is Your Life*, September 30, 1959; Val Adams, "ONE MORE TIME: THIS IS YOUR LIFE," *Boston Globe*, January 1, 1983; Stephen Farber, "ONE-NIGHT ENCORE FOR 'THIS IS YOUR LIFE,'" *New York Times*, April 16, 1987; "TV Fight of the Month," *Sports Illustrated*, October 12, 1959; Mabel Barbee Lee to Lowell Thomas, November 5, 1959; *Lowell Thomas and the News*, October 1, 1959; Richard F. Shepard, "Lowell Thomas' Life," *New York Times*, October 2, 1959; John Lardner, "The Air: Travel," *New Yorker*, October 24, 1959. For Marianna Thomas' later theory on why Lowell was upset with the program—"he was fearful that Edwards would delve too deeply into LT's personal life"—see Bill Booker to Fred Crawford, June 18, 1996.

14. To Strive, To Seek, To Find, and Not to Yield

1. "Prosper Buranelli, Aide of Lowell Thomas, Dead," *New York Times*, June 20, 1960; "Prosper Buranelli Dies, Expert on Crosswords," *New York Herald Tribune*, June 20, 1960; interview with Bernard Buranelli, March 7, 2016.

2. Interview with Lowell Thomas Jr. and Mary "Tay" Thomas, Anchorage, Alaska, November 12, 14, 2012; Tad Bartimus, "At 60, Lowell Thomas Jr. Takes on His Dream Job as Alaskan Bush Pilot," *Hartford Courant*, November 25, 1983.

3. "The Movie," *Lowell Thomas and Lawrence of Arabia, Making a Legend, Creating History*, http://www.cliohistory.org/thomas-lawrence/movie/; Joseph F. Dmohowski, "Unfinished Business: Michael Wilson's 'Seven Pillars of Wisdom' Screenplay," *Film History* 24: 1, 56–73; James Chapman and Nicholas John Coll, *Projecting Empire: Imperialism and Popular Cinema* (New York: I. B. Tauris, 2009), 87–111; Adrian Turner, *The Making of David Lean's Lawrence of Arabia* (London: Dragon's World, 1994), 51; Natasha Fraser-Cavassoni, *Sam Spiegel* (New York: Simon and Schuster, 2003), 215–252; Lowell Thomas to Sam Spiegel, January 7, 1963; *Lowell Thomas and the News*, May 1963.

4. "1,200 Hail Lowell Thomas; Message Sent by Johnson," *New York Times*, November 23, 1965; "Hodges and Party Visit Antarctica," *New York Times*, November 20, 1962; Lowell Thomas and Lowell Thomas Jr., *Famous First Flights That Changed History* (New York: Doubleday, 1968); "PLANE ENDS FLIGHT OVER BOTH POLES," *Chicago Tribune*, November 18, 1965; Allyn Baum, "ANTARCTIC FLIGHT CALLED HISTORIC," *New York Times*, October 2, 1963; J. R. Reedy, "First Flight Across the Bottom of the World," *National Geographic*, 125, 3, 1964; Lowell Thomas to Hilde, Kurt and Christl Thalhammer, November 14, 1963.

5. Lowell Thomas to Cardinal Spellman, December 17, 1963; "Lowell Thomas Out of Hospital," *New York Times*, November 22, 1963.

6. Mrs. Lowell Thomas Jr., "An Alaskan Family's Night of Terror," *National Geographic*, July 1964; Lowell Thomas Jr. with Lew Freedman, *Lowell Thomas Jr.: Flight to Adventure and Beyond* (Portland, OR: Alaska Northwest Books, 2014), 181–190.

7. Interview with Casey Murrow, Vermont, August 19, 2015; Joseph E. Persico, *Edward R. Murrow: An American Original* (New York: McGraw Hill, 1988), 266–269, 355–358, 499; A. M. Sperber, *Murrow: His Life and Times* (New York: Freundlich Books, 1986), 324; Alexander Kendrick, *Prime Time: The Life of Edward R. Murrow* (Boston: Little, Brown, 1969), 308, 313, 363–364; Edward R. Murrow to Lowell Thomas, December 23, 1949; *Lowell Thomas and the News*, April 27, 1965.

8. Lowell Thomas to Frances Thomas, November 29, 1958; February 19, 1961; November 8, 1962; February 10, 1964.

9. Lowell Thomas to Lowell Thomas Jr., May 25, 1953; Lowell Thomas to Miriam Macmillan, October 2, 1964; Lowell Thomas to John Harding, February 12, 1965; Lowell Thomas to Pherbia Thornburg Jr., February 3, 1969; Lowell Thomas to Mamie Eisenhower, March 24, 1969; Lowell Thomas to Earl Thacker, November 20, 1969.

10. Lowell Thomas to Steve, April 13, 1964; "THE WORLD OF LOWELL THOMAS," *Variety*, September 28, 1966; *BBC Handbook: 1968* (Aylesbury, Bucks: Hazell Watson & Viney, 1968), 41; Val Adams, "Lowell Thomas and B.B.C. Plan Color Series on Distant Places," *New York Times*, December 1, 1965; "Cap Cities Sets 2nd Network Docu," *Variety*, February 12, 1969; "'Patrol into the Unknown,' A Lowell Thomas Expedition," *Boston Globe*, January 25, 1970; Christl, *Adventures with the New Guinea Headhunters* (New York: Doubleday, 1965), 5, 251; Lowell Thomas, "Taken to the Cleaners or The Saga of the Beautiful Blonde's Missing Pants," April 17, 1963; Lowell Thomas to Christl Thalhammer, May 9, 1964.

11. Hawver, *Capital Cities/ABC: The Early Years*, 73–90; "FRANK SMITH, 56, RADIO-TV LEADER," *New York Times*, August 8, 1966.

12. Marianna Thomas to Fred W. Crawford, April 12, 20, 1995; February 23, 1996; Marianna Munn Thomas, "Life With the Late, Great Lowell Thomas"; Lowell Thomas to Marianna Munn, postcard from the Camelot Inns, contents noted but not dated by Fred W. Crawford.

13. Interviews with Thomas Murphy, February 5, 2013, August 17, 2015; Hawver, *Capital Cities/ABC*, 90127; Alex S. Jones, "CAPITAL CITIES HUNTS BARGAINS," *New York Times*, August 22, 1984.

14. "Lowell Thomas, promoter, National Aviation Hall of Fame, Enshrined 1992," http://www.nationalaviation.org/thomas-lowell/; McCandlish Phillips, "Lowell Thomas Honored at Fete After 40 Years as a Newscaster," *New York Times*, October 22, 1970.

15. Lowell Thomas to Dr. Frick, September 30, 1971; Lowell Thomas to Erling, January 25, 1972; Robert Beverley Evans to Lowell Thomas, February 20, 1973; Lowell Thomas to Alma, August 8, 1973; Lowell Thomas to Mabel Barbee Lee, August 1, 1972; Lowell Thomas to James H. Doolittle, January 22, 1974.

16. Richard Norton Smith, *Thomas E. Dewey and His Times* (New York: Simon and Schuster, 1982), 322, 630–643.

17. Special thanks to two researchers—Melvis Acosta and Nicholas Chhoeun—for tracking down the dates of these changes. Jerry Parker, "Tonight, It's Just 'So Long,'" *Newsday*, May 14, 1976; *Lowell Thomas and the News*, June 3, 1974, May 14, 1976; "Lowell Thomas, Last Broadcast on CBS Radio," https://www.youtube.com/watch?v=EhXUoul56DM.

18. Franklynn Peterson, "Pioneering Newscaster Lowell Thomas Still on Job," *Hartford Courant*, August 25, 1974. See also, Lowell Thomas to Anna-Grace, July 8, 1974.

19. Lowell Thomas Jr. with Lew Freedman, *Lowell Thomas Jr.: Flight to Adventure and Beyond*, 209–218; Lowell Thomas to Robert Atwood, April 22, 1964; "Lowell Thomas Jr. Tells Blacks That He Opposes Mixed Marriages," *New York Times*, November 27, 1977; Albin Krebs, "Notes on People," *New York Times*, December 3, 1977; Tad Bartimus, "At 60, Lowell Thomas Jr. Takes on His Dream Job as Alaskan Bush Pilot," *Hartford Courant*, November 25, 1983; telephone interviews with Larry Smith, Charles Wohlforth and Bella Hammond in Alaska, August 2016; email from Anne Thomas Donaghy, September 2, 2016.

20. "Frances Ryan Thomas, 81," United Press International, *Boston Globe*, February 17, 1975; Jerry Parker, "Tonight, It's Just 'So Long,'" *Newsday*, May 14, 1976.

21. Allen D. Breck, *From the Rockies to the World: A Companion to the History of the University of Denver* (Denver: University of Denver, 1997), 181; "Fates and Fortunes: Gift from an Alumnus," *Broadcasting*, March 17, 1975; "POSTINGS: A PLUM IN PAWLING," *New York Times*, February 27, 1983; Leon F. Drozd Jr. to Ross Pritchard, November 13, 1978; Lowell Thomas to Ross Pritchard, August 25, 1981; Cliff Carpenter to Lowell Thomas, February 3, 1980.

22. *Lowell Thomas and the News*, May 14, 1976; "Lowell Thomas, Last Broadcast on CBS Radio," https://www.youtube.com/watch?v=EhXUoul56DM; Jerry Parker, "Tonight, It's Just

'So Long,'" *Newsday*, May 14, 1976; Les Brown, "Lowell Thomas Is Giving Up Nightly Radio Show," *New York Times*, May 1, 1976; Andy Wickstrom, "History Reels Across Your Screen," *Chicago Tribune*, April 18, 1986; "LOWELL THOMAS, A WORLD TRAVELER AND BROADCASTER FOR 45 YEARS, DEAD," *New York Times*, August 30, 1981.

23. Marianna Munn Thomas, "Life With the Late, Great Lowell Thomas"; notes on telephone conversation with Marianna Thomas by Fred W. Crawford, August 14, 1991; "Harold D. Krickenbarger Sr., Obituary," *Dayton Daily News*, December 10, 2005; Albin Krebs, "Notes on People," *New York Times*, January 5, 1977; "Lowell Thomas to Wed in Hawaii," *Chicago Tribune*, January 4, 1977.

24. Lawrence van Gelder, "Lowell Thomas," *New York Times*, February 5, 1978; Marianna Munn Thomas, "Life With the Late, Great Lowell Thomas"; "Lowell Thomas Dutchess County Estate Offered by Sotheby Parke Bernet International Realty Corporation."

25. Lawrence van Gelder, "Lowell Thomas," *New York Times*, February 5, 1978; Barbara Bush, *A Memoir* (New York: Simon and Schuster, 1994), 138–140; James Lilley, *China Hands* (New York: Public Affairs, 2004), 201–204; David S. Broder, "Lowell Thomas: Real Tibet Gone," *Washington Post*, October 5, 1977.

26. Hawver, *Capital Cities/ABC*, 132–237; Gregory James, "Paper Strike in Wilkes-Barre Grows Bitter," *New York Times*, November 19, 1978. "PAPERS' FEUD ROOTED IN 3-YEAR STRIKE," *New York Times*, October 6, 1981; Alex S. Jones, "CAPITAL CITIES HUNTS BARGAINS," *New York Times*, August 22, 1984; "From Cripple Creek to Capital Cities," *Forbes*, October 1, 1976.

27. Lawrence van Gelder, "Lowell Thomas," *New York Times*, February 5, 1978.

28. Marianna Thomas to Fred W. Crawford, April 12, 20, 1995.

29. Certificate of Death, Pherbia Thomas Thornburg, November 24, 1980; "Pherbia Thomas Thornburg," *Pawling News-Chronicle*, November 26, 1980; Certificate of Death, Raymond Thornburg, January 17, 1981; "S. Raymond Thornburg," draft of obituary, January 1981.

30. Interview with James Morrison, July 15, 2016; "Remembering Lowell Thomas, with Walter Cronkite," in George Plimpton, ed., *As Told at the Explorers Club* (Guilford, CT: Lyons Press, 2005), 431–445; Lowell Thomas to William F. Buckley Jr., February 27, 1978; interview with Richard Moulton, April 17, 2016.

31. Interview with David Lowell Thomas, June 21, 2014.

32. Joan Hanauer, "Thomas: Newsman, Newsmaker," *Los Angeles Times*, October 1, 1975; McCandlish Phillips, "Lowell Thomas Honored at Fete After 40 Years as a Newscaster," *New York Times*, October 22, 1970.

33. Interview with James Morrison, July 15, 2016; Fred D. Crawford interview with James Morrison, June 18, 1991; Tom Brokaw to Fred D. Crawford, October 21, 1991; interview with Tom Brokaw, November 19, 2015.

34. Marianna Thomas to Fred W. Crawford, February 23, 1996; Jerry Schwartz, "Hundreds of Mourners Say 'So Long' to Lowell Thomas," *Hartford Courant*, September 3, 1981; "Lowell Thomas, A World Traveler and Broadcaster for 45 Years, Dead," *New York Times*, August 30, 1981.

Epilogue: He Loved the Face of the Earth

1. "Remembering Lowell Thomas, with Walter Cronkite," in George Plimpton, ed., *As Told at the Explorers Club* (Guilford, CT: Lyons Press, 2005), 431–445; Douglas Edwards, "Lowell Thomas Was Truly the Granddaddy of Us All," *New York Times*, September 20, 1981.

2. Interviews with Thomas Murphy, February 5, 2013, August 17, 2015; Hawver, *Capital Cities/ABC*, 31, 312–332; William J. Casey, director of the CIA under President Ronald Reagan, had been an early investor in Capital Cities. That gave rise to conspiracy theories, some involving Lowell Thomas (recalling the Soviet charges about his role in Tibet), when Capital Cities acquired ABC in 1985; see Andy Boehm, "The Seizing of the American Broad-

casting Company," *L.A. Weekly*, February 14, 1987; Dennis W. Mazzocco, *Networks of Power* (Boston: South End Press, 1994), 60–62.

3. Andy Wickstrom, "History Reels Across Your Screen," *Chicago Tribune*, April 18, 1986.

4. Google Books Ngram Viewer, https://books.google.com/ngrams/graph?content=F.+Scott+Fitzgerald%2CFred+Astaire%2CCharles+Lindbergh%2CLowell+Thomas&year_start=1935&year_end=2000&corpus=17&smoothing=3&share=&direct_url=t1%3B%2CF.%20Scott%20Fitzgerald%3B%2Cc0%3B.t1%3B%2CFred%20Astaire%3B%2Cc0%3B.t1%3B%2CCharles%20Lindbergh%3B%2Cc0%3B.t1%3B%2CLowell%20Thomas%3B%2Cc0. Compared with that of actors, novelists or other notables from that period, discussion of Thomas' journalistic contemporaries—such as Walter Lippmann, Ernie Pyle and Dorothy Thompson—has also plummeted; Google Books Ngram Viewer, https://books.google.com/ngrams/graph?content=Walter+Lippmann%2C+Dorothy+Thompson%2CF.+Scott+Fitzgerald%2CErnie+Pyle%2CFred+Astaire%2CCharles+Lindbergh&year_start=1935&year_end=2000&corpus=17&smoothing=3&share=&direct_url=t1%3B%2CWalter%20Lippmann%3B%2Cc0%3B.t1%3B%2CDorothy%20Thompson%3B%2Cc0%3B.t1%3B%2CF.%20Scott%20Fitzgerald%3B%2Cc0%3B.t1%3B%2CErnie%20Pyle%3B%2Cc0%3B.t1%3B%2CFred%20Astaire%3B%2Cc0%3B.t1%3B%2CCharles%20Lindbergh%3B%2Cc0; Google Books Ngram Viewer, https://books.google.com/ngrams/graph?content=Walter+Cronkite%2CBarbara+Walters%2CTom+Brokaw&year_start=1980&year_end=2008&corpus=17&smoothing=3&share=&direct_url=t1%3B%2CWalter%20Cronkite%3B%2Cc0%3B.t1%3B%2CBarbara%20Walters%3B%2Cc0%3B.t1%3B%2CTom%20Brokaw%3B%2Cc0.

5. Photograph in *Dayton Daily News*, March 30, 2006. Thomas material is also displayed at the Lowell Thomas Center in the John Kane house in Pawling, at Akin Hall on Quaker Hill and with the Lowell Thomas Papers at Marist College in Poughkeepsie.

6. Email from Ruth Zalewski, "Victor Lowell Thomas Museum," to Kulsoom Kahn, April 23, 2016.

7. Lowell Thomas to J. Edgar Folk Jr., August 18, 1980.

8. For a more detailed version of my take on these matters, see Mitchell Stephens, *Beyond News: The Future of Journalism* (New York: Columbia University Press, 2014).

9. Stanley Johnson, "Lowell Thomas Marks 80th Year, Finds Life Is Still an Adventure," *Los Angeles Times*, April 7, 1972.

Index